DELIBERATE ACTS

Tsukukiwyungwa ("squatting down in serious discussion"). Hostile men on the plain below Oraibi shortly after the 1906 split. Photograph by Jo Mora, courtesy of Special Collections (John R. Wilson Collection), Cline Library, Northern Arizona University, Flagstaff.

DELIBERATE ACTS

Changing Hopi Culture Through the Oraibi Split

Peter M. Whiteley

The University of Arizona Press, Tucson

THE UNIVERSITY OF ARIZONA PRESS

© 1988 by Peter M. Whiteley. All Rights Reserved.

Manufactured in the U.S.A.
This book was set in 11/13 Linotron 202 Sabon.

Designed by Kaelin Chappell

Library of Congress Cataloging-in-Publication Data
Whiteley, Peter M.
    Deliberate acts : changing Hopi culture through the Oraibi split /
Peter M. Whiteley.
      p. cm.
    Includes index.
    ISBN 0-8165-1037-7 (alk. paper)
      1. Hopi Indians—History. 2. Hopi Indians—Politics and
government. 3. Hopi Indians—Religion and mythology. 4. Indians of
North America—Arizona—History. 5. Indians of North America—
Arizona—Politics and government. 6. Indians of North America—
Arizona—Religion and mythology. I. Title.
E99.H7W47 1988
979.1'00497—dc19   87-30240
                                                                                                CIP

British Library Cataloguing in Publication data are available.

For

Honwungwa
Kookyangwungwa
Tepwungwa
Honanwungwa
Iswungwa
Paa'iswungwa
Piikyaswungwa
Tsuuwungwa
Paaqapwungwa
Kwaawungwa
Tawawungwa

And to the memory of Jack Whiteley

Les événements retentissants ne sont souvent que des instants,
que des manifestations de ces larges destins et ne s'expliquent
que par eux.
Resounding events are often but instants,
but manifestations of a larger destiny by which alone
they can be explained.
—Fernand Braudel (*La Méditerranée et le monde méditerranéen à l'époque de Philippe II*)

It is no mystery,
We're making history.
—Linton Kwesi Johnson (*Making History*)

Contents

List of Illustrations — xi
List of Tables — xiii
Preface — xv
1. Introduction: The Question and Its Context — 1

PART I. ORAIBI SOCIETY

2. Currents of History — 11
3. Oraibi Society in the Late Nineteenth Century — 44
4. From Oraibi to Bacavi — 71

PART II. BACAVI SOCIETY

5. Demography, Human Geography, and Economy — 121
6. Kinship and Social Structure — 162
7. Ritual, Politics, and Some Broader Contexts — 192

PART III. INTERPRETATIONS
8. Hopi Analysis and Anthropological Analysis 243
9. Intentional Actors and Sociocultural Interpretation 285

PART IV. REFERENCE MATERIAL
Appendixes
1. Commissioner Leupp's Program for Dealing with the Existing Hopi Troubles 295
2. Letter from Reuben J. Perry to the Commissioner of Indian Affairs, 11-17-1906 299
3. Agreement Signed by Hostiles Returning to Oraibi 307
4. Letter from Horton H. Miller to the Commissioner of Indian Affairs, 11-12-1909 309
5. Telegram from Horton H. Miller to the Commissioner of Indian Affairs, 12-4-1909 315

Notes to the Chapters 317
References Cited 331
Index 365

Illustrations

Photographs

Hostile men shortly after the 1906 split	Frontispiece
Oraibi in the 1890s	12
Oraibi's chief kiva	62
First arrest and imprisonment of Hostile leaders	80
Hostiles at Alcatraz, 1894–95	87
Meeting at Hostile encampment in Hotevilla	112
Hostiles being run-marched to Ganado, 1906	115
Bacavi from the air, 1940	122
Bacavi's plaza, 1910s	123
Bacavi's first kiva, circa 1925	126
Kooninkatsinam (Havasupai Kachinas) in Bacavi, 1924	197
Soyohim (mixed) Kachinas in Bacavi, circa 1911–15	199
First Mennonite church building in Bacavi	218
Arizona politicians and *Tasapkatsinam* (Navajo Kachinas), circa 1915	252

Maps

1.1.	Hopi reservation	3
1.2.	Third Mesa	4

5.1.	Bacavi, circa 1915	124
5.2.	Bacavi, 1940	128
5.3.	Bacavi, 1981	129

Figure

| 5.1. | Comparative Bacavi population curves | 137 |

Tables

3.1.	Oraibi Clans and Phratries	50
3.2.	Oraibi Ceremonies and Societies	60
3.3.	Oraibi Kivas Prior to 1900	63
5.1.	Bacavi's Population Structure, 1981	130
5.2.	Bacavi's Overall Population by Off- or On-Reservation Residence, 1981	130
5.3.	Bacavi's Population Structure, 1910	132
5.4.	Bacavi's Population Structure, 1937	132
5.5.	Bacavi's Population Structure, 1950	133
5.6.	Bacavi's Overall Population by Off- or On-Reservation Residence, 1950	134
5.7.	Bacavi's Population Structure, 1968	135
5.8.	Bacavi's Comparative Population Structure by Age	136
5.9.	Bacavi's Comparative Adult Age and Sex Distribution	136
5.10.	Economic Statistics of Bacavi Household Heads, 1922	156
5.11.	Economic Census, 1935	159

6.1.	Bacavi Household Composition, 1981	166
6.2.	Oraibi Household Composition of Pre-1906 Populace	169
6.3.	Bacavi's Phratries, Clans, and Lineages, 1981	173
6.4.	Bacavi's Clans and Lineage Fragments, 1910	176
6.5.	Bacavi Marriages, 1910–81	188
6.6.	Bacavi Marriages by Decade	189
6.7.	Summary of Bacavi Marriages	189
7.1.	Bacavi's Clan and Ceremonial Groups, 1910	202
7.2.	Distribution of Third Mesa Politico-Religious Leaders, 1906–9	208
7.3.	Distribution of Third Mesa Politico-Religious Leaders in Relation to Population Size, 1906–9	209

⌐ Preface

> So, you *studied* us, huh? Were we *interesting*?
> —*An older Hopi man, on learning of my prior research.*
>
> Hopi? Oh, *everyone* has done fieldwork there.
> —*An older New York anthropologist, on learning of my prior research.*

It's pretty tough to write about the Hopi these days. Myriad anthropological sojourns since the 1870s have spawned peculiar relationships. Hopis are intrinsically suspicious of anthropologists as people who pry too much, reveal cultural secrets, and make a living by exploiting Hopi culture. Anthropologists, on the other hand, seem intrinsically suspicious of each other: 1980s Hopi ethnography is surely plagiarist of and inferior to orthodox ethnographies conducted when the Hopi were still *really* Hopi (whatever this may mean). For better or worse, such orthodox ethnographies have ensconced themselves as exemplars of American cultural anthropology. Though not too many anthropologists read about the Gururumba, everyone *knows* about the Hopi: is there an introductory textbook that does not mention them?

With this in mind, I must offer some preliminary explanations. First, on the Hopi side. The communication of knowledge in Hopi society is not an open free-for-all; much knowledge is privileged and valuable, and the average citizen does not have rights of access. Some forms of knowledge, especially pertaining to ritual, are highly sensitive and should never be discussed publicly (anthropologists have mostly ignored this, of course). Other forms are less sensitive but should not be specifically discussed in written texts because they intrude too much on the lives of individuals, by turning them into fixed literary images widely disseminated in the society that surrounds and impinges at every turn. For these reasons, certain kinds of information are not found in the following pages. My discussions of ritual, such as they are, are very superficial, and apart from as they pertain to the contemporary situation, are mostly taken from already published sources. I do discuss aspects of knowledge concerning the Oraibi split which were once secret and esoteric, but which are not, according to my Hopi consultants, any longer. I do not use personal names of living or recently deceased Hopi people, except for a few prominent individuals who are well known in published works or via the media. I am careful to obscure the specific identities of consultants. This has been difficult for me, since the authority of certain consultants would clearly have added weight to their cited statements. I am not earning any money from this book: all author's royalties will go to a local, Hopi community resource—the least I can do to repay hospitality. I am still subject to the charge that I am making my career off the Hopis: this is undeniably true, and I only hope that in so doing, my writings have significance for Hopi people.

On the anthropological side, I must attempt to inscribe the "authority" of my statements. This work is based upon my research into Bacavi's history, conducted while living in the village continuously from June 1980 to August 1981, together with research at numerous archives thereafter. In view of the justified Hopi skepticism of anthropologists, I was very fortunate to be allowed to live in the village and for this I am deeply grateful. Since I remained in the Southwest for four years after my initial research, I have been back to Hopi numerous times and learned additionally from Hopi consultants.

Like Gary Witherspoon (e.g., 1977), although assuredly without the extent of his experience, I am uncomfortable with the idea of myself as "the anthropologist" drily extracting "data" from "informants." This would mock friendship and at the same time make me look as though I were somehow responsible for Hopi knowledge; I am not—I have been merely a vehicle through which some of it has come to be written down.

Historical ethnographies have come into something of a vogue (see, e.g., Geertz 1980; Rosaldo 1980; Fowler 1982; Price 1983; Sahlins 1981, 1985), and of course, ethnohistoric interest in American Indian societies is deeply rooted in the ethnographic tradition. The present work shares features with this genre, especially in its attempt to elucidate social processes via the conjoint historical insights of the documentary record and Hopi interpretations. But it was largely a Hopi interest in history that directed my attention to the subject. I began with an interest in social structure through time (following, particularly, Leach 1954 and Turner 1957) and in acculturation studies of American Indian societies (e.g., Linton 1940; Spicer 1961). I imagined that Bacavi would have reconstituted society on the Oraibi model and was gradually acculturating toward the dominant society. In part, this turned out to be true, but in many ways it was not. I was surprised to find that questions concerning the extent of ceremonial reconstitution often met with a quizzical incredulity and responses to the effect, "Of course that ceremony wasn't recreated in Bacavi—that was the whole point of the Oraibi split." Intrigued, my attention gradually turned toward internal perspectives to see what they revealed of Hopi society through time. I think they reveal a great deal, so much that my search for theoretical stimuli to illuminate the study moved away from anthropological perspectives toward these Hopi ones. Since the research was completed (if one ever does this), certain of the insights developed found resonance with some current anthropological concerns, some of which I have interspersed through the text for comparative purposes. But, as far as I am concerned, the ideas developed here remain largely Hopi in inspiration.

Intensive research at Hopi lasted fourteen months and focused upon compiling a historical reconstruction of Bacavi from its origins on. Formal and informal interviews were held in both Hopi and English. Interviews in Hopi were translated with the aid of interpreters. I made a concerted effort to learn as much Hopi as possible; the level attained was enough to serve as a working research tool, but I cannot claim expressive fluency. Even my oldest consultants could speak some English, and our joint vernacular became a mixture of the two languages. Several consultants, highly articulate in both languages, were critically aware of the problems of conceptual intertranslatability between Hopi and English; in consequence, a good deal of time was spent in the explanation of Hopi concepts via the mixture mentioned.

Most of the consultants were from Bacavi and ranged in age from twenty to more than eighty-five years. In addition, consultants included members of other villages, as follows: Hotevilla, Kykotsmovi, Oraibi, Upper and Lower Moencopi (on Third Mesa); Shongopavi (on Second Mesa); and "Polacca" (the generic term for First Mesa residence). I considered it important to gain extra-Third Mesa viewpoints on the Oraibi split, on the status of Third Mesa society as a whole, and on Bacavi.

Several archival resources were researched for materials pertaining to the Oraibi split, its origins and aftermaths, and to Bacavi, in order to contextualize events and processes as "thickly" as possible. The following archival institutions were investigated in person: the Bureau of Indian Affairs Hopi Agency offices in Keam's Canyon (of greatest utility for the Agency Superintendent's letterbooks from 1899 to 1912); the Museum of Northern Arizona, Flagstaff; the National Archives in Washington, D.C., and Laguna Niguel, California; the National Anthropological Archives, Smithsonian Institution, Washington, D.C.; the Peabody Museum of American Archaeology and Ethnology, Cambridge, Massachusetts; the Mennonite Library and Archives, Bethel College, North Newton, Kansas; the Latter-Day Saints Genealogical Archives and Church Historian's Office, Salt Lake City, Utah; several federal, state and local archival resources in Arizona, New Mexico, Utah, and Colorado; the Southwest Museum, Los Angeles; the Museum of the American Indian, Heye Foundation, New York City; and minor sources too numerous to mention. In addition, Fred Eggan loaned me microfilms of Keam's Canyon letterbooks supplemental to those at the Hopi Agency, up to 1916; Margaret Wright provided a copy of Mischa Titiev's census notes of Oraibi; and Shuichi Nagata sent me a rare copy of a 1950 village census—for all of these I am very grateful.

Finally, another type of resource should be mentioned: the published ethnographic literature on Oraibi and Third Mesa specifically, and on Hopi more generally. The modern student of Hopi society is both blessed and cursed with the great weight of former anthropological studies. The extensive accounts of various aspects of Hopi society and culture greatly facilitate a basic, general knowledge. The writings of H. R. Voth (see Laird 1977 for a complete record) between 1900 and 1912, which are mostly concerned with Oraibi religious ceremonies, provide good insights into contemporary Oraibi life. Voth was the Mennonite missionary at Oraibi for seven years between 1893 and 1902. The depth of his familiarity with Oraibi culture was considerable, although his aggressive prying into religious secrets has become legendary and did not endear him to Oraibi people. The true giant of Third Mesa studies is Mischa Titiev. His accounts (particularly 1944 and 1972) of Oraibi society form the backdrop for much of the present work. In addition, for the purpose of analyzing the composition of the factions in Oraibi, his census notes (n.d.), which focus upon the period immediately prior to the split, are of paramount significance and provide a benchmark for much of my own research on the Bacavi faction. Fred Eggan's classic study of western Pueblo social organization (1950) remains the exemplar in studies of Hopi social structure and is drawn upon extensively in the present work. I am critical of a number of Titiev's and Eggan's analytical conclusions, but the criticisms do not and could not detract from the enormity of their respective contributions to Hopi ethnology.

Acknowledgments

My interest in Hopi really awakened in 1978, when I ventured to Hotevilla for the Snake Dance. Like so many others before, I was transfixed. I wanted to learn more of these people: how, by what lights, could they sustain themselves in such radically "other" practices against the ever-increasing tide of the dominant society's homogenizing ways? To me, a rather typical European "orientalist" (if I may generalize this term to include the mythical geography of the "Wild West") in search of the exotic, this Hopi ritual was not some reinvented, quasi-authentic spectacle, but the "real stuff": the truly traditional, persistent, and genuinely exotic "other"—in postmodern America yet. Whatever my callow motivational impulses, the subsequent efforts at understanding have benefited enormously from the tutelage, support, and assistance of many people, both Hopi and non-Hopi.

The research upon which this work is based began in 1980 and remained intensive through 1982. Since then until 1986, additional information has accumulated more intermittently. With a project of such duration, and with a range of different influences, it is impossible to express my gratitude to all for whom it is most genuinely felt. In particular, values of cultural and personal privacy make it inappropriate to thank Hopi individuals by name in this context. My dedication offers a generalized tribute to a number of Hopi clans, and I would here underline an *Iskwakweh* to the people of Bacavi and of Third Mesa more generally, who generously gave of their time, wisdom, and affection: working with a rather poor student, they graciously attempted to teach some of the significances of Hopi life. But still, this generalized "thank you," though necessary, troubles me. "The people of Bacavi and of Third Mesa" seem an amorphous mass of "others" in contrast to the individualized non-Hopis whose names appear below. To be sure, I have a relationship not with "the people of Third Mesa" but with certain individuals in varying measures and manners: it is to these people that my deepest appreciation, respect, and thanks are directed.

To Harry Basehart I owe a great intellectual and affective debt, which, happily for me, continues to pile up. Also at the University of New Mexico, Karl Schwerin, Alfonso Ortiz, Scott Rushforth, and Margaret Szasz all provided deeply appreciated correctives to excessive transgressions against principles of cultural interpretation, false arguments, and the sanctity of the English language. I have sedulously outwitted some of their best efforts, however, and they bear no responsibility for sins of commission and omission which remain. Fred Eggan has graciously and generously assisted in a number of ways—practical, intellectual, and ethnographic— even despite my seemingly ungrateful hacking away at some of his published ideas, which nevertheless continue to stand at the heart of the best of Hopi ethnography.

John R. Wilson has provided extraordinarily selfless and generous support, both financial and moral, without which much archival research, in particular, would have been impossible. I gratefully acknowledge other financial and/or infrastructural sup-

Preface

port for research, writing, or both, from institutions and individuals as follows: the Village of Bacavi, Sigma Xi, Byron Harvey III, the Frieda Butler Foundation, the University of New Mexico Graduate Students' Association, the School of American Research and the Weatherhead Foundation, Northern Arizona University Library, the American Philosophical Society, and Sarah Lawrence College. I also offer warm thanks to the staffs of the many archives mentioned earlier, for extensive research assistance. In addition, I am most grateful to Louis Hieb and Shuichi Nagata for helpful textual criticism.

I would also like to thank the following organizations for their generous permission to reprint various passages from their publications or collections: Northland Press in cooperation with the Museum of Northern Arizona, Flagstaff, for use of excerpts from Edmund Nequatewa's *Truth of a Hopi*; the Peabody Museum of Archaeology and Ethnology for excerpts from Mischa Titiev's *Old Oraibi, A Study of the Hopi Indians of Third Mesa*; and The University of Chicago Press for excerpts from Fred Eggan's *Social Organization of the Western Pueblos*.

Finally, my greatest thanks are to Jane Campbell, for more than words can tell.

Peter Whiteley
December 1986

DELIBERATE ACTS

1
⌘ Introduction:
The Question and Its Context

The Hopi have attracted a great deal of outside interest for a long time. The country is spectacular; Hopi religious rituals are beautiful, dramatic, and suitably exotic; and the Southwest has been a tourist mecca for almost a century. Leo Crane, eight-year veteran of the Hopi Agency, wrote:

> During those eight long years I met on the reservation thousands of visitors—students and their mentors; painters and etchers and sculptors of distinction, and those who thought they were; ethnologists, philologists, and sociologists; ballyhoo men from Eastern department-stores and half-wits taking an outing; journalists and authors and publishers; geologists and common "water-witches"; motion-picture men and others wearing puttees; actors and lecturers; composers, musicians, and vocalists; museum scouts and "scratchers"; clergymen and soldiers; Oxford men, Harvard men, men from Bonn; retired statesmen and unretiring politicians; representatives of foreign governments; persons from the far-famed city of New York; tourists and caparisoned dudes, and simple guides; plain gentlemen and plainer roughnecks. (Crane 1925:191)

If this was true in 1920, so much more is it in the late 1980s. Regular bus tours deposit hordes of gaping visitors, many of whom, out of their own environments, abandon common decorum and courtesy. Hopi artifacts and ideofacts abound in general southwestern American culture and beyond. Hopi religious symbols have been expropriated and commercialized in almost every form imaginable, from the *Talavai* (Morning) Kachina who adorns the Arizona National Bank to the egregious "Kiva" pornographic bookstore in Albuquerque. Such grotesqueries are so commonplace as to never raise an eyebrow (except a Hopi one: how would Christian Americans feel about the "Angel Gabriel Usury" or "Our Lady of Sorrows Exotic Leathers"?).

Hopi is not, then, a pristine society isolated from the mainstreams of twentieth-century Western culture: it is enmeshed in them, although a great deal of distinctively Hopi practices persist and give primary meanings to people's lives. Incidences of "crossover" culture (from both directions) are legion, from the Hopi "K-Town [Kykotsmovi] Break Dancers," who are doubtless already out of style, to white, post-hippie hippies who, having read *Book of the Hopi* (Waters 1963), attempt to enact quasi-Hopi identities and occasionally intrude upon ceremonies. Fortunately, those great levelers, Hopi ritual clowns, take revenge, exposing the manifold incongruities that pervade Hopi life in the late twentieth century.

Internally, Hopi society is a complex configuration. It consists of approximately nine thousand people, each of whom has a predominant affiliation to one of thirteen sedentary villages located on or around three adjacent mesas (the westernmost settlements of Moencopi are conceptually, if not geologically, a part of Third Mesa). The mesas extend as the southernmost fingers of Black Mesa of the Colorado Plateau; each finger is about eight miles from the next, separated by drainages that form valleys roughly five hundred feet below the mesa tops (see Maps 1.1 and 1.2). There are significant differences in culture and social structure in the villages of different mesas. Each village on each mesa is, theoretically at least, an independent, self-governing unit. The extent of their independence is today significantly marked by the ongoing difficulties of the Tribal Council (originally convened by the U.S. government after the Indian Reorganization Act of 1934) in obtaining representatives from all the villages.

I am concerned here with Third Mesa society, particularly as it is

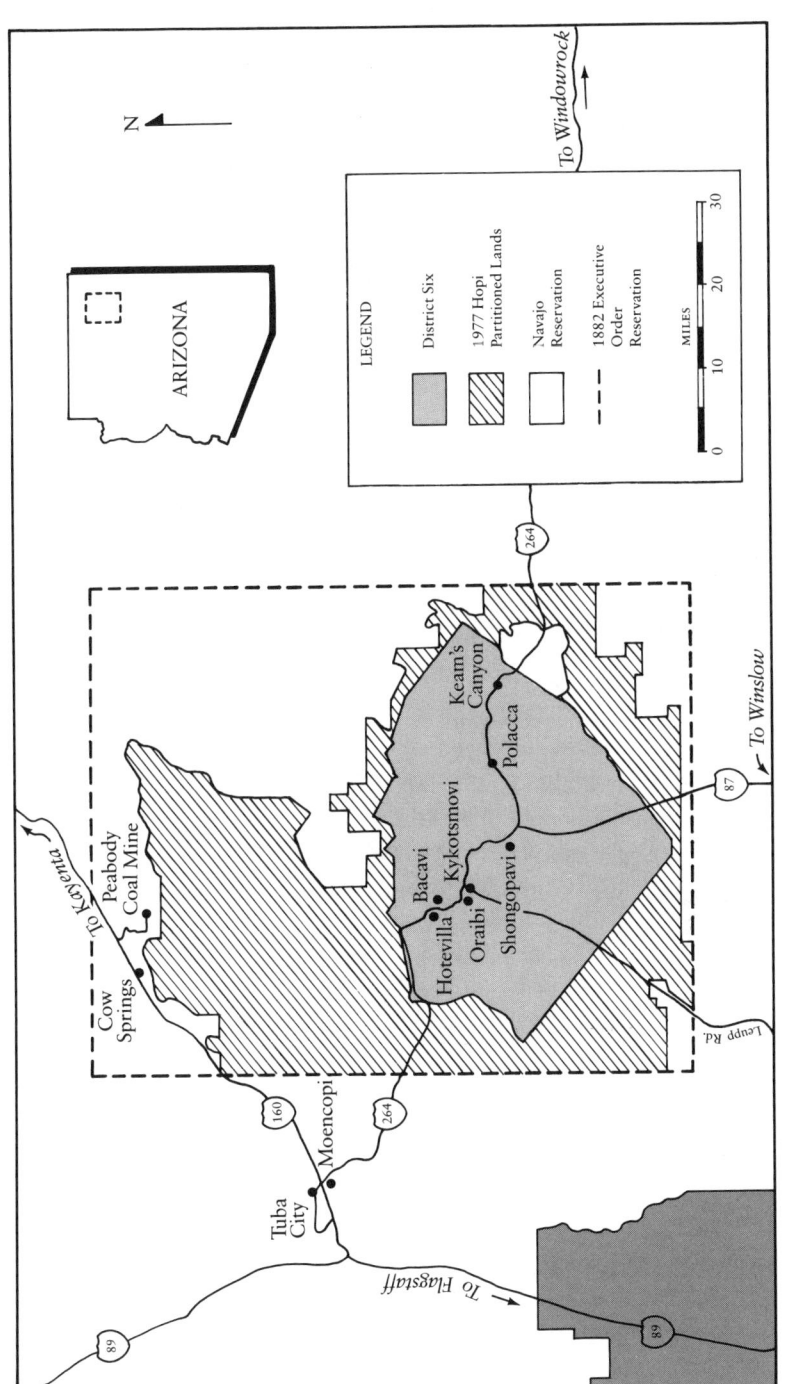

Map 1.1 Hopi Reservation

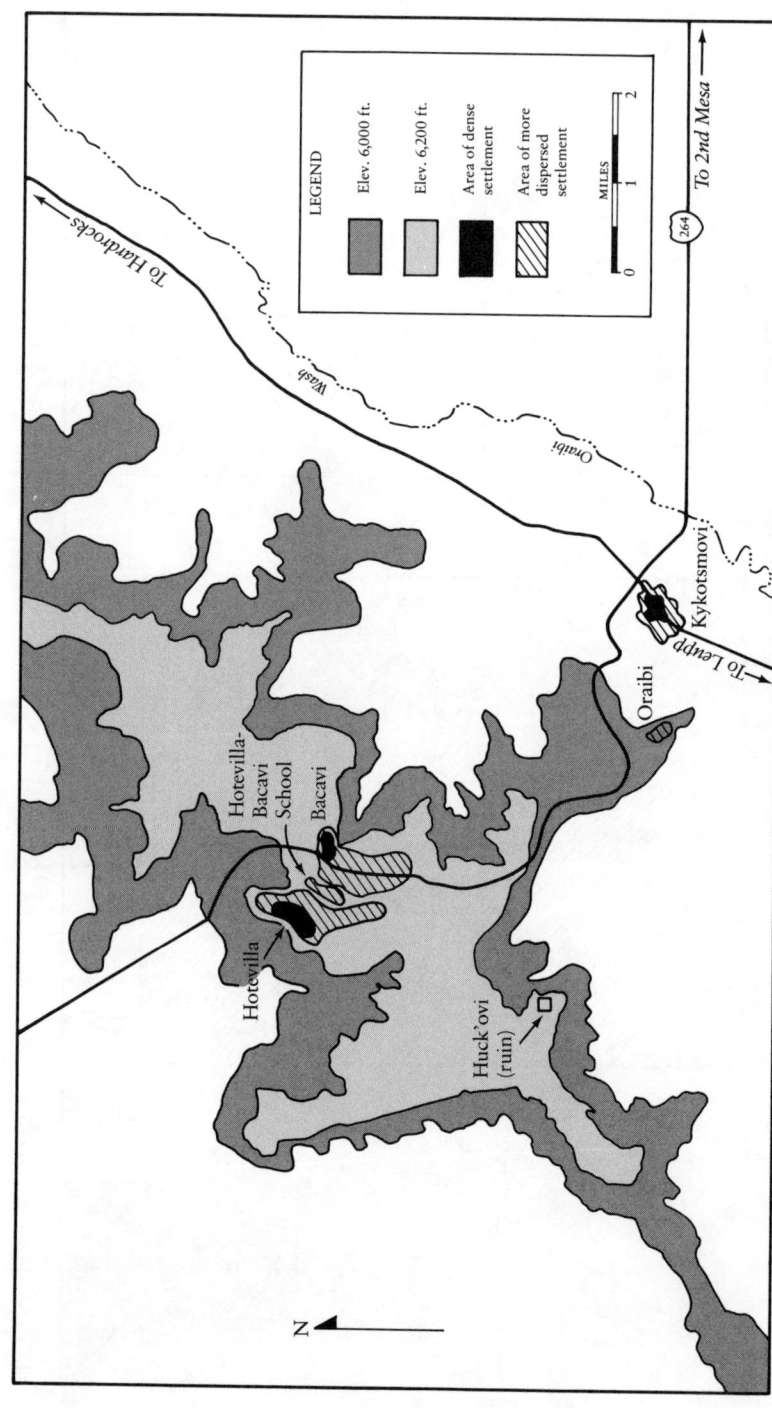

Map 1.2 Third Mesa

embodied in Bacavi and as it was in the past in Oraibi.[1] Third Mesa is located between the Oraibi and Dinnebito valleys, which are centrally cut by washes of the same names. The village of Bacavi traces its origins to the split of Oraibi in 1906. At that time, Oraibi was the only village on Third Mesa, with the partial exception of its small farming colony, Moencopi, some forty-five miles away. In modern times, Third Mesa includes six villages: Oraibi, Kykotsmovi, Bacavi, Hotevilla, Upper Moencopi, and Lower Moencopi.

Oraibi had long been the largest Hopi village and was consistently regarded in Spanish chronicles and early American reports as the most important—the "capital of the province." Further, since the Pueblo Revolt of 1680, the general stance of Oraibi to Euro-Americans had been almost without exception one of hostility and obdurate rejection of their attempts to impose religious and political dominion.

The Oraibi split, so the conventional story holds (e.g., Dockstader 1979:526–29), was the result of a division of the town into factions: "Hostiles" and "Friendlies," as the government called them. The Hostiles wanted nothing to do with the white man and resented most of all his policies to forcibly educate their children in an alien cultural system. The Friendlies were more conciliatory and saw the tangible virtues of such education in the items of American manufacture that were becoming increasingly accessible to them—especially when they toed, or appeared to toe, the government line. The gradual division into factions began, it is held, with the visit of the Oraibi *Kikmongwi*, or village chief, Loololma, to Washington, D.C., in 1890 and his consequent conversion to American ways. This forced his people either to follow his change of heart or to oppose him. Disagreements reached such a head that the Hostiles were forced out of the village after a volatile pushing contest in September 1906.

There are a number of very good reasons to question this conventional view. Some questions have already been posed with a variety of results: these can be basically summarized as shifting the attribution of cause from acculturative pressure to another uniform cause, such as internal, social structural instability (e.g., Titiev 1944) or population pressure upon diminishing resources (e.g., Bradfield 1971). I find that none of these alternatives provides fully efficacious explanations, as will become evident.

The story continues that the Hostiles, after being forced out of Oraibi, founded the new village of Hotevilla four miles to the northwest. Here the conventional versions get mixed up. The prevailing view is that, shortly after the establishment of Hotevilla, there was a further division of the Hostile party. The "less conservative" decided to go back to Oraibi. They were, however, refused permission to reenter, so in the spring of 1907 they established another village a mile from Hotevilla, named "Bacavi" after some springs in the canyon below. Titiev's version (1944:212) is closer to the mark. He states that the less conservative faction was accepted back into Oraibi with assistance from the government, but that they left again the following year, in October 1907, to found Bacavi, since the arrangement had been only a temporary one to provide them with shelter through the winter.

In fact, notwithstanding all published sources to the contrary, this faction's members remained in Oraibi after readmission in November 1906 until November 1909, when they not so much left of their own accord as were forced out after another flare-up of antagonisms with the Friendly faction. They then established Bacavi, securing aid from the Indian Agency in Keam's Canyon in the form of tools, lumber, and windows. They agreed to, even repeatedly asked for, a school at the foot of the mesa below the village; repeatedly asked that they be allotted land in severalty under the program then being pursued by the government (which had likewise been a major bone of Hostile contention); and agreed to allow the Mennonite Church to establish a mission adjacent to the village.

We are thus faced with two thorny inconsistencies, which the conventional views have either neglected or obscured for the sake of arguments that accord more with a preconceived set of anthropological axioms than they do with the facts at hand. The first problem concerns the length of time spent by the returned Hostiles back in Oraibi. The idea that even after the severity of the division the Friendlies might agree to the temporary presence of these Hostiles for the winter is plausible. Three years requires too great a strain on its plausibility. The second inconsistency is even more troublesome. Supposedly, the division had come about over acceptance or rejection of the "white man's ways." Yet after three years, some of the Hostiles actively sought government aid in its previously most despised forms, that is, they became more "Friendly" than the "Friendlies." We might explain this as the spiritual, material, and philosophical defeat of this subfaction (as Titiev 1944: 212 does), perhaps because they were too few and/or too weak to viably maintain their opposition. But their small numbers have been exaggerated. The Hostiles returning to Oraibi numbered around one-third of the total Oraibi Hostile faction, accounting for between 150 and 160 out of 485; at this period, Shongopavi, on Second Mesa, which is in the 1980s the village with more traditional ritual and political structures intact than any other, numbered around 200 people. Further, the returning Hostile subfaction included a contingent of *pavansinom* (ritually and politically "important people") far in excess of its proportional size and including some of the very leaders of Hostile opposition.

How are we to explain such inconsistencies? The answers, I maintain, lie in two places. First, in the very functioning of Hopi social structure, particularly in the realm of Oraibi politics, as this is revealed by Hopi consultants; and second, in an abundance of documented historical contexts that have previously been ignored. To get at the answers is my fundamental objective. I shall go about it with a comparative analysis of Bacavi social structure through time with its original baseline in Oraibi in the late nineteenth century. My perspective is how one fragment of a well-established society went about creating a new social order, after that of which it had been a part was drastically fragmented. In comparing the new society with the old, my aim is to explain how far the former was modeled upon the latter, and where it was not, to discern the underlying processes of modification.

1
ORAIBI SOCIETY

2
Currents of History

The view of Oraibi through the prehistoric and historic records is "through a glass darkly." Very little archaeological research has been conducted because the pueblo has been unwilling to have its cultural privacy invaded by those whose sense of history is incompatible with ancestral sanctity. Historically, the record is one of shreds and patches: brief, sporadic glimpses by transient sojourners, most of whom were uninterested in cultural detail. It gets clearer as it gets more recent; the second half of the nineteenth century sees a marked increase in the number of intruders interested, for a variety of reasons, in recording something of their experience. Nonetheless, overall there is no possibility of constructing a systematic diachronic record of Oraibi through documentary resources; these records are just too few and far between.

My intent here, then, is simply to give a context for the events of the late nineteenth and early twentieth centuries. However desultorily, the documentary record does reveal cultural and structural continuities. It suggests structural precedents for later sociopolitical actions and deeply established traditions in the Hopi *Weltan-*

A view of Oraibi in the 1890s, from the west. Photograph by F. H. Maude, Southwest Museum, Los Angeles.

schauung for the interpretation of events. As Marshall Sahlins insists, "People organize their projects and give significance to their objects from the existing understandings of the cultural order" (1985:vii). The reduplication of patterns of action revealed in the historical record of Oraibi suggests that events attained meaningful forms through their interaction with preexisting schemes of interpretation (Sahlins's "structure of conjuncture"). Furthermore, these interpretive schemes and the social structures in which they are embedded appear to persist. I am certainly not claiming that Oraibi society was stable and unchanging for centuries, but simply stating that significant diachronic regularities can inform our understanding of more recent historical events. At the least, we can be sure that the configuration of Oraibi society in 1900 was not the incidental product of recent contingencies, but the contemporary reproduction of an age-old community that had existed in situ since prehistory.

Historically, Oraibi reveals features that significantly distinguish it from the other Hopi villages. It seems always to have been the largest village and was regarded by outsiders as the most important. According to Hopi tradition, Shongopavi on Second Mesa was the first village to be established (cf. Nequatewa 1936:35–37), but Oraibi is the oldest continuously inhabited village (in all of North America as well), since Shongopavi moved its village site after the Pueblo Revolt of 1680 (Hargrave 1930:2). These three factors—size, prominence, and long-term occupancy—undergird Oraibi's distinctive social structural pattern and its long-held political stance toward antagonistic foreign powers. Let me elaborate these ideas with some glimpses of Oraibi through the historical record.

Oraibi in Prehistory

On the basis of ceramic evidence, Hargrave (1932:1) claims Oraibi has been occupied since at least A.D. 1150. Dendrochronological cutting dates of some Oraibi beams start in the 1350s (Bannister, Robinson, and Warren 1967:20–24), but given the paucity of archaeological research, occupation may be considerably earlier than even Hargrave's date. Brew summarizes the late prehistory of the Hopi area in general:

Sites representing the late Basketmaker and early Pueblo phases of the prehistoric culture are to be found throughout the Hopi country. . . . That the villages of 1,500 and 1,600 years ago were occupied by direct ancestors of the modern Hopis is a matter for discussion, but the cultural remains present a clear, uninterrupted logical development culminating in the life, general technology, architecture, and agricultural and ceremonial practices to be seen on the three Hopi mesas today. (Brew 1979:514)

In short, Puebloan settlement in the area is long-established and the antiquity of Oraibi is impressive.

The Spanish Period: 1540–1821

The Hopi's first recorded Spanish contact was the Coronado expedition of 1540. I emphasize "recorded" because of the erroneous general assumption that nonliterate societies exist in oblivious informational vacuums until rescued by inscription into western literate records. There is archaeological debate over the existence of regular trade networks between the Southwest and Mesoamerica prehistorically (e.g., McGuire 1980; Mathien 1981). Nevertheless, it seems very plausible that the Hopi received intelligence of the Spanish presence to the south of them prior to actual contact.

Coronado learned of the Hopi villages at Zuni, where he made a first headquarters: "They informed him about a province with seven villages of the same sort as theirs, although somewhat different. . . . This province is called Tusayan. It is twenty-five leagues from Cibola. Their villages are high and the people are warlike" (Winship 1896: 488). He dispatched Pedro de Tovar and Fray Juan Padilla with a force of about twenty soldiers to investigate "Tusayan" on 15 July 1540 (Winship 1896:343). There were hostilities at the first village, which was probably Awatovi (although this is disputed: see Montgomery, Smith, and Brew 1949:5–7; Reed 1942). After a show of Spanish strength, the Hopi force capitulated and allowed the visitors into the village. Castañeda's narrative of the expedition vaguely implies that all Hopi villages were visited, but the implication is a vague one and it cannot be ascertained whether the party visited Oraibi or not: ". . . Aquel dia se recogio *la gente de la tierra* y binieron a dar la obidencia y dieron abiertamente *sus pueblos* y que entrasen en ellos a tratar comprar y bender y cambiar" (Winship 1896:429, my emphasis).

The following month, the second party, led by Garcia Lopez de Cárdenas, was sent from Zuni in search of a great river (the Colorado) of which the Tovar-Padilla expedition had learned. Again, the chronicles reveal no mention of individual villages. The route may have been via Oraibi (James 1974:37), although this is in doubt (cf. Hargrave 1932:4).

Castañeda provides some general observations of interest. On Hopi political structure, he notes: "It is governed like Cibola, by an assembly of the oldest men. They have their governors and generals (sus governadores y capitanes—p. 429)" (Winship 1896:489). This point is developed further in the description of Zuni (Cibola): "They do not have chiefs as in New Spain, but are ruled by a council of the oldest men. They have priests who preach to them. . . . These are the elders. . . . They tell them how they are to live, and I believe that they give certain commandments for them to keep" (Winship 1896:518).

Castañeda also estimates population for Hopi and Zuni: "There may be as many as 3,000 or 4,000 men in the fourteen villages of these two provinces" (Winship 1896:518). This may be an important index. Most sixteenth- and seventeenth-century population estimates are suspected of overinflation for ulterior reasons, that is, to procure more support—military, missionary, and material—for the fledgling frontier colony. But Castañeda's estimate probably antedates such motives. In light of the massive decimation of Amerindian populations by Old World diseases (Dobyns 1966, 1983; Denevan 1976) it should not be regarded as an index of precolumbian population (the New World smallpox pandemic of 1520–24, in particular, probably had a severe impact on the Pueblos [cf. Dobyns 1983:13–14]). Castañeda counted only adult males, a procedure that served militarily to determine potential resistance. For total population, Charles Polzer, general editor of *Documentary Relations of the Southwest*, suggests (personal communication 1981) a maximum multiplier of four. This would yield twelve thousand to sixteen thousand Hopi and Zuni people. If we give eight thousand to Hopi, which is noted by two other chroniclers as having a somewhat greater population than Zuni (Winship 1896: 574,587), we might not be too far off the mark to estimate Oraibi in 1540 at a minimum of fifteen hundred to three thousand inhabitants (Oraibi's proportional population was higher than that of the other Hopi villages from at least 1583, as noted below). If this figure is anywhere near accurate, it suggests that at contact Oraibi was a very substantial pueblo.

The next recorded visit was by Antonio de Espejo's expedition of 1582–83. Chronicler Pérez de Luxán (1929:39) describes the province of "Mojose"[1] as consisting of twelve thousand persons in five villages. Espejo visited Awatovi first and the other four villages (Walpi, Mishongnovi, Shongopavi, and Oraibi) soon after. On 24 April 1583 they "reached the pueblo of Olalla,[2] which is the largest in the province" (Luxán 1929:102). They were received well and presented with eight hundred blankets.

Don Juan de Oñate visited Hopi in 1598. His purpose was to secure formal submission to the Spanish Crown and to survey the area and peoples recently brought under his jurisdiction as governor of the new colony of Nuevo Mexico. Oñate visited Oraibi on 14 November (Hargrave 1932:4). He lists chiefs of the Hopi villages, albeit somewhat confusedly. Although Oraibi was the last visited, both the village and its chief are listed first (Hammond and Rey 1953:360), which may suggest that the Spanish had begun to regard Oraibi as politically preeminent.

Oñate visited the "Province of Mohoqui" again in 1604–5 on his expedition to and from California. Father Escobar's diary of the expedition contains some interesting observations:

It [the province] has only five pueblos, four of them half in ruins and destroyed, containing not more than five hundred occupied houses.... There is very little firewood and still less water. Everywhere in this province there are excellent estufas [kivas] in each pueblo, so that with a small amount of wood they keep very warm the whole winter.... They have no temples for their worship, although some of the houses in which they live, it was noticed, were devoted to their ceremonies and worship.... I do not think these houses are often visited, and not by all the people, but from what I could gather, only by the leading and oldest Indians. (Hammond and Rey 1953: 1014–15)

An intertwining of religious and political structures and (in conjunction with Castañeda's observations above) a basis in gerontocracy are inferable from this account. Although four of the towns were in ruins, five hundred occupied houses would still suggest a total population of about three thousand.[3] Although considerably diminished from the earlier estimates, possibly due to introduced diseases, this is substantially larger than most nineteenth-century figures.

In August 1629, the next recorded official visit, three Franciscans arrived at Awatovi and established a mission, later building two more at Shongopavi and Oraibi. As early as 1598, the Hopi had been assigned a missionary, but it is generally doubted that he ever visited them (Montgomery, Smith, and Brew 1949:8). Evidently, the colonists were too busy establishing themselves in the Rio Grande valley: in the 1620s both Hopi and Zuni were exempt from tribute for the garrison in Santa Fe (Bancroft 1889:159).

The Benavides Memorial of 1634 records Hopi opposition to the missionaries' arrival:

Here the friars were received with some coolness, because the devil was trying in all possible ways to impede and obstruct the promulgation of the divine law.... He now took for his tool an Indian apostate from the Christian pueblos; he, preceding them, told the people of Moqui that some Spaniards, whom they would meet shortly, were coming to burn their pueblos, steal their property and behead their children, and that other Spaniards with the tonsures and vestments were nothing but impostors and that they should not allow them to sprinkle water on their heads because they would be certain to die from it. (Benavides 1945:217)

The Hopi planned attacks on the missionaries and their military escort, but the latter, sensing the antagonism, twice forestalled nighttime ambush attempts (Benavides 1945:217).

In 1640 Fray Bartolomé Romero, guardian at the mission of San Francisco de Oraibi, recorded that he had been at Hopi for ten years: "If those ten years were spent at Oraibi, which we do not know, then the mission there must have been established soon after San Bernardo de Aguatubi" (Montgomery, Smith, and Brew 1949:12).

General receptivity to the Franciscans was low (cf. James 1974:44–50). Father Porras died in 1633 at Awatovi under suspicious circumstances, and the few extant mission records indicate some good reasons for Hopi antipathy. Corruption and brutality ran rampant in the New Mexico missions. The "most flagrant case on record during the entire seventeenth century" (Scholes 1937: 144) occurred at Oraibi in 1655:

In the summer of that year several Indian captains from the Hopi Pueblos appeared before Custodian Ibargaray ... to denounce the actions of their priest, Friar Salvador de Guerra.... Several Indians were summoned to testify, and they told a harrowing tale. They stated that an Oraibi Indian named Juan Cuna had been discovered in some act of idolatry. In the presence of the entire pueblo, Father Guerra gave him such a severe beating that he was bathed in blood. Then inside the church, the Friar administered a second beating, following which he took burning turpentine and larded the Indian's body from head to feet. Soon after receiving this brutal punishment the Indian died. The Indians also testified that several other persons ... had been whipped and tarred with hot turpentine. (Scholes 1937:144–45)

This incident was not extraordinary (cf. Montgomery, Smith, and Brew 1949:15–16); Oraibi's later obdurate resistance to the Spanish is hardly surprising.

In 1664 there is a further record of the Oraibi mission: "The pueblo of Oraibi has a very good church, very good provision for public worship, a choir with many (musical) instruments, a good *convento*, and 1236 souls under its administration" (Scholes 1929: 49). Total population for the other four pueblos is listed at eighteen hundred persons, again indicating Oraibi's numerical strength. Since these estimates probably derive from the missions themselves, they may be quite reliable.

In 1680 in a concerted action, all the Pueblos revolted against the Spanish regime, sacking the missions and settlements and driving the colonists down the Rio Grande to El Paso. At the mission of San Miguel de Oraibi (there is no apparent reason for the change in patron saint) two priests were reported killed (Hackett and Shelby 1942:111). According to Third Mesa traditions, the killing occurred inside the mission by Warrior Kachinas provided by the Badger clan; the priests were then thrown off the mesa edge. Wikvaya, narrating a tale to H. R. Voth, details some motives:

> The padres . . . continued to oppress the Hopi and made them work very hard, and demanded contributions of food, etc. from them. They would also disregard all the feelings of the Hopi as to their own (the Hopi's) religion. They would trample under foot the chastity of the Hopi women and maidens. So finally the Hopi became angry and began to discuss the advisability of getting rid of their oppressors. (Voth 1905a:270)

Following the Revolt many refugees came from the Rio Grande pueblos and built at least three villages in the Hopi country. Bancroft quotes an account that

> 4,000 men, women and children . . . went via Zuni to Moqui, and having induced that people to give them a home gradually gained possession of the country and towns, reducing the original Moquis to complete subjection, extending their conquests far to the Southwest, and seating their young king, Trasquillo, on the throne at Oraibi. (Bancroft 1889:186 n. 13)

Bancroft remarks on the exaggerated nature of this account, but it again serves to indicate Oraibi's significance from the Spanish viewpoint.

De Vargas's reconquest of New Mexico in 1692 affected the Hopi less than the Rio Grande pueblos. De Vargas visited Awatovi, Walpi, Mishongnovi, and Shongopavi, receiving submission before a large white cross he erected in the plazas, though the party had to placate forces of armed men at Awatovi and Walpi (see Espinosa 1940:209–28). He did not go on to Oraibi. His official reasons were sent to the Viceroy: ". . . and in order not to risk losing the said horses and mules, and thereby find ourselves on foot and without mounts in such hostile land; and since the said pueblo of Oraibi is the only one remaining in this said province; for these reasons I postponed for the present the said entry" (Espinosa 1940:228). Possibly, De Vargas feared that the threats encountered at Awatovi and Walpi might be translated into action at Oraibi. At any rate, Oraibi never was reconquered by the Spanish military nor received absolution from the priests for its role in the Revolt.

Despite the nominal subjugation of the other Hopi villages, all except Awatovi rejected Spanish attempts to reestablish missions. This period immediately following the Reconquest provides some fascinating insights into Hopi political action. Under the leadership of Oraibi's "Francisco de Espeleta," who had been raised and taught to read and write by José de Espeleta (Hackett 1937:385), one of the missionaries killed at Oraibi, the Hopi effectively prevented reentry by the Franciscans. Shortly after reestablishment of the Spanish regime in Santa Fe, Espeleta began to maneuver:

The Moquis, noting the submission of other nations, and dreading war more than they feared or loved Christians, sent ambassadors in May 1700 to treat with the governor, professing their readiness to rebuild churches and receive missionaries. At the same time, Espeleta, Chief of Oraibe, sent for Padre Juan Garaicoechea to come and baptize children. The friar set out at once with Alcalde Jose Lopez Naranjo, and went to Aguatuvi, where he baptized seventy-three young Moquis. On account of a pretended rumor that the messengers to Santa Fé had been killed, he was not permitted to visit Oraibi or the other pueblos at this time; but Espeleta promised to notify him soon when they were ready for another visit. (Bancroft 1889:221–22)

Bandelier's description of the visit to Santa Fe gives more detail:

On the 11th of October of the same year [1700], one of the leading chiefs of Oraibi appeared at Santa Fe with 20 other delegates and presented themselves to the Governor, Pedro Rodriguez Cubero, as a formal embassy from the Moquis not as subjects and vassals of the crown, but as delegates of a foreign power sent to conclude a treaty of peace and amity. (Bandelier 1892:371–72)

Bancroft adds:

> He [Espeleta] now proposed a simple treaty of peace, his nation, like Spain, to retain its own religion. Cubero could offer peace only on condition of conversion to Christianity. Then the Moqui chief proposed as an ultimatum that the padres should visit one pueblo each year for six years to baptize, but postponed permanent residence till the end of that period. This scheme was likewise rejected, and Espeleta went home for further deliberation. (Bancroft 1889:222)

The documentary accounts suggest that Espeleta, as "cacique" of Oraibi, represented all the Hopi villages (cf. Twitchell 1911:419 n. 422). They are not full enough to warrant a conclusion that he was the head of an integral Hopi political order (Upham's interesting account [1982] of protohistoric western Pueblo political organization notwithstanding). What is clear, however, is that Espeleta and the other delegates were united in opposing a Spanish return, while remaining keenly aware of their military inferiority. What from the Spanish point of view appears to be chicanery—that is, the promise to accept missionaries, the open offer of acceptance and welcome, the unexpected rejection on trumped-up grounds, and a complete change of course a few months later, but all conducted with much diplomacy and overtly conciliatory compromise—was from the Hopi standpoint masterly political negotiation to forestall military confrontation. The elusive protocol seems remarkably similar to later encounters with the U.S. government (see Chapter 4).

Shortly after Espeleta's visit to Santa Fe, the village of Awatovi, on Antelope Mesa, was destroyed by Hopis from other villages (see Montgomery, Smith, and Brew 1949 for a thorough account). According to Hopi tradition, the agent provocateur was the Awatovi Village Chief, who colluded with the leaders of the other villages (e.g., see Voth 1905a:245–55; Fewkes 1898:603–5). Hopi accounts differ regarding proportional participation by the various villages, but Oraibi is always held to play a significant role. A Spanish account attributes major responsibility to Espeleta:

> At this time his people being infuriated because the Indians of the pueblo of Aguatubi had been reduced to our holy faith and the obedience of our king, he (Espeleta) came with more than one hundred of his people to the said pueblo, entered it, killed all the braves, and carried off the women,

leaving the pueblo to this day desolate and unpeopled. (Hackett 1937: 385–86)

The symbolic import of the destruction of Awatovi over its reacceptance of the Franciscan church must have been powerful for Hopi and Spaniard alike. The fact that the Hopi were prepared to annihilate the male population of one of their own villages suggests an astonishingly intense form of cultural self-regulation in preference to direct confrontation with the external foe. It may be that this course of action was considered the most effective method of preserving independence with the least long-term cost. The Pueblos in general are known for a stringent conservatism enforced by religious elites. Certainly, in the case of Awatovi, the devastating effects of deviation from cultural norms cannot have escaped the attention of any potential convert or any potential converter.

The recalcitrant stance toward the Spanish became entrenched. Hopi country became "the refuge of the irreconcilable, the diehards among the Pueblos of the east who could not bring themselves to bear the Spanish yoke" (Montgomery, Smith, and Brew 1949:20). All attempts to subjugate the Hopi by Spanish civil and ecclesiastical authorities met with failure. In 1701 Governor Cubero sent a punitive expedition over the destruction of Awatovi, and though a few Hopis were killed or captured, the force was easily repulsed by the Hopi and their refugee allies.

In 1713 two Zunis reported on a visit to Hopi that "the Moquis [were] eager for peace and alliance with the Zunis, but the *controlling element under the chief of Oraibi* had no desire for friendship with the Spaniards" (Twitchell 1911:428, my emphasis). Again, Oraibi's political importance and increasing reputation as the hard core of resistance is apparent.

In 1716 a force under Governor Phelix Martinez visited Walpi with the intention of conquest. They encountered fierce opposition and beat an ignominious retreat, having first laid waste some cornfields. According to contemporary documents, Martinez waited upon the decisions of "the Chief Cacique of the Pueblo of Oraibe called Fabian" before instigating the campaign (Bloom 1931).

Ecclesiasts met with the same stance as militia. In 1724

Father Fray Antonio Miranda and Fray Francisco Yrasabal entered the said province of Moqui apostolically in the month of May, making their way into the great pueblo of Oraibe. Although the fathers preached to them that they should accept the evangelical law which they had professed and submit themselves to the pale of the church, they were only able to obtain some hopes for the future—nothing more. (Hackett 1937:387)

In 1730 Fray Francisco de Archundi preached in vain at Oraibi for a day, and Bancroft (1889:239–40 n. 34) records other equally bootless clerical visits.

Throughout the first half of the eighteenth century there was an ongoing conflict between the Franciscans and the Jesuits over the province of Moqui. As early as 1716 the Bishop of Durango, on the authority of the viceroy, attempted to put the Jesuits in charge, but failed. In 1719 the king approved this transfer of power and in 1725 the viceroy issued a decree to put it into effect (Bancroft 1889:365). In practice the Jesuits never reached Hopi and displayed no great desire to do so. They were more interested in securing a presidio in the Gila Valley, whence to expand into California (Bancroft 1889:364). The threat of Jesuit encroachment, however, significantly affected Franciscan efforts. The 1740s saw a flurry of Franciscan visitors anxious to demonstrate a commitment to the Hopi and an ability to produce results. In 1742 Fathers Delgado and Pino visited Hopi and returned to the custodia of Albuquerque with four hundred forty-one "saved souls" (Hackett 1937:388–89). Most probably were Rio Grande refugees who wanted to return home for a variety of reasons (Montgomery, Smith, and Brew 1949:30–33).

In 1744 and again in 1745, Delgado visited all six Hopi towns (Shipaulovi and Hano had been founded in the aftermath of the Revolt). The inhabitants listened courteously to his preachings but characteristically put off any baptisms to some unspecified future. He counted, fairly thoroughly by his own account, 10,846 persons in all the villages (Hackett 1937:414–25). In 1745 a small party led by Father Rodriguez de la Torre received a similar rebuff; his attempts to preach were flummoxed by a "cacique endemoniado" who orated in counterpoint, denying the validity of his statements (Bancroft 1889:256). The same year, the province of Moqui was officially returned to the religious jurisdiction of the Franciscans.

The 1740s were a turbulent time for the Hopi. Brew (Montgomery, Smith, and Brew 1949:30–33) suggests that the Rio Grande refugees had, for the most part, outstayed their welcome. In consequence, there was considerable friction, even "daily wars" (Hackett 1937:472). Further, a prolonged drought exerted great pressure on Hopi resources (Montgomery, Smith, and Brew 1949:32). Whatever the causes, many refugees returned to the Rio Grande pueblos during this period (notably in 1748, when a group founded Sandia pueblo [Tamarón y Romeral 1954]), leaving Hano on First Mesa as the only non-Hopi pueblo in the area.

One of the last records of the Spanish period contains significant ethnographic detail. In 1775 Father Silvestre de Escalante spent eight days visiting all the villages, which by this time were the ones familiar in 1900: Walpi, Sichomovi, and Hano on First Mesa; Mishongnovi, Shipaulovi, and Shongopavi on Second Mesa; and Oraibi on Third Mesa. Escalante wrote several letters and kept a daily journal (Thomas 1932:302–8). He stayed in Oraibi for two days from 27 June:

The third mesa is to the west northwest. The pueblo of San Francisco de Oraybi . . . is on it. It has eleven rather large and well-arranged tenements, with streets to all directions, and there must be at least eight hundred families. It is governed by two captains and a cacique. . . . All the pueblos have an abundance of sheep, whose wool is usually black. They also have some cattle, and there is much more of this at Oraybi. This includes a good herd of horses. (Adams 1963:134–35)

Escalante remarked on the coolness of his reception at Oraibi:

Here there were no manifestations of courtesy and pleasure as in Gualpi. . . . I was surprised that no one came to see me during the whole afternoon, not even for the sake of novelty. . . . I sent for the cacique and captains to prepare them for the sermon I wanted to preach to them the next day. Only the chief captain and his lieutenant or companion came, with some old men. Through the interpreter I indicated my good will, to which they did not respond as they should have. I inquired for the cacique, and they said he was out hunting (which I later learned was untrue) and so I should tell them once and for all what I wanted to discuss with them. I replied that when the cacique came we would talk about it, that I was in no hurry, for my sole purpose in coming was to see them and converse with them about things which were very important to them. The chief captain (with obstinacy) said that he was superior to all, that the cacique would approve whatever he might decide, and that if I did not state my purpose in coming then and there they would not come to me again. (Adams 1963:124–25)

Escalante proceeded to preach to them through the interpreter:

I gave them to understand that I had been sent by God to proclaim for Him the eternal glory to which He was inviting them even though they had offended Him for so long, and the torments with which He would punish them if they did not abandon their abominations and, becoming Christian, keep His Holy Commandments. I exhorted them with all the force and clarity I could, and they replied briefly that even if what they had heard from me was true they had no desire to be Christians. (Adams 1963:125)

So he raised his threats of fire and brimstone to a new level, but

the said Captain replied with haughtiness and arrogance that he was ruling as governor, as king and that he did not want the Spaniards ever to live in his land; and for me not to weary myself in going about giving advice to his people, for none would give ear to me because he had already given orders to this effect and they must perforce obey him. (Adams 1963:127)

Escalante stormed out of the room, whereupon his antagonists suddenly became conciliatory:

They thought some harm might result to them from my anger and so they begged the interpreter to calm me down, saying that conversion to Christianity should not be by force, that although being Christian was repugnant to them, they wanted to remain on friendly terms with me and the Spaniards. I returned having recovered my equilibrium, and explained that I had not been angry with them, but that my profound sorrow because they did not want to be saved, when they could be, was breaking my heart, in which I cherished them all. At this point the meeting came to an end, and I retired to my lodging feeling very sad. Immediately after they left there, they proclaimed that no one was to listen to my counsels because my aim was to subject them to the Spaniards. They also sent the same admonition to all the other pueblos, telling their leaders what reply they were to make to me. (Adams 1963:126)

The foregoing narrative burgeons with interpretive significance. Oraibi's political stance and strategy of negotiation emerge with some clarity. The would-be missionary is psychologically manipulated with a supple political facility. His imperial intentions, and moreover his will to realize them, are entirely defused. When the ebullient and culturally self-righteous Escalante presents himself for acknowledgment, he is barely greeted. When he arrogantly orders the "cacique" (probably the *Kikmongwi*) to come and hear him, he is deceitfully eluded by other leaders who return his arrogance. When he says he is in no hurry, they rush him into his sermon. When they disdainfully reject it, he threatens powerful supernatural aid. They reply with even greater disdain. He becomes angry and frustrated and stalks out. They show solicitous concern and offer to compromise. He is mollified and slightly encouraged, but as the meeting ends he feels "sad." Immediately afterward, he learns that they have matter-of-factly informed the people to ignore him.

Other important observations emerge in Escalante's narrative. At First Mesa he attempted further missionary activity:

I tried to find out the sentiments and inclinations of individuals, instructing and exhorting those I could when there were no people about to prevent them from declaring themselves. I found, as in the other pueblos, some rebellious and others intimidated, although the malicious faction is everywhere larger and more numerous. (Adams 1963:130)

By itself, this passage may not entitle us to infer active factionalism, but such inference is strengthened by another remark Escalante makes concerning missionaries of the 1740s: "[Frailes Delgado and Yrigoyen] succeeded in bringing down some families from Oraibe ... because God, in order to save these souls, allowed *a grave discord over the election of a chief in Oraibe. On this account the pueblo was divided into two parties*, who took arms against one another" (Thomas 1932:159, my emphasis).

Finally, Escalante has some suggestive remarks on internal Hopi political organization. Referring to the conversion of some refugees in the 1740s, he notes, "the principal men ... promulgated by common agreement formidable penalties not only against those who brought about their conversion but also against those *who, not being captains, caciques, or Old Men of Authority*, were proved to have been talking with intent with the fathers in matters of religion" (Thomas 1932:160, my emphasis). In another passage (Thomas 1932:152), Escalante refers to "the inordinate religious control which the caciques and chiefs have." These observations point up a rather different kind of political system than the egalitarian model frequently presented in the ethnographic literature.

In July 1776 Oraibi received another Franciscan visitor, Francisco Garcés. The Oraibis refused to listen to him, store his baggage, house him or feed him; he spent two nights sleeping in one of the streets. The following morning, 4 July 1776, Garcés awoke to music and dance. After a while,

> I saw coming nigh unto me a great multitude of people, (the sight of) which caused me some fear of losing my life. There came forward four Indians who appeared to be principals, of whom the tallest one asked me with a grimace (risueño[4]), "For what hast thou come here? Get thee gone without delay—back to thy land!" (Coues 1900:390)

As Brew notes: "On the very day that representatives of a new American nation were proclaiming their independence at Philadelphia, July 4, 1776, the old nation of Oraibi was reaffirming theirs" (Montgomery, Smith, and Brew 1949:36).

A few months later, in November 1776, Fray Francisco Domínguez reported briefly that he was well received in Oraibi (Adams and Chávez 1956:289). In September 1780, fearing a Hopi-Apache alliance, the governor of New Mexico, Don Juan Bautista de Anza, set out with 125 men, the first substantial military expedition of record since the abortive reconquest attempt of Martinez in 1716. Anza determined that his first serious consultation should be at Oraibi, "which is the capital of this province of Moqui" (Thomas 1932:21). In response to his solicitations

> the cacique affirmed that he and his nation had always recognized as their God the very one the Spaniards had, although they were not baptized; that though most of his people were among the heathen, he and those who remained had so resolved to die, except the ones who wished to go to New Mexico and become Christians. With regard to trade, the chief assured the governor that he appreciated his kindness and would take advantage of it if they re-established themselves. However, this he thought was impossible because they had lost so much from drought and, he added bitterly, from the continuous war made upon them by the Utes and Navajos. Anza at once offered to mediate but the hardy old chieftain spurned the idea, preferring death at the foes' hands. Even Anza's proffer of a horse loaded with supplies the cacique refused, lacking the wherewithal to return the gift in kind as his customs demanded. Additional conversations only revealed further the stiff-necked pride of the cacique. (Thomas 1932:28)

Anza's approach was more diplomatic than those of Escalante and Garcés. In turn this elicited more courteous replies, but the message remained the same. Despite "hunger, pestilence and war," "the chief priests of the nation were inexorable in their purpose of remaining heathen, preserving their customs, and remaining in their desolated pueblos" (Thomas 1941:109).

Anza's desolate picture of the Hopi villages may be exaggerated (as Brew [Montgomery, Smith, and Brew 1949:37] thinks). He reports only thirty to forty families at Oraibi, where five years earlier Escalante had reported eight hundred. Anza spent a maximum of six or seven hours in Oraibi (see Thomas 1932:233–36), hardly sufficient to make an accurate population estimate during this, the harvest season. Nevertheless, Dockstader (1954:155) reports that the drought impelled Hopis to live at Zuni and with the Havasupai during this period. Refugees to the latter were very likely from Oraibi; through the late nineteenth century some Havasupais continued to live in the vicinity of Moencopi (considerably further east than their present reservation confinement).

Notwithstanding the complete rejection of everything Anza offered that might have affected cultural sovereignty, the following day at his camp near Awatovi, "a considerable number of Moqui joined us, the larger part from Oraibe seeking the opening of trade" (Thomas 1932:236). A parallel pattern is discernible here with the "Hostiles" in the late nineteenth century and many "traditional" Hopi in modern times. There is much interest in the benefits deriving from American society when these are made accessible to the Hopi on their own terms and do not result in indebtedness or binding relationships to non-Hopi agencies. In the late twentieth century, for example, in Hotevilla many people enjoy television by hooking up to pickup truck batteries, "pirate" water-lines run into the village from a central reservoir, and houses are lighted with propane from individually owned tanks. But the village as a whole has vigorously rejected attempts by utility companies to bring electricity or standard water-lines into the village, fearing that a potential corporate indebtedness would compromise their independence.

Most available documentary records of Hopi in the Spanish period concern missionary or military contacts. The extent of contact with private individuals is not recorded, but it is noteworthy that Garcés (Coues 1900:464) reports annual visits to Oraibi in the 1770s by a blacksmith. Clearly, such unofficial contacts would have significantly affected Hopi perceptions of the Spanish, although in what ways can only be speculated. Garcés also notes (Coues 1900:464) that the Hopi were key traders in an indigenous southwestern trading network for certain introduced commodities: awls, dibbles, hoes, and knives. Again this suggests that interaction with the Spanish was rather more complex than the records of official church and civil visits indicate.

After Anza's visit no more Spanish *entradas* were recorded into Hopi. Five important points about Hopi may be noted from the Spanish period. The first is Oraibi's size and importance in relation to the other Hopi villages. The second concerns Hopi government, which is characteristically described as comprising a "cacique," one or two "captains," and a council of "old men of authority" (e.g., Thomas 1932:162). The cacique is clearly the *Kikmongwi*, or Village Chief. The chief captain is most likely the *Qaletaqmongwi*, or War Chief, who represents the War Twin, *Pöökong*, and his assistant the representative of the other War Twin, *Palengawhoya*. The other "captains" may be other members of the *Momtsit*, Warriors' society. The "old men of authority" (though the inference here may be too general) are likely several of the *wimmomngwit*, heads of the "religious" societies. Third, the political authority of leadership consistently appears more sharply delineated than in the anthropological picture of egalitarianism frequently drawn of the Hopi. Repeated suggestions of Oraibi's influence over the other villages raise questions about the conventional village autonomy asserted in the ethnographic literature. At least from the Spanish viewpoint (and of course they had their interpretive models of correct political order, so the inference may be unwarranted), Oraibi exerted some authority in a (formally unspecifiable) pan-Hopi polity. Fourth, Oraibi continually and emphatically rejected all attempts at "directed culture change" after the 1680 Revolt. Finally, they resisted would-be "directors" with deliberate strategies and an eminent political sophistication. These attest to an incisive paradigm of political interpretation (regarding both their own society and the invading one) that was highly successful in generating schemes for managing particular attempts at dominion.

After the Revolt, the Spanish were never able again to bring the Hopi under their yoke, and Oraibi was always seen as the mainstay of Hopi intransigence. Oraibis repeatedly led Spanish representatives to believe that they were on the very brink of capitulating, but always actually maintained complete cultural sovereignty. Brew notes with not a little irony:

Against the background of the record of the eighteenth century, an entry of 1819 is either pathetic or amusing, depending on the point of view of the reader. Reporting Spanish-Navajo hostilities of 1819 from contemporary documents, Bancroft states: "A notable feature of this affair is the fact that the Navajos, being hard pressed, settled near the Moqui towns, and the Moquis sent five of their number to ask aid from the Spaniards. This was deemed a most fortunate occurrence, opening the way to the submission of this nation after an apostasy of 139 years. It was resolved to take advantage of the opportunity, but of the practical result nothing is known." (Montgomery, Smith, and Brew 1949:40)

It seems reasonable to infer that Oraibi's leaders, had they known of this resolution, might have risked a cautious smile.

The Mexican Period: 1821–46

Technically, the Hopi were subject to the Mexican government as they had technically been subject to the Spanish Crown. But Mexican authority was never actually imposed upon the Hopi, who were too difficult and distant to administer in these extremely lean times for the frontier province of New Mexico. Hargrave (1932:6) records that contact with the Mexicans during this period was "limited to raids upon the Hopis in order to secure slaves." Slave-raiding had long been a feature of Hispano-Indian relations and continued until shortly after U.S. abolition in 1865 (Aitken 1931: 377). New Mexican raiders took women, children, and livestock: "Indian women and children were sold after church on Sundays in the villages of Rio Arriba county and a healthy eight-year-old girl sometimes fetched $400" (Aitken 1931:377). Nequatewa (1944) describes a raid on Oraibi (which probably occurred in the 1860s—cf. Curtis 1922:11) recounted to him by one of the captives, and other accounts are recorded by Harrington (1931:227–30), Aitken (1931:378–81), and Curtis (1922:11–14). The account given to Aitken includes the murder by the slave-raiders of the Oraibi *Kik-*

mongwi and several priests conducting the *Soyalangw* ceremony in the chief kiva (this may coincide with the 1866 raid discussed below).

In 1823 a large expeditionary force (of fifteen hundred men) against the Navajo, led by Governor José Antonio Vizcarra, spent part of July and August in Hopi country (Brugge 1964). Oraibi was visited several times—initially by three hundred troops in the middle of the night, after a rumor of Navajo presence there (Brugge 1964:233)—though the only significant observation concerns the paucity of water in the Oraibi vicinity.

This period also sees the first Anglo-American visitors. In 1826 Lieutenant Ohio Pattie refers to a meeting with "Mokee" Indians during his travels across the West (Pattie 1905:130). The mountain man Bill Williams "lived among the Hopi in 1827" (James 1974: 75), and though he left no written record, "this Williams mingled with them in their social customs & religious rites, & became familiar with their rules & usages" (Yount 1942:195). George C. Yount visited Hopi in 1828 and provides some ethnographic observations of general interest (Yount 1942:1966). Williams, whose intentions seem benign from Yount's report, was very probably in a party of trappers from the Rocky Mountain Fur Company which passed through some Oraibi gardens in 1834. They plundered the gardens and evidently shot fifteen or twenty Hopis who protested (Donaldson 1893:24).

There had been reports of Ute, Navajo, and Comanche raids on the Hopi since the second half of the eighteenth century, and these, especially Navajo, increased significantly in the nineteenth century. One reason for the scant documentary record on the Hopi during this period is that "they were surrounded by deserts and the fierce Navajos and these were sufficient to stop visitors or adventurers; only armies could reach them" (Donaldson 1893:24).

The Anglo-American Period: 1846–82

A few minor contacts with Anglo-American groups are briefly recorded through the 1830s and 1840s (see Dockstader 1954:157). The first formal meeting between the Hopi and the U.S. government occurred in October 1850. The newly appointed superintendent of Indian Affairs for the Territory of New Mexico, James S. Calhoun, had tried to visit Hopi in that year but was denied an escort (Abel 1915:415). So the Hopi came to him, and in light of political traditions suggested above, their purpose is interesting:

> Their object, as announced, was to ascertain the purposes and views of the government of the United States toward them. They complained bitterly of the depredations of the Navajos. The deputation consisted of the cacique of all the pueblos, and a chief of the largest pueblo, accompanied by 2 who were not officials. From what I could learn from the cacique, I came to the conclusion that each of the seven pueblos was an independent republic, having confederated for mutual protection.... I understood further they regarded as a small pueblo Zuni, as compared with Oriva.... They supposed Oriva could turn out 1,000 warriors. (Donaldson 1893:25)

Calhoun received another Hopi delegation the following year (Abel 1915:415). In 1851 and 1852 Dr. P. G. S. Ten Broeck, assistant surgeon in the U.S. Army, visited First Mesa; his descriptions are informative, though it appears he did not visit Oraibi (Donaldson 1893:25–27; Schoolcraft 1854, 4:72–91). In 1852, long before any official government visit, the Hopi established contact with President Millard Fillmore. They communicated via an intermediary: "In the month of August, 1852, a message reached the President of the United States, by a delegation of the Pueblos of Tesuque in New Mexico, offering him friendship and intercommunication; and opening, symbolically, a road from Moqui Country to Washington" (Schoolcraft 1853, 3:306). The Hopi message was a "unique diplomatic pacquet" containing ritually valuable objects including prayer-sticks, honey, tobacco, and a pipe for the president to smoke—a basic sacramental act (Schoolcraft 1853, 3:306–9). This Hopi communiqué to the highest representative of the United States casts doubt on the widespread assumption that cognitively superior European "discoverers" have always taken the initiative with indigenous peoples—who, conversely, are assumed to be communicatively isolated in shadowy realms of backwoods ignorance. It also calls into question the suggestion that the Oraibi split of 1906 resulted from pressures of a dominant society whose intentions were barely even apprehended, let alone comprehended, in Hopi society. I shall return to this issue in Chapter 8.

Several expeditions had peripheral contact with the Hopi in the early 1850s. In 1851 Antoine Leroux (guide for the Sitgreaves expedition down the Zuni and Little Colorado rivers) reported a visit and gave total population as 6,720, with 2,400 at Oraibi (Whipple 1855:13). In November 1853, however, the Whipple expedition received intelligence from three Zunis of a severe smallpox epidemic that had decimated the Hopi population (Donaldson 1893:28). Oral traditions record so many dead that they could not be buried and were pushed off the mesa edges. In 1856 Major H. L. Kendrick, commander of Fort Defiance (which had been established in 1851) distributed some farming implements—including spades, axes, hoes, plows, and hatchets—to the Hopi villages (Hammond 1957, 1:21).

In 1858 Lieutenant J. C. Ives led a Corps of Topographical Engineers expedition to the Hopi villages. This is the first recorded visit of Anglo-Americans to Oraibi since official annexation of New Mexico by the Treaty of Guadalupe Hidalgo in 1848. They reached Oraibi on 12 May:

> A large number of the citizens came to see us. I subsequently learned that one of them was the chief, but he did not accost any one nor seem desirous of making acquaintances. It was apparent that he was out of humor, and the chief that had guided us [from Mishongnovi] informed me that the other, *who seems to be the senior of all*, had objected to any of the tribe accompanying the expedition north, on the ground that there was no water, that the country was bad, that we would have to travel several days before we would come to a river and that if we did reach it the mules could not get to the bank. Arguments and promises were vain. The Oraybe continued to express disapproval, and *his influence seemed to be all-powerful*. His ill temper increased as the discussion proceeded, and at last he left in a sulk and went home. I then had a talk with the other [the Mishongnovi chief]. He was friendly in his manner, but said that *he could not go while his superior objected* and intimated, if I understood him aright, that the Oraybe captain had some reason for not being well disposed towards Americans. (Ives 1861:124, my emphasis)

This passage again suggests Oraibi's relative importance and its skepticism of Euro-Americans—possibly compounded by the 1834 massacre (above). But, having ascertained that the Ives party was harmless,

> the Oraybe chief, gratified at the fulfillment of his prediction in regard to the impracticability of the trip northward, has been to visit us [at "Oraibi

Gardens," below present-day Hotevilla] and comported himself with much amiability. He told me that he would send a guide to show us the best route to Fort Defiance, and I accordingly regaled him with the best the camp afforded. (Ives 1861:126)

The same year, 1858, saw the beginning of Mormon visits to the area, especially to Oraibi. Mormon colonization of Utah began in the 1840s, and by 1856 Utah, or the "Kingdom of Deseret," had a population of seventy-seven thousand (Journal History of the Church 12-18-1856), many of them poor immigrants from the industrial slums of northern England. They probably learned about the Hopi from Paiutes or Hispanos. Although the detail is sketchy, the Mormons seem to have elaborated a mythology about these town-dwelling people to the south of them and had great expectations of their first meeting. Mormon interest in the Hopi dates from at least 1852 (Peterson 1971:180), and contemporary Mormon journals occasionally carried articles on the legendary "Moquitches" (e.g., *The Millennial Star* 1853:167–68; *The Deseret Evening News* 11-21-1853).

The first Mormon attempt to reach Hopi, in 1855, failed (Flake 1965:13), but in 1858 Jacob Hamblin, with a party of thirteen missionaries, reached Oraibi in the late fall (Flake 1965:16). The missionaries included a Welsh interpreter, in accordance with the notion that the Hopi might be descended from Welsh colonists who had come to North America in the twelfth century:

I have the history of the ancient Britons, which speaks of Prince Madoc, who was the son of Owen Guynedd, King of Wales, having sailed from Wales in the year 1160, with three ships. He returned in the year 1163, saying he had found a beautiful country across the western sea. He left Wales again in the year 1164 with fifteen ships and three thousand men. He was never again heard of. (Harris 1879:160)

After several missionary visits, it was decided that some Hopi words were identical with Welsh: "I was told by some intelligent Welsh Mormons that the Moqui chiefs could pronounce any word in the Welsh language with facility, but not the dialect now in use" (Posten 1864:150). Subsequently the Hopi came to be regarded, like all other Indians, as Lamanites, one of the Lost Tribes of Israel.

Thus, although "heathen," the Hopi were treated with considerable respect, initially at least, by Mormons, through their inclusion within two distinct mythological traditions of joint ancestry. This contrasted with the often contemptuous attitudes of other Anglo-Americans. Even within the latter's intellectual discourse—which was mostly removed from the frontier—Indians had only recently made it into the same species as Europeans, with Darwin's (1859) thorough grounding of the theory of evolution and Huxley's (1863) specific refutation of the polygenist theory of human origins (prevalent into the 1850s). At that, Indians had grasped only the bottom rung of the evolutionary ladder, which was headed by Europeans.

The Hopi developed separate categories of person for these two types of newcomers—*momonam* (Mormons) and *pahaanam* (other Anglos)—and they trusted the former considerably more than the latter. After a visit to Oraibi in 1881, Captain John G. Bourke (1884:330) noted that "the Mormons have great influence over the Oraybe Moquis, who decline to have any relations whatever with other Caucasians" (and cf. Cushing 1922:262).

Hamblin's first visit left some significant accounts:

> The natives say the Americans have been among them but had not acted very good. They said Bro. Hamblin looked like an American, but he might be good; they received him kindly but were very jealous; they asked him if he was not afraid they would kill him. He answered, no, and asked them if they killed their friends; they replied no. They did not believe in killing.
>
> They have seven cities or towns; they invited Bro. Hamblin to a big dance [possibly *Wuwtsim*]; each one of the natives brought to the dance something to denote his occupation. They showed Bro. Hamblin through their buildings; in one town he visited every house; their houses are very neat on the inside.... They dress in buckskin and blankets.... They informed Bro. Hamblin that at one time they were very rich, but that the Navajoes had robbed them of a great deal of their property; they also informed Bro. Hamblin that they did not suffer the Americans to enter their towns; they said they had heard of the Mormons from other Indians. When Bro. Hamblin was about leaving, he asked the chief what he should bring to trade with them, when he returned; they told him to bring wool cards, sheep shears, dye stuffs, hoes, spades. (Journal History of the Church 12-31-1858)

Four missionaries were left behind (two at Oraibi) in order to learn Hopi customs as a preliminary to preaching. However, they left after only three weeks on account of poor supplies (Gibbons 1858).

By the time of Hamblin's next visit to Oraibi in 1859, the Hopi had obtained hoes and spades from other American visitors and felt it unnecessary to trade with the Mormons for more (Journal History of the Church 11-30-1859). The earliness of these technological introductions is noteworthy. Missionaries Thales Haskell and Marion Shelton spent the winter of 1859–60 in Oraibi. Haskell's journal (Brooks 1944:69–98) contains some interesting ethnographic glimpses, but disappointingly, they are too brief to offer deep insights into Oraibi social life.

Mormon expeditions became a regular feature in the 1860s:

The Mormons sent no fewer than fifteen official missions to the Hopis [between 1858 and 1873]. On at least three occasions, missionaries were left on the mesas with instructions to stay and preach for periods extending up to a year, but none of them seems to have remained for more than five months. All told, about 85 white men participated in one or more of the fifteen expeditions, with total personnel for the trips approaching 125 men. Jacob Hamblin made every trip. Thales Haskell and Ira Hatch and one or two others also returned many times. Expeditions were usually made in the fall or winter and, as a general rule, lasted no longer than two or three months.... Between 1865 and 1869 preoccupation with Navajo raids in southern Utah and fear of hostile bands along the route apparently kept the missionaries at home. Otherwise, the Mormons sent an expedition to the Hopis nearly every year. (Peterson 1971:181–82)

In 1862, Hamblin persuaded three Oraibi men to accompany his party back to Salt Lake City (Journal History of the Church 1-8-1863), where they spent about four months. They met with Church President Brigham Young and became the first Hopis to be photographed (Peterson 1971:191 reproduces the picture). Moreover,

the President seemed much pleased with the results of the last Mission to the Moquis Pueblos; he immediately declared his intention of building forts on the East side of the Colorado, and place [sic] sufficient missionary force there to protect Lamanite industry, should they see proper to be gathered under the wings of Israel's Eagles. Brother Hamblin will probably raise about 100 men, such as we wanted for that purpose, in the southern country this spring, selecting such men who are willing to work for Israel, and do not worship the almighty dollar. (Journal History of the Church 2-15-1863)

Colonization attempts did not, in fact, begin for another ten years. Meanwhile, Tuuvi, an Oraibi man (possibly one of the visitors in 1862–63) and his wife, Katsinmana, visited Utah for about a year around 1870 and were evidently converted to the Mormon faith while staying with the Hamblin family in Kanab (Flake 1965:

35–36).[5] Tuuvi welcomed Mormon settlement of the Moencopi area as a means of protection from the Navajo (e.g., Lee 1955: 295–96). The first attempt to establish a colony in 1873 failed, but some colonists stayed long enough to start farming: "Tube took Bro. Blythe and some of the brethren around and allotted them about 10 or 12 acres of land to farm" (Solomon 1873–74:35). John D. Lee lived at Moencopi and later close by at Moenavi from 1873 to 1874. Lee had been formally excommunicated from the Mormon church over his role in the 1857 Mountain Meadows massacre (he was executed for it in 1877), and he was technically in hiding, though he retained much informal contact with southern Utah Mormons. Lee's diary for 1873–74 (1955, 2:263–342) reveals extensive contacts with a few Oraibis installed at Moencopi and records numerous parties passing through the area, including prospectors, the Wheeler survey, and Mormon settlers. He reports that a party of Oraibi men traveled to Kanab, Utah, in 1873 to trade for horses, noting that "one of them spoke good English" (1955, 2:284). Lee also recorded a short word list of the "Orava Language" (1955, 2:284). The extent of cultural interchange between the Mormons and some Oraibis is indicated in his account of a gathering in August 1873:

Rachel A. [one of his wives] and I rode to the Upper Moen cropa on a visit to Tuba, Taltee and others of the oriba dignataries. We were very courteously Entertained. Mrs. Tuby and Mother got up a Spendid dinner for us of Mutton Stake, 3 kinds of wheat Bread of their own grinding, Fried cakes, Tea & sugar, vegatable Squash, Water & Musk Mellons. After dinner, Mr. Taltee, the Alcalda (who by the way speaks the Mexica[n] language) handed Me a Portfolio containing a No. of recommendations from U.S. officials, also Several Bank Notes &c. We passed off the day verry agreable. (Lee 1955, 2:286)

Lee gave Tuuvi an iron stove (1955, 2:265) and may have introduced other manufactures to which he had access (such as bacon, coffee, clothing, tools, and a wagon). At his Moencopi farm he planted (as well as maize, beans, and squash) peas, potatoes, beets, radishes, lettuce, alfalfa, onions, turnips, wheat, and barley; this may have been the first access Hopis had to several of these cultigens.

The first successful settlement of Mormons at Moencopi occurred in 1875 (Flake 1965:44). In 1876 they moved a short distance away and established "Tuba City" (named for Tuuvi). They had considerable contact with Tuuvi and some other Oraibi Hopis who were beginning to spend more time at the small farming colony of Moencopi. However, the missionary impetus dwindled:

> Ironically once a substantial number of Mormons had moved to Hopiland, the interest that had sustained the Hopi Mission for fifteen years soon abated ... with a few exceptions such as Tuba City's Christian Lingo Christensen, the Mormon Missionary impulse lay dormant as far as the Hopis were concerned after 1880. (Peterson 1971:192–93)

Very few Hopis converted: Peterson (1971:193) estimates "no more than a dozen," but Flake (1965:50), probably more accurately, reports no more than four or five. Moreover, Tuuvi practically became an outcast from Oraibi society for his espousal of Mormonism (Flake 1965:50–51), and Katsinmana later renounced her conversion. Although initial relations may have been good, the permanent Mormon presence at Tuba City put a severe strain on them, and occurrences of violence against Hopis, especially over the water supply, appear in the documentary record (e.g., Christensen 1877–85:20–22). Evidently, the Mormons introduced silver dollars as a medium of exchange (Brainard 1935: 126).

In the 1870s several Mormon settlements such as Holbrook, Joseph City, Sunset, and Woodruff were established along the Little Colorado River to the south (Flake 1965:39–81). They offered an alternative source of Anglo influence to the gradually increasing presence of government representatives. However, fearing Mormon expansionism throughout the West, in 1875 the government began a campaign of harassment, focusing upon the practice of polygamy (e.g., Brooks 1942:90). Gradually, the Arizona settlers began to withdraw to Utah. In February 1903 the Mormons left Tuba City, virtually forced out by the government with a compensatory settlement of $45,000 (Flake 1965:81).[6]

In 1861 U.S. Indian Agent John Ward visited Hopi and reported a total population of twenty-five hundred, eight hundred of whom were at Oraibi. In 1865 Ward indicated the lack of significant government involvement with the Hopi:

> The only succor worthy of notice which these people have received from this superintendency, so far as I am aware, is that which has been extended to them during this winter. I can safely say that there was never a tribe of

Indians so completely neglected and so little cared for as these same Moqui Indians; indeed for some time they seem to have belonged nowhere. For several years previous to the creation of Arizona territory, they were not mentioned in the annual reports of my predecessor. (Donaldson 1893:34)

Two years earlier Arizona Territory had been created from the western half of New Mexico, and the Hopi were transferred to the Arizona Superintendency of Indian Affairs. The transfer was apparently an enigma to the Hopi, "owing to their mutual relations and extensive acquaintance with our Pueblo Indians, and the fact that they consider themselves as belonging to this country" (Ward, quoted in Donaldson 1893:34). Nevertheless, Hopis soon responded to this transfer with visits to Prescott, the new territorial seat, beginning in April 1866 (*Arizona Miner* 4-25-1866). Over the next four years several more Hopi parties arrived, principally from Oraibi (*Arizona Miner* 7-23-1870).

Possibly a major reason for Hopi visits to white settlements during the 1860s was a severe drought. As early as 1863, Mormon visitors reported their difficulty in obtaining food supplies at Oraibi: "They would rather give us a little than to sell, for they have been subject to great famines here. Twenty-four of their men and twenty-two of their women have died through starvation within the last two years" (Journal History of the Church 1-8-1863). Two years later the situation had worsened considerably:

The crop failure during the last two years has reduced the Zunis and Moquis to a state of beggary. The very fact that most of them, men, women, and children have come on foot a distance of at least 300 miles through deep snow during one of the most severe winters of many years, for the purpose of procuring something to eat and what little they can pack to their homes, is of itself sufficient evidence of their deplorable condition. (Ward, April 1, 1865, quoted in Leathers 1937:31)

Again in 1867, the condition of the Hopis was "wretched in the extreme" (U.S. Government 1867:153). Matters improved by 1869 (U.S. Government 1869:90–91), but overall the 1860s seem to have been a devastating period.

In November 1863 another kind of Anglo party spent some time in the Hopi villages. The Navajo "roundup" was in full swing, and Kit Carson arrived to recruit men from all the villages to aid the military expedition—all villages, that is, except Oraibi: "Before my arrival at Oraibi I was credibly informed that the people of that village had formed an alliance with the Navajos, and on reaching there I caused to be bound their Governor and another of their principal men and took them with me as prisoners" (Twitchell 1917:350–51). Evidently, within a few days Carson "became convinced that he had been misinformed about the attitude of the Oraibi people toward the Navajo, and his Hopi captives were released" (James 1974:83). In 1864 Lieutenant Robert Thompson of the New Mexico Volunteers was sent on a reconnaissance expedition to the Hopi villages. The Oraibis were evidently cowed by his approach:

When he got there, the people, whom he thought from appearances might number 600–700, and their chiefs, had fled and could not be induced to return. Thompson estimated that Oraibi had about 400 acres in cultivation, mostly planted to corn, and that its people probably raised some 3,000 to 4,000 bushels per year ... he thought the pueblo might have from 3,000 to 4,000 sheep and goats. (Hammond 1957, 1:41)

New Mexican slave raids were noted above. In December 1866, eighty New Mexicans raided Oraibi, where they "killed three, wounded four, drove off 558 head of livestock, and carried into captivity five girls and six boys" (Bailey 1966:121). An Oraibi party journeyed to Santa Fe to enlist Special Agent John Ward's assistance, and the captives and a few stock were returned. The raiders, however, went unpunished (Bailey 1966:122).

During the late 1860s and 1870s recorded visits to Hopi increase significantly; I shall not attempt to document them all here. From 1850 to 1863 the Hopi had been officially under the Pueblo Indian Agency in New Mexico (apart from a short period from 1858 when they were under the Navajo Agent at Fort Defiance [Hammond 1957, 1:28, 31]), though Ward in 1861 was the only agent to reach Hopi. From 1864 several agents, in absentia at Santa Fe, Fort Wingate, or Fort Defiance, were appointed to the Hopi; most did not visit their constituency. Donaldson recounts subsequent agency history:

In 1868 Major A. D. Palmer was appointed special agent for the Moquis and went to Arizona in pursuance of his appointment in 1869. He served during 1869–70. W. D. Crothers was agent in 1871–1872. The Moqui

Pueblo Agency was really established in 1870. In 1873-1874 W. S. Defrees was agent for the Moqui Pueblos, as they were called, and erected the first agency building at what is now Keam's Canon, Arizona. In 1875-76 W. B. Truax was the Agent. The separate agency was abandoned between October, 1876, and February, 1878. After this time the agency was continued with the Navajo agency. William R. Mateer was agent in 1878-79, John H. Sullivan in 1880-1881, J. D. Fleming in 1882, F. W. Vandever 1889-1890, and A. D. Shipley in 1891. (Donaldson 1893:36)

Contacts between these agents and the Hopi villages were variable in character, but early on the hostility of Oraibi was noted:

My reception by these people was of a cordial character, apart from the Oreybes, who manifested much hostility to me, saying they did not wish to have anything to do with the Government, and, I regret to say a portion of them continue to be hostile. I also found the relation between the six villages and the Oreybes was not of a friendly character.... The chiefs said they had no unkind feeling toward the Oreybes, but the chief of the Oreybes was angry with them because they were friends to the white man and the Government. (Crothers 1871:704)

Initially the Oraibis spurned all annuity goods, and although some later relented, "the chief refused to accept anything" (Crothers 1871:704). This might be an indication of internal dissidence, for the following year, "I will state here that the census of the Oreybes was not as satisfactorily taken as I should have desired, there being a want of harmony among the chiefs, a portion of the chiefs desiring a count taken, and a portion opposing, not wishing to have anything to do with Americans" (Crothers 1872:324).

In general, Oraibi's hostility to the government persisted throughout the 1870s. In 1877 an annuity issue of clothing "was made to six villages and one family of the Orribies" (Irvine 1877: 160), and in 1878 "the Oraibies still refuse to be enrolled" in the census[7] (Mateer 1878:8). Between 1872 and 1876 a small school was desultorily operated in Keam's Canyon, but it is very doubtful that any pupils were from Oraibi. Agent Mateer, after his arrival in February 1878, called a council of Hopi chiefs, but Oraibi refused to attend. So

he visited Oraibi village, whose chief, Lo-lu-lul-a-my, said . . . "if the Gov. wanted anything from him why did'nt [sic] the President come and see him himself." The chief told how, during the Navajo war [of the early 1860s], the Americans and Mexicans had abused them, taken their stock and abused their wives, and he was in no mood to have anything to do with Mateer. (Hammond 1957, 1:80)

This is the earliest record I have found indicating Loololma as chief (see Chapter 4). At this juncture, his antigovernment stance is clear.

The Oraibis were certainly more hospitable to some groups than to others. John Wesley Powell's Colorado River expeditions of 1869–1872 made at least two visits to the Hopi towns and in 1870 spent two months there "studying the language and customs of the people" (J. W. Powell 1972:16). Powell's accounts are the earliest to give some sensitively observed ethnographic detail. He was invited to the kiva ceremonies for either the *Owaqöl* or *Lakon* society in Mishongnovi, and collected an Oraibi word list (Fowler and Fowler 1971:273–74, 278–81) and a lengthy version of the Hopi creation myth, which clearly comes from Oraibi. One of his hosts in Oraibi, Talti, who was Tuuvi's "brother in-law" (Lee 1955, 2:293) and may have been Crier Chief (*Tsa'akmongwi*), gave Powell considerable information. A plan was hatched to take Talti to Washington, but last-minute confusion during the departure from Santa Fe wrought its failure. Overall, the Powell party received a fine welcome in Oraibi; the presence of Mormon pioneer Jacob Hamblin as guide may have facilitated their reception. They were feasted and engaged in extensive trading, all of which, from Powell's description (1895:35ff.), seems most convivial. Perhaps the most striking illustration of cordial relations was their departure:

October 24th—Today we leave Oraibi. We are ready to start in the early morning. The whole town comes to bid us good-by. Before we start they perform some strange ceremony which I cannot understand, but, with invocations to some deity, they sprinkle us, our animals, and our goods with water and with meal. Then there is a time of handshaking and hugging. "Good-by; good-by; good-by!" (J. W. Powell 1895:44)

In 1872 another of the Colorado River expeditions visited Oraibi and was similarly welcomed. Walter Clement Powell (J. W.'s brother) reported:

He [Talti] received us kindly, and, in referring to the matter [of the aborted trip to Washington], simply said that the white man had waited as agreed, and there was no cause to complain. This Chief's special occupation is that of Town Crier. Every evening from his housetop he announces the programme for the following day. The Government consists of 3 persons, the principal Chief and 2 subordinates, who arrange the order of public festivals, ceremonies, and general affairs. Oryba contained 600 inhabitants. (W. C. Powell 1949:482)

In 1874, during a campaign against the Western Apache, a military party under General George Crook visited Hopi for about ten days (Bourke 1891:230). Cushing (n.d.:39), presumably from hearsay evidence, suggests that there was a demonstration of military might at Oraibi, after the Oraibis first refused to give up the gunpowder Crook accused them of trading to the Apaches. Lieutenant John G. Bourke, the southwestern soldier-ethnologist who accompanied Crook, makes no mention of this, confining his remarks on Oraibi to the abundance of available water and peach trees (Bloom 1934:8).

The last record of meeting I wish to briefly mention (I shall return to it in Chapter 4) was by ethnologist Frank H. Cushing in December 1882. Cushing barged uninvited into an Oraibi kiva (quite possibly the chief kiva during the *Soyalangw* ceremony) to trade and was greeted with much hostility. In the ensuing encounter, he discovered two factions in the village, those siding with the *Kikmongwi*, Loololma, and those led by the "Chief Priest of the tribe and a *Wizard*" (Cushing n.d.:13), who was head of the Spider clan (Cushing n.d.:20). During a tense confrontation (during which Cushing's guide from Hano, Tom Polaccaca, kept his hand on his pistol), Cushing learned a considerable amount about the factionalism. Shortly afterward, he was forced to leave Oraibi.

Around the time Cushing was in Oraibi, on 16 December 1882, President Chester Arthur ratified an executive order creating a reservation for the Hopi. According to Hopi tradition, each side of the rectangular reservation boundaries was marked by a relay of four Hopi runners under the direction of the Hopi Agent, J. H. Flemming. Starting at the southeast corner, the first runner carried a U.S. flag to the southwest corner and passed it to the next, who ran to the northwest corner, and so on (Waters 1963:288 records a variant). In practice these boundaries had little immediate effect on Hopi life; though they may have deterred Anglo-American settlement, they had no impact upon the increasing Navajo encroachment onto traditionally Hopi lands.

Of particular emphasis in this chapter has been Oraibi's historic role as the strongest and most unbending antagonist of Euro-American imperialism and its strategies for dealing with alien powers attempting to impose dominion. The strategies were flexible, depending upon the nature of interaction; neither was the stance monolithic (as the Powell visit illustrates), except in its determination to preserve autonomy. The picture of political authority through which the strategies were played out raises questions about conventional views of Hopi political organization and, by extension, the entire scheme of social organization (see Chapter 3). Oraibi's metropolitan status in the eyes of outsiders is continuously evident. Fray Agustín de Morfi, for example, writing in 1782 (from Escalante's reports) noted: "It is like the capital of the [Moqui] province the largest and best arranged of all and perhaps of all the Interior Provinces [of Nuevo Mexico]" (Thomas 1932:108). Two hundred years later, Albert Yava from First Mesa echoed these sentiments from an internal perspective: "For a long time Oraibi was very important ceremonially. The Oraibis always thought of themselves as the center of everything, and they sort of looked at the other villages as outlying provinces" (Yava 1978:111).

3
◨ Oraibi Society in the Late Nineteenth Century

Foregrounding the Signifier

Anthropology has been suffering from a "crisis of representations" in recent years (see, e.g., Marcus and Fischer 1986). One can no longer write ethnography without an awareness that the standard descriptive terms invoke an authority that rests on a bedrock of rhetorical genre conventions (cf. Clifford 1983). More generally, this "crisis" is intrinsic to the ethnographic project, and the current emphasis is merely a gathering of speed. Disputes (together with their implications for interpretation) over the meanings of ethnographic terms (totem, lineage, ritual, tribe) have been virtually continuous in anthropological discourse.

In discussing Oraibi society, I use such terms as clan, phratry, religious society, lineage, household, kiva group, ceremony, and so on. The sheer weight of prior Hopi ethnography makes it impossible to ignore such terms (although their applications have not always been consistent). Voegelin and Voegelin (1970:47), for example, refer to a "consensus of anthropological opinion" regarding the hierarchical arrangement of Hopi kin groups (into phratries, clans, lineages, and households)—a consensus ascertained from the reading of "900 bibliographic items." The attendant conceptual entrenchment is difficult to subvert without a concerted revisionism, which is beyond my present scope (I have made a first step elsewhere: Whiteley 1985b, 1986). Yet what does this consensus actually mean?

A significant task of ethnography has been the identification of basic institutions. What groups is society made of? What are its basic building blocks? To understand British history, for example, familiarity with the institutions of monarchy, courts of law, the Church of England, tradesmen's guilds, the monogamous, bilateral nuclear family, and so forth, is essential. Identification of basic institutions in "other" cultures has been guided by four broad divisions of human activity assumed as universal: kinship, economics, politics, and religion. David Schneider (1984:184) traces these cornerstones of social science to "European folk theories," and he impugns their cross-cultural validity.

Schneider reasonably suggests that this four-fold matrix is ineffective analytically because it categorically separates fields of social action that are not so separated in many of the societies anthropologists study. His suggestion serves as a warning to the pages that follow. For the sake of simplicity, I have elected to rely on the matrix (although with, I hope, a continuously critical awareness). In describing the general principles of Hopi social structure and how these were specifically manifest in turn-of-the-century Oraibi, I make heavy use of the established Hopi ethnographic canon, as well as my own (much later) fieldwork. The result is a mixture—I trust not a muddle—of representations: redescriptions from texts, reinterpretations, both interspersed with diacritical inserts from "first-hand" observations and dialogues. I have found it difficult to control the tense of general descriptions. Frequently the "ethnographic present" refers to a time long gone in Oraibi; the descriptions nevertheless retain currency for such villages as Shongopavi and Mishongnovi, so I use a combination of present and past tenses. What follows, then, should be regarded as an ideal-typical representation of some formal attributes and specific features of Hopi social structure as this was manifested in Oraibi, not a comprehensive empirical account.

General Social Structure

Analyses of Hopi social structure are myriad. The most centrally important in the history of Hopi ethnography are those of Fred Eggan (1950) and Mischa Titiev (1944); Connelly (1979) provides a useful synopsis. Eggan (1950:18–19) succinctly summarizes the general features of Hopi village structure:

A preliminary examination reveals that each village is divided into a series of matrilineal, totemically named clans which are linked or grouped in nameless, but exogamous phratries. Each clan is composed of one or more matrilineal lineages, which, though nameless, are of great importance. The basic local organization is the extended family based on matrilocal residence and occupying a household of one or more rooms in common. In addition there are various associations, both societies and kiva groups, which are involved in the performance of the calendric ceremonies.

According to Eggan and others, the key principle in Hopi social structure is a balance effected between discrete groups of different orders, organized on the basis of kinship, residence, and ritual. The balance is achieved by the interweaving of these groups so that different combinations are brought together for different purposes. The combinations create a multiplicity of rights and duties which counterbalances the divisive tendencies of individual allegiances to just one type of social group. An individual is thus a member of several different social groupings simultaneously, and the solidarity of the maximal unit, which for the present purposes is best considered as the village, is effected by the conjunction of the smaller units through their mutually cross-cutting membership. Eggan (1950: 116) describes this process:

Hopi integration may be viewed from the standpoint of the major organizations: kinship, clan and phratry, society and kiva. Each of these organizations has various devices for increasing or maintaining its own social solidarity. Each system of organization also overlaps the others in terms of membership, so that an integration of the whole is achieved; the bonds holding individuals to household, clan, society, and kiva groupings interweave in complex fashion.

These "major organizations" can profitably be divided into those in which status is ascribed and those in which it is achieved. Natal household, lineage, clan, phratry, and village memberships are ascribed. Affinal household, society, and kiva memberships are achieved, at least in the sense that they are not entirely predetermined. Through the ascribed statuses, ties are effected between groups on a vertical axis—from household to village—of increasing inclusiveness. The achieved statuses create ties that intersect the ascriptive structure.

Let me try to clarify this by examining the major structural units within the village in turn.

Kinship and Residence Units

THE HOUSEHOLD

The household is "the smallest distinct unit of Hopi society" (Connelly 1979:545). For Titiev, it consists of a segment of a matrilineage: "The basic feature of this grouping is the fact that a mature woman, her daughters, and occasionally, her granddaughters, occupy a common residence through life and bring up their children under the same roof" (Titiev 1944:7).

Since men alter their household of residence and production upon marriage but not their position in the ritual duties of their natal household, they are "peripheral, with divided residences and loyalties" (Eggan 1950:30). The household is thus a matrilocal residential and economic unit, which partially includes inmarried affines and outmarried, uxorilocal male kin. Typically, it consists of a woman and her husband, married daughters and their husbands, unmarried sons, and children of the daughters. This group occupies a set of adjoining rooms in the village (Eggan 1950:29).

The developmental cycle leads to new household formation: "Proliferation of descent lines may lead to forming of separate households, but these often continue in amiable relations with the prime group" (Connelly 1979:546). This process may segment the lineage and provide the mechanism for the formation of new lineages (Titiev 1944:46–48).

The relationship among households can be hierarchical: each matrilineal clan has a primary household with a "clan-house," where the clan's *wu'uya* (totemic sacra) are kept. The social status of other households in the clan varies in accordance with genealogical proximity to the primary household. The latter forms the "core lineage segment" and possesses prestige deriving from its custody of the "heart of the clan" (the *wu'uya*) and from the fact that it is usually within this group that clan or ritual roles are inherited. As for the rest, "in a crisis situation, such as drought, crop loss, declining domestic water supply, or overpopulation, the peripheral household groups may be pressed to emigrate" (Connelly 1979: 546).

Older consultants from Third Mesa suggest that the ranking of households—at least between the primary household and the rest—was more clearly demarcated there than at First Mesa and Second Mesa (cf. Eggan 1950:105). Eggan (personal communication 1982) links this clearer household individuation to pressure upon land rights in the Oraibi Valley. Oraibi's population was consistently greater in the historic period than any other village, with the corollary (at least in the late nineteenth century) of larger clan size and a larger number of clans.[1]

The household is the primary residential, productive, and reproductive unit. It is also a significant ritual unit, but much more so in those primary households that controlled major rituals.

THE LINEAGE

Anthropologists (e.g., Eggan 1950; Titiev 1944; Connelly 1979) have agreed that, although it is unnamed in Hopi, the lineage is a distinct segment of the clan with important functions. It may be confined to a single household but more often occupies a number of households. Eggan (1950:109) regards the lineage as the most fundamental unit in the Hopi kinship system: "The lineage, unnamed as it is, is of primary importance to the Hopi because it contains the *mechanism* for transmitting rights, duties, land, houses, and ceremonial knowledge, and thus it is vital with respect to status."[2]

The lineage is a less obviously visible body than the household in that it unites noncoresidential kin. Indeed, Titiev (1944:58) finds its formal boundaries difficult to specify:

Lineage—an exogamic, unilateral group of matrilineal kindred, demonstrably descended from a common ancestress. Since such demonstrations cannot always be made among the modern Hopi, and since the lineage lacks both name and *wuya* and may be scattered over several households, it is the vaguest of the Hopi divisions. Its importance lies primarily in its theoretical implications as a nascent clan, and in the tendency for inheritance to follow the lineage pattern.

Emphasis upon the lineage as basic is best regarded as an anthropological model rather than a full reflection of the empirical situation. In practice, it is impossible to identify consistently and unambiguously a lineage when the same group of people may simultaneously comprise clan, lineage, and household. In part this is a function of numbers: for example, if the sole representatives of a clan consist of the women of one household and their male relatives for whom this is the natal household, this group can be regarded as both lineage and clan, even if it consists of only two or three people. At the other extreme, as in the case of the highly populous Greasewood clan at Third Mesa, lineages and households within the clan may proliferate. Titiev (1944:48) acknowledges this: "Today one can find instances of one clan containing a single lineage and a solitary household; of one clan containing a single lineage but several households; or of one clan containing what seem to be several lineages whose members are scattered among a number of households."

For Eggan, who gives it the most importance, the lineage—as a genealogically distinguishable segment within a clan—is the primary corporate action group. He regards it as in practice the most significant unit, jurally, economically, and ritually (Eggan 1949). But there is a contradiction here:

> The clan is the outstanding unit of social organization; in Hopi conception it is "timeless" and permanent, extending back to the period before the emergence and forward to include as yet unborn children. . . . The Hopi have utilized the clan as a primitive "corporation," holding land, houses, and ceremonial knowledge and property "in trust" for future generations. (Eggan 1950:110)

Which, then, is the primary unit—lineage or clan? What if the two are empirically identical and occupy a single household? (I have developed these criticisms elsewhere: see Whiteley 1985b, 1986.) Hopi kinship groups by no means operate on a completely ad hoc basis. But neither do they fall neatly into descent-theory categories of "universal" applicability in which the societal functions of "lineages" and "clans" are clear and mutually distinguishable.

Table 3.1. Oraibi Clans and Phratries

Phratry	Clan Hopi Name	Clan English Name	No. of Households	Population F	Population M	Population Total
I	Tapngyam	Rabbit	13	33	28	61
	Katsinngyam	Kachina	2	5	6	11
	Kyarngyam	Parrot	5	16	15	31
	Angwusngyam	Crow	1	2	0	2
II	Honngyam	Bear	5	6	13	19
	Kookyangngyam	Spider	3	16	15	31
III	Tuwangyam	Sand	9	28	31	59
	Kuukutsngyam	Lizard	4	28	30	58
	Tsuungyam	Snake	2	2	4	6
IV	Tawangyam	Sun	9	24	23	47
	Kwaangyam	Eagle	6	12	9	21
V	Tepngyam	Greasewood	14	37	36	73
	Paaqapngyam	Reed	7	32	17	49
	Awatngyam	Bow	4	7	8	15
VI	Masngyam	Maasaw	7	29	19	48
	Kookopngyam	Kookop ("Fire")	3	8	14	22
	Hoongyam	Cedar	1	0	2	2
	Leengyam	Millet	1	5	6	11
	Isngyam	Coyote	10	24	22	46
	Paa'isngyam	Desert Fox (Water Coyote)	10	27	30	57
VII	Pashonanngyam	Real Badger	5	14	23	37
	Masihonanngyam	Gray Badger	3	6	27	33
	Tasaphonanngyam	Navajo Badger	3	7	4	11
	Poliingyam	Butterfly	1	2	3	5
VIII	Piikyasngyam	Young Corn	7	25	20	45
	Patkingyam	Divided Water (Water-House)	7	17	19	36
	Siva'apngyam	Rabbitbrush	1	1	2	3
IX	Kelngyam	Chickenhawk	2	5	5	10
	Atokngyam	Crane	1	1	4	5
	Patngyam	Squash	2	3	6	9
TOTAL	30		147	422	441	863

SOURCE: Titiev 1944:52 (Chart VI).

NOTE: I have eliminated the "Gray Hawk" and "Agave" clans, from Phratries IV and VI, respectively, since Titiev gives no population figures or households for either. I have changed some of his spellings to accord with modern orthographic conventions. I have changed English translations (Water Coyote to Desert Fox, Water-House to Divided Water) in accordance with my consultants' interpretations. I have left *Tsuungyam* as "Snake," its predominant rendering in the literature and in modern Hopi-English. The literal meaning of *tsu'a*, the species referred to, is "rattlesnake," the generic term for snake being *lölöqang*.

Hopis regard internal clan segments as de facto groups that may or may not exist within specific clans. The "clan" (the accepted English gloss for -*ngyam*), not the lineage, is the primary cognized model. The presence of *some* discrete lineages or lineage-segments within particular clans is, nevertheless, important for some purposes—in particular at Oraibi, for the political structure. I shall return to the question of politics below.

THE CLAN

I have cited Eggan's concept of the clan above. Titiev (1944:58) settles on the following definition:

Clan—A totemically named, exogamous, unilateral aggregation of matrilineal kindred, comprising one or more lineages all of which are supposedly descended from one ancestress. Each clan has at least one *wuya* stored in *the* clan house. If this *wuya* forms the nucleus of a pueblo ritual, the controlling clan furnishes the officers who conduct the ceremony. It is the only kinship group for which there is a native term, and since land is held in the name of the clan, this unit is the cornerstone of Hopi society.

For turn-of-the-century Oraibi, Titiev (1944:52) lists thirty-one clans grouped in nine phratries (Table 3.1). Clan-totem associations refer mostly to animals, plants, or clan deities. The *wu'uya*, or totem (in deference to Lévi-Strauss's 1962 deconstruction of "totemism," I mean this term in a very general sense), may have tangible representation in a fetish or ritual objects of different kinds. Mythological acquisition of a particular totem follows a variety of styles. The following (abbreviated) example was given to me for Badger:

We were living at Kiisiwu [Shady Springs, about fifty miles to the northeast of Oraibi]. The people had heard of Oraibi and they decided to try to move there. So we picked up and migrated over here. Our leader went to see the Oraibi *Kikmongwi* to ask for permission to live in the village. He refused. So we set up camp in a valley below Oraibi [subsequently called Honansikya, Badger Valley]. That first night, the leaders wanted to pray. So they set up a *pongya* [sand altar], right there on the ground. They started to pray. Right in the middle of their *pongya* a Badger emerged from the ground. That's when we became Badgers.

Titiev (1944:69) regards clan solidarity as stronger than that of the village:

Despite a nominal allegiance to the Village chief, each clan is to a large extent autonomous, choosing its own officers and transacting its own affairs with a good deal of independence. Since a clan owns land, houses, gardens, and water-rights, it is virtually a self-sufficient unit. Only the rule of exogamy and the custom of matrilocal residence force it to cooperate with other groups.

From the Hopi viewpoint, the clan is significantly situated in the cosmological order. Its oral traditions associate a clan conceptually with natural species and supernatural forces. These associations are underpinned in ritual action, since many clans "own" ceremonies (or specific ceremonial roles or practices) in the annual liturgy of religious works. Eggan (1950:80–89) and especially Bradfield (1973:198–305) have analyzed the holistic associations between clans, phratries, and the natural and supernatural orders.

In Hopi thought a fundamental principle of clan differentiation concerns each clan's aboriginal arrival and acceptance into Hopi society. Clans are regarded as having been independently migratory units that arrived at different times and from different directions (cf. Fewkes 1900; Mindeleff 1900). Each clan in each village has its own version of clan history. Since Oraibi is my concern, I shall take a Third Mesa perspective and treat Oraibi as the point of arrival.

Oraibi was first occupied by the Bear clan. Subsequently, other clans approached the village seeking permission to settle there. The Bear clan leader (who was also the Village Chief, or *Kikmongwi*) asked what beneficial power they had to contribute. The clan proceeded to demonstrate its ritual (or its defensive capabilities, etc.), and if this was successful, the Bear leader assigned it a place to build in the village and an area in the Oraibi valley to farm. For example:

One of the first clans to arrive with those mentioned was the Bow clan, which came from the southwest. When the village chief asked the leader of this clan what he brought with him to produce rain, he said, "Yes, I have here the Sháalako Katcinas, the Tangík Katcinas, the Túkwunang Katcina and the Sháwiki Katcina. When they dance, it usually rains." "Very well," the chief said, "you try it." So the Áoatwungwa [Bow clan individual] arranged a dance. On the day before the dance it rained a little, and on the last day when they had their dance it rained fearfully. All the washes were full of water. So the village chief invited them to move to the village and gave them a large tract of land. He told them that they should have their ceremonies first.... Others came later. Small bands living throughout the country when they could hear about the people living in Oraibi would sometimes move up towards Oraibi and ask for admission to live in the village. In this way the villages were built up slowly. (Voth 1905a:24–25)

Mythological history and its reenactment in ritual or its reiteration in tradition constitute crucial features of clan identity in Hopi thought. Clan traditions are matters of continuous intraclan discourse that repeatedly reaffirms marks of distinction. Such marks occupy manifold frames of reference: mythico-historical, theological, ritual, geographical, archaeological, botanical, zoological, meteorological, and so forth. In short, clans in Hopi thought are cosmological, not simply sociological, entities.

PHRATRIES

Aggregations of related Hopi clans are generally referred to by anthropologists as phratries. Titiev's (1944:58) definition is:

Phratry—a nameless division of kindred made up of two or more clans which share certain privileges, mainly ceremonial, in common. The outstanding features of the phratry are that it delimits the greatest extension of kinship terms based on any given relationship, and that it marks the largest exogamic units recognized by the Hopi.

Both Eggan (1950:78) and Titiev (1944:51–52) report that Hopi assignment of clan names to individuals fluctuates extensively. In contrast, assignment of individuals to phratries, and accounts of which clans co-occur in particular phratries, are highly consistent. "Phratry lines are more clearly distinguished than clan ties" (Titiev 1944:53), and by inference, "the phratry grouping has exerted an enormous stabilizing influence in Hopi society" (Eggan 1950:78).

The Hopi rationale for the grouping of clans into phratries is variable (see Eggan 1950:64–80). Some are associated mythologically with the origins of their totems. The usual example cited is Phratry I (which at First Mesa and Second Mesa includes others besides Bear and Spider). During their migrations, a group of people came upon a dead bear and decided to take this animal for their *wu'uya*. Other groups arrived successively at the eponymous site and did or saw something with the bear carcass, from which each one took its name. Some cut a strip of hide for a carrying strap and became the *Peqösngyam* (Bear-Strap clan); others saw a bluebird sitting on the skeleton, and became *Tsorngyam* (Bluebird clan); the last group (others include Gopher and Greasy Eye-Cavity clans) found a Spider spinning her web between the bones and took *Kookyangsowuuti* (Spider Grandmother) for its *wu'uya*.

Clans in other phratries are associated (or distinguished, by the fission of an originally unitary clan, e.g., *Piikyas-Patki*, Greasewood-Reed, *Kookop-Maasaw*) on the basis of other mythico-historical pretexts. Eggan (1950:80–89) relates phratry organization to Hopi natural classification, and Bradfield (1973:198–305) extends this to "foci of interest" in the natural environment. Each phratry, Bradfield maintains, has responsibilities for the vital sustenance of a group of natural entities. Reflexively, the Hopi logic for grouping entities together (e.g., all types of soil with all species of snakes and lizards) provides the rationale for the grouping of derivatively named clans into a phratry.

Bradfield greatly oversimplifies clan relationships within phratries for the symmetry of his argument. The important point, though, is that in Hopi epistemology not only are natural elements "good to think" (as Lévi-Strauss 1966 would have it) as metaphors for the classification of social groups, but the metaphor works both ways. In a variety of verbal and ritual genres (which go far beyond the annual liturgy of the major ceremonies), social groups act upon the natural groups with which they are linked and influence their existential condition (preferably for the better of the world, though witchcraft is ever-present). In this way the natural elements are "good to act," and the logic of phratry groupings is grounded in behavioral practices as well as mental representations.

Connelly (1979:542–43) depicts phratries as combinations of a "prime" clan and lesser, "orbital" clans:

Within the phratry the position, expected behavior, and responsibilities of clans are defined in relation to the prime clan. . . . The clusters of associated clans thus surround the prime clan in an orbital arrangement of dependency and support, and a clan's social distance from the center is determined by the significance of its contribution.

For pre-split Oraibi, distinction between prime and orbital clans is not always possible. Conflicting claims to primacy are common.

Parrot in Phratry I and Bow in Phratry V are clearly preeminent, but other phratries are more doubtful. Further, relative closeness of clans in phratries varies: in Phratry VI, Coyote and Desert Fox are closer than either is to any other; in Phratry III, Snake and Lizard, of which the former is clearly primary, are very close, whereas Sand is more distant from both, occupying an independent ritual niche with its own measure of prestige.

Thus, although there definitely were prestige differentials among Oraibi clans, they did not follow a neat hierarchy. Rank criteria are multiple: whereas some concern descent-group membership, others depend on quite different social contexts. I shall return to this in discussing Oraibi politics.

In sum, phratries are the largest kinship groupings that enforce exogamy. Economically, they have no importance, except perhaps as mutual-aid organizations in times of crisis. Ritual linkages within and between phratries are part of a broader cosmological classification, which is associated also with the religious societies (see below). Clans and phratries are not merely units of an abstract social structure devoid of cultural or environmental context. They are intrinsic to the Hopi conceptualization of a world in which nature and culture are radically interwoven.

Households, lineages, clans, and phratries are, then, the major institutional units based on kinship and residence that have been identified in the conventional wisdom on Hopi social structure. As I have suggested, they are best regarded as elements of a model rather than as consistent empirical forms. Actual Hopi kin groups slide back and forth between these modal types with a theoretically embarrassing fluidity. In Hopi thought, clans are the primary kin groups, but even these are subject to widespread compositional variation and variable criteria of inclusion (see Whiteley 1986).

The Oraibi Economy

Titiev (1944:181–200) surveys economic patterns at Oraibi in some depth, and Beaglehole (1937), Forde (1931), and Kennard (1979) are good basic sources for the Hopi economy more generally.

Late-nineteenth-century Oraibi had a mixed economy, based on maize-beans-squash agriculture and sheep husbandry. Horses and burros—as draft animals—and cattle—for food and trade—were also important, and Oraibi had the largest herds of the Hopi villages. Agriculture and animal husbandry were primarily male activities. Fruit trees (principally peaches and apricots, but also pears and apples), comprising extensive orchards, were tended by both men and women individually. Several series of irrigated, terraced gardens, under the control of individual women, featured a number of secondary crops, such as onions and chilis. Hunting, especially of rabbits, and gathering of a great variety of wild resources were subsidiary economic activities. The former was a male activity; the latter was engaged in by both sexes. Euro-American goods were increasingly entering Oraibi's economy through trade by barter, for cash, or for labor. At this period, however, they were relatively minor features of the overall economy.

Lineages and clans have been regarded as particularly important organizing groups for economic activities. I have criticized this view at length elsewhere (Whiteley 1985b) and will reiterate only a few points here. The conventional wisdom has it that each clan farmed "clan-lands" in the Oraibi Valley, and most economic activities were articulated by the clan or segments of it. My contention is that this view reflects preconceived theoretical axioms rather than Hopi reality. The supposed clan-lands were very small in relation to population size. According to my older consultants, administration of clan-land (at Oraibi at least) was nothing like the nice, symmetrical division between lineage and household plots which Ernest Beaglehole describes for Second Mesa (1937:15–16). Indeed, clan-land was in the hands of that leading family or lineage segment that controlled the ritual prerogatives for which the clan was mythologically admitted into the village. Such lands were intimately connected with the ritual prerogatives themselves and are known as *wimvaavasa*, literally "ceremonial/ritual farming fields." Areas within the tract might or might not be apportioned to other clan members at the discretion of the core lineage segment. Usually other clan members simply farmed in a large "free area" in the Oraibi Valley (cf. Titiev 1944:63).

Likewise, other economic activities were not controlled by clans, according to my consultants. Rather, the economy was organized primarily by households. Cooperative economic ventures (planting or hunting parties, for example) drew upon a wide range of relatives—patrilateral and affinal as well as matrilineal—and nonrelatives.

The Ritual Structure

Religious Societies

General discussions of Hopi religious practices are found in Eggan (1950), Titiev (1944), Bradfield (1973:46–305), and Frigout (1979). Voth (1901, 1903a,b, 1912a,b; Dorsey and Voth 1901) offers detailed accounts of particular Oraibi ceremonies.

Eggan (1950:89) provides a useful summary statement:

The ceremonial organization of the Hopi is highly complex and includes the Katcina cult, the men's societies concerned with Tribal Initiation, the Winter Solstice ceremony, and the various societies concerned with rain, war, clowning, and curing. The ritual activities are organized in terms of a ceremonial calendar, and each major ceremony is associated with a clan, a society, and a kiva.

The ceremonial calendar at Oraibi in the past (and in modern times at other villages) runs roughly as follows. The beginning of the year, reckoned in lunar months, falls in October-November; it is marked by the *Wuwtsim* ceremonies, including those of the *Aa'alt* (Two-Horn society), *Kwaakwant* (One-Horn society), *Taatawkyam* (Singers' society), and *Wuwtsimt* (usually untranslated, but roughly "Manhood" society). These four societies perform in tandem. Each is regarded as complementary to the other three, although *Aa'alt* and *Kwaakwant* have a specially paired ritual relationship. Each society is predominantly associated with a particular religious concern: the *Wuwtsimt* and Singers with fertility, the Two-Horn with hunting and game animals, and the One-Horn with the dead and with supernatural protection of the village.

In the following month, at the time of the winter solstice, *Soyalangw* occurs. This complex ceremony (see Dorsey and Voth 1901) convenes the most important priests in the village. They plan the events of the coming year and perform a variety of rituals concerned with reversing the northward movement of the sun, the regeneration of human, animal, and vegetal life, and meteorological harmony. After *Soyalangw*, game-animal dances—particularly Buffalo—occur, although these are less formal "social dances" not conducted by initiated religious societies.

Soyalangw opens the Kachina "season" at Oraibi. Kachinas are personated in periodic performances from December through July. The Kachina concept is multifaceted. Kachina spirits include those of mammals, birds, insects, plants, particular deities, mythological figures, positive and negative social values—and often a number of these categories simultaneously. Some more important ones, the *mong-* (chief) *katsinam*, represent clan deities. Kachina performers appear in groups to dance at night in the kivas from January through March, and during the day in the *kiisonvi* (plaza) thereafter. They are generally associated with the securing of moisture—first snow, then different types of rain—for the agricultural cycle. During the plaza dances, Kachinas may be accompanied by an unmasked troupe of *tsutskut*, sacred clowns, who conduct a ceremony in counterpoint (see Hieb 1972). The two most important Kachina ceremonies are *Powamuy* (the "Bean Dance") and *Niman* (the "Home Dance"). *Powamuy*, in February, is a complex pageant concerned, among other things, with purifying the earth and prefiguring the planting season. *Niman*, in July, marks the last performance of the year of the Kachinas, as they are ritually sent back to spiritual homes in the San Francisco Peaks and other mountainous areas.

The Kachina season is followed by a series of religious society performances. First, in August, in even years at Oraibi, came the Snake-Antelope ceremonies performed by the *Tsuutsut* (Snake society) and *Tsöötsöpt* (Antelope society); in the alternate years, the *Sakwalelent* (Blue Flute) and *Masilelent* (Gray Flute) societies conducted the Flute ceremonies. Both sets of ceremonies are multifaceted and densely symbolic. They feature magical attempts to bring rain at the driest time of the year (which occurs at the final period of crop maturation), the marking of the sun's post-solstitial passage, and the dramatization of the mythological entrance into the village of particular clans.

More "social dances," referred to generically in English as "Butterfly Dances" but including many other varieties, follow in late

August or early September. After these come the women's society ceremonies: *Lakon, Owaqöl,* and *Maraw* (which are untranslated). The former two (referred to as "Basket Dances") stress fertility and the celebration of the harvest. *Maraw,* which has a contrapuntal relationship to the male *Wuwtsim* society and includes burlesques of male rituals, is particularly associated with fertility and the fruits of warfare.

The ritual cycle is coordinated with the natural cycle, which dictates parallel cycles of secular human activities. *Wuwtsimt* and *Soyalangw* serve as master ceremonies that bring together many religious concerns, renewing and reorienting the world and human society's position within it. Overall (and oversimply), agricultural fertility and productivity, human fertility, game-animal fertility, war, curing, and social harmony are the major issues upon which ritual interest is trained.

Differing levels of importance attach to the ceremonies and the societies, although ranking is not exact. In a general sense, the ranking of societies from most to least important is as follows:

First-order societies
Aa'alt, Kwaakwant, Wuwtsimt, Taatawkyam; Sosyalt (the *Soyalangw* society); *Mamrawt (Maraw)*
Second-order societies
Sakwalelent, Masilelent; Tsuutsut, Tsöötsöpt; Lalkont; Owaqölt
Third-order societies
Powamuy, Katsina

These levels describe general structural similarities, not strict equivalencies within categories. All Hopis are initiated into one of the two third-order societies, usually between ages six and ten. After that, they are eligible (though there is a sexual division between the societies) for initiation into a second-order society; some may never join one, others may be initiated even in old age. At roughly ages sixteen to twenty, all males were traditionally initiated into one of the *Wuwtsim* societies, and many females into the *Mamrawt.* For males, initiation into the *Sosyalt* was then possible. In a sense, the *Sosyalt* is on a higher plane still, but in practice the *Wuwtsim* societies are regarded as socially the most important.

Table 3.2. Oraibi Ceremonies and Societies (ca. 1890)

Time of Year	Ceremony and Society	Controlling Clan	Home Kiva
November	Wuwtsim	Sparrowhawk	Hawiovi
	Wuwtsimt	Sparrowhawk	Hawiovi
	Taatawkyam (Singers)	Parrot	Taw
	Aa'alt (Two-Horn)	Bow	Naasavi
	Kwaakwant (One-Horn)	Maasaw	Kwan
December	Soyalangw	Bear	Sakwalenvi
February	Powamuy ("Bean Dance")		
	Powamuy	Badger	Hotsitsivi
	Katsina	Kachina	Maraw
July	Niman ("Home Dance")	Kachina & Badger	(Rotates)
August			
Odd Years	Flute		
	Blue Flute	Spider	Sakwalenvi
	Gray Flute	Patki	Hawiovi
Even Years	Snake-Antelope		
	Snake	Snake	Snake
	Antelope	Spider	Naasavi
September–October			
Odd Years	Owaqöl	Sand	Hawiovi
Even Years	Maraw	Lizard	Maraw
	Lakon	Parrot	Hawiovi

SOURCE: Eggan (1950:103) and Frigout (1979:575).
NOTE: Both Eggan (1950:103) and Frigout (1979:575) have the Kachina society as housed in Hawiovi. This does not accord with the Hopi scheme of keeping the two major levels of initiation (Kachina and *Wuwtsim*) separate. I thus follow Voth's (1901:72) statement that "Katsina initiation . . . is performed in the Marau kiva." For *Niman*, Eggan and Frigout have just Kachina as the controlling clan. I follow my consultants and Titiev (1944:128) to include Badger.

Each society conducts its ceremony at the appointed time of the year. The ceremony is owned by a particular clan that should provide the chief-priest for the society (Table 3.2). Other members of the society may belong to any clan; they simply need to be sponsored by someone already a member. Initiation into a religious society thus effects new ties for the individual—both to society cohorts and, through the agency of the sponsoring ceremonial "father" or "aunt," to another phratry, by virtue of the extension of patrilateral kinship terms.

For example, for Kachina initiation, a boy may choose his own "godfather," or his parents may do this for him. The godfather must be of a clan other than his own or his father's and preferably outside these two phratries. If the individual agrees to be a godfather, he asks his sister, mother, or another clanswoman to act as the boy's ceremonial aunt, or "godmother" in Hopi English. The godfather baptizes the boy and gives him a new name deriving from his (the godfather's) clan. From then on the boy addresses all phratry relatives of his godfather with the same kinship terms (see Eggan 1950:31–42) he uses for his own paternal relatives. He usually keeps the same godfather for subsequent initiations and so tends to join the societies to which his godfather belongs.

Let me make this more specific. If my mother is Greasewood clan and my father Snake clan, I am linked at birth by kinship terms and behavior to two entire phratries, since I use the same terms of reference and address for phratry as for clan relatives: for example, all females of the Greasewood, Bow, and Reed clans are, then, my "mothers," "sisters," or "nieces"; all Snake, Lizard, and Sand clan males are my "fathers." For Kachina initiation, my chosen godfather is Rabbit clan, which links me to all Rabbit, Parrot, Kachina, and Crow clan men as "fathers" and women as "aunts." The same principle may (i.e., if I have a different godfather) apply again to another set of clans when I am initiated into the Antelope society, *Wuwtsimt*, and so on.

The major Oraibi ceremonies with their controlling clans and kiva centers are shown in Table 3.2. Other societies included the *Momtsit* or "Warriors" and the *Nasotanwiwimkyam* or "Stick-Swallowers" (both owned jointly by the Spider and *Kookop* clans). These societies became inactive around the turn of the century (one elderly consultant recalled seeing the last public *Momtsit* performance as a young child), but they feature in the Oraibi split as nexuses of ties between "Hostile" faction initiates (see Chapter 4). Society initiation charges the acolyte with lifelong responsibilities. Even if the ceremony as a whole passes out of use, he must personally observe certain ritual formalities at the appropriate times of the year. Thus *Momtsit* members retained a common bond that outlasted ceremonial desuetude.

Kiva Groups

The other major ritual units are the kiva groups. A Hopi kiva is a rectangular ceremonial chamber, generally thought of as "owned"

Sakwalenvi ("Blue Flute Place"), Oraibi's chief kiva, to the left. This was a center of Hostile ritual and political activity, especially in the 1890s and 1900s. To the right is Hotsitsivi ("Zigzag Place"), otherwise known as Powamu kiva or Honan ("Badger") kiva. Photograph by Jo Mora, courtesy Special Collections (John R. Wilson Collection) Cline Library, Northern Arizona University, Flagstaff.

or taken care of by a particular clan, clan segment, or clan member. But the social significance of kivas is variable:

The kivas, and their relations to clan, society, and ceremony, have never been clearly defined for the Hopi, and there is much confusion in the literature on the subject.... Kivas are built or repaired to meet ceremonial needs, so that a member of a clan controlling a particular ceremony frequently takes the initiative in construction and the obligation of maintenance.... But while the kiva is thought of as "belonging" to a particular clan or clans, membership is not by clan. (Eggan 1950:96)

Furthermore, clan association with a kiva may alter fairly often if that kiva is not the home of a major ceremony. If a kiva is not taken care of by its "owner," another kiva member may repair it. It then passes into his charge and is renamed after his clan, its "baptismal" ceremony involving a social dance. As with people, kivas retain a variety of names and nicknames, so that straightforward clan identification is frequently impossible. Bacavi's main kiva, for example, has at least six interchangeable names.

The majority of ritual action occurs in kivas. More generally, kivas functioned (more so in the past than in modern times) as male clubs, workshops, occasional sleeping places, and general meeting places for business or pleasure.

There is a sense of ranking among kivas. Oraibi had thirteen—considerably more than any other village—and there was a marked division between "common" kivas and those reserved for major ceremonies. Oraibi's kivas with their controlling clans at the turn of the century are listed in Table 3.3.

The first eight were the prominent kivas, the remainder "common" kivas (Titiev 1944:245 n. 4). Sakwalenvi was traditionally the *mong-* (chief) kiva, as it housed *Soyalangw*. However,

> previous to the year 1900 the Soyal ceremony had been performed in the *Sakwalanvi* (Blue Flute) kiva, which up to that time was universally recognized as the *Monwi* (Chief) kiva, in as much as the village chief Lolulomai was identified with that kiva. But the majority of the members of that kiva became Conservatives, and Lolulomai and his followers withdrew to the *Ponovi* (Circle) kiva, which has ever since been denominated by Liberals as the *Monwi* Kiva, and there the Soyal has since been held. (Dorsey and Voth 1901:11)

Each kiva has its own chief, the *kivamongwi*, who is often the chief-priest of a ceremony based in that kiva:

> A kiva chief has several ritual duties attendant on his office, such as acting as father of the Katcinas on certain occasions, smoking formally with messengers who come to announce impending ceremonies, and sponsoring the Niman (Homegoing) dance in the years when that obligation, which rotates annually, falls to his kiva. In addition, he is leader of many secular pursuits which are performed by kiva units, including communal

Table 3.3. Oraibi Kivas Prior to 1900

	Main Name of Kiva	Controlling Clan(s)
1	Sakwalenvi (Blue Flute Place)	Spider
2	Hawiovi (Going Down Place)	Bow and Sand
3	Taw Kiva (Singers' Society Kiva)	Parrot
4	Naasavi (Middle Place)	Bow
5	Kwan Kiva (One-Horn Kiva)	Cedar-Kookop-Maasaw
6	Hotsitsivi (Zigzag Place)	Badger
7	Tsuu Kiva (Rattlesnake Kiva)	Snake
8	Maraw Kiva (—)	Lizard
9	Hano Kiva (—)	Squash
10	Wiklavi (Fold-of-fat Place)	Spider and Kookop
11	Pongovi (Circle Place)	Coyote
12	Is Kiva (Coyote Kiva)	Coyote
13	Katsin Kiva (Katsina Kiva)	Kachina

SOURCE: Titiev 1944:245.

hunts and cotton-spinning bees, and it is up to him to see that the chamber is kept in good repair and is well stocked with firewood during the winter months. (Titiev 1944:104)

Kiva members join for a variety of reasons: "Kiva *membership* is not primarily by clan—while men may join other ceremonies and participate in other kivas which are more congenial or more convenient, their basic affiliation is with the kiva into which they are initiated during the Tribal Initiation [*Wuwtsim*]" (Eggan 1950:96). Seven kivas were "Tribal Initiation" kivas in Oraibi (Titiev 1944: 242). Secondary kiva membership may have followed the general pattern of kiva membership at Third Mesa in the 1980s, which is largely a matter of individual choice and may change through life accordingly. Kiva groups effect ties that cut across kinship groups and religious societies, adding other strands of coactivity which link individuals in other social combinations.

Political Organization

I have largely followed the conventional accounts of Hopi social structure so far. With political organization, I must depart from these. Anthropologists have, by and large, written about the Hopi as an apolitical, egalitarian society in which social control is maintained by the crosscutting ties immanent in the social structure:

Hopi society, despite appearances, is not highly integrated. As it has no political superstructure, the clan and phratry groups tend to assert their position at the expense of the village. Hopi society has been held together by kinship ties, marriage bonds, and associational structures which cut across clan lines. (Eggan 1949:143)

The Hopi never developed a political society. (Eggan 1964:182)

The larger units of Hopi society lack all semblance of political organization ... the political framework of the pueblo itself is extraordinarily weak.... Whatever other talents they may possess, the Hopi do not have the gift of statecraft. (Titiev 1944:67–68)

It would appear from these statements that there were no administrative processes in operation at all and that the villages functioned entirely without political articulation (apart from ad hoc factionalism). Instead, they greeted each new day on automatic pilot, the ability and means to deal with social and political problems, both the everyday and the unique, somehow emanating noiselessly from social structural "principles."

Hopis recognize divisions of rank which they regard as very significant in the conduct of everyday (and not so everyday) affairs. The cardinal division is between *pavansinom* and *sukavungsinom*. *Sinom* is a plural meaning "persons" or "people." In this context *pavan* is most aptly rendered "most powerful" or "most important." I have been offered Hopi etymologies for *sukavung*, but these are debatable and I think it best to work with the usual Hopi-English gloss for *sukavungsinom*: "grassroots people" or "common people." Conversely, the usual gloss for *pavansinom* is "ruling people."

References to this general "class" division, as Hopis term it, are extremely few in the literature, although it is a matter of everyday Hopi discourse. Shuichi Nagata confines the following discussion to a footnote (1970:44 n. 2):

> The Hopi term *pavansinom* seems important here. *Pavan* means force, strength, and perhaps supernatural power (Voegelin and Voegelin, 1957: C4.4), and *pavansinom* is contrasted to *shikabunsinom* or "ordinary people." The former refers to the clans owning ceremonies or members of such secret societies as Momchit. The people using *poaka* or witchcraft[3] are also called *pavansinom* and now the Tribal Council is so called because of its power. One informant noted that the *pavansinom* tended to marry each other for fear of clan secrets being stolen by nonimportant people.

Richard Brandt (1954:23–24) elucidates the division (although he has a different term for *pavansinom*):

> The Hopi speak of themselves as a "class" society. The language contains terms marking traditional stratifications: *mongsinom*,[4] meaning "people who have the title or dignity of chiefs," and *sukaavungs sinom*, meaning "common people." If a Hopi is asked to which class a given individual belongs, he will give a definite answer, depending upon the traditional tribal offices held by him or his family or his clan connections with persons holding such offices. (These offices almost always have some relation to the ceremonial system; individuals holding certain offices are usually at the same time vested with ownership of certain ceremonies and have the right to decide if and when their ceremony is performed.) Thus, if a Hopi

is asked which are the "higher" clans, he will mention Bear, Spider, Bow, Corn-Cloud, and so on, with some variations except for the first. Members of the upper classes have prestige in the sense that the lower classes look up to them as "blue bloods" associated with the tribal leadership.

Criteria of *pavansinom* status are more complex than the above quotations imply. Although there is a sense in which all Bear clan members are *pavansinom* in comparison, say, to the Sun clan, the same distinctions may also be made within the Bear clan. Thus the Bear clan segment that provides the *Kikmongwi*, owns the *Soyalangw* ceremony and provides leading officers for it comprises the "real" *pavansinom* within the Bear clan. Other Bear clan members may be regarded, from this perspective, as *sukavungsinom*.

Within the upper division, there are several other terms of distinction also. For example, the Bear clan segment that provides the *Kikmongwi* are the *kiikyam*.[5] Clans in the same phratry as Bear are *mongwisiuta*, "those in line with the chief," or, again, "the ruling people." The few individuals most active in leadership (including the factional heads in pre-split Oraibi) can be called *pavanmomngwit*. The religious society heads, including the *Kikmongwi*, are *wimmomngwit*.[6]

The *Kikmongwi* was the most important of a series of formally instituted offices. Titiev (1944:64–65) details its functions and notes a lack of coercive power: "the Village Chief is looked upon rather as a guide and an advisor than as an executive; and as an interpreter of tradition rather than as a legislator." The *Kikmongwi* had various aides, including the head of the *Piikyas* clan, who provided general support, and the *Tsa'akmongwi*, or Crier Chief, who formally announced ceremonial occasions (Titiev 1944:60 n. 11).

The *Qaletaqmongwi*, or War Chief, head of the *Momtsit*, was a position of great importance, especially prior to the cessation of warfare. Titiev (1944:65–66) describes his role as "maintaining the discipline, and he was the nearest approach to a policeman in each Hopi town. . . . The basis of his authority lay in his military leadership." I believe the War Chief's role at Oraibi has been underestimated ethnographically because of the factional dispute. In the 1890s the War Chief led the Hostile faction against the *Kikmongwi*, head of the Friendly faction (see Chapter 4). Most Third Mesa ethnographic research has been conducted with members or descendants of the Friendly faction, who, I suggest, downplayed the significance of their antagonist.

The War Chief was the earthly representative of *Pöökong*, the elder of the "War Twins," and was often helped by an assistant representing the younger, *Palengawhoya*. The *Qaletaqmongwi*'s role was complementary to that of the *Kikmongwi*. By comparison with the War Chief in other pueblos (cf. E. Brandt 1980, 1985), I suggest the *Qaletaqmongwi* had executive authority for the protection of the village from external forces. His coercive authority in internal affairs does not seem to have constituted a systematic disciplinary regime. A useful analogy to the complementary roles of *Kikmongwi* and *Qaletaqmongwi* may be drawn from ceremonies having both a *mongwi* (chief-priest) and a *qaleetaqa* (guardian). The *mongwi* directs the ritual performance, while the *qaleetaqa* serves to protect the participants from external intrusion. Thus *Kikmongwi* is to *Qaletaqmongwi* as "inside chief" to "outside chief." In times of peace and harmony, the *Kikmongwi*'s role is considerably more significant; in times of external stress or internal crisis the *Qaletaqmongwi* comes to the fore.

Titiev, who worked a great deal with Tawaquaptewa, the Oraibi *Kikmongwi* and head of *Soyalangw*, characterizes the "most important" political officers as officiants in the *Soyalangw* ceremony:

> Participating in the Chiefs' Talk [*Monglavaiyi*] were the officers who had just brought the Soyal to a close. The Village Chief (kikmongwi) of Oraibi spoke first, and was followed in order by the head man of the Parrot clan; the Pikyas clan chief; the Tobacco Chief (Pipmongwi), normally the head of the Rabbit clan; the Crier Chief (Tca'akmongwi), usually leader of the Greasewood clan; and the War Chief (Kaletaka), who may be from the Badger or Coyote clan.[7] In every respect these men are the most important officials in the pueblo. (1944:59–60)

It is instructive to contrast this view with that of Yukioma, leader of the Hostile faction prior to the split. Describing mythological emergence, Yukioma lists the leaders as follows:

> So they commenced to climb up the reed, first the different chiefs, the Village Chief (Kík-mongwi), who was also at the same time the Soyál-mongwi, the Flute chief (Lán-mongwi), Horn chief (Ál-mongwi), Agave chief (Kwán-mongwi), Singer chief (Táo-mongwi), Wúwüchim chief

(Kél-mongwi), Rattlesnake chief (Tcú-mongwi), Antelope chief (Tcöb-mongwi), Maraú chief (Maraú-mongwi), Lagón chief (Lagón-mongwi), and the Warrior chief (Kaléhtak-mongwi or Pöokong). And then the people followed and a great many went out. (Voth 1905b:19)

Yukioma's narrative conforms to my consultants' accounts (most, though not all, descendants of the Hostile faction) of leadership structure. These are the leaders referred to collectively as *wim-momngwit* (see above), chief-priests of the religious societies, of which the four *Wuutsim* societies are accorded the most importance. In the words of one older consultant, "the *Wuutsim* societies are the Hopis' government."

This alternative view of Oraibi government may unjustifiably deemphasize the importance of the *Soyalangw* officers, but conversely, neglect of the *Wuutsim* leaders is certainly unwarranted. They served not as subservient assistants to the *Kikmongwi*, but rather as independent participants in a group of decision makers; the *Kikmongwi*'s position was first among equals. It is well-known, for example, that during ceremonies the society chief-priest is in charge of the village, temporarily superseding the *Kikmongwi*.

Pavansinom are primarily those members of the core lineage segments with principal ceremonial offices. Their authority rests in the religious societies and is repeatedly validated in myth and ritual. Ritual action, because of its intent to affect instrumentally the conditions of existence, is simultaneously political action. The core lineage segment, rather than the clan as a whole, is the actual owning group of a particular ceremony or office and maintains strict proprietary control (cf. Lowie 1929:330; Parsons 1933:23; Titiev 1944:46). Control and usage of this "property" defines the core segment as *pavansinom*. Political and supernatural power accrue to them through exclusive access to esoteric ritual knowledge.

As Nagata points out, those attributed the power of witchcraft are sometimes considered *pavansinom*. Further, a medicine man, *tuuhikya*, may be included in this category although he is outside the formal ceremonial structure. His power is achieved, in the sense that it requires public affirmation through medical success, although it may be attributed to acquisition through inheritance within a kin group. Because he controls transformative powers, a *tuuhikya* can be regarded as a *pavansino* and simultaneously suspected as a *powaqa* (witch). Others who manifest exceptional abilities (with the raising of particular cultigens, for example) may be thought of as *pavansinom* and/or *popwaqt* (witches). The coalescence of these two categories illustrates further the nature of *pavansinom*. They are not unambiguously benign and their power may be used for selfish, antisocial purposes (the distinctive features of a *powaqa*) as well as for communal benefit.

In sum, the term *pavansinom* is perhaps most accurately rendered "powerful people." The power—to make significant transformations in the world—derives from various sorts of esoteric knowledge, the primary locus of which is in ritual. Initiation into a religious society confers power, but the greatest proportion adheres to the chief-priests. Their specialized knowledge is kept with strict secrecy from ordinary participants. The respect attributed by ordinary Hopis to *pavansinom* is not for institutionalized office per se, but for the supernatural capabilities it entails.

Hopi political decision making is not *legislative* over social relations but *deliberative* over the course of events in the world (cf. Titiev 1944:66–67). Hence, the responsibility of *pavansinom* is perceived as extremely serious and not to be undertaken lightly. It is not unusual for individuals to refuse ceremonial office because the duties (and their associated dangers) to mankind and the cosmos are felt to be too great (cf. Brandt 1954:24–25). The distinction is not necessarily sought after and carries no economic advantages: "the priests and chiefs are not privileged persons . . . they engage in the same labors and lead precisely the same life as the other villagers" (A. M. Stephen, in Donaldson 1893:17). Their authority lies in the ritual capacity to plan the future course of events (see Chapter 8 for a fuller discussion). In this way, as it was phrased to me, "the *pavansinom* have the destiny of the people in their hands."

In summary, the leading institutions of turn-of-the-century Oraibi comprised a series of kinship and ritual subgroups with intersecting memberships. The economy was based primarily on agriculture and sheepherding. A complex religious structure was largely orchestrated by initiated religious societies. Oraibi was politically differentiated, on the basis of ritual knowledge and authority, into an elite and a commoner class, unmarked by economic differences.

Direct Anglo-American influences on Oraibi's lifestyle were as yet limited:

> No one can ever see the Hopi pueblos as they appeared to the writer on his first visit to them in 1890 . . . one might easily fancy himself back in the time of the discoverers. There were in 1890 no iron stoves, tables, chairs, lamps, or any of the so-called comforts of civilization. Many rooms were entered through the roofs. . . . Purchases from the store were limited to the simplest staple necessities, as calico, flour, sugar, tobacco, and coffee. There was no wagon road from the plain to the villages on top of the mesa, narrow, steep trails being the only means of access . . . the Hopi rarely went to the railroad to trade. They possessed horses and a few cattle and a considerable number of sheep and goats. The Hopi lived mostly on corn, beans, squashes and other vegetables. Matches, tobacco, yeast, cakes and candy were in great demand. . . . The supply of rabbits, deer, and other game was small, and almost every animal of mammalian form was at times eaten. The introduction of common household utensils has taken place in the last thirty years. A few fabrics of whiteman's make were in use, but native blankets, sashes, rabbit-skin rugs, and the like predominated . . . practically all their cloth was made by themselves, with the exception of the calico pantaloon, or the shirt of scanty proportions which they wore on their shoulders. There was a demand for flour bags before their contents were consumed, as material for shirts, and it was no uncommon sight . . . to see an adult man wearing a shirt made of a flour bag with the three X's and the commercial name of the mill on his back, the letters being regarded as ornamental. . . . About every Indian, certainly every farmer, at that time owned a burro. . . . The Hopi in 1890 had few wagons and no plows. Everybody travelled on foot, burro, or horseback. (Fewkes 1922:270–72)

Oraibi society in 1890, then, was relatively untrammeled by the strictures of Anglo-American dominion. Not for much longer would this be the case.

4
From Oraibi to Bacavi

> Love may be a "many-splendored thing," but crisis is certainly a "many-levelled thing" in all cultures.
> —*Victor Turner (1982:70)*

The number of extant texts on the Oraibi split breaks double figures (see Laird 1977). Titiev (1944:69–95) provides the most comprehensive coverage. In part this chapter duplicates details of some published sources, but I primarily use hitherto unconsidered documentary sources from a variety of archives. These provide extensive material evidence for the multiple contexts in which the split took place, and they reveal many basic errors—of fact and interpretation—in the extant accounts. I occasionally intersperse (indicated) Hopi consultants' accounts with the documentary record below, but these are mostly reserved for Chapter 8.

We left the historical record of Oraibi in 1882 at the time of Cushing's visit. This year also coincides with the expanded penetration of white society into the broader environs of Hopi country:

The summer of 1882 brought a crucial change: tracks of the Atlantic and Pacific Railroad advanced west from Gallup and then west from the Painted Desert towards the San Francisco Peaks and a raw new lumber town that would be named Flagstaff. In the wake of the road gangs the towns of Holbrook and Winslow sprang up, at once serving as supply centers for the entire territory, north and south. (McNitt 1962:188)

Cushing's account of his 1882 visit to Oraibi is important, both as an ethnographic document and for the political scenario he describes. The origin of the factions that split Oraibi has frequently been attributed to the return from a visit to Washington of several Hopi leaders, including the Oraibi *Kikmongwi*, Loololma. The argument (e.g., Titiev 1944:72ff; Clemmer 1978:39,54; Dockstader 1979:526; James 1974:130–31) suggests that Loololma was initially opposed to the U.S. government and white influence in general. Following this visit, however, he reversed his stance. Thenceforth, many Oraibi people opposed him, regarding his reversal as a betrayal. Some continued to support him, however, and thus were the factions, "Hostiles" and "Friendlies," founded.

A thorough search of the archival records reveals that no such visit to Washington occurred prior to 1890.[1] Cushing (1922:253–68; n.d.) clearly describes two factions at Oraibi in 1882.[2] He colorfully details a volatile encounter with a " 'wizard' faction" (n.d.:43) opposed to Loololma: "He [Loololma] talked to me, cried, and begged that I ask Washington for soldiers to help get rid of the witches. He told me they were the ones who opposed the acceptance of annuities, and caused all the trouble in Oraibi, keeping his people poor" (1922:267). Further, Loololma names his leading antagonists: "Kui-ian-ai-ni-wa. Pi-tchi-fui-a (his [Loololma's] would be successor). Mui-in-wa. Kuh-ni-na (the Cozonino). Pa-tuis-ni-wa (the caller). He-vi-ma. Mui-shon-ai-ti-wa" (Cushing n.d.:40–41).

Although I am unable to identify all of these people, several were prominent in the Hostile party subsequently, especially in the 1890s. "Pi-tchi-fui-a" is very likely Patupha (*Kookop* clan head), one of the last initiates (possibly *the* last) of the Oraibi *Porswimkyam*, an eminent Medicine society, and a member of *Momtsit*, the Warriors' society (Titiev n.d.:22). He was a principal Hostile leader of the 1890s and was regarded as a very powerful medicine man.[3] "Kuh-ni-na" was the nickname for Duvewuhioma, Spider clan, a member of *Wuwtsim* at the chief kiva, and a chief-priest of the Antelope society (Titiev n.d.:3).[4] "He-vi-ma" (Heevi'ima[5]) was another *Kookop* clansman, Yukioma's (see below) mother's sister's son (Titiev n.d.:46a), very likely the chief of *Momtsit* and thus *Qaletaqmongwi*, or War Chief. A government official stationed at Oraibi in the 1890s consistently referred to Heevi'ima as *the* leader of the Hostiles (Mayhugh 1892–94:passim). "Mui-shon-ai-ti-wa" is probably correctly identified by Parsons (Cushing 1922:267 n. 16) as Masangöntewa, Snake clan, chief-priest of the Snake society in the 1890s.[6] He was head of the Snake kiva's branch of *Wuwtsim* and also a member of the *Momtsit* (Titiev n.d.:18a). The remaining names I am unable to identify with certainty.[7]

The social statuses of these individuals suggest continuity in the Hostile leadership from at least 1882, particularly concerning the prominence of two clans, Spider and *Kookop*, whose *pavansinom* (see Chapter 3) figure significantly. Common religious society affiliations include *Momtsit*, Antelope society, Blue Flute society, and those initiated into *Wuwtsim* at Sakwalenvi, the chief kiva. The *Momtsit* was jointly owned by the Spider and *Kookop* clans, the Antelope and the Blue Flute societies by the Spider clan, and Sakwalenvi kiva was controlled by the Spider clan (*Wuwtsim* initiation at Sakwalenvi was prerequisite to participation in *Soyalangw*). Other clusters of affiliation ramify from this corpus. Masangöntewa, as head of the Snake clan, Snake society, and Snake kiva, had close ceremonial ties with the Antelope society, since the Snake-Antelope ceremonies were performed jointly. By the mid-1890s, all "Friendly" members of these societies had withdrawn, so the ritual sodalities themselves became factional nuclei.

Leaders of the opposing factions in 1882 represented substantially similar social positions to those present at the split of 1906. Further, Loololma clearly favored a conciliatory stance toward the government eight years prior to his visit to Washington. Thus, although this visit may have been a powerful catalyst of dispute, it was not the originating source of the factions.

In 1883 the Moqui Pueblo Agency was abolished (McCluskey 1980:382). Although managed only desultorily since its beginnings in 1869–70, the complete removal from Keam's Canyon significantly diminished government influence. Until 1899 the Hopi were in a subagency under the Navajo Agency at Fort Defiance.

There was, nonetheless, much interest in having a permanent school established. In September 1884 John H. Bowman, the agent at Fort Defiance, earnestly recommended it and trader Thomas Keam was eager to provide the use of some buildings at no cost (Bowman 9-27-1884). No action was taken upon these recommendations, so in 1886 a petition requesting a school, with the names of twenty Hopi leaders, was sent by Agent S. S. Patterson to the commissioner of Indian affairs (U.S. Government 1886:lxxx). Most of the signatories were from First Mesa, and none was from Oraibi.[8]

A boarding school at Keam's Canyon was opened in the fall of 1887. No pupils were obtained from Oraibi, but Agent Patterson was optimistic: "Even the Oriba Chief, whose people until recently despised the face of a white man, told me the other day that he would send two of his own children to the school, and would secure the attendance of several others from his village" (Patterson 1887: 178).

Schooling became a key issue in the factional division of Oraibi. The great majority initially resisted the Keam's Canyon school (which would take their children thirty-five miles away for most of the year). The government's education program was explicitly designed to indoctrinate Anglo-American values and prevent indigenous enculturation:

In the fifty years before the publication of the Meriam Report, the federal government pursued a policy of total assimilation of the American Indian into the mainstream society.... Congress and the Indian Bureau adopted a plan to remold the Indian's conception of life, or what came to be known as his "system of values." If this could be changed, assimilationists reasoned, the Indian would then become like the white man. The Indian's system of values was expressed in the education of his children and in his attitude towards the land. Consequently, the assimilationists chose to attack these two concepts as the major targets of the campaign. (Szasz 1974:8)

Agent Shipley's philosophy specifically reflected this position at the Keam's Canyon Boarding School:

It appears to me that if any marked degree of advancement toward modern civilization is to be made with this people, it must be accomplished through a system of schoolwork. It is the early impressions, imbued within any child, that largely makes the man.... A great deal may be accomplished in this connection toward breaking up and destroying their crude forms of worship, superstition, etc. and thus gradually supplant them with a knowledge of true Christian principles. (Shipley 1892:212)

Faced with such policies the Oraibi majority balked, and may well have averted immediate punitive measures by the strategy of delay noted in Chapter 2: "The Oribas, who have never sent a child to school and never accepted but very little annuity goods, during my last visit promised to send half a dozen of their children to school" (Vandever 1889:262).

The problem of school attendance persisted, however. In arranging the visit of Hopi leaders to Washington in 1890, the commissioner of Indian affairs made the trip conditional upon a "guarantee to fill the Moqui school with Moqui children" (Morgan 3-8-1890). This condition was not met, but the visit to Washington, after repeated delays, got under way on 16 June 1890 (Vandever 6-4-1890). It was led by C. E. Vandever, the Navajo agent, with Thomas Keam as interpreter. As well as meeting President Benjamin Harrison, the Hopi leaders—Loololma from Oraibi, Simo and Ahnawita from Walpi, Honani from Shongopavi, and Polaccaca from Hano—took in the capital's theater, Carlisle Indian School in Pennsylvania, and some industrial workshops in Vandever's hometown of Terre Haute, Indiana (Vandever 1890:171–72). They returned to Hopi about a month later.

The commissioner's intent in arranging the trip was to persuade the leaders to accept Anglo-American control. According to Hopi accounts (cf. Hopi Hearings 1955:269–72, 289–90), the leaders ritually smoked over an agreement with President Harrison. The agreement provided that the Hopi should accept three things: the education program, Christian missionaries, and allotment of land as specified by the Dawes Severalty Act of 1887.

Upon the leaders' return, in part to induce support for the government and in part to provide an example for the rest of the people, gable-roofed, stone houses—intended as prototypes of allotment farmsteads—were built for them. Loololma's was built below Mumursva Springs, about three miles west of Oraibi. Hopis refer to these houses as *palakiki*, "red houses," on account of their rusted tin roofs; they still stand out as obtrusive landmarks of early government presence.

Education and Allotment

If Loololma was incompletely convinced of the virtues of the white man's ways before his visit to Washington, he apparently was no more. Allegedly he proclaimed, "My people are blind. Their ears are closed. I am the only one. I am alone. They don't want to go in the white men's ways, although I am Chief" (Office of Indian Affairs 6-30-1890). Loololma and a few of his supporters agreed to send their children to the school, but this accounted for very few pupils from Oraibi, as School Superintendent Ralph P. Collins reported:

> The Indians were informed in council September 1 that school would be opened September 15, and that they should have their children here promptly. The numbers varied from 2 to 18 until November 2, while I labored with them diligently, by every peaceful means in my power, to get them to send their children to school. (Collins 1891:552)

In consequence, more drastic measures were brought to bear. On 1 November 1890 a party consisting of T. J. Morgan, commissioner of Indian Affairs; Brigadier General A. D. McCook, commander of the Department of Arizona; Julian Scott, special agent for the eleventh census; and others arrived at Keam's Canyon. A conference was called at the Canyon the following day.[9] One of the first issues was the school:

> Lalolamy also said that he had been opposed to the schools until his visit to Washington, when he saw in going and coming so many great cities, so many people, so many great cornfields, so many wonderful things which he had never before seen or even dreamed of, and learning that these things grew out of the system of education existing among the white people, he had changed his mind and would use all his influence in the future in persuading his people to send their children to school. There were some men among his people who were bitter against the Keam's Canyon School and all other schools, but most of them wanted schools at their villages, and it might be necessary to resort to force to effect their acceptance of these educational benefits. (Donaldson 1893:56)

Morgan, therefore, decided on a quota system: "The Commissioner informed the Moquis that they must fill this school, and that each village must furnish its quota and that they must have 25 here at once, 25 in another week, and 25 more in two weeks from that time, making 75 in all" (Collins 1891:552).

This meeting perhaps signals the true beginning of government intrusion into the Oraibi factional division. The commissioner's commands were backed with threats of physical coercion:

When the two weeks had expired and no children had arrived I waited another week, being informed in the meantime by Lololomi that he was being opposed by a large party in his village (Oreiba) in his efforts to get children. Then, in company with Mr. Julian Scott, special agent of the Census Bureau, and Mr. Keam, the trader here, and five Moquis friends, I went to Oreiba, called a council and was informed that all except Lololomi and a few of his friends would not come into a council. We then went to the leader of the opposing faction and brought him to the council place, and informed him that he and his people would be given fifteen minutes in which to produce the children which the commissioner had told them they must furnish, and that unless they did so he would be taken away a prisoner. (Collins 1891:552)[10]

The opposing leader may well have been Heevi'ima.[11] He was arrested, and on the way to Second Mesa the party encountered his "brother," the "great medicine man of all the Moquis" (Donaldson 1893:58), Patupha, and arrested him, too.

For several days thereafter, Loololma and his supporters sent in a few children. However,

the opposition was more active than ever, and they arrested Lololomi, and confined him three days with threats to kill, etc. Thinking I had done all in my power, I telegraphed the Indian Office and a company of troops was sent, and upon their arrival, Lieut. Greerson and troop, Special Agent Parker, Mr. Keam, and myself went to Oreiba and demanded enough children to fill the school. . . . When the troops marched into the village we found all the people assembled in its center. Every man, woman, and child shook hands with every officer, private, and civil official there, and they formed the children in line and I took as many as I wanted. (Collins 1891:552)

With troops in Oraibi, the threat posed by the school passed from a notional status to hard reality. However, Collins's account notwithstanding, the Hostiles were not prepared to take the intrusion lying down.

The following spring (1891) the first allotment surveyors arrived. Allotment proved to be an even greater aggravation than the school. Anthropologist Jesse W. Fewkes was present at First Mesa:

The Chiefs were very much disturbed and resented the white people looking over the land through tubes and—in their eyes a more grievous sin—mysteriously putting wooden sticks in the ground. They desiring to know the meaning of this, it was explained to them that the white man was preparing to grant each family a plot of land which would be registered in Washington and be protected as the property of their children forever. (Fewkes 1922:273–74)

Thomas Donaldson, expert special agent for the 1890 census, is more trenchant: "They could not comprehend why they should be dispossessed of land owned and occupied for homes by their ancestors and themselves for certainly 350 years, and perhaps thousands of years" (Donaldson 1893:37). The established system of land tenure reflected the vagaries of topography and ecology. Geometric subdivision by allotment was entirely unsuited to these conditions, as the Hopi, but evidently not the surveyors, realized.

A rider attached to allotment was that the Hopi should move away from the mesa-top villages and build houses on individual allotments in the valleys. This had been an official desire since the 1870s; various government agents had recommended village dispersal as essential for assimilation.[12] The villages were recognized as cultural and religious enclaves (as well as simply residence sites), and thus strongholds of resistance to the penetration of acculturative influence.

After the surveyors had left, the Oraibis—probably the Hostiles (Mayhugh 2-19-1894:18)—pulled up all the stakes around Third Mesa (Fewkes 1922:274). The survey had also accentuated resentment toward the school:

In June, 1891, the opposition of the Moquis to the Keam's Canyon school continued, and it was reported that the Oraibis would fight before permitting their children to be taken to it. It was given out that they were tearing up the surveyor's stakes, destroying survey monuments, and threatening to raid the school. (Donaldson 1893:37)

As a result, troops were called in to arrest the Hostile leaders. A small detachment, under Lieutenant L. M. Brett, reached Oraibi on 21 June 1891, but they met with more than they had bargained for:

Came to Oraibi to arrest several Oraibis, who have destroyed the surveyor's marks and threatened to destroy the school. When we entered the village we were confronted by about 50 hostiles armed and stationed behind a barricade. They openly declared hostility to the government, and a fight was barely averted. A strong force should be sent here with Hotchkiss guns, as I anticipate serious trouble if the hostiles are not summarily dealt with. (Donaldson 1893:37)

Brett's terse communiqué hardly does his antagonists ethnographic justice. In fact, he was confronted with the opening stages of a formal declaration of war. Titiev (1944:77–79) and Fewkes (1922: 275–76) describe this in considerable detail, so I will not reiterate it at any length. Several personated war deities appeared before the soldiers, including *Maasaw, Kookyangsowuuti, Pöökong,* and *Palengawhoya*. Each of these figures has a specific relationship with the cluster of elements described above as central to the composition of the Hostile leadership. *Maasaw* is the *wu' uya,* or ancestral emblem, of the *Kookop* clan; he is a multifunctional personage— half man, half deity—associated, among other things, with fire and death. He was personated by Patupha, the *Kookop* clan medicine man (Titiev 1944:78). *Kookyangsowuuti*, Spider Grandmother, is the Spider clan's *wu'uya* and was represented by Lomahongyoma (Titiev 1944:78), a leading member of this clan and emerging figurehead of the Hostile faction. *Pöökong* and *Palengawhoya,* the War Twins, are supernatural prototypes of the War Chief and his assistant; in this instance they were represented by two Snake/ Lizard clan members (Titiev 1944:78).[13]

Lieutenant Brett's recommendation was acted upon. On 1 July, four companies of troops under Colonel H. C. Corbin reached Oraibi, with two Hotchkiss guns in tow (Fewkes 1922:276–82 and Donaldson 1893:37–39 discuss the campaign at length). At dawn, the troops marched into the village to find it deserted: the people had assembled near the point of the mesa. Nine Hostile leaders were taken to Fort Wingate.[14] Five were released early in 1892 (U.S. Government 1892:585) and the other four remained at Fort Wingate until the end of that year.[15] While in Oraibi, trader Thomas Keam and Superintendent Collins requested that the Hotchkiss guns be trained on a portion of the village to destroy it; this, they thought "might be the means of getting them to move off the mesa" (Shipley 7-6-1891:3). The troops did fire off the guns into some peach orchards and cracked a large rock north of Oraibi; the rock is widely known among Hopis today for the event it commemo-

First arrest and imprisonment of Hostile leaders, Fort Wingate, New Mexico, 1891–92. *Back row (left to right):* Lomayestewa (Spider), Heevi'ima (*Kookop*), not known, Lomahongyoma (Spider), Patupha (*Kookop*); *front row:* Yukioma (*Kookop*), rest not known. These identifications are the author's (the original photograph does not include names). The four unidentified include Qötswistewa (Rabbit), Talangainewa (*Kookop*), and Puhu'ima (Sun). Photograph by unknown photographer, 26 January 1892, Southwest Museum, Los Angeles.

rates. But Agent Shipley refused to accede to Keam's and Collins's request.

The government continued to demand that children be sent to school, and at Oraibi the demands continued to be resisted. When school opened in 1892, Superintendent Collins noted the absence of Oraibi children: "I believe that these men are doing this for the sole purpose of showing their opposition to the Government, as the reports seem to indicate that the children themselves want to come back, and that they will not give them up without trouble" (U.S. Government 1892:166).

The Government moved a step closer: by mid-August 1892, "a day school building is finished on the plain near Oriba" (U.S. Government 1892:586). The Oraibi Day School opened in March

1893, though not without "much opposition on the part of the Indians" (Goodman 1894:998). The school managed to maintain an attendance of about thirty, but "not a pupil has been enrolled from among the 'hostiles'" (Goodman 1894:998).

The allotment program also persisted. Special Allotting Agent John S. Mayhugh spent the better part of two years at Hopi between 1892 and 1894. Allotment was resented by Hopis of all political allegiances and was also opposed by knowledgeable whites. Acting Agent Lieutenant E. H. Plummer forwarded to Washington a petition against allotment signed by 123 Hopi men (Plummer 4-10-1894). The petition, which contains totemic signatures by individual names and clan affiliations, was largely the work of Thomas Keam, Alexander Stephen (the ethnologist living at First Mesa), and missionary H. R. Voth. They secured signatures of support from General A. D. McCook, now commander of the Army's Department of the Colorado, and anthropologists James Mooney, Frank Cushing, and John Wesley Powell, among others. Over fifty of the Hopi signatories were from Oraibi, and all of them were "Friendlies,"[16] which would suggest that the latter were not entirely accepting of government policies.

The allotment program was discontinued at Hopi in February 1894 (U.S. Government 1895:20). Despite the widespread opposition represented by the petition, only the Oraibis, and of these especially the Hostiles, had consistently refused to take the allotments that Mayhugh provisionally assigned (e.g., Mayhugh 2-14-1893). As for the Friendlies, Mayhugh's correspondence reveals that Loololma occasionally expressed a desire to accept his allotment (perhaps as eighteenth-century Oraibi leaders expressed to missionaries a desire for Christianity), but would never actually accept the one assigned, voicing a variety of reasons.

Mayhugh's observations are significant in that he spent more time at Oraibi than any prior government official. He performed the first successful census of Oraibi in 1892 (Mayhugh 6-9-1892); previously, refusal to participate in government censuses—successfully conducted at the other villages since the 1870s—had been virtually unanimous. Of the 853 Oraibis he enumerated, 299 were Hostile (Mayhugh 6-9-1892, 2-14-1893). Records of the early 1900s repeatedly describe the Hostile faction as outnumbering the Friendlies, in some cases by as much as two to one. We might infer that the factions underwent considerable changes of allegiance in the years prior to the split.

Mayhugh also provides some interesting details on the nature of the factionalism. He repeatedly refers to Heevi'ima, the War Chief, as Hostile leader and does not mention Patupha, Yukioma, or Lomahongyoma. Moreover, he distinguishes between the factions not as "Friendlies" and "Hostiles," but as "Loololma's band" and "Heevi'ima's band." Initially, Heevi'ima steadfastly refused to talk to him, but toward the end of his stay

> I councilled with Hay be mer and some of his head men after I finished the work of allotment at Oraibi and still found him much opposed to taking his land in severalty yet he seemed more pleasant and talked more reasonable upon the subject. . . . There is quite a difference now in his demeanor to what it was when he with his band pulled up the stakes of survey and levelled down the mounds when the military had to be called in to protect the surveyors in finishing the Government survey. (Mayhugh 2-19-1894)

I noted above that the Oraibi signatories of the petition against allotment were Friendlies, headed by Loololma. Yet Mayhugh claims that he persuaded Loololma and his supporters to accept provisional allotments. While Heevi'ima became approachable and, Mayhugh thought, potentially amenable to allotment, Loololma, he repeatedly noted, was evasive, equivocating, and often deliberately misleading. Far from the opinion of Polingaysi Qoyawayma (Elizabeth White) (1964:32) that "Lololma was a weakling," Mayhugh (2-14-1893:3) found him a "very cunning old chief" and (9-19-1893:2) "smart and intelligent." Loololma told Mayhugh on more than one occasion that he could not take his allotment for fear of being killed by Heevi'ima (e.g., Mayhugh 7-12-1893). At the same time, Mayhugh records that in practice (i.e., were it not for allotment), the factions "get along peaceably and harmonious" (Mayhugh 9-19-1893:5).

It seems we have a few contradictions here. On the one hand, Heevi'ima is at least as approachable as Loololma: on one occasion, Mayhugh describes Heevi'ima's asking him for matches, tobacco, and a drink of water, and shaking his hand (Mayhugh 9-19-1893:3). On the other hand, Loololma, supposedly the "Friendly" representative, seems frequently less amenable than Heevi'ima, and his behavior is reminiscent of the manipulative strategies described in Chapter 2. Even Mayhugh's awareness of the factional division is used as a means to put him off: while Loololma expresses grave fears for his own safety, Mayhugh notes the factions' peaceable relations. Heevi'ima rejects allotment, but "I think before the expiration of the time required by law to make forced allotments he may take his land" (Mayhugh 2-19-1894:18). Loololma expresses approval of allotment but then leads his faction in signing a petition against it.

My point, Mayhugh's predicament notwithstanding, is that unless an individual had already been branded "Friendly" or "Hostile," it is difficult to tell which is which. Neither side was particularly "friendly": acceptance or rejection of "the white man's ways" does not seem a clear issue. Another contemporary observer, Daniel Dorchester, superintendent of Indian schools, reported:

> The Oriba village . . . has always been the farthest removed from the whites and the most conservative. About one-half the village is reported as hostile to education to white men's ways and to the United States Government. . . . The hostile ones say to the white men, "We want you to keep away." The other half are friendly and say, "We want to do what Washington tells us." They are all heathens of the worst type, and exceedingly selfish with one another, as well as with outside persons. Like many white people, the main aim of the better class, in relation to Government, is to make all they can out of it. The more advanced are tenacious for their old customs. They favor new houses, say they want them, but have no idea of giving up their old religion, by going into the new buildings. (U.S. Government 1892:584)

Thus, from at least two first-hand viewpoints, Oraibi factionalism was rather more complex than a simple ideological opposition over the Anglo-American presence.

H. R. Voth, Mennonite Missionary

In August 1893 (Goodman 1894:997) another influential figure, Reverend H. R. Voth, appeared on the scene. Voth and his wife settled on the east side of the Oraibi Wash about two miles from the village. He devoted himself to learning Hopi and by 1894 had "acquired a very good knowledge of the Moqui language and seems to have acquired a good and strong influence over the inhabitants of the village" (Plummer 1894:101). Views of Voth's work at Oraibi vary, but what is certain is that he was an extremely important representative of white society during the period prior to the split. (Essays on Voth's missionary and ethnological activities include Eggan 1979 and James 1974:146–58.)

Voth spent seven years at Oraibi, from August 1893 until April 1902 (*The Mennonite* 4-24-1902:2), with short visits thereafter; he was absent from August 1898 until June 1900 (*The Mennonite* 9-1900:93). Voth is universally reviled in contemporary Hopi discourse, though less for his missionary than his ethnological activities. The latter were expressly conceived as a means to penetrate and subvert Hopi religious precepts:

> I knew that much we could need in our religious work was hidden in the songs, prayers, speeches and symbolism of their secret religious performances. And in order to get it genuine I would have to get it where it was—in the religious ceremonies in their underground chambers (kivas). What little I could pump out of the priests, was as I soon found, misleading, distorted, and unreliable. The priests were not very anxious to furnish me anything that I wanted to use to undermine their religion. (Letter to the General Conference of Mennonites, cited in James 1974:153)

By a mixture of persuasion, friendship, medical and material aid, and downright aggression, Voth gathered ritual information and collected ritual artifacts. Though impressed by the complexity of Hopi beliefs, he continued to denigrate them:

> What a pantheon, what a religious system, what a rich language, what traditions, what organization! And yet how utterly little to satisfy the longings of the soul, to give peace to the heart for this life and a hope for eternity. Stacks of straw and chaff with here and there a grain of truth as is the case in all religious systems. (Letter to the General Conference of Mennonites, cited in James 1974:153–54)

Voth's subjection of Hopi religion to open scrutiny ran directly counter to Hopi practice. As noted in Chapter 3, ritual knowledge is guarded with great secrecy: it is the "currency" of power in Hopi society. Effective ritual depends on small, strictly controlled groups with privileged access to occult procedures. Voth's repeated intrusions into private rituals (from which he was forcibly ejected on occasion) and theological arguments with the priests (cf. James

1974:154) would at the least have disturbed the mental harmony deemed essential for ritual success.[17]

Voth began to publicize his findings in a series of monographs (see Laird 1977) on Oraibi rituals. He also constructed replicas of ritual altars which were exhibited at the Field Museum in Chicago, the Alvarado Hotel in Albuquerque, and the Grand Canyon's "Hopi House," the last of which Voth took a prominent role in organizing in 1905 (Harvey 1979:xiv). Voth's replicas were so accurate that occasionally Hopis who saw them demanded their return (Eggan 1979:6). I concur with Eggan (1979:7) that it is a mistake to blame the Mennonites for Oraibi's discord (as Laura Thompson 1950 does), but Voth's influence is, nonetheless, a factor to be reckoned with. His public distribution of esoteric lore (with concomitant vitiation of ritual power and priestly authority) cannot have gone unnoticed in Oraibi ("Hopi House" is quite close by, for example).

At the same time, Voth made some friends in Oraibi. He was clearly in sympathy with some Hostile views and occasionally served as intermediary with government agents. As the only resident white who could speak Hopi fluently, he was trusted by some to interpret government policies. His signature on the petition against allotment is not the only instance of protest against government action. This aspect of his role has been generally overshadowed by negative impressions. Voth's daughter, Martha Dyck (interviewed in 1982), describes him as "a harsh man, definitely not gemütlich," who occasionally used physical violence against Hopis. Mennonite historian Alfred Siemens (1962) provides his denomination's view (cited in Eggan 1979:3):

> The first Mennonite missionary to the Hopi, H. R. Voth, was an aggressive evangelist and anthropologist. He gathered many Hopi artifacts, made intensive studies of their customs, vocabulary and religion, and wrote carefully and voluminously about them. But he, as had the Catholic fathers before him, also antagonized them. The present missionaries feel they are still the objects of a resentment that was aroused by pioneer missionaries.

An enduring symbol of Voth's presence lies in the burnt-out shell of the church he built on the mesa top—over considerable Hopi protest for its proximity to active shrines—in 1901–2. The church was struck by lightning around 1912 (James 1974:157) and again in 1942 (Dockstader 1979:528). The prevailing Hopi view is that, through supernatural intervention, Voth's monument received its just deserts.

Continuing Factionalism and the Division of the Ritual Order

In the fall of 1894, tensions flared again between the factions. Since the 1870s, the area around Moencopi had been cultivated continuously by several Oraibi men (see Chapter 2). Gradually, the colony began to grow (Nagata 1970 provides a thorough account of Moencopi history). The group farming there was Friendly (Tuuvi, who died around 1887, was a close ally of Loololma). However, ruins in the Moencopi area were the traditional claim of clans now predominantly Hostile: Spider, Snake, and *Kookop* (cf. Voth 1905a:23). In order to safeguard their claim (and possibly at the instigation of Mormon settlers[18]), a group of about fifty Hostiles, led by Heevi'ima, went to Moencopi and planted the land with wheat.[19] Captain Constant Williams, acting Indian agent for the Navajo and Hopi appointed in the middle of this crisis, held a meeting in Oraibi on 6 November 1894:

> Lo ma hung yo ma and He bi ma replied for the Hostiles and fully and freely admitted the truth of Lo lu lo mai's statements. They said for themselves that they do not want to follow the Washington path; that they do not want their children to go to school; that they do not want to wear white man's clothes; that they do not want to eat white man's food; that they do want the white man to let them alone and allow them to follow the Oraibi path; and they totally denounced the Friendlies for departing from the Oraibi path. They said that they had taken the Moen-copie fields because they had anciently belonged to them, although they admitted that the Friendlies had had peaceful possession of them for many years; they added that in the spring they intended to take away the fields now cultivated by the Friendlies around the mesa of Oraibi. And they concluded by saying that they also wished to have troops come. I asked them if they could not adjust their differences in a peaceable talk and they replied "no, that this trouble can never be settled until the soldiers come."[20] (Williams 11-15-1894a:2)

From Oraibi to Bacavi

Hostiles at Alcatraz, 1894–95. This photograph is also published in James (1974: 115) and Dockstader (1979:527), where there are a number of misidentifications (see note 21, this chapter). The following identifications are based on those identifications appearing in James and Dockstader which coincide with the names of those arrested (recorded in Williams 11-29-1894); the author's comparison of other names in Williams's list with other photographs; and older consultants' identifications. *Back row (left to right):* unidentified, Polingyaoma (Kachina), Heevi'ima (*Kookop*), Masatewa (Snake/Lizard), unidentified. *Middle row:* Qötsventewa (Bow), Piphongva (Badger), unidentified, Lomahongyoma (Spider), unidentified, Lomayestewa (Spider), Yukioma (*Kookop*). *Front row:* Duvewuhioma (Spider), unidentified, Patupha (*Kookop*), Qötsyaoma (Desert Fox), unidentified, Sikyaheptewa (*Patki*), unidentified. The remaining names in Williams's list are Talangainewa (*Kookop*), Talasyaoma (Badger), Nasingainewa (Eagle), Lomayaoma (Coyote), Tawaletstewa (Badger), Aka'usi (Navajo, adopted into the Eagle clan), Qöiwisö (*Kookop*). Photograph by Isaiah W. Taber, George Wharton James Collection, Southwest Museum, Los Angeles.

The Hostiles also threatened to drive the Friendlies "from this country into Mexico" (Williams 11-15-1894a:1)—the earliest record I have found that one faction might be forced out of the village.

Williams decided to comply with the request for troops in order "to bring them to their senses" (11-15-1894b). With two troops of cavalry, he reached Oraibi on 25 November and arrested nineteen of the Hostile party. They were shipped to the military prison on

Alcatraz Island, where they remained at hard labor until September 1895.[21]

Williams also provides the earliest record found of Lomahongyoma as leader of the Hostiles: he states that the Hostiles "are under Loma hung yo ma (with He bi ma as his principal adviser)" (11-15-1894a). Williams (and also Voth [7-8-1895]) regarded Lomahongyoma as amenable to compromise: "he will, in time, become a leader in the right way and earnestly work for the true interest of his people. He is an hereditary chief and if he can be brought over the result will be good" (11-29-1894:3). The *Kookop* clan leaders were singled out rather differently:

I respectfully recommend that Hebima, Yukioma, and Patopa be separated, as soon as practicable, from the rest and sent to some remote place where they may have no opportunity to communicate with their people. . . . These men are obstinate in their adherence to their old savage ways; their influence, which is very great, has always been, and always will be, exerted against the enlightenment of the Moquis. (11-29-1894:2)

Lomahongyoma became a direct rival to Loololma for the position of *Kikmongwi*. His pedigree was unsurpassed. "He had been chosen head of the Spider clan" (Titiev 1944:73), which was of the phratry that traditionally provided the *Kikmongwi*; he was head of the Blue Flute ceremony, the most important Spider clan ritual prerogative; he was kiva chief at Sakwalenvi where the *Soyalangw* ceremony (which traditionally belonged to the *Kikmongwi*) was centered and "in that ceremony he held an important post as a singer of sacred songs" (Titiev 1944:73); he was a member of *Momtsit* (the Warriors' society), of which his own mother's brother, Talai'ima, had been head (Titiev 1944:73). Clearly, Lomahongyoma belonged to the core lineage segment of the Spider clan and was an eminent *pavansino*.

Several reasons suggest that Lomahongyoma was the Hostiles' *Kikmongwi*, rather than a de facto leader who achieved prominence by political maneuver. First, as we have seen, the *Kookop* leaders, especially Heevi'ima and Patupha, were consistently recognized in contemporary documents as the primary Hostile instigators. Second, Acting Agent Williams, who clearly recognized Heevi'ima's influence, comments indicatively, "I have told Lomahungyoma that hereafter but one chief would be recognized at Oraibi, to wit, Lololomai" (9-29-1895). Third, Yukioma, the later

Hostile leader, in an interview with Voth, states: "a soldier chief asked us whether we wanted Loloma to be our chief, and he said to us if they would treat us that way again and take away our children again, then Lomahongyoma should be chief alone" (Voth n.d.a:1). Voth (Dorsey and Voth 1901:9) also refers to Lomahongyoma specifically as the rival to Loololma.

At some point in the 1890s, and linked to this chiefly rivalry, the division touched the ceremonies. Friendly members of societies controlled by Hostiles, and vice versa, began to withdraw:

So, as a matter of fact, we find today that the religious organizations are divided into two opposing factions, the performance of any given ceremony being conducted, with but few exceptions, by the members of either one or the other party. The gap has even widened to such an extent that in certain instances the withdrawing members have held independent performances, even without or with an improvised altar; and in the fall of 1900 the seceding members of the *Wowochimtu* fraternity, and in January, 1901, the Blue Flute Society, refused to participate in the ceremonies at all, an occurrence hitherto entirely unknown among the Oraibis. (Dorsey and Voth 1901:10)

Titiev discusses the ceremonial division at length (1944:80–83) and concludes that "two separate ceremonial cycles were conducted annually" (1944:83). This, I believe, is overgeneralized. It certainly was not the case that each society and ceremony was replicated: there was no Friendly Antelope, Blue Flute, or Snake society,[22] and no Hostile Gray Flute, *Lakon*, or *Maraw*. As for Titiev's list of rival society officers (1944:83), the contexts for which they were rivals are unclear and some suggested incumbents are questionable: Sikyave'ima, for example, whom Titiev lists as Hostile *Kwan* chief, never assumed this mantle in Bacavi and my consultants found the suggestion implausible. Some ceremonies, nevertheless, were replicated. Another indication that Lomahongyoma was setting himself up as *Kikmongwi* is that he became leader of a rival *Soyalangw* ceremony to Loololma's. Loololma had been forced out of the *Soyalangw* headquarters at Sakwalenvi and had to use Pongookiva for his ceremony (Dorsey and Voth 1901:11).

The factional division thus reached a new height with the emergence of a rival for the most important position in the traditional politico-religious elite. Surpassing simple factional opposition to the *Kikmongwi*'s policies, the projection of a rival claimant had the dual effect of delegitimizing the incumbent and legitimizing opposition at the highest level.

In 1896 the commissioner again issued orders that all children be put in school (Williams 1896:113). This compulsory ruling was to have severe effects at Oraibi over the next few years. For the time being, it was still possible for the prisoners returned from Alcatraz to "refuse to send their children to school, assigning religious scruples as a reason for their not doing so" (Williams 1896:113). The Oraibi Day School maintained an attendance of about thirty pupils, all offspring of Friendly parents, and coercive measures temporarily lapsed.

The Smallpox Epidemic

Another confrontation with government officialdom occurred in 1899 following a smallpox epidemic. The epidemic began in December 1898 and was severe. All schools were closed and a quarantine was maintained at Oraibi by stationing a string of Indian police (mostly Navajos, First Mesa Hopis and Hopi-Tewas) between Second Mesa and Third Mesa. This measure prevented the disease from spreading to Oraibi,[23] but the enforced segregation of those with nonwestern concepts of disease aetiology constituted another instance of intrusion upon Hopi autonomy.

Six hundred thirty-two people from First Mesa and Second Mesa (a little more than half the population) caught the disease, and 187 of them died (Hazylett 1899:159). By April 1899, the worst of the epidemic was over and a "cleanup" began. Clothing was burnt, houses were fumigated and disinfected, and a full-blown vaccination program was undertaken. "Four or five hundred" Oraibis consented to vaccination; the Hostiles refused (Hazylett 5-8-1899), but this caused little concern since the disease had not broken out at Oraibi. However, opposition to the cleanup at Shongopavi led to the calling out of troops. The official report states that "the troops soon subdued them without any serious injury to anyone" (Hazylett 1899:159). Correspondence reveals rather more. The leading dissidents were gathered in one house and to "persuade" them to come out, the soldiers started to demolish the house about them.

Since the dissidents had no firearms the soldiers put theirs aside, but as a result a severe hand to hand conflict was indulged in which several Indians were badly used up, before the leaders were captured and taken down, when the rest followed submissively enough. They were all bathed in a carbolic acid bath, issued new clothing and their village thoroughly disinfected and fumigated, and by evening they were all allowed to return to their houses with the exception of seven of the leaders, who were arrested and escorted to this agency by the troop. (Hazylett 6-6-1899:4)

These seven, plus one other, were kept at hard labor at Fort Defiance for five months. Despite the usual reports (e.g., Hazylett 9-4-1899) that by the end of their confinement the prisoners had "come around" to the "Government way," several of those imprisoned were instrumental in the relocation of the Second Mesa Hostiles to Oraibi some seven years later.

Superintendent Burton and the Reestablishment of the Moqui Agency

July 1899 saw the arrival of Charles E. Burton, new superintendent of the Keam's Canyon school and special disbursing agent. Control of the Moqui Reservation was officially passed into his hands and the Moqui Subagency at Fort Defiance was abolished.

Burton was a young man (aged twenty-seven upon his arrival) and zealous in pursuit of assimilation for those in his charge. Almost immediately he instituted a plan to put all Hopi children into the schools. He met, however, with considerable resistance:

The hostiles are a very serious drawback to the progress of civilization, not only refusing to send their children to school but by severe criticism preventing others from sending to school and in other ways making the progress they should make. These should be forced to send their children to school. (Burton 1900:475)

Two weeks after he wrote this report, Burton made good his recommendation: "I have the honor to report to you that the day before yesterday I went to Oraibi with Mr. Kampmeier, the Day School teacher at the place, and two policemen and brought away eight of the hostile children and the hostile chief with only a very slight show of force" (Burton 9-15-1900). Burton's "slight show of force" came to be a regular feature. He kept the Hostile leader and later his "lieutenant" (probably, from the context, Lomahongyoma and Yukioma) at the Keam's Canyon Agency under "surveillance" for the next several months.

His efforts to put all the children into school were very successful, so much so that the Oraibi Day School became dangerously overcrowded, as Kampmeier (1901:522) reported:

> When I took charge of this school on November 15, 1899, this school had an enrollment of 17, which I have succeeded with your [i.e., Burton's] help to increase to 114, about 60 per cent of the school population of this Indian village. . . . The best way to describe the buildings at this school, excepting the teacher's cottage, would be to leave a blank space under this sub-heading. I will say, however, that the schoolhouse is entirely too small, unfit, and extremely dangerous.

For the first time, Burton and Kampmeier's forceful tactics were bringing Hostiles' children into school. But Burton's zeal was less educational than designed to impress his superiors: "The hostile element here is very hard to manage, but more children than could be well cared for were enrolled to prove to the Department that the hostile people could be made to put their children in school" (Burton 1901:518). Hopi oral traditions are abundant with details of Potni's (Burton's) and Kepma's (Kampmeier's) excesses. Every morning, children were hidden in a variety of ways (in rolled sheepskins, in house cellars, etc.) or sent herding sheep early to prevent abduction by Indian police.

Burton's correspondence reveals an increasingly obsessive man, extremely sensitive to criticism. He attempted to have Thomas Keam ejected from the reservation (Burton 2-20-1900) and incurred the dislike of many visitors, including ethnologist George Dorsey and H. R. Voth (Burton 11-23-1903), who both protested his brutal treatment of children. He was particularly concerned with clamping down on Hopi religious ritual:

> I recommend that all the employees in the government service be forbidden to attend these dances except such as may be detailed to prevent evil practices. . . . I also desire to regulate the attendance from the outside. . . . The schools are interfered with, the time and energy of the Indians wasted, immorality encouraged, old superstitions and customs kept alive, civiliza-

tion and citizenship hindered by these and other practices and I heartily endorse and recommend any steps that will put a stop to them. (Burton 3-7-1900)

Since the 1880s, anthropologists, tourists, artists, photographers, and scientists of one kind or another had been visiting Hopi, mostly to see the Snake Dance, which had been widely publicized by Bourke's *Snake Dance of the Moquis* (1884) (though see Laird 1977 for myriad other accounts). Tours to the Snake Dance (with the Grand Canyon thrown in) were advertised in leading Eastern newspapers, especially from the late 1890s, and a few years later became great social events (Theodore Roosevelt visited in 1913), with huge crowds of camera-wielding tourists. The Fred Harvey Company, which operated an entertainment franchise along the Atchison, Topeka, and Santa Fe Railroad, cornered much of the market in the early 1900s with its "Indian Detours" (Thomas 1978). Visitors to Hopi often commented on the inequities of government practice and encouraged the Hopi to maintain traditions. Burton repeatedly called for authority to control visitors on the reservation, though without much success. Miltona Keith, field matron at the Oraibi Day School, typifies the agency attitude toward tourists: "I wish the Department could realize the influence of some of the tourists who came here. Their own costumes have a very demoralizing effect and they encourage the Hopi in wearing their hair long and clinging to Hopi clothing, customs, and superstitions" (Keith 1904:140).

In time, missionaries (specifically Voth's successor, J. B. Epp, who arrived in 1901), tourists, and longer-term visitors with an interest in Hopi culture often sided with the Hostile faction against government policies. The "whitemen," then, did not present a united front and this must have had an impact on how they were perceived.

In a long, rambling reply to the report of an inspector who had been sent to investigate the schools and the reservation, Burton defended himself against the charge that he had interfered with Hopi ceremonies, but his true sentiments emerge with clarity:

I have not tried to break up their religious ceremonies including their snake dances. I have not given the dances my approval and stood for hours in open mouthed ecstasy at a revolting and immoral and heathenish uncivilized exposure of human forms. . . . I did prohibit one cruel barbarous ceremony that of great hulking bucks taking a handful of Spanish daggers and whipping the little barebacks of small children some of them not two years old till the blood run down in great streams.[24] . . . I did do this, Mr. Commissioner, and as long as I am superintendent, I expect to do so unless you expressly forbid me to do so under which circumstances my resignation will surely be tendered. (Burton 4-2-1901:12)

Mr. Burton, it seems, was a man with decidedly Victorian views.

In early 1902 Burton received encouragement from the commissioner for his plans to stamp out Hopi ceremonies. His reply noted: "If the Moqui dances are to be prohibited, it will be necessary to destroy their underground kevas [sic] where the ceremonies are carried on. This destruction will put an end to it at once and I strongly recommend that I be given authority to make that the first move" (Burton 1-27-1902). And, to prevent protests by visitors, "I recommend that no scientific people be allowed to visit the reservation for one year" (1-27-1902). Fortunately, Burton was never authorized to proceed, despite his fervent declaration that "I expect to open the ball as soon as I hear from this letter" (1-27-1902).

Burton committed other transgressions against Hopi proprieties. In 1901 there was another smallpox scare, when five Navajos living near Keam's Canyon came down with the disease. It remained confined to this Navajo camp, forty miles from Oraibi. However, all the Hopi were quarantined and another total vaccination program was instituted. Only Oraibi resisted. So

the village was surrounded two hours before dawn by a force of 16 police and employees. After sunrise every person in the village was ordered to the clear ground outside the town. . . . The entire population then passed through a gauntlet of vaccinators, and all who had not been vaccinated before were compelled to submit. (Burton 1901:518)

Four men who held out had their hair cut and were forcibly vaccinated (Burton 3-24-1901). Burton's proclivity for haircuts as punishment received a boost when this was made official Indian Affairs policy in the winter of 1901–2. He proceeded to cut the hair of all Hopi men, according to his own account; missionaries at both Second Mesa and Third Mesa protested in vain (Burton 1-26-1903). This was a matter of great and long-remembered resentment among Hopi men, not only for obvious reasons, but because long hair was highly valued as a ritual mark of manhood entitled by *Wuwtsim* initiation.

News of Burton's excesses began to penetrate beyond the reservation. In 1902 Gertrude P. Gates was sent as an "underground" representative of Charles F. Lummis's "Sequoya League" (an Indian-rights group) to investigate stories of cruelty at the Oraibi Day School. In February 1903, when Belle Axtell Kolp resigned her position as teacher at the Oraibi Day School after only five weeks, on account of the brutality she encountered, Lummis began a crusade to have Burton removed from office. Lummis was an influential man: he was a personal friend of Theodore Roosevelt, whose support he solicited for the campaign against Burton. He published a series of articles condemning Burton's actions in his magazine *Out West*, and a wider public took note. One of the articles, a notarized affidavit by Kolp, was particularly revelatory:

> When I began work at Oraibi, the daily attendance at the school was about 125 children.... When I left, there were 174 children in school, and still two teachers—one of them having in her charge 96 children, whose ages ranged from less than four years to others who were 18 or 20.... These children, with others were taken forcibly from their homes by an armed body of Government employees and Navajo Indians, under the leadership of C. E. Burton—not for the purpose of "making better Indians," but for the benefit of those in charge. (Lummis 1968:43–44)

Kolp describes an incident in which the principal, T. Ballinger, was seen to "break sticks on the boy's [sic] backs when whipping them in the school dining room" (Lummis 1968:48).

The particular raid that Kolp described was celebrated by Burton (2-9-1903). His report is worth quoting at length for the perspective it provides into Oraibi-government relations prior to the split:

> At day break we went up silently to the village and began a search through the houses for the children. As we found them, we took them to a kiva near the center of the village and left them under guard by a policeman. Our diligent search was only rewarded by 10 children. When we had finished we proceeded to the kiva and started with the children. About fifty of the Hostiles attacked us and attempted to take the children away from us. After struggling with them till we reached the edge of the mesa where the trail descends abruptly to the school fearing that they would crowd us over the edge to our death, I ordered the police and employees to

draw their guns, which we did and stood off the mob, having managed to get the children started down the trail to the school. One Moqui was knocked down in the struggle and several were tapped over the head with the pistols but no-one was hurt in the least. The leaders then began to parley saying that the Missionaries had told them that we had no right to take their children without their consent, that the law did not give us the right; that the Missionaries had read them your [the commissioner's] two orders concerning the cutting of their hair and had told them that we had no right to do it, etc. etc. Imagine if you will our position, immediately on the edge of a lofty precipice and only a trail where one could go at a time and that trail icy and snowy. I feared that if we turned to go down they would make a rush and push us over. Fifty against seven (two having gone with the children)! After considering for a moment I ordered all to advance and drive them back. We did so and after some scuffling the Indians wavered and fell back to the village. We then turned and quietly proceeded down to the school.

That afternoon I sent the 10 children to Keam's Canyon, and the next day, I secured twelve extra policemen. The next morning we proceeded to the village and arrested 17 of the leaders of the mob, and started them to the Canyon. (Burton 2-9-1903:2–4)

Burton's "True West," pistol-tapping approach received a severe reprimand following an investigation prompted by Lummis's articles:

He was warned that in the future, no threats or force of any kind were to be employed regarding haircutting and that he must trust entirely to persuasion and example. The report recommended that Kampmeier, who had already been transferred, be dismissed from the Indian Service, as he was in 1904, and that Ballinger be removed to a less responsible place. (James 1974:129)

Burton's relations with watchdog whites deteriorated. Mrs. Gates, a wealthy society lady from Pasadena, spent several weeks each year from 1902 to 1906 living at Oraibi. Burton initiated a lengthy correspondence with the Indian Office about her anti-government influence. Evidently, she participated in a Butterfly Dance at Oraibi in 1903 (older Hopis recollect that Tawaquaptewa [see below] was her partner), and many Hopis from other villages came to watch (U.S. Government, Dept. of the Interior 1903–4:passim). With racist, florid, prurient (and in this case, at least, totally inaccurate) rhetoric, Burton protested that

[Mrs. Gates] was dancing with a lot of Indian men, stripped to the waist, as she admitted to me (but in fact stripped *down* to the waist and stripped *up* to the waist), and that she was by these actions destroying the influence exerted by employees for years.... Imagine if you please, a modest, refined woman surrounded by a score of naked, painted, sweating, filthy, stinking Indians and you will have an accurate picture of the scene. (Burton 7-10-1903:7)

Burton was fighting a losing battle, however. Even some of his own employees went against the party line. In 1904 the painter Louis Akin, who was teaching at the Oraibi Day School, and Additional Farmer Wood were both wearing their hair long, sporting Hopi dress, and otherwise copying a Hopi lifestyle (Burton 6-25-1904); Akin was living in Oraibi itself during this period (cf. Babbitt 1973:4–14).

The influence of liberal whites should not be underestimated. As well as getting rid of the Oraibi Day School principals, it seems likely that their cumulative pressure led to Burton's transfer. Burton's management of the schools did not much improve. The next principal of the Oraibi Day School, Glen C. Lawrence, was accused of the same brutality as his predecessors (Burton 7-28-1904), which resulted in his transfer (Burton 10-6-1904). Burton himself was transferred in late 1904 without consultation. Characteristically, the poor fellow threatened his resignation: "I have been maligned without any chance to defend myself" (Burton 11-10-1904).

Subsequently, Gates proposed a more equitable scheme of voluntary education at the Oraibi Day School. Although abandoned in 1906 and claimed a failure by Burton's successor, Theodore G. Lemmon, the "Viets-Gates experiment" (after Gates and A. H. Viets, inspector of day schools and new principal teacher at Oraibi) was tried through the 1905–6 school year (Lemmon 8-30-1906).

Climate

In 1905 Matthew Murphy, superintendent of the Western Navajo Reservation at Tuba City, reported that "these Indians have just passed through a period of drought that must have rivaled the seven dry years of Egypt" (1905:180). Official correspondence suggests that during the 1890s the climatic situation was stable. In the aftermath of the smallpox epidemic, the government seriously considered destroying all stored produce in the Hopi villages (e.g., Hazylett 4-18-1899). They desisted, but during their investigations found that the granaries were full with a surplus to last two years (Hazylett 1899:158). The harvest in 1897 and possibly 1898 was good: "last year the Moquis had very good crops, and, from present indications, they will have better ones this year" (Williams 1898:124).

However, Voth records partial harvest failures at Oraibi in 1899 and 1900 (*The Mennonite* 9-1900), and the worst year seems to have been 1902: "No rain has fallen this year. Many of the Indians could not plant at all, owing to the hardness and dryness of the ground. Suffering is bound to come" (Burton 1902:154). Missionary Epp recorded an almost total failure of the harvest (*The Mennonite* 12-11-1902). In spring 1903 he imported two train-carloads of corn from Kansas to distribute in Oraibi (Gates 4-21-1903; J. B. Frey 1915:22). Nevertheless, the lack of indigenous productivity must have had a profound effect upon Hopi thinking. Many religious practices are aimed at ensuring productive climatic conditions, and failure meets with interpersonal recriminations. The severe shortage of rainfall must undoubtedly have been of critical concern.

Burton notes (1903:123) that 1903 was a good year for rainfall, and in 1905 Superintendent Lemmon's correspondence repeatedly records heavy snow and rainfall. Nevertheless, in 1906 the springs failed badly: "It is the first time since I came that the springs have been failing. I have put in every minute that I can to get away to study the conditions at water sources" (Lemmon 6-16-1906). Even a preponderance of moisture in 1905 would not yet have permeated the mesa-top sandstone enough to replenish the talus-slope springs (see Gregory 1916 on local hydrography). Hopi accounts record lines of women waiting for hours at the springs for enough water to fill their jars. This was another matter of vital concern, with significant repercussions on the social judgment of ritual efficacy. It resulted in skepticism of the supernatural intentions of ritual leaders and pervasive witchcraft accusations. I shall return to these issues in Chapter 8.

Changes in Factional Leadership

In 1905 land again became the subject of dispute. Almost immediately after he took over the agency, Lemmon was called upon to look into the matter: "the unfriendly's [sic] have their bristles up and threaten innumerable dire and calamitous things from all of which I infer there is something of a family row on hands. . . . I will see that people who try to do right shall not be *driven out of the village*" (Lemmon 1-26-1905, my emphasis). Again, the possibility is raised that one faction might be expelled. It seems reasonable to infer that this had become a common topic in Oraibi discourse.

Lemmon visited Oraibi for half a day and discovered little. He learned shortly thereafter that "the trouble was growing worse over the land" (Lemmon 2-14-1905) and further that there was a plot to kill Tawaquaptewa, the new *Kikmongwi* and leader of the Friendlies following Loololma's death around 1904 (see below). Lemmon was "begged" to come out to Oraibi to protect him (Lemmon 7-23-1905:2). Upon arrival, Lemmon arranged a meeting with Tawaquaptewa and Lomahongyoma in the Oraibi Valley, where they discussed the land situation. Lemmon then convened a general council in Oraibi and announced: "For the present year you will farm the lands you did last year and in November or December I will call a council and we will decide on a division that will last till the shifting sands or the receding of the wash makes another division necessary" (Lemmon 7-23-1905:5). Although I found no further references by Lemmon in November or December 1905 to a division of lands, an older consultant reported a meeting of Lemmon, Tawaquaptewa, and Lomahongyoma in which it was decided that all land north of a line across the Oraibi Valley (he showed me the points of demarcation) would go to the Hostiles, and all south to the Friendlies. Although Lemmon does not mention this explicitly in his accounts of the February meeting, his purpose (from arranging to meet in the Oraibi Valley) seems fairly clear.

Lemmon regarded Lomahongyoma as the main Hostile leader, and Yukioma "ranked second." He set about to try to create a rift between the two and based this on the notion that Lomahongyoma, as the head of ceremonies with some Friendly participants, might have conflicting loyalties: "seeing a double tie in Lomahogioma I orated till I had him in a good humor and Yukioma in a bad humor" (Lemmon 7-23-1905:4). As a result, "in less than two hours after I left I was informed that a part of the conservatives had deposed Lomahogioma and raised up Yukioma in his place. I had succeeded to the fullest measure I had hoped. I had split the unfriendly faction" (Lemmon 7-23-1905:5).

Lemmon's claim is rather doubtful, although Yukioma did indeed replace Lomahongyoma as principal leader of the Hostiles sometime before 1906. According to Yukioma in an interview around 1905:

They asked for our children again and they took Lomahongyoma to Keam's Canyon where they cut his hair and kept him a while, then Lomahongyoma became willing to listen to the chief's talk. So they all came to Oraibi and then Lomahongyoma told us all to have pity on them and send our children, he was willing. But our people did not want to send their children because we had not learned it that way from our forefathers. . . . I asked Lomahongyoma whether he was really willing. He said, yes, he pitied his people. If we were willing we would not be ill-treated; we would not be kicked; we would not be punished. (Voth n.d.a:1–2)

Yukioma then proposed to the people that he should be leader, "but no-one said a word." The basis of his claim was that, "although these others were the chiefs, they did not own the village here, and the land, it was I who really owned it, because I represent the old Masauwu"[25] (Voth n.d.a:1).

Shortly after this, another meeting was held at the Oraibi Day School, during which Lomahongyoma repeated his acquiescence and Yukioma formally replaced him. According to several of my consultants, after the meeting at the day school people were making their way back up the hill to Oraibi, when (by prearranged plan) Naquave'ima (Eagle clan) took hold of Lomahongyoma's shoulder and announced, "You shall no longer lead us." Taking hold of Yukioma's shoulder, he said, "From now on, you shall be our leader." In 1911 Yukioma recounted a sequence of events which suggests, by comparison with the documentary record, that this transition occurred in early 1901.[26]

Thus significant changes were occurring in the leadership of both factions. Yukioma had become head of the *Kookop* clan, by his own account, "in Burton's time" (Scott 12-5-1911:8). Patupha, the previous clan head, died probably in 1899 or 1900. Heevi'ima may well have been getting too old (judging by the 1895 photograph of the Hostiles at Alcatraz) to be such an active force as previously (he died probably between 1907 and 1910). Hence, Yukioma's rise to prominence in the Hostile leadership was supported by his assumption of clan leadership. Yukioma received considerable support from Naquave'ima and from Lomahongyoma's brother, Lomayestewa, who may have been trying to assume Lomahongyoma's claim, since Lemmon reports that in 1906 Lomayestewa "robbed his brother of his ceremonial regalia to farther humiliate him" (9-20-1906:6). Lemmon (7-23-1905:6) also suggests that Lomahongyoma was formally ousted from Sakwalenvi, the chief kiva, of which he was head.

On the Friendly side, Loololma died, probably around 1904,[27] and was succeeded by a young nephew, Tawaquaptewa. Several consultants (including descendants of Loololma) indicate that two of Tawaquaptewa's older brothers had originally been considered (and one had been "trained" by Loololma). Hence, the subsequent choice of Tawaquaptewa had a specific intent. Titiev confirms this: "It is the opinion of some of the old Hopi that Tawaquaptiwa was chosen in preference to his older brothers because he was young and impetuous, and Lololma evidently had hoped that he would be energetic enough to bring matters to a head and so end the incessant bickering at Oraibi" (1944:83).

Navajos and Traders

Although there had been several attempts, and more pleas by Indian agents, to have Navajos removed from the Moqui Reservation, from at least 1890 (Vandever 1890:170) they continued to be a powerful, dominating force. They encroached on Hopi springs and stole crops and stock.

In 1899 Burton (9-11-1899) reported the murder of a Hopi man near Oraibi by a Navajo. The following year, Burton recommended that Navajos be barred from the trading posts at Keam's Canyon and near Oraibi. Frederick W. Volz had opened a store near the Oraibi Day School, below the mesa, around 1898. Apparently, he was largely an absentee landlord, since his main trading post was at Canyon Diablo. He left his brother, William, and "a Mexican— who has not a good reputation in any respect" (Burton 10-19-1900:2) in charge. Burton (10-19-1900:3) tried unsuccessfully to have them removed, reporting their exploitation and aggression against Oraibi people and that their presence encouraged Navajo depredations:

The Oraibi Indians personally and through their chiefs protest against the store as detrimental to their interests in many ways. They claim that the only roads to the store are through their corn fields and that the Navajos going and returning to the store rob melon and pumpkin patches, allow their burros and ponies to eat and otherwise destroy their corn and that they much rather that the store would not be there. Their complaints about the Navajos are perfectly true.

Burton (1899:383) also voiced more specific complaints about the Navajos:

Many Navajos from the Navajo Reservation have settled along the water courses and at the watering places on Moqui land. Why this has been allowed I cannot understand, as the Navajo Reservation is the largest in the United States and the Moqui Reservation is comparatively small. These places taken by the Navajos are the very best ones on the reservation and control most of the water supply.

During the years of drought, especially, the Navajo presence must have been particularly threatening. Moreover, Burton (9-10-1900: 2) characterizes Hopi-Navajo relations as thoroughly unequal:

Mr. Commissioner, something must be done for the relief and protection of these people. The Navajos have imposed upon them for so long and treated them so cruelly that the Hopi will not defend himself and I will not stand it much longer, and I am sure that blood will be spilled and lives lost if assistance is not given us.

This picture conforms to the general Hopi feelings of Navajo oppression still current in the 1980s. The legacy of early government inaction on Navajo encroachment is embodied in the ongoing Hopi-Navajo land dispute.

The influence of white traders at Oraibi is somewhat obscure. Volz maintained his store until 1905 or 1906, partly under the sponsorship of southwestern trading-post magnate Lorenzo Hubbell (McNitt 1962:270). After this the store passed to Hubbell outright and was run by his nephew, Antonio Armijo (Lemmon 8-20-1906). Burton, perhaps not the best source on temperament, described Volz as "a man of violent temper and on various occasions in the past has struck and beaten Indians who were at his store or in his employment" (10-6-1904). Earle Forrest (1961:9) records that Volz made a business of taking parties to the Snake Dance at Oraibi.

The trading post was, at any rate, another nexus of white influence, providing increased access to American goods. Burton encouraged a policy of Hopi ownership and operation of stores. Sam Pawiki opened the first at Oraibi in 1902 (Kampmeier 1902:155). In 1905 Lemmon (3-2-1905) recorded the following traders at Oraibi: William Volz, Thos. Tawaquaptewa, Sam Pawiki, and Naquiestewa. The last three, including the new *Kikmongwi*, were all Friendlies. Gradual absorption into the national economy had moved a little farther forward.

The Second Mesa Hostiles Move to Oraibi

And so to 1906. We have noted in passing some resistance at Second Mesa. The Hostiles there were not so numerous as at Oraibi and receive far less attention in the documentary record, but they maintained opposition throughout this period. Nequatewa (1936: 60–65) provides a good account of the events that led to a split at Shongopavi. Tawahongnewa (Bluebird clan), one of those incarcerated in the aftermath of the smallpox epidemic of 1898–99, was the Hostile leader. His natal village was either Shongopavi or Mishongnovi and he was married into Shipaulovi, where he built an initial cadre of resistance to the government. (In view of his subsequent tie to Lomayestewa at Oraibi, it is significant that there is a special closeness between the Spider and Bluebird clans: Bluebird is also a member of the chiefly phratry, although there were no living members at Oraibi by 1900.) The Hostiles moved from bases in Shipaulovi and Mishongnovi to Shongopavi shortly after the smallpox epidemic (Nequatewa 1936:62). According to modern Hopi accounts, they built houses in a section still recognized as separate from the main village nucleus.

In early January 1906 the Shongopavi Hostiles were withholding children from school (Lemmon 4-20-1906:4). Lemmon sent some police to arrest the leaders. They succeeded in making some arrests, although Tawahongnewa led an attack on them (Lemmon 4-20-1906:11). Lemmon decided to arrest the other assailants. On 26 February, a day planned for a dance (probably *Powamuy*), he set off with a force of Hopi and Navajo police. He found no sign of the dance: all the Hostile men were assembled in a kiva. They agreed to come out after he threatened to pour ammonia into the kiva and tear it up. Among their number, Lemmon noticed Yukioma (4-20-1906:17). A fierce fight ensued, during which one Hopi man was killed (Lemmon 4-20-1906:32). Toward the end of the fight, sixty Hostiles arrived from Oraibi (Lemmon 4-20-1906:23–24). Lemmon and his force retreated.

Two days later they were back and confronted a large group of Hostiles, many of whom were from Oraibi, in a Shongopavi street. Lemmon was requested to come alone and parley:

> Then I issued the only order about shooting that I issued at all. I told the Captain of police that if he heard any shooting around there where I was going to call up all the men and not stop killing as long as there was a living Hopi man in the village. If there was treachery, I determined to leave my successor a Hopi reservation almost without unfriendly Hopis. (Lemmon 4-20-1906:25–26)

These orders were not acted upon. Lemmon failed to arrest the five Shongopavi men he was looking for, and he asked for three hostages instead. Three men volunteered, at least two of them from Oraibi: Lomayestewa (Spider) and Quoyahoinewa (Sand) (Lemmon 4-20-1906:30, 9-20-1906:6). Lomayestewa told Lemmon "he was going to take all the unfriendly Hopis to live with him and the other unfriendlies at Oraibi" (4-20-1906:29). It was suggested to him by Peter Staufer (see below), an agency employee accompanying Lemmon, that the Hostiles move away from both Oraibi and Shongopavi and build a separate village (Lemmon 4-20-1906:31).

Shortly after this fracas, on 1 March 1906,[28] the Shongopavi contingent, consisting of about fifty-two people, moved to Oraibi, where they were ritually greeted by Lomayestewa and Yukioma, and led into the village with blessings of cornmeal. If things had been bad in Oraibi before, they now grew immeasurably worse: the Shongopavi Hostiles "began agitation to drive Tawaquaptiwa, the chief of the friendlies out of the village that Tawahongniwa might take the ceremonial priesthood and rank that has belonged to Tawaquaptiwa since the death of Lololomi" (Lemmon 9-20-1906:9). Tawaquaptewa was not amused:

Chief Tewaquaptewa went to Keam's Canyon, protesting to the superintendent that the Hostiles from Shungopovi were going to build houses in Oraibi, although they were not wanted and there was neither water nor corn land sufficient for the people already there. He said that if they attempted to build houses, the walls would be torn down as fast as they were put up; also that the time for the initiation ceremony was drawing near, and he didn't want the Shungopovis in Oraibi at that time; they would not be permitted at the initiation. They had to go, and at once. Moreover, Tewaquaptewa was outraged because the Shungopovi priests had usurped the authority of the Oraibi priests to consecrate cornmeal for ceremonial use. (H. Sekaquaptewa 1969:67–68)

Many Hopis cite this influx from Second Mesa as the precipitating cause of the Oraibi split. This finds confirmation in the contemporary report of the split by missionary Epp:

The *immediate* cause leading to the wild action of the "friendly" party of Oraibi is, to my observation, *very clearly* an incident that occurred at the neighboring village of Shumo'pavi and some of the consequences of it. . . . [After leaving Second Mesa] these fugitives remained *from month to month* at Oraibi; *planting* there; and using of the very scant supply of water, and in different other ways making themselves *very obnoxious* to the "friendlies" of Oraibi. (Epp 9-20-1906, emphasis in original)

The Commissioner Visits

Lemmon was called to Washington for most of March and April, although exactly why is uncertain. His long report (4-20-1906) of the Shongopavi conflict immediately followed his return, and it appears that the commissioner, Francis E. Leupp, doubted his competence. Leupp visited Oraibi personally, probably in early June (Lemmon 6-16-1906), without apprising Lemmon of his presence (he came directly to Oraibi from Winslow, avoiding Keam's Canyon). His purpose was to assess the Oraibi troubles at first hand. Leupp describes his meetings with Tawaquaptewa and Yukioma in some detail in his annual report (1907:120–22). Yukioma contemptuously rebuffed his threats:

With a sneer the chief responded that such talk was all nonsense; that he had heard it many times before, but nothing came of it; that his people did not wish anything to do with the whites; that their fathers had warned them not to let their children go to school and learn white ways; that he intended to follow the advice of the fathers rather than of Washington, and that if his people got into any trouble they would be rescued by their "white brother who lives in the far east where the sun rises" [see Chapter 8]. (Leupp 1907:120)

Leupp's luck with Tawaquaptewa was no better. Since he had arrived in stealth, unaccompanied by Lemmon, and specifically since he denied the existence of a government plan to drive the Hostiles from Oraibi (which, Tawaquaptewa assured him, had been repeatedly vouchsafed by Lemmon), Tawaquaptewa seriously doubted his claim to be commissioner. Then

he repeated his reference to the alleged government plan for driving out the Hostiles and dividing up their estate among the Friendlies, adding this time that the Hostiles had grown steadily more aggressive and increased in numbers because of the Government's inaction, and that unless I took some steps to punish the Hostiles and show my appreciation for the Friendlies there would presently be no Friendlies left. (Leupp 1907:122)

From this fruitless visit, Leupp decided that the only solution was a "demonstration with troops which would convince the ringleaders of the Hostile faction that they would gain nothing by further hostility" (1907:122). But before he could put this into practice, it was too late.

The Split

The immediate events of the split have been recounted in numerous texts. Titiev's (1944:69–95) remains the most comprehensive account. A serious ceremonial disruption occurred during the Hostiles' *Niman* (Home Dance) in July. A group of Friendlies, led by Tawaquaptewa, blocked the path of the Kachinas as they tried to leave for the *Niman* shrine (Titiev 1944:84). They were thus denied the ability to send the Kachinas to their spiritual home. Peter Staufer (9-18-1906), general mechanic and peripatetic lay Mennonite missionary, who was the longest-serving government employee on the Hopi Reservation (since 1890), records that participation by Second Mesa Hostiles in this *Niman* began the final aggravation leading to the split. A new "ceremonial organization" (inferably led by Tawahongnewa) denied Tawaquaptewa his traditional right to consecrate cornmeal for the departing Kachinas.

The Snake Dance was repeatedly postponed. Normally, it would have taken place about twenty days after *Niman*. Earle Forrest (1961:32), who was present, records that the postponements were connected with factional troubles. It appears that the Snake-Antelope ceremonies (which by now had solely Hostile participants) were in some way linked to the split, which occurred two days after the public "Snake Dance." This was within the post-performance period of sacredness, during which participants must still observe ritual proscriptions.

It is probable the Second Mesa Hostiles had some part in the ceremonies. This would account for reported disputes over the performance and for the intention, announced by the Friendlies, to eject them from Oraibi the day after it. In his first long report of the split, Lemmon noted:

During my absence [at the beginning of September] at Grand Junction there was a clash and a fight about the close of which one shot was fired. This I understand was over some difference over the Snake Dance.... I expected trouble up there at the time of the dance and arranged to be present, the dance taking place on Wednesday. While we were waiting for the dance to come on Mr. Frederick I. Monsen, who has attended the snake dance here before, remarked upon the tone of Hopi action being so widely at variance with anything he had ever known. (Lemmon 9-9-1906:1)

I will not duplicate in detail extant accounts of the split itself. Titiev (1944:85–86), H. Sekaquaptewa (1969:70–84), and Nequatewa (1936:65–68) provide the best published sources. Perhaps the best manuscript account by a Hopi eyewitness occurs in the

Hopi Hearings (1955:273–87). In addition, there is a wealth of materials in the Indian Office files at the National Archives (U.S. Government 1906–10). These are referred to in H. Sekaquaptewa (1969:84), though little use is made of them. Otherwise, to my knowledge, no other publication mentions them, which is surprising in view of the number of texts on the split. The materials include extensive correspondence of officials delegated to Oraibi and a number of detailed reports of the split by whites present in the village at the time. The following is a bare synthesis of these and my own consultants' accounts, although the latter are principally addressed in Chapter 8.

On 6 September a plan was announced to drive out the Second Mesa Hostiles the following day (Keith 9-16-1906:1). Evidently, Tawaquaptewa had learned they were plotting to assassinate him and this proved the last straw. Throughout the night both factions held councils, the Friendlies in Tawaquaptewa's house on the northwest side of the village, and the Hostiles in Naquave'ima's house on the east side (cf. Titiev 1944:85). At dawn, one of the leading Snake priests, Puhunimptewa (Snake clan), went to the mission in Oraibi Valley and informed those present—Reverend Epp, Mrs. Gates, and her wagon driver, E. Gannett—of the plan to drive out the Second Mesa Hostiles. They set out for the village immediately and picked up Elizabeth Stanley, acting principal of the Oraibi Day School, and Miltona Keith, field matron, on the way (Gates 10-25-1906:1–2). Evidently, Lomahongyoma was working at the mission when Puhunimptewa arrived, and his own son rushed in to inform him of the impending trouble. Clearly, he thus had no part in the final Hostile council.

The whites went straight to Tawaquaptewa's house, and Miss Stanley, the senior government representative, advised against the use of weapons. They then went to Naquave'ima's house. All the Second Mesa Hostile men and several of the Oraibi Hostile men, about fifty in total, were there:

We were just about to try to get a promise from them not to use arms or knives when suddenly a few of Tewaquaptewa's men with him at the head rushed in *unarmed* and demanded that we leave the room saying that we had been too long. When we started to talk to the unfriendlies we had been warned to hurry with our talk for it was getting late and they, the friendlies, were in a hurry. We left the room and in almost no time a commotion arose ... the friendlies were carrying out the struggling hostiles. Great commotion prevailed. The friendlies seemed to be pushing, pulling, and carrying the unwilling hostiles who were kicking, striking, and pulling the hair of their adversaries. The unfriendlies were taken to the northern outskirts of the village and put down. ... Later in the day I asked Frank Jenkins who is considered to be the least biased of any of the interpreters what had occurred in the house after we left. According to his version Tewaquaptewa ordered the Shemopovis to leave the village where upon Yukeoma the chief of the Oraibi hostiles said they should not leave and that the hostiles of Oraibi would aid the Shemopovis. Tewaquaptewa answered "You will go too, then." Each of the few friendlies who could gain access to the already crowded room grabbed a Shemopovi to put him out and was in turn grasped from behind by an Oraibi hostile. Frank tells me that in the room the unfriendlies were about four to one. To my surprise when I had dispatched a letter to Supt. Lemmon and was free to observe passing events the men who had been put over the line stayed there without apparent objection. Women and children gathered over there. ... [Friendly] men went to the various houses and told the inmates they must leave. (Keith 9-16-1906:4–6)

The Hostiles assembled a little to the northwest of the village, by some flat rocks near the shrine of Atsamali. Tawaquaptewa agreed to allow three at a time to return to the village to collect their belongings. The Hostiles were periodically charged upon by groups of Friendlies trying to force them to move on (Gates 10-25-1906:7). Around mid-afternoon

a long discussion followed between the two factions. The unfriendlies said they knew somebody had to go for it is a prophecy but each wished the other to go. Finally Yukeoma drew another line and said that which ever party was put across should go. The unfriendlies were put over and started for Hoti vella without more ado while the friendlies turned back. (Keith 9-16-1906:11)

The push-line was later commemorated by a carving in the flat rocks (a photograph appears in James 1974:137).

Evidently, each side expected the other to make an attack; the prophecy (see Chapter 8) held that the party that left would return to destroy the village. It was also rumored that a Friendly party would go to Hotevilla to drive the Hostiles farther on. According to my consultants, an attack was seriously considered by the Hostiles. Naquave'ima did not go with the rest to Hotevilla immediately.

Instead he went to the ruin of Huk'ovi, from where, by the prophecy, the attack on Oraibi was to be launched. Kewanimptewa, later chief of Bacavi, was approached in camp at Hotevilla by six men who asked if he would lead the attack. He refused. The attack never came, but correspondence indicates that Tawaquaptewa greatly feared one within four days after the split.

The Government's Response

Government interference in the aftermath of the split is only thinly discussed in the literature. Writers have been concerned to document the immediate details of the split and the immediate consequence of the settling of Hotevilla, but beyond this, they are vague at best. As early as 9 September, Lemmon's report gives recommendations that were repeated in the reports of subsequent investigators and that find numerous echoes in the events of later Third Mesa history. In particular:

1. That they [the Hostiles] be brought back and required to build themselves two villages on other parts of the reservation. . . .

2. That the present leaders be transported. . . .

5. That a smaller village be made the home of the most superstitious and priest ridden, that the more intelligent may have homes in the better village away from the old ones.

6. That in lieu of their present chiefs they be required to elect a governor and some petty officers each year for five years. . . . (Lemmon 9-9-1906:6–7).

The first outside investigator on the scene was Matthew Murphy, superintendent of the Western Navajo Agency. Since Moencopi was in his jurisdiction, he was already familiar with the basic situation; he had given a specific order (which was ignored) that no one should go from Moencopi to aid the Oraibi Friendlies. Murphy's recommendations included:

1. That the tribal government of Oraibi be abolished; that the chiefs of both factions be deposed; that the village be placed under the jurisdiction of an Indian judge to be appointed by the superintendent in charge, subject to the approval of the Commissioner of Indian Affairs. . . .

From Oraibi to Bacavi

3. That the leaders of the Hostile faction, and others whose influence and conduct is exerted to retard the progress of the tribe, be removed from the country; that the leaders, especially Yukeoma and Towahongnewa, be permitted never to return to the Hopi country. . . .

5. That the other members of the Hostile faction be returned to their homes in Oraibi, after they have acknowledged the authority of the judge provided for in recommendation (1) above. . . .

8. That regular soldiers be sent to Oraibi to carry out these recommendations, or any other policy that may be adopted. . . .

11. That the lands belonging to these Indians be surveyed and allotted at as early a date as possible. (Murphy 9-20-1906:3–5)

Murphy also proposed that two new villages be established and that Tawaquaptewa be sent to a nonreservation school for three years. All these recommendations were in some form pursued.

On 29 September, with the information he had amassed, Commissioner Leupp produced a "Program for Dealing with the Existing Hopi Troubles" (Appendix 1). It was submitted to President Roosevelt on 4 October by Leupp's deputy: "[I] received his unqualified approval of the program and oral instructions to proceed at once, through the proper channels, to secure a sufficient military force to carry it into effect" (Larrabee 10-5-1906:2). The Oraibi situation was being deliberated, then, in the highest echelons of government; as well as Roosevelt, the secretaries of war and interior were both personally involved in putting Leupp's program into effect (U.S. Government 1906–10:passim).

Reuben Perry, superintendent of the Navajo Agency at Fort Defiance, was selected to take charge. Troops at Fort Wingate were made ready (Williams 10-12-1906). Perry arrived at Oraibi on 23 October (Perry 10-24-1906) and held preliminary meetings over the next two days:

Yukeoma, unlike the Friendly chief, says he and his people desire the old way and that they are opposed to schools and to the white man's way and all they desire the government to do for them is to return them to the village, behead the Friendly chief, bother them no more about school and let them have their own way. He urged me yesterday and today to cut the Friendly chief's head off and end the trouble. (Perry 10-25-1906:2)

The reference to head-cutting is also related to the prophecy.

Yukioma's desire to return to Oraibi and have the other faction

A meeting at the Hostile encampment in Hotevilla, shortly after the split. The leading man on horseback may be Supervisor Reuben Perry; his leading Hopi interlocutor does not appear to be Yukioma and remains unknown to the author. Photograph by Jo Mora, courtesy Special Collections (John R. Wilson Collection), Cline Library, Northern Arizona University, Flagstaff.

put out is worth noting. Older Hopis recall that the six weeks in camp at Hotevilla before the troops arrived was a period of turbulent discussion. Evidently, Yukioma wavered: Should they try to return to Oraibi, go on toward Kawestima (their prophesied destination), or begin building at Hotevilla? Finally, it was Naquave'ima who made a strong stand to remain at Hotevilla.

Meanwhile, "Supervisor" (the title established for his intermediary role) Perry summoned two troops of cavalry which arrived on 27 October (Perry 10-29-1906:1). With threats of force, he persuaded the Hostile men to come for a meeting at the Oraibi Day School on the next day:

I opened council by telling them the mistake they had made in following Yukeoma blindly and not accepting the good advice given by you [Leupp] on the recent visit to the place. I explained in detail what you desired me to say to Yukeoma, then deposed him from chiefship and had him placed under arrest, told him and his people that he was to leave the Hopi country forever. His official advisers who have been ringleaders in opposition to government schools, etc. and who would take his place in carrying on his hostile ideas were also placed under arrest after giving them an opportunity to agree to conform to the desires of the government and after their having declined. (Perry 10-29-1906:1–2)

Perry's accounts omit some details, which are amply recorded in Hopi oral tradition. During his second visit to Hotevilla, Perry set up a duel between Tawaquaptewa (whom he had taken along) and Yukioma (cf. Hopi Hearings 1955:255,282). Tawaquaptewa was given a pistol and Perry told him to shoot Yukioma. Similarly, during the meeting at the Oraibi Day School, Perry tried to get Yukioma to shoot Tawaquaptewa in public. Perry's intention, apparently, was to publicly expose the unwillingness of both leaders to live up to the consequences of the prophecy they kept telling him about, and thereby undermine their authority:

[Perry] told Tewaquaptewa from this day on the traditions and the theory of fulfilling the plans would be erased, and he will be stripped of his authority from that time on because he could not carry out his theory that he has talked about . . . then it was told to both men [Tawaquaptewa and Yukioma] that from that time on they should not cause any more trouble . . . and they would no longer be known as leaders of the people. (Hopi Hearings 1955:282–83)

Initially, Perry thought Leupp's idea to return the Hostiles to Oraibi for the winter needed modification. The women and children should do this, he suggested, but the men should remain encamped: "it seems impossible for men of both factions to live peaceably in village" (Perry 10-30-1906). Nevertheless, possibly under Leupp's orders, sterner measures were enacted. With troops, the remaining Second Mesa Hostiles (i.e., those who had not been arrested on 28 October) were returned from Hotevilla to Shongopavi on 3 November. On 4 November, the Hotevilla camp was surrounded and eighty-two children were seized, later to be taken to Keam's Canyon Boarding School (Perry 11-5-1906). Again on 7 November, the troops came and Perry issued an ultimatum: "Offered permit [sic] men to take families and return to village who would agree to keep children in school and obey orders of government. About 25 accepted but 53 refused. The latter were placed under arrest and are held by troop" (Perry 11-7-1906).

The "25" who accepted returned to Oraibi under escort on 8 November, after signing an agreement (Appendix 3). In fact, rather more than twenty-five returned, now dubbed *pensoiyungqam*, "pencil-takers" (referring to the agreement) by those who remained. Perry records 151 all told (see Appendix 2) and he made a complete census (U.S. Government 1906–14). They included Lomahongyoma, Heevi'ima, and several other prominent people.

Of those who refused to sign, almost all the men (there were about seven exceptions) were put to hard labor in Keam's Canyon for a minimum of ninety days. The remaining children of school age (twenty-eight) were seized in another raid on 9 November and taken to Keam's Canyon (Perry 11-10-1906). By far the majority of those who remained at Hotevilla were women (sixty-three) and small children (twenty-one); they were left to get through the winter as best they could. Oral tradition records that they survived principally by hunting (rabbits especially), at which some women became very proficient. Of the Hostiles arrested, seventy-two were kept at Keam's Canyon (Lemmon 11-13-1906); seventeen (seven from Second Mesa) were sent to Fort Huachuca in southern Arizona (Miller 5-25-1908); and eleven (six from Second Mesa)—all of them well over school age—were sent to Carlisle Indian School in Pennsylvania (Perry 1-17-1907).[29]

According to the agreement, the returned Hostiles would remain in Oraibi only for the winter; the following spring, they should start building one or more new villages. Perry had the Friendlies sign an agreement also, on 9 November:

We the Oraibi Indians, known as "Friendlies," hereby agree and promise as follows: That we will not molest but will live in peace and harmony with the people of the "Unfriendly Oraibi Indians" that have come back to the village and have signed the agreement with the United States Government to hereafter obey and respect said Government and all articles stated in that agreement. (U.S. Government 1906–14)

Tawaquaptewa, who appears from the correspondence to have been anxious to abide by government decisions, heads the list of signatories.

The Returned Hostiles

Leupp had second thoughts about the returned Hostiles having to leave again the following spring: "those who have yielded on the school question are now living at peace in the old village of Oraibi,

From Oraibi to Bacavi

Hostiles being run-marched from Keam's Canyon to Ganado, November 1906. From Ganado, most were sent to Fort Huachuca in southern Arizona, the rest to Carlisle Indian School in Pennsylvania. Photograph by Jo Mora, courtesy Special Collections (John R. Wilson Collection), Cline Library, Northern Arizona University, Flagstaff.

and I don't know of any reason for removing them as long as they behave themselves" (Leupp 12-5-1906:4). As a result, most of them remained in Oraibi long after the spring of 1907.

Perry fulfilled another of Leupp's clauses by replacing the traditional leadership with a "Board of Control." This consisted of the principal teacher of the Oraibi Day School; Qoyangainewa, who had been War Chief in Loololma's *Soyalangw* and one of three "Indian Judges" (one per Mesa) appointed by Burton in 1900; and Kewanimptewa, "a bright young man selected by me from the Hostiles" (Perry 11-17-1906:3). Kewanimptewa (Sand clan, married to Lomahongyoma's sister's daughter) came to be regarded as the leader and spokesman for the returned Hostiles.

Tawaquaptewa was sent to the Sherman Institute, an Indian school in Riverside, California, for three years but maintained contact with Oraibi and was very jealous of his authority (e.g., Perry 1-30-1907; Titiev 1944:93). He returned to Hopi at least once before his three-year term was up. On a school recruiting trip with Sherman's disciplinarian, he "sneaked into Moencopi village [and] tried to incite a riot between the "friendly" and "hostile" factions of Moencopi" (Murphy 9-1-1907).

At Oraibi, meanwhile, "the Hostile parties, who returned to the village, have been very orderly, kept their children in school and obeyed the teacher and their young judge [Kewanimptewa]. They desire to remain in the village if the Friendlies become willing" (Perry 1-30-1907:3).

By modern accounts, the Friendlies were by no means willing. They tolerated the Hostiles only, it seems, for fear of provoking government ire. Before leaving the reservation for the last time in April 1907, Perry recommended that Peter Staufer, the agency mechanic, be stationed at Oraibi permanently: "He speaks the language well, has the confidence of both factions and I believe will be able to keep all outside affairs in good shape. . . . Little frivolous matters are coming up all the time at Oraibi and to the Indians seem to be of great importance and they have to be settled" (Perry 4-5-1907:2).

What these "little frivolous matters" were we can only guess. Older Bacavi people report that there was considerable harassment of the Hostiles by the Friendlies. They were confined to the usage of one kiva (Iskiva) and maintained a ritual separation. Lomahongyoma conducted the Blue Flute ceremony in 1907 (cf. Forrest 1929:315), although Tawaquaptewa protested via the mail (Titiev 1944:250). In addition, the returned Hostiles performed at least one *Powamuy* with initiations—also restricted to one kiva and devoid of Friendly participants. Their other ritual activities are not known to me. The active, legitimate priests of the Snake and Antelope societies were mostly at Hotevilla, where they first conducted a ceremony in 1908 (cf. Forrest 1961:13–14). The Friendlies staged a Snake Dance at Oraibi in 1908, although there is a hint this was more for tourist purposes than out of religious conviction. There were no Antelope men, their place being taken by four Snake men; several of the Snake men were new recruits who showed palpable fear of the snakes; and overall the performance "was only a burlesque of that held there in former years" (Forrest 1929:139).

Tawaquaptewa returned from Riverside permanently during the summer of 1909. He greatly resented the conduct of Oraibi's affairs during his absence and in particular the continuing presence of the Hostiles. His return coincides with a severe exacerbation of tensions. Superintendent Miller (who had replaced Lemmon in January 1907) acceded to his demand that Qoyangainewa resign as judge and appointed Tawaquaptewa himself to the position on 1

September (Miller 10-30-1909). Toward the end of October, Tawaquaptewa made it plain he did not want the Hostiles present during *Wuwtsim* in November. Around this time, two young women of the Hostile faction (one Spider clan, the other Bear) died in rapid succession. Witchcraft (which always works best among close kin) was identified as the cause.

On 27 October, Miller received a delegation of Hostile leaders—Kewanimptewa, Sikyave'ima, Nasiquaptewa, and Sumatzkuku—who reported a meeting held the previous night:

Chief Tewaquaptewa had many of his followers, both men and women, present and they stated that they did not desire these returned Hostiles to remain in the village. . . . The delegation said they were sure the Friendlies would undertake to drive them out of the village because there was to be a ceremony for the initiation of some of the young men. (Miller 10-30-1909:1–2)

Furthermore, "Rev. J. B. Epp, missionary, Mr. Armijo, trader, the old friendly judge Quoinginiwa, his sons and daughters, and their families are to be driven away from Oraibi as well as the returned Hostiles" (Miller 10-30-1909:4). C. A. Gossett, principal of the Oraibi Day School, wrote to Miller on 29 October, 1 November, and 3 November, reporting a rapid escalation of tensions and urging Miller's presence (Gossett 10-29-1909, 11-1-1909, 11-3-1909). Similarly, Reverend Epp was beginning to panic: "The time to interfere, on the part of the Government authority, *is now!* . . . In about two weeks the chief's brother, Burt Fredericks . . . will return to Oraibi, and then *something is to be done! But the bomb may burst any day!*" (Epp 11-1-1909, emphasis in original). Epp fled Oraibi for Moencopi on 5 November in fear of his life (Epp 11-5-1909).

Miller arrived at Oraibi on 4 November. The returned Hostiles, he learned, were prepared to leave, albeit reluctantly. Borrowing Miller's buggy, Kewanimptewa and Sikyave'ima (Reed clan) sought out a new village site. They decided on the mesa top above Bacavi Springs, about a mile from Hotevilla. On 8 November they took Miller to show him their choice:

I found it to be a very desirable site for a village because of the bountiful supply of good pure water. . . . Kewanimptewa gave me thirty-two beans representing the number of children of their faction now attending the

Oraibi School and asked that I recommend the establishment of a school at Bä-cä-bi (this being the name of the spring where their new village is to be located). (Miller 11-12-1909:6–7; see Appendix 4)

Kewanimptewa also persuaded Miller to have his people allotted lands before any others on Third Mesa (the allotment program had been resuscitated in February 1908) and secured a promise of material aid for constructing the new village (Miller 11-12-1909:3). On 9 November the Hostiles began to quarry rock at Bacavi preparatory to building houses (Miller 11-12-1909:7).

Miller attempted to persuade Tawaquaptewa to allow the Hostiles to remain unmolested in Oraibi until their new homes were complete. But shortly after his return to Keam's Canyon, there was a final confrontation and the Hostiles were forced to leave immediately. Supervisor Perry's presence was requested (Abbott 11-12-1909), and the newspapers carried lurid tales: "It is said that the government has been notified and the soldiers are waiting instructions to march to the Hopi villages to subdue the restless braves, who have worked themselves to a high pitch of excitement. War dances are held nightly, it is reported, at the villages" (*Los Angeles Herald* 11-23-1909). Perry did not appear, however, and no troops were called. On 4 December, Miller somewhat cryptically telegraphed the commissioner: "Kewanimptewa's faction voluntarily moved to new location two weeks ago. Men, women and children are constructing homes no disturbances or rumors of trouble since my report of November twelvth" (Miller 12-4-1909).

And so Bacavi was founded. The first winter was extremely hard. The people lived in crude shacks and rough shelters built into the rocks on a ledge of the mesa until they could begin work on permanent houses the following spring.

II
BACAVI SOCIETY

5
Demography, Human Geography, and Economy

Foundations

The villages of Bacavi and Hotevilla are located at a slightly higher elevation than the other Hopi villages because they are farther away from the tips of the mesas. These two villages are about a mile from each other, at roughly opposite points on either side of the southwest-trending mesa. Hotevilla faces northwest into the Dinnebito Valley, and Bacavi is located at the apex of the Bacavi Valley, a tributary drainage to the Oraibi Valley. Bacavi overlooks a long staircase of walled, terraced gardens on the northeast-facing canyon slope adjacent to a series of springs. These gardens were in use by Oraibi prior to Bacavi's establishment.

Technically, the village name, more properly *paaqavi*, means "reed" (*Phragmites communis*). Formerly an abundance of reeds grew in the vicinity. The *-vi* ending—which refers to place, as in other village names (*Orayvi, Songoopavi, Munqapi,* etc.)—is fortuitous; it is not the usual place-name suffix but simply the singular ending for this species of reed. Technically (Malotki 1982 personal communication), it is illegitimate to give *Paaqavi* locative and abla-

Bacavi from the air, 1940. The church buildings are visible at the left. Photograph from the Spence Collection, Department of Geography, University of California, Los Angeles.

tive case endings applicable to other village names. But in everyday usage Hopis often do so and thus the -*vi* has become a quasi-suffix.

The earliest written reference to the name Bacavi I have found is a Mormon diary entry of August 1877: "In the afternoon passed a spring called Ho Lu Ville [Hotevilla] some 8 miles north of Oriba villages.... This evening passed a small spring bearing the name Pah Kap Vee. This is tolerable good water" (Gibbons 1877:n.p.).

The nucleus of Bacavi looks southeast into the Bacavi Valley and lies at an altitude between 6,290 and 6,300 feet. By "nucleus" I mean the area in the immediate vicinity of the plaza complex and associated house rows, and some single houses nearby. The house-building patterns of the village have led to its gradual expansion away from this nucleus. Some houses considered part of Bacavi are up to a mile away from the center. Originally, however, the nucleus comprised the entire village.

The founders moved to the site under arduous circumstances at the beginning of a hard winter. Until the following spring they lived in temporary dwellings in two clusters with a large open space between. A few constructed lone shelters nearby. One cluster abutted the mesa edge where sandstone is interspersed with patches of sand and loam. Here, people used the irregular sandstone formations on a broad, shallow ledge close to the mesa edge, to which they added rocks and other available materials, or else they dug pit-houses into the loam. These shelters were extremely small: a family of five or six crowded into a floor-space of twenty-five or thirty square feet with a roof only four or five feet from the floor. The other settlement cluster was located about one hundred twenty yards away. It consisted of a row of pit-houses dug four feet into the soil with two or three feet of rock wall above the surface, roofed with brush, branches and clay. Nearby were two Navajo-style, forked-stick hogans, or *homoki* (sing.) in Hopi.

The space between the clusters was left open intentionally. The leaders wanted to build an expansive, rectangular *kiisonvi* (plaza) with single-storied houses and well-planned streets. Kewanimptewa worked with Antonio Armijo, manager of Hubbell's store in Kykotsmovi, to design the village after a Hispanic pueblo. The agency supplied lumber, windows, wheelbarrows, and other equipment, and some carpentry expertise. Construction began in the spring of 1910. Dense stands of juniper had to be cleared, although one tree was left standing and distinguished Bacavi's plaza for several years. It was used ritually as a *pahoki* (prayer-feather house).

Bacavi's *kiisonvi* (plaza) from the east, 1910s. Photograph by Edward S. Curtis, *The North American Indian*, vol. 12, *The Hopi*.

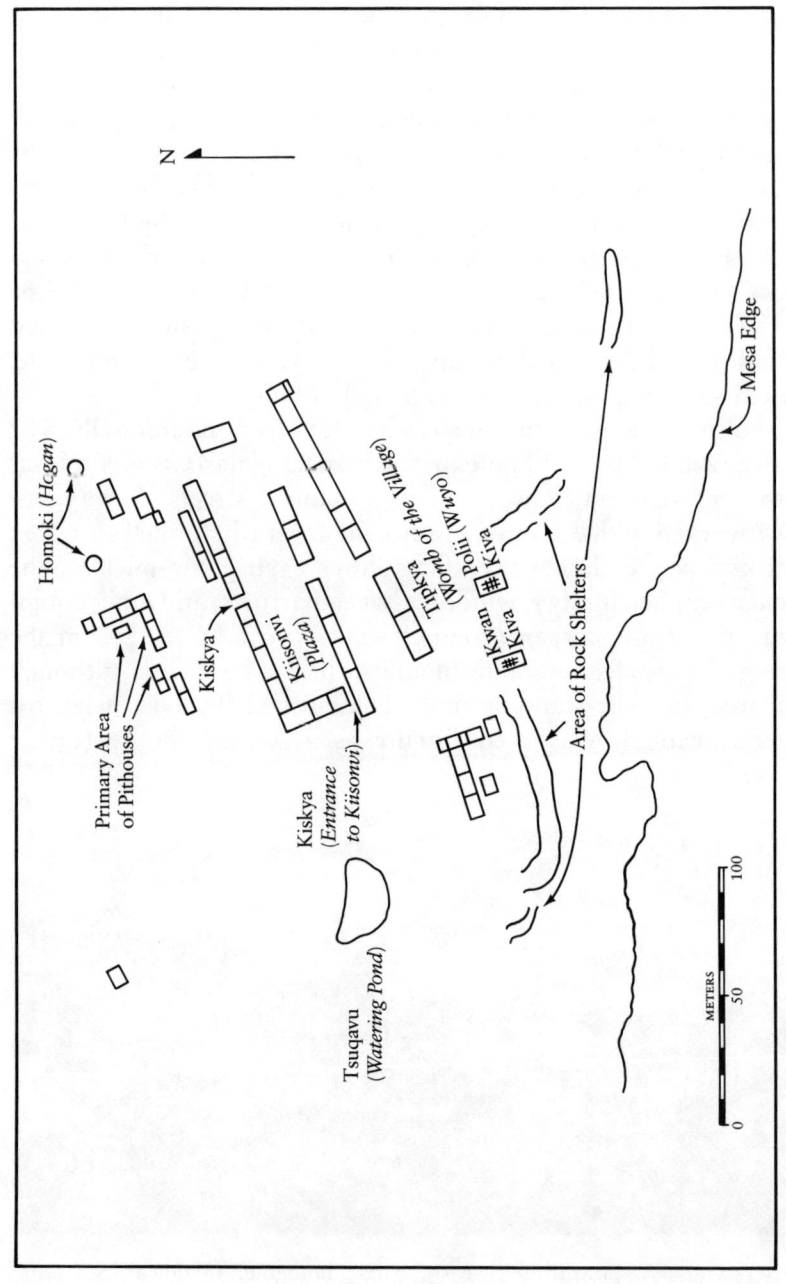

Map 5.1 Bacavi, circa 1915

The *kiisonvi* was aligned, like Oraibi's, on a northeast-southwest axis. A more formal *pahoki* was installed underground and *kiikiskyam*, passageways into the *kiisonvi*, were consecrated for the entry of Kachinas during ceremonies. The plaza houses were planned in terms of who would live where. Although one isolated house is located at the far northeast end, in effect the *kiisonvi* is only three-sided. Dances always occur in a space bounded by these three sides and an invisible line running between the passages on two of the three sides (see Map 5.1).

The planning of particular domiciles in part concerned traditional clan roles. A specific house was designated for a Bear clan family, because Bear people act as first blessers of the Kachinas and need, therefore, to be prominently situated. Another house was designated for a Rabbit clan family in connection with phratry responsibilities (Bacavi had no Kachina clan family) for the formal announcement of Kachina dances from the housetop by a *Kooyemsi* ("Mudhead" Kachina). A ladder is always kept in place at this house for the purpose. Kewanimptewa and his Spider clan wife, Qömamönim, moved into a house that became associated both with his chiefship and with the Spider clan. The house was the repository for the Blue Flute sacra and thus took on the characteristics of Oraibi's *Kookyangwungwki* (Spider clan-house). The reasoning for the location of other families is rather less clear, although there is a definite notion that other houses were formally specified also.

After the nucleus of dwellings was completed, work began on kivas. Bacavi has three kivas. The first built is commonly referred to as *Wuyokiva*, "old kiva," after the fact that when it was built, a number of old men used to spend much time there. Its proper name is *Poliikiva* (Butterfly kiva), deriving from the sponsor of its building, Nasiquaptewa (Badger clan). Since this was Bacavi's *mong*-(chief) kiva, where Lomahongyoma conducted *Wuwtsim*, the name Sakwalenvi, after Oraibi's *mongkiva*, was also used. The kiva was originally built especially for the *Powamuy* ceremony, but when Bacavi subsequently put on *Wuwtsim*, it also acquired the name *Wuwtsim* kiva. The second kiva, a few yards away (both are at the southwest corner of the nucleus of the village), was built shortly afterward by Talaswuhioma (Badger clan). It was named *Kwan*-

Bacavi's first kiva: *Polii'kiva* (Butterfly kiva), also known as *Sakwalenvi, Wuyo'kiva,* etc. Photograph by E. Carson, ca. 1925, Arizona Historical Society, Tucson.

kiva (One-Horn kiva) since it housed the *Kwaakwant* (One-Horn society) while they still operated in Bacavi. The third kiva was built in the late 1930s by Polingyaoma (Kachina clan) and was called *Alkiva* (Two-Horn kiva). Polingyaoma had led the Two-Horn society performances in Bacavi, although these had ceased by the 1930s. The title then was mostly honorific and referred to the fact that some Two-Horn society sacra were kept in a small house nearby. *Alkiva* is commonly referred to as *Kwiningyaq,* "at the northwest." Other aspects of the village were formally planned and ritually established, including several specific shrines, such as the *Katsinki* (Kachina house, usually translated "Kachina resting place"), the *tipkya* ("womb of the village"), and several dedicated to particular Kachinas. No attempt was made to replicate the full complement of Oraibi's shrines.

Changing Human Geography

Bacavi's physical structure has expanded considerably since the village's origin, owing to gradual population increase and technological change. An initial pattern of building close to the nucleus has given way to a tendency to dispersed homesites. This is in part due to the density of land claims close to the nucleus. The first settlers had small fields up to the edges of the nucleus. As more fields were established farther away, these plots ceased to be used and became available for homesites. Each of these plots, larger than necessary for a single house, was inherited by one person or a small group, who retained rights in the area. Thus much seemingly available space is already spoken for. Several newer homesites are a mile away from the nucleus in an area regarded as village land, which the village's governing body assigns by plots. Maps 5.1–5.3 show the gradual expansion of village houses away from the nucleus at various stages. Maps 5.2 and 5.3 are taken from aerial photographs of the village in 1940 and 1981.

Bacavi and Hotevilla have been expanding toward each other for many years, and their outskirts now intersect. Some Bacavi people deliberately built next to what Bacavi considers the village boundary, in order to make good its claim to the area and allay fear of encroachment by its numerically more powerful neighbor.

Demography

For the most part, Bacavi has never had a population greater than two hundred fifty. The cardinal population characteristic is a division by residence. Extensive nonresidence owes primarily to involvement in the wage economy. For a number of historical reasons (not the least of which is the national society's education system) Hopis are inextricably involved, by their own perception too, in the cash economy. Many have at some time in their lives sought wage employment, which has historically entailed that they leave the reservation.

Precise numbers for Bacavi's 1980s population are virtually impossible to determine (see Whiteley 1983:268–84 for a fuller discussion). Of an overall total of 434 people born or enrolled in the village (calculated from a 1977 village census and my own 1980–81 household census), about 237 people are normally resident (see Tables 5.1 and 5.2). Of the remainder, 44 live in other Hopi villages, and 153 reside off the reservation in towns and cities throughout the Southwest and beyond. Of those resident in other villages, some maintain extensive ties with Bacavi, whereas others have become completely immersed in their adoptive villages. A variety of positions between the two extremes make dis-

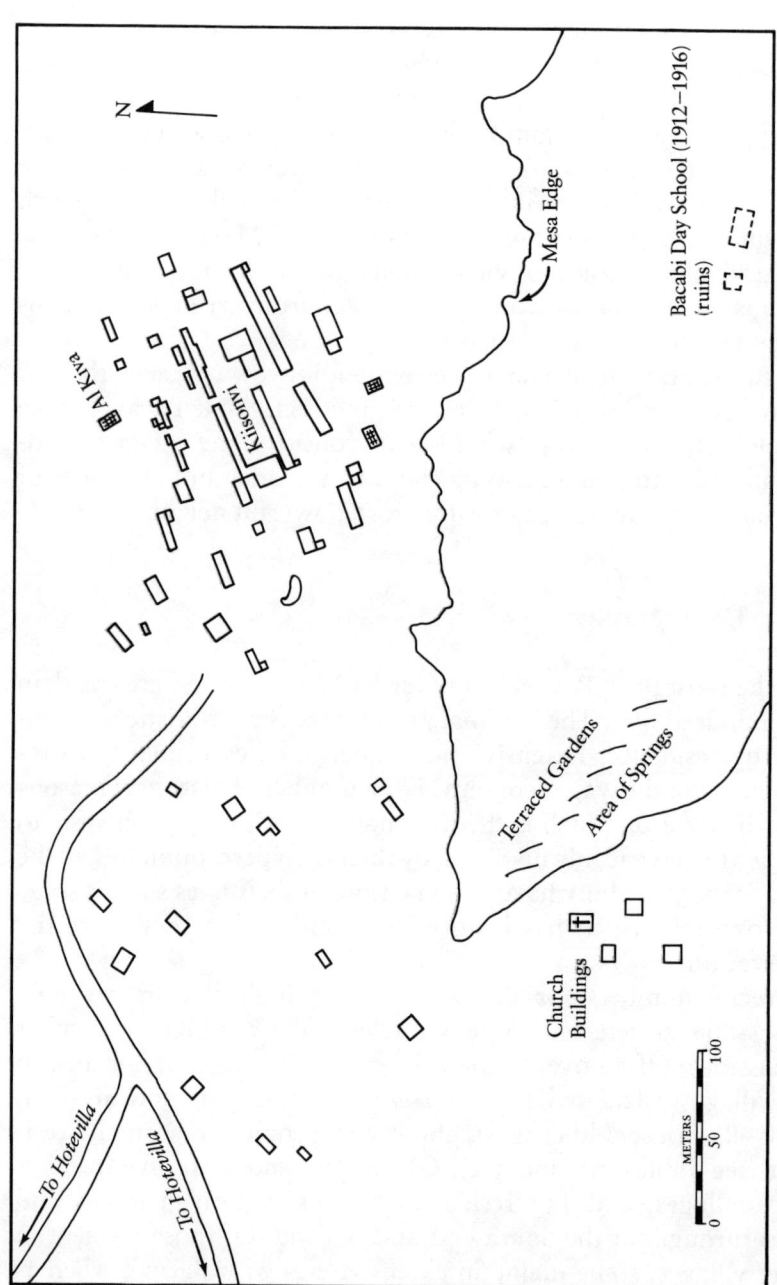

Map 5.2 Bacavi, 1940

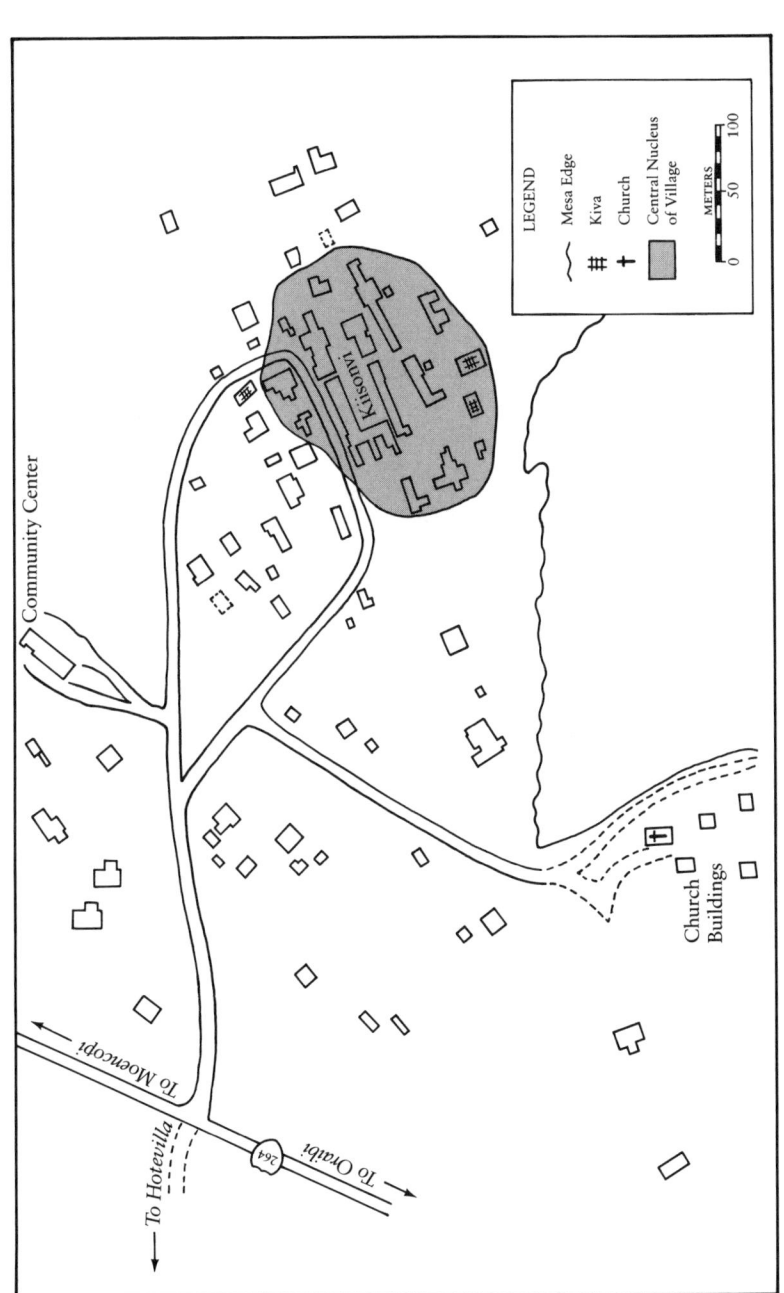

Map 5.3 Bacavi, 1981

Table 5.1. Bacavi's Population Structure, 1981

Age	Males	Male Total, %	Females	Female Total, %	Combined	Combined Total, %
0–10	32	14.4	29	13.7	61	14.1
10–20	48	21.5	42	19.9	90	20.7
20–30	50	22.4	45	21.3	95	21.9
30–40	27	12.1	31	14.7	58	13.4
40–50	22	9.9	25	11.8	47	10.8
50–60	19	8.5	11	5.2	30	6.9
60–70	13	5.8	11	5.2	24	5.5
70–80	9	4.0	12	5.7	21	4.8
80–90	3	1.3	5	2.4	8	1.8
TOTAL	223	100	211	99.9	434	99.9

Table 5.2. Bacavi's Overall Population by Off- or On-Reservation Residence, 1981

Age	Males	All Males in Age Category, %	Females	All Females in Age Category, %	Combined	Combined Males and Females in Age Category, %
At Hopi						
0–10	21	65.6	16	55.2	37	60.7
10–20	33	68.8	24	57.1	57	63.3
20–30	32	64.0	25	55.6	57	60.0
30–40	16	59.3	14	45.2	30	51.7
40–50	15	68.2	17	68.0	32	68.1
50–60	14	73.7	8	72.7	22	73.3
60–70	10	76.9	10	90.9	20	83.3
70–80	8	88.9	10	83.3	18	85.7
80–90	3	100.0	5	100.0	8	100.0
TOTAL	152	68.2	129	61.1	281	64.7
Away from Hopi						
0–10	11	34.4	13	44.8	24	39.3
10–20	15	31.2	18	42.9	33	36.7
20–30	18	36.0	20	44.4	38	40.0
30–40	11	40.7	17	54.8	28	48.3
40–50	7	31.8	8	32.0	15	31.9
50–60	5	26.3	3	27.3	8	26.7
60–70	3	23.1	1	9.1	4	16.7
70–80	1	11.1	2	16.7	3	14.3
80–90	0	0	0	0	0	0
TOTAL	71	31.8	82	38.9	153	35.3

crete village identity in some cases obscure. Similarly, of the off-reservation populace, some return periodically and have houses in the village. They will return permanently on retirement from off-reservation jobs. Others return more seldom or never at all, and some of these were born elsewhere. The latter thus have only nominal allegiance to the village through tribal census enrollment. Further, of the 237 residents, 42 are resident by marriage, and some of them maintain extensive ties with their natal villages.

Approximately 65 percent of Bacavi males and 55 percent of females (I cannot explain the sexual discrepancy) under age 30 remain at Hopi. The 30–40 age-group category has the largest proportion of nonresidents, and for women this is especially marked with almost 55 percent (the only instance in which nonresidence surpasses 50 percent). The reasons are clearly economic: this is the age group in which, in 1981, most sought wage employment away from Hopi. Residence increases significantly for both sexes (especially women) over age 40, and continues to rise throughout the upper age grades to 100 percent in the 80–90 category.

Historical Demography

Bacavi's population has grown since the village's founding. Although off-reservation migrations were initially nonexistent and for a long time minimal, outmarriage (to other Hopis) and residence outside the village have been continuous.

Bacavi's founding population, as shown in Table 5.3, is based on a combination of three sources: annual agency censuses of the village, Titiev's census notes of Oraibi (n.d.), and my own diachronic household census of Bacavi. The 1937 population structure, shown in Table 5.4, is based upon the agency's village census for that year (U.S. Government 1937) with modifications from my own research. Population accretion from in-migration subsequent to the original settlement was rather low.

Table 5.4 includes four nuclear families that moved to Bacavi between 1915 and 1932. They had to secure permission to move in from the Village Chief, Kewanimptewa, who set aside a homesite

Table 5.3. Bacavi's Population Structure, 1910

Age	Males	Male Total, %	Females	Female Total, %	Combined	Combined Total, %
0–10	18	28.1	24	38.1	42	33.1
10–20	19	30.0	15	23.8	34	26.8
20–30	2	3.1	2	3.1	4	3.1
30–40	6	9.3	8	12.7	14	11.0
40–50	8	12.5	4	6.4	12	9.4
50–60	1	1.5	1	1.6	2	1.6
60–70	4	6.3	4	6.4	8	6.3
70–80	2	3.1	2	3.1	4	3.2
80–90	3	4.7	3	4.8	6	4.7
90–100	1	1.5	...	...	1	0.8
TOTAL	64	100.1	63	100.0	127	100.0

NOTE: Ages attributed to individuals in agency censuses were, apart from children, the result of guesswork by the census takers. They are taken from the 1910 census but have been cross-checked with the 1900 census (U.S. Government 1900) and with the Allotment Census of 1892 (Mayhugh 1894). Where there are discrepancies, ages have been averaged.

Table 5.4. Bacavi's Population Structure, 1937

Age	Males	Male Total, %	Females	Female Total, %	Combined	Combined Total, %
0–10	13	17.1	14	20.9	27	18.9
10–20	18	23.7	13	19.4	31	21.7
20–30	11	14.5	10	14.9	21	14.7
30–40	10	13.2	9	13.4	19	13.3
40–50	8	10.5	5	7.5	13	9.1
50–60	5	6.6	4	6.0	9	6.3
60–70	8	10.5	9	13.4	17	11.9
70–80	2	2.6	3	4.5	5	3.5
80–90	...	...	...	...	...	...
90–100	1	1.3	...	...	1	0.7
TOTAL	76	100.0	67	100.0	143	100.0

and a plot of land close to the village for each one (the pattern in this instance follows the mythico-historical admission of clan groups to Oraibi). Bacavi, according to its founding philosophy, was to be an "open" village, where anyone could move if they wished. Those who did come had certain "restrictions of citizenship" imposed upon them, as *nutungksinom* (last-arriving people). Most of these later migrants were originally Friendlies, and the restrictions primarily concerned the assumption of political roles in the village with authority over the original settlers.

Table 5.5. Bacavi's Population Structure, 1950

Age	Males	Male Total, %	Females	Female Total, %	Combined	Combined Total, %
0–10	16	23.0	16	22.6	32	22.7
10–20	14	20.0	14	19.7	28	19.9
20–30	8	11.4	8	11.3	16	11.3
30–40	6	8.6	8	11.3	14	9.9
40–50	4	5.7	3	4.2	7	5.0
50–60	9	12.8	7	9.9	16	11.3
60–70	4	5.7	3	4.2	7	5.0
70–80	7	10.0	8	11.3	15	10.6
80–90	2	2.8	4	5.6	6	4.3
TOTAL	70	100.0	71	100.1	141	100.0

SOURCE: Hopi Indian Agency (1950).

Table 5.5, showing Bacavi's population structure in 1950, is taken from a 1950 agency census (Hopi Indian Agency 1950) with a few minor adjustments. Although the 1950 total is comparable with 1937, considerable movement had taken place: sixty of the 1937 populace do not appear in 1950; sixty-five of the 1950 populace were not recorded in 1937. Of the latter, one family and one individual had returned from a period of off-reservation residence. Despite such movements, we can still see trends in the maturation of the original populace: the comparatively high proportion of individuals in the 70–80 category (reflecting the 30–40 category in 1910) in contrast to the small number in the 60–70 category (20–30 in 1910). In-migration of non-Bacavi people was very low. Ten spouses moved into the village between 1937 and 1950. Otherwise there was no in-migration, and in fact, of the four couples (with their families) that had moved to Bacavi neolocally since 1910, two had moved away.

The 1950 census is the first with a significant number of off-reservation residents (who are not recorded in Table 5.5). Although the pattern of off-reservation residence had begun as early as the 1920s (frequently only for short periods), the 1937 figures reveal only a very small number (less than ten) in this category. Table 5.6 shows the figures for off-reservation residence in 1950. The marked increase of off-reservation residence, then, clearly begins in the 1940s. Kennard (1965:26) and Nagata (1970:181) have both pointed up this pattern as a result of World War II: a considerable

Table 5.6. Bacavi's Overall Population
by Off- or On-Reservation Residence, 1950

Age	Males	All Males in Age Category, %	Females	All Females in Age Category, %	Combined	Combined Males and Females in Age Category, %
At Hopi						
0–10	16	94.1	16	84.2	32	88.9
10–20	14	77.8	15	83.3	29	80.6
20–30	10	62.5	9	64.3	19	63.3
30–40	9	69.2	9	90.0	18	78.3
40–50	4	50.0	4	50.0	8	50.0
50–60	9	81.8	7	100.0	16	88.9
60–70	4	100.0	3	100.0	7	100.0
70–80	7	100.0	8	100.0	15	100.0
80–90	2	100.0	4	100.0	6	100.0
TOTAL	75	78.1	75	82.4	150	80.2
Away from Hopi						
0–10	1	5.9	3	15.8	4	11.1
10–20	4	22.2	3	16.7	7	19.4
20–30	6	37.5	5	35.7	11	36.7
30–40	4	30.8	1	10.0	5	21.7
40–50	4	50.0	4	50.0	8	50.0
50–60	2	18.2	...	0	2	11.1
60–70	...	0	...	0	...	0
70–80	...	0	...	0	...	0
80–90	...	0	...	0	...	0
TOTAL	21	21.9	16	17.6	37	19.8

number of Hopis were in the military or moved to towns to join the labor force. After the war, many chose to stay away, at least temporarily.

It would have been preferable also to show figures for points between 1950 and 1981. I have not been able to acquire data of equivalent quality for this period. The year 1937 was the last that the agency was required to submit annual village censuses. Later figures, which are available, are much more limited (see Whiteley 1983:292–95). Table 5.7, showing figures for 1968, derives from a general BIA census, which I have not been able to cross-check independently, and is provided for broad comparative purposes only.

The most noteworthy feature of the 1910 population structure is

Table 5.7. Bacavi's Population Structure, 1968

Age	Males	Male Total, %	Females	Female Total, %	Combined	Combined Total, %
0–15	34	47.9	34	45.9	68	46.9
16–24	10	14.1	6	8.1	16	11.0
25–34	9	12.7	11	14.8	20	13.8
35–44	5	7.0	4	5.4	9	6.2
45–54	5	7.0	7	9.5	12	8.3
55–64	2	2.8	3	4.1	5	3.4
65–74	4	5.6	6	8.1	10	6.9
75+	2	2.8	3	4.1	5	3.5
TOTAL	71	99.9	74	100.0	145	100.0

SOURCE: Woods (1969).

the irregularity in age distribution. The two categories in Table 5.8 (0–20, 20+) are designed to distinguish between children, adolescents, and young married adults on the one hand, and older and/or married adults on the other. Table 5.9 shows a distribution between older and younger adults. Of Bacavi's original populace, almost 60 percent were children and adolescents.[1] There was also a high proportion of older adults (by comparison with 1937 and 1981). Further, the great majority (26 out of 32, or 81.3 percent) of adults between ages 20 to 60 fell into the 30–50 age range (Table 5.3); only a few were between 20 and 30 or 50 and 60. There was, then, a roughly trimodal distribution, with concentrations in the 0–20, 30–50, and 60+ age ranges (see Figure 5.1).

Several older consultants remarked that among the Hostiles who returned to Oraibi from Hotevilla there were, on the one hand, a number of pregnant women and women with small children, and on the other hand, a good number of older people. This finds confirmation in Supervisor Reuben Perry's census of returned Hostiles taken on 9 November 1906 (U.S. Government 1906–14). We can infer that Bacavi was founded largely by nuclear families that had been established for at least ten years, and by older people. All of the latter had close kin among the former. This picture conforms quite well with a contemporary documentary source: "[Kewanimptewa] also gave me twenty-four beans which represented the number of young married women (heads of families) who would build houses at the new village, and stated that there would also be old

Table 5.8. Bacavi's Comparative Population Structure by Age: Young vs. Adults, 1910, 1937, 1950, 1981

Age	M	F	Combined	Percent of Total
		A. 1910		
0–20	37	39	76	59.8
20+	27	24	51	40.2
TOTAL	64	63	127	100.0
		B. 1937		
0–20	31	27	58	40.6
20+	45	40	85	59.4
TOTAL	76	67	143	100.0
		C. 1950		
0–20	30	30	60	42.6
20+	40	41	81	57.4
TOTAL	70	71	141	100.0
		D. 1981		
0–20	47	38	85	35.9
20+	73	79	152	64.1
TOTAL	120	117	237	100.0

Table 5.9. Bacavi's Comparative Adult Age and Sex Distribution, 1910, 1937, 1950, 1981

Age	M	F	Combined	Percent of Total
		A. 1910		
20–60	17	15	32	62.7
60+	10	9	19	37.3
TOTAL	27	24	51	100.0
		B. 1937		
20–60	34	28	62	72.9
60+	11	12	23	27.1
TOTAL	45	40	85	100.0
		C. 1950		
20–60	27	26	53	65.4
60+	13	15	28	34.6
TOTAL	40	41	81	100.0
		D. 1981		
20–60	60	59	119	78.3
60+	13	20	33	21.7
TOTAL	73	79	152	100.0

Human Geography and Economy

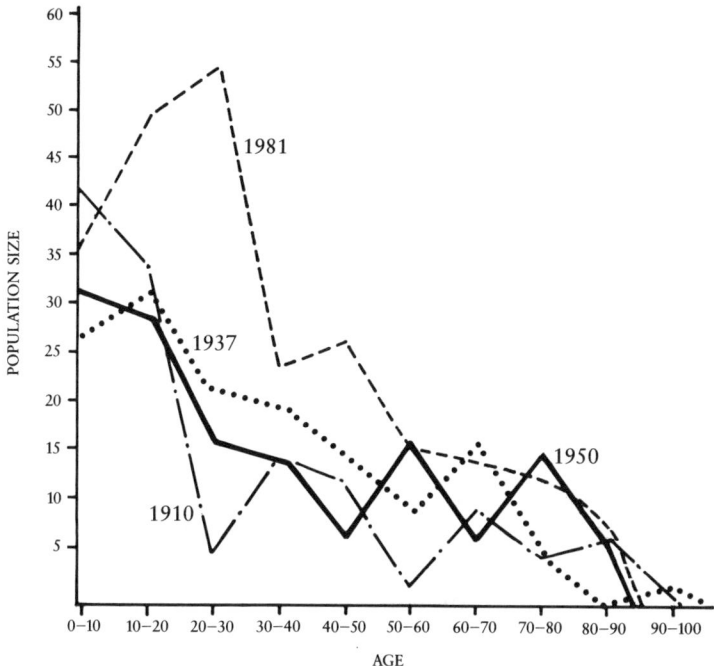

Figure 5.1. Comparative Bacavi population curves.

men and women who would come with their sons and daughters to this village" (Miller 11-12-1909:7; see Appendix 4).

The Changing Economy

Modern Bacavi is considerably changed from turn-of-the-century Oraibi. Many of the changes are directly related to changes in American society. These include, most obviously, technological introductions—cars, pickups, tractors, metalled roads, propane gas, electricity, water lines—and other economic changes resulting from increased participation in the national economy. In turn, these have impacted greatly upon other social and cultural changes, but I believe it is mistaken to regard all of the latter as deterministically "caused" by the former. My reasoning will become evident in Chapter 8.

Several authors have described economic change at various Hopi villages (e.g., Beaglehole 1937; Thompson 1950; Kennard 1965, 1979; Nagata 1970). Of these, Nagata's account of Moencopi is the most comprehensive. Although there are some significant differences with Bacavi (especially Moencopi's greater local access to wage labor), many changes are similar, and the reader is therefore referred to Nagata's work (1970:98–222) for a fuller account of economic change. My aim here is to describe the general properties of Bacavi's economy, noting features distinctive to the village and general changes since Nagata's work in the 1960s.

The Contemporary Economic Structure

The central dichotomy in the twentieth-century Hopi economy is between the traditional subsistence system and the impinging elements of the national system. Involvement in the cash economy is pervasive in the 1980s, though the forms of cash income are very varied. As noted, much off-reservation residence is motivated by opportunities for wage employment. Consistent sources of wage work have been few and far between at Hopi. But temporary work (for the agency, mission, school, and trading post) has been available at Third Mesa since the turn of the century, and cash barter goes back at least to the Mormon colonies: "When I was a child the Mormons came to trade with us and paid us in silver dollars, the first we had ever seen. We children played with them, rolling them around on the floor for money meant nothing to us" (Brainard 1935:126).

The twentieth century has seen a gradual shift in relative importance of the two sectors of the Hopi economy. Especially after World War II, there was a basic change "from what was primarily a subsistence economy supplemented by cash and trade goods to a cash economy supplemented by the persistence of traditional subsistence activities" (Kennard 1965:25).

Locally grown agricultural produce remains important in most Bacavi households, although its relative importance varies. Corn is the dominant Hopi religious symbol: it is closely associated with fundamental aspects of Hopi identity and more generally with the very process of human life. Thus although farming has lessened considerably, it is a rare household indeed that does not have some corn on hand, even if only for special occasions. Not every household is actively engaged in farming, however; a good number acquire corn from relatives.

The Decline of Agriculture

Overall, the 1960s and 1970s saw a remarkable decrease in farming throughout District Six (see Map 1.1).[2] In 1981 a survey of farm plots by the Hopi Agency disclosed 1,477 acres under cultivation (Hopi Agency Branch of Land Operations 1981). This shows a dramatic decline from the next most recent figure—6,355 acres—from 1974 (Bureau of Indian Affairs, Branch of Land Operations, Hopi Agency 1974). The 1974 survey used cumulative figures from a 1964 survey and a partial survey in 1973, and qualifies its estimate of plots as "annually or intermittently cultivated." Thus, in contrast to the 1981 figures, this may overestimate actual usage in 1973. We cannot infer, then, that the phenomenal decrease (from 6,355 acres to 1,477) occurred wholly within this eight-year period.

My own calculations (see Whiteley 1983:311–14) from the 1964 survey (Bureau of Indian Affairs, Branch of Land Operations 1964) result in a total for Third Mesa (including the Oraibi Valley, Dinnebito Valley, and the mesa top [Bacavi farmers use all these areas]) of 2,256 acres of cultivated land. The comparable area in 1981 showed 842.1 acres—a decline of almost two-thirds. R. M. Bradfield's survey of the Oraibi Valley in 1966 (Bradfield 1971) gives 920 acres under cultivation; the 1964 agency survey shows a total of 1,051 acres for the comparable area. In 1981 the agency survey counted 670 cultivated acres in this area, roughly a one-third decline since 1964.

For further comparison, a 1945 survey showed 3,706 acres under cultivation at Third Mesa, with an overall Hopi total of 7,130 (Day 1946:25). In 1936 cultivated land at Third Mesa was recorded as 3,306 acres with 6,084 overall (Land Management Unit No. 6 1937:41). Using Stephen's figures (Stephen 1936:954–

55), Bradfield (1971:41) suggests that in 1890–91 Third Mesa cultivated 2,480 acres of a Hopi total of 5,600 acres.

Third Mesa's declining usage since the 1960s is not disproportionate. In 1974 First and Second Mesa fields totaled 3,580 acres. The 1981 figures show 629.6 acres cultivated—an even steeper decline than for Third Mesa (about four-fifths as opposed to two-thirds).

Even allowing for survey error, the decline has been remarkable and rapid. It is difficult to venture a conclusion for this pattern. One reason may be that the late 1970s and early 1980s were very dry, which may have discouraged some farming on a purely temporary basis. Klara Kelley (1982 personal communication) reports a significant decline in Navajo farming in the Black Hat (New Mexico) area in the 1970s and attributes this to the increased aridity. However, it is clear that there are also sociocultural reasons at Hopi. A necessary condition, of course, is that the wherewithal to make a living exists elsewhere in the overall economy. But this is not a sufficient condition, since many (probably the majority) who are engaged in farming do not absolutely need to be in order to survive (of which they are quite well aware), because of their simultaneous participation in the cash economy. Hence, the decision to continue to farm has personal and cultural motivations, as well as economic ones. Such motivations include the centrality of corn in Hopi religious thought; but where the symbolic connection between corn and human life was previously founded in the sheer conditions of existence, it has now become a more abstract statement of Hopi ethnicity.

Of Bacavi's sixty-three households, one-third continue to be actively engaged in subsistence farming. Of the remainder, fourteen are either matrifocal households, matrilineage-segment households with no adult male labor force, or single-individual households. At least twenty-four households are regularly supplied with some corn by farming relatives in other households, some of which are in other villages. Of the remainder, my data are not sufficient to judge the regularity of their supply of corn, but my impression is that it is extremely unlikely that any never uses corn at all. Despite the overall decline in Hopi agriculture, Bacavi itself remains significantly involved in farming and in the redistribution of crops to nonfarming households. Nagata (1970:106–8) has documented a more severe decline at Moencopi, and agriculture appears to be less prevalent, proportionally, also among Kykotsmovi people. What this suggests is that on Third Mesa Bacavi and Hotevilla are the predominant farming communities, since Oraibi (some of whose members are active farmers) has such a small population. Since I do not have the data to support this contention statistically, it must remain inferential.

Gardening and Orchards

Use of the terraced gardens has diminished markedly at Bacavi (in contrast to Hotevilla, where they have continued to flourish). In 1981 only one Bacavi terrace was in use (by the husband of its owner), of an approximate total of twelve groups of terrace plots (exact figures are unclear since adjacent terraces sometimes belong to the same woman). Gardens are owned by women individually. After the founding of Bacavi, the existing terraced staircase was distributed among the new residents, the distribution reflecting social rank. For example, in the topmost terraces close to the highest spring (the best spot), were the plots of Kewanimptewa's Spider clan wife, of a Bear clan woman, and of two prominent Snake clan women.

Decline of the terraced gardens coincides with the availability of piped water into the village around 1970. Several women established small gardens adjacent to their houses, greatly facilitating irrigation. Thus the disuse of the terraced gardens does not represent a complete demise of the gardening economy: the locus of activity has shifted, owing to technological change.

The decline of orchards, especially of peach and apricot trees, is another significant change in the subsistence economy. Fruit trees used to grow in abundance around the outskirts of the village. Some still bear fruit but many are dead, and the same is true of orchards at other villages. According to my consultants, the decline eventuated in the 1950s from three causes: a particularly hard winter that killed many trees, a fatal disease around the same time, and perhaps most important, less care for the trees (again as a result of economic alternatives). Some Bacavi people have maintained fruit trees into the 1980s, but the situation is much changed from the 1940s, when July and August would see the mesa edges covered with peaches drying in the sun, and dried peaches and *piiki* (rolled wafer bread) were daily staples.

Sheep, Cattle, and Hunting-Gathering

Sheepherding has fallen off even more dramatically than agriculture and horticulture. In 1981 there were six remaining sheepherders at Third Mesa, three each from Bacavi and Hotevilla. In 1982 two of them (one from each village) gave up herding, owing to advanced age. According to my Third Mesa consultants, only two men (one from Shongopavi and one from Mishongnovi) continued to herd sheep at Second Mesa, and two at First Mesa, in 1981. These figures contrast sharply with earlier periods. At Third Mesa there were fifty-three sheepherders in 1960 (Hopi Agency 1960), seventy in 1949 (Hopi Agency 1949), and ninety in 1944, immediately after the stock-reduction program (Hopi Agency 1944).

Total numbers of sheep have also decreased greatly. Available figures do not permit a diachronic representation for Bacavi; they usually cover the Hopi total or total by entire Mesa. Perhaps the first reliable estimate (apparently based on a fairly thorough survey), in 1890, recorded a total of 22,300 Hopi sheep and goats, "the largest herds being at Oraibi" (Vandever 1890:170). In 1917 Agent Leo Crane (1917:20) estimated 25,000 head of Hopi sheep. In 1930 a Department of Agriculture survey recorded 20,511 sheep and goats (Zeh 1930:5a). Immediately after stock reduction, in 1943, 4,317 sheep and goats was Third Mesa's share (Hopi Agency 1944) of a Hopi total of 12,627 (Thompson 1950:38).

There was much bitterness over the stock-reduction program, especially at Third Mesa (see, e.g., Hopi Hearings 1955:passim). Average reduction at Third Mesa was 44 percent of each owner's stock, in contrast to 20 percent and 22 percent at First Mesa and Second Mesa, respectively (Thompson 1950:38). Several Hotevilla men went to jail for refusing to cooperate in the program. Bacavi reluctantly agreed to cooperate; its plaza was used as a central corral into which sheep were herded, counted, and slaughtered. In general, a severe blow was dealt to this aspect of the traditional economy and a good many herders quit, as labor in some cases began to exceed productivity. The decrease in number of herders from 1944 to 1960 bears this out.

Nevertheless, total abandonment was not immediate: figures for sheep and goats remained consistent through 1960, when 4,075 were recorded at Third Mesa, with 9,619 throughout District Six (Hopi Agency 1960). Again, the most drastic period of decline occurred in the 1960s and 1970s. In 1981, judging by the size of two Third Mesa herds and the modern practice of single-individual herding, it seems most unlikely that the total number of sheep and goats at Hopi exceeded 1,000, and it was probably considerably less.

The rapid demise of this sector of the subsistence economy is again attributable to a combination of more general economic changes and changes in Hopi valuation of sheepherding (with, of course, the impact of a draconian government policy). Five out of the six Third Mesa sheepherders in 1981 were older men who had herded throughout their lives; only one herder, who worked with his father, was below 60 years of age. Apart from the last pair, shepherds herded mostly by themselves. In the past, sheepherding was shared by a group of male relatives who took turns by the day. In the 1980s, since the other traditionally major activities for men—farming and ceremonies—have somewhat abated, the remaining herders are able to devote more time to their sheep than previously. Moreover, sheepherding tends to be regarded by the younger generations as toilsome work and the herders have difficulty enlisting aid.

The decline of sheepherding is a major social and economic change: it was formerly the second most important male economic activity. It is less significant, however, than agriculture in terms of highly valued cultural practices. Sheep symbolism is virtually nonexistent in Hopi religion and it had always been customary to trade for mutton with visiting Navajos (a practice that has continued).

In contrast, cattle herding has gradually increased. This activity represents a bridge between the subsistence and the cash economies. The historical record shows that cattle have been present since at least the 1770s, when, in particular, "there is much more of this at Oraybi" (Adams 1963:135). The same discrepancy was apparent a century later: "The East and Middle Mesa Village people have but very few cattle possibly not over from 150 to 200 head while the Oraibi village people have over 350 head among them. The number of Beeves slaughtered I am informed by Chief Lo lo lo my is equal to the annual increase" (Mayhugh 2-19-1894:8).

Mormon accounts (e.g., Journal History of the Church 3-12-1870) suggest that cattle were a prime target for Navajo and Apache raids. According to my older consultants, Oraibi grazed cattle in the nineteenth century as far north as Cow Springs (the name is in fact a literal translation of the Hopi term for the place, *wakasva*).

As cattle stocks expanded in the twentieth century, they became commercial commodities. In 1981 six Bacavi households maintained herds and about ten individuals altogether were involved in cattle herding. Cattle are owned individually, primarily by men. Ten herders were also recorded at Bacavi in 1960, with a total of thirty-four cattlemen on Third Mesa (Hopi Agency 1960). In the immediate postreduction period, only three Bacavi men, out of a Third Mesa total of seventeen, had cattle (Hopi Agency 1944). BIA stockmen persuaded several herders to switch from sheep to cattle, which give a higher return for fewer animals and have a less deleterious effect upon pasture.

Cattle are sold at auction every year. Most Hopi cattlemen sell them at reservation auctions (notably at a large cattle market below Second Mesa). Outside buyers from nearby towns and ranches purchase them at prices slightly, though not much, less than they would pay elsewhere (the Hopi stockmen's union sponsors the sales and protects the rights of the sellers). In the past, cattle were driven to places such as Sunrise (near Leupp), where they were sold and then driven on to the railroad, a little farther south. Numbers of cattle and cattle owners in Bacavi have remained fairly stable since 1960, although there have been some changes of ownership.

Hunting and gathering are still practiced at Bacavi in the 1980s. Apart from formalized rabbit hunts (which occur regularly at Hotevilla and somewhat less frequently at Bacavi), information on traditional hunting and gathering activities is rather limited (see Laird 1977 for published sources). The modern pattern is for an individual or a group of two or three to go hunting or gathering for a specific item. Hunting is always done by males and may involve off-reservation trips for larger game, whereas rabbits are commonly hunted in the vicinity. Shotguns, rather than rabbit-sticks or bows, are used nowadays. Gathering is done by both men and women, in groups or singly, for plant foods (e.g., pine nuts, yucca fruit, wild "spinach") and raw materials (yucca leaves, clay, spruce branches, etc.) for traditional manufactures. These activities contribute minor additions to the overall economy, although they were always secondary features. This sector of the economy has probably changed less, relatively speaking, than agriculture and herding.

Employment and the Cash Economy

The 1970s saw a great expansion in the Tribal Council bureaucracy (for example, in the creation of new departments of Health, Manpower, Natural Resources, and Education) which had effects in a number of different programs in the villages. Permanent jobs at Hopi increased markedly. There was a parallel increase in short-term and temporary employment in two areas. First, adoption of various federal programs, such as under the Comprehensive Employment Training Act and the Youth Conservation Corps Act, gave some permanent and considerable temporary employment to many. Second, the Tribe's[3] pursuit of various developments on the reservation (such as the Cultural Center at Second Mesa, the Civic Center between Second Mesa and Third Mesa, Hopi police facilities between Polacca and Keam's Canyon, and most recently the Hopi High School) opened up much short-term employment, especially involving construction.

Other major employers on the reservation are the Hopi Agency, the Public Health Service Hospital, the Roads Department (all located in Keam's Canyon), and the Cultural Center. Since completion of State Highway 264 in 1959, employees have been able to commute from Bacavi to Keam's Canyon, and several Bacavi people do this on a daily basis. In 1970 the agency was the largest single employer on the reservation (Hopi Tribal Council 1970), but in the 1970s the Tribe took over this role.

The U.S. Forest Service is a significant source of employment. Several people have permanent jobs with the Forest Service at various nearby off-reservation locations (such as Happy Jack near Flagstaff, or Show Low near Winslow). From the 1940s, temporary firefighting crews have been organized annually among southwestern Indian peoples. Every summer a new Hopi crew is selected, trained, and subsequently shipped to any forest fire occurring in the western states. Competition to get onto the crew is great, since the pay is high and the temporary nature of the work does not require long absences from Hopi.

Closer to Bacavi, the Hotevilla-Bacavi Community School provides a source of some employment, and did so especially during its period of independence from 1978 to 1983 (see Chapter 7). The number of Hopis employed in 1980 was three times higher than in 1970 (Rhodes 1982:3–3).

Periodic efforts to establish small business concerns in Bacavi have given employment to a number of residents. In 1970 the Olga Manufacturing Corporation leased Bacavi's Community Center and hired several Bacavi employees before closing, after only a few months, for financial reasons. In 1980 the Hopi Electronics Corporation, managed by a man from Polacca, seriously considered leasing a building in Bacavi but eventually located at Second Mesa.

Local community projects such as construction of the sewage system, Community Center, village warehouse, water system, and electricity system recruited short-term Bacavi labor between the 1960s and 1980s. These projects were conducted under Tribal, BIA, or Public Health Service sponsorship.

The national and international art market's expanded interest in southwestern Indian arts and crafts has increased opportunity for self-employment. Items particularly in demand in the 1980s are silver jewelry and Kachina dolls (male crafts), basketry and pottery (female crafts; pottery is mostly restricted to First Mesa), and paintings (primarily male). The success of Charles Loloma (from Hotevilla) is unique in its magnitude, but several other artists and craftsmen have begun to make good livings from their work. Margaret Wright (1972) has documented the development of Hopi silvercraft and discusses a number of Bacavi smiths. Exact numbers (probably fewer than a dozen) are difficult to calculate, since several smiths work peripatetically from year to year. Kachina dolls have found a lucrative market since the 1970s. In the 1960s a doll usually sold for ten or fifteen dollars, a price that seemed "inordinately high" to outsiders (Nagata 1970:196). In 1981 even a novice carver could sometimes get one hundred dollars or more for a doll. Better-known carvers can command one thousand dollars or more, although they often sell to retail stores at a third to half the store-marked price. Several Bacavi men make a living by carving dolls and taking them to off-reservation towns to sell. Wicker plaques and yucca baskets (the former a Third Mesa specialty) provide a significant source of income for some Bacavi women. Plaques usually fetch from fifty to two hundred dollars but are generally less saleable commodities than Kachina dolls, one of the most popular southwestern art forms. Annual exhibitions, such as the Hopi Craftsmen's Show at the Museum of Northern Arizona, or the Santa Fe Indian Market, reinforce the wide interest in and market values of Hopi arts and crafts.

Other forms of cash income in 1981 came from government benefits, such as Old Age Assistance, Social Security, and Aid to Dependent Children.

Since 1981, federal budget cuts have ravaged employment opportunities at Hopi established during the 1970s. The new Tribal departments have cut back extensively, and several operate on a month-by-month basis under continual threat of closure. Long-term effects and the Hopi response remain to be seen. The loss of government jobs may stimulate new movements off the reservation, a return to greater involvement in the subsistence economy, or the expansion of private Hopi business concerns.

Technology

The national society's technological developments have impacted upon Bacavi variously: some have supplanted traditional practices and others have been added to them. Since the early 1970s, most Bacavi households have had in-house plumbing and electricity. All have bottled propane gas for cooking, a practice that began in the 1950s. Coal and wood are still used extensively for heating, although a few houses are centrally heated with propane. Coal is brought in pickup truckloads from the Peabody Mine at Black Mesa (where Hopis and Navajos may gather their coal free), a round trip of five hours over dirt roads. Wood must be gathered at increasing distances from the villages. From Bacavi, people frequently go to cut wood in the Big Mountain area (at least until the escalation of antagonism over the Navajo-Hopi Relocation Act) or near Piñon. In addition, Navajos sometimes bring truckloads of coal or wood for sale around the village. Hopi-Navajo relations have generally deteriorated with the Relocation program. Nevertheless, it has always been the case that despite ongoing antagonisms, some individuals and families on both sides have maintained close ties. In the 1980s Navajos continued to visit a highly respected Bacavi medicine man and still came to the village to trade mutton for corn or cash. Much of the attention given to the land dispute by the national media has clouded the realities of multiplex relationships between the two peoples.

A telephone system was introduced into the village in the 1970s, though only a few households had their own telephones in 1981. Motor vehicles have come into increased use especially since the paving of Highway 264 in 1959. The first trucks in Bacavi were bought in the 1930s. Only ten households were without trucks or cars in 1981; eight of these comprised people over 60 years of age, and the other two, young people in their early 20s or younger. Tractors have been increasingly used since the 1960s. An agency pamphlet from 1968 records "about a dozen very small farm tractors" (Hopi Indian Agency 1968:6) in use among all the Hopi villages. In 1981 about eight Bacavi households had their own tractors and other farm machinery.

Introduction of motorized vehicles led to the declining significance of horses, mules, and burros. Only five Bacavi households owned horses in 1981, in contrast to ten in 1960 (Hopi Agency 1960). With burros and mules, the decline has been much sharper; the last burro on Third Mesa died in Bacavi in the spring of 1981. There were very few burros left at Second Mesa, and probably none at First Mesa. By contrast, in 1960 a total of ninety-seven mules and burros were recorded in District Six (Hopi Agency 1960).

Some aspects of subsistence agriculture have nonetheless remained remarkably similar to the traditional pattern. Some farmers use planting machines, but these are generally not preferred. Although a few men from Hotevilla still used the greasewood digging stick in the 1980s, most Bacavi men have adopted an improvised, steel-pipe version that is easier to use (Nagata 1970:139–40 reports the same for Moencopi). Weeding between corn rows is accomplished with hoes or a modified, wheeled, hand plow. Otherwise, apart from tractor plowing, Bacavi farming techniques follow long-established methods. For example, many farmers disapprove of chemical pesticides and refrain from using them even when much of their crop is destroyed by one of the numerous types of pests. Scarecrows, some modified by the addition of a dead raven to warn off his confreres, and all-night vigils with shotguns at the ready for ravens, coyotes, and porcupines, are the preferred methods of pest control. The wide use of steel traps is seen as a continuation of the use of traditional rock-slab traps.

Changes in household technology (as well as the typical array of basic appliances in an average American household) include the addition of grinding machines, facilitating the most arduous female labor of grinding corn. For some weddings, however, the more traditionally oriented households insist that their new *me'öwi* (female in-law) grind corn in the old fashion with mano and metate for four days. Otherwise, the corn-grinding songs and traditionary images of Hopi women leaning over grinding bins have generally become memorate representations (reproduced in art forms) of female identity.

Cinderblocks, cut lumber, and other commercially available materials have come to be preferred for buildings since the 1950s. When Bacavi rebuilt Poliikiva in the late 1970s, the use of cinderblock was seriously considered, although native rock was finally chosen. Several kivas in other villages have cinderblock additions. Although Hopi aesthetics (as well as those of tourists, who frequently deplore the nonpicturesque effects of cinderblock during their half-hour visits) continue to value the appearance of the older rock houses, the ease and convenience of cinderblock are attractive factors.

As early as the 1920s, after some men had learned Anglo masonry techniques, new houses tended to be built with rectangularly cut stone blocks and concrete rather than the traditional rough-hewn stone and adobe. The first gable-roofed house in Bacavi was built in the 1920s. Since the 1970s, a number of houses, paid for in installments by the occupants, have been constructed under a Federal Housing and Urban Development program. They are "standard issue," southwestern, suburban-style dwellings, built to a design somewhat (though not much) tailored to local tastes. Nevertheless, most of the houses in the village had traditional mud-and-brush roofs over a framework of logs and smaller branches into the 1960s. In that decade many of these houses had leak-proof roofs put on top of, rather than in place of (for reasons both aesthetic, i.e., to preserve the log-and-brush ceilings, and insulatory), the old-style roofs. Many inhabited houses have changed little from their original construction. In the 1980s it is still standard practice to replaster with adobe the walls of the plaza houses before a summer Kachina dance, "challenging" the rain to wash off the fresh work.

Founding a New Land Base

The spring of 1910 saw the need to establish an agricultural base for Bacavi. Many men continued to cultivate in the areas of the main Oraibi Valley and elsewhere which they had farmed prior to the split. However, it was clear that additional fields and orchards closer to the village would be more convenient. Peach orchards, bean fields, and melon patches were especially desired in the immediate vicinity. The terraced gardens on the canyon slope were assigned to individual women.

Farther away, cornfields were opened on the mesa top and more were planted in the Bacavi Valley and adjacent drainages—especially the eastern slope of the Dinnebito Valley, and below Paqaptsoqvi ("reeds-on-ledge springs"), a tributary drainage to the Bacavi Valley. The new areas followed the established preference for a good, even distribution of runoff from precipitation. Another area developed was at Pangwuvi (literally, "bighorn sheep place"; the English name is No-Trail Mesa), about ten miles to the southwest of Bacavi. This area was first used before the split by Polingyaoma (Kachina clan), one of Bacavi's founders. In time, several

Human Geography and Economy   151

Badger clan men (including Polingyaoma's father) from Bacavi opened fields close by. Bacavi had a disproportionately high number of Badger clan men originally and it is possible that others were invited to farm in the vicinity by their clan brothers. Because of this, some people (frequently Badger clan members) regard the area as Badger "clan-land," but this is disputed by users who are the sons and grandsons of the first farmers.

Apart from this doubtful case, none of the new fields had any clan associations. Oraibi clan-lands were granted by the *Kikmongwi* in exchange for a ritual contribution to the village by gradually in-migrating clan groups. Bacavi never attempted to reestablish this pattern, although some elements of the clans' ceremonial roles persisted. The reasons are several. The first concerns the idea that the Oraibi split terminated certain ritual prerogatives (see Chapter 8). Since the basis of clan-lands was ritual and the ritual order had been destroyed, the very idea of clan-lands, *wimvaavasa* (ritual/ceremonial fields), was anathema. (Hotevilla did not establish clan-lands either.) All newly established fields and orchards were individually owned and patterns of inheritance vary; patrilineal succession is widespread. This pattern departs significantly from the established view of land inheritance, but as I have argued elsewhere (Whiteley 1985b), the established view needs considerable modification. Bacavi people definitely perceive a significant difference in the lack of clan-lands among the newly opened areas, but such lands are regarded as only part of the old system at Oraibi. Although clan-lands are still recognized and farmed in the Oraibi Valley as a vestigial aspect of this system (by farmers from Oraibi, Kykotsmovi, Bacavi, and Hotevilla), they have ceased to have much ritual significance. Old claims to use-rights on this clan basis are often circumvented by appeal to their changed status. The Tribal Council built on land traditionally in the Badger clan, and the Civic Center took Sand clan-lands. Had the traditional system remained intact, such encroachment would have been unthinkable. As it was, heated arguments occurred, but in both cases the traditional claims were overridden by invoking the idea that the old system had come to an end with the split.

Bacavi's establishment of new fields also coincided with the resuscitated allotment program. After abandonment in 1894, allotment was reinstigated in February 1908 (Miller 11-21-1908) as part of the government's "solution" for the split. Matthew Murphy, a former superintendent of the Western Navajo Agency at Tuba City, was appointed special allotting agent. Correspondence reveals considerable antagonism between Murphy and Hopi Agency Superintendent Horton Miller (e.g., Murphy 11-23-1910) and Miller's successor A. L. Lawshe (e.g., Lawshe 12-19-1910). Murphy's competence was repeatedly called into question, even by his supervisor (Gunderson 3-24-1910), for, among other things, nepotism within his crew and inadequate work.

Murphy succeeded in allotting Moencopi in 1908 (Murphy 11-23-1910), the only allotments that were adhered to subsequently. His initial allotments at Oraibi were made prior to the split of 1909. He assigned the returned Hostiles to lands south of the Mennonite mission in the Oraibi Valley, and the Friendlies to lands north of the mission. Relocation of the Hostiles to Bacavi caused him to modify these allotments. Since the Bacavi people had agreed to cooperate with the government, they were willing to go along with allotment. Kewanimptewa was anxious to have allotments drawn up near the new village as early as possible in 1910, so that they could begin planting (Murphy 2-12-1910).

Murphy changed his mind on allotments several times. In April 1910, after the planting season had begun, he reported (4-18-1910) that he could not allot Bacavi, Oraibi, or Hotevilla until land disputes had been resolved. Evidently Murphy's equivocation led to confusion among Bacavi people and they decided to plant where they chose. According to some Hotevilla consultants, Bacavi's choices entailed driving Hotevilla people off fields they had already opened. Some Bacavi people acknowledge this view; others dispute it.

Termination of the allotment program was officially recommended as early as May 1910 by an Interior Department inspector sent to investigate (Norris 5-19-1910). Nevertheless, it puttered on until final abandonment in March 1911 (Valentine 4-17-1911). During this time, Murphy offered several plans for the allotment of Bacavi. He tried to persuade the Oraibis to take the land in the Oraibi Valley south of the mission, which had first been set aside for the returned Hostiles. Conversely, he proposed to allot the Bacavi people north of the mission, although he could not persuade some Oraibi men who had already begun to farm there to move south. In late November 1910 he assigned Bacavi allotments, numbering some 134,[4] in the northern section of the Oraibi Valley as far as Hardrocks (Murphy 11-23-1910). He proposed the building of a dam and canal system at the northern apex of the Oraibi Valley in order to irrigate fields in the Bacavi allotments. This idea (which Murphy had discussed favorably with Bacavi people) received round condemnation from the engineering and irrigation sections of the Office of Indian Affairs (Code 12-16-1910), the superintendent of irrigation calling the plan "a very wild and chimerical one" (Robinson 12-12-1910).

Disapproval of the plan meant that yet another survey would have to be made. Kewanimptewa had the Oraibi Day School principal write to Superintendent Lawshe, who forwarded the letter to the Commissioner with his comments. Kewanimptewa's frustration with Murphy is evident:

[Kewanimptewa] says that he was appointed judge . . . and that he supposed that he was given the position because the officials in charge had some confidence in his integrity, and for this reason, thinks that his word should possess some weight. He says that Mr. Murphy consulted with him in regard to the allotment of the land and then disregarded the advice that he had given. That, more than once, Mr. Murphy has given the Bacabi people their allotments, and that they were all happy, but that later he took the land from them and gave them other land that they do not wish and that now they are very unhappy. That twelve men had been thus given land and were told by the Allotting Agent that the Navajos wished the land that had been given to them and that they would have to take other land. He says, also, that some land was taken from the Bacabis after allotment and given to other Hopis. In view of this, he asks that you relieve him as judge, and appoint someone whose word may be of some value. That the money is not much and that he does not care for the place if he may not be of service and have the confidence of the officials.

I must insist, in the interest of good administration that this complaint of Kewanimptewa be listened to, and that the Allotting Agent be required to satisfy the reasonable demands of the Bacabi people. (Lawshe 12-19-1910, emphasis in original)

These issues became moot with abandonment of the allotment program shortly thereafter, but the question of Bacavi's lands remained of great concern. According to my consultants, Murphy had issued a few written allotment titles to Bacavi people (although they were never ratified), and some of them have been used subsequently as "proofs" of claims to certain areas. To try to consolidate ownership of the northern Oraibi Valley, Kewanimptewa began fencing it. He and several Bacavi men placed a barbed-wire fence across the Oraibi Valley to mark the southern boundary (part of it still stood in 1981). However, the fencing was never completed, apparently on Tawaquaptewa's advice that Bacavi would be forever restricted to that area if they finished it. The remaining wire (obtained from the agency) was divided among several individuals who used it to fence their own fields (by now established independently of the allotment program). From the very beginning, then, Bacavi's landholding has displayed some rather different features from the system in Oraibi.

Early Economy

Agriculture and sheepherding initially remained the most important means of subsistence. Involvement in the cash economy took the form of occasional wage work for the agency. Construction of the Bacabi Day School in 1910–11 and the Hotevilla-Bacabi Day School in 1914–16 used Bacavi labor. Similarly, labor required to operate the school brought some cash income. Access to the Bacabi Day School (below the mesa in the canyon) was difficult, especially for heavy loads. Wagonloads of firewood were taken to the edge of the mesa and thrown off. In the 1910s freighting between towns and the agency, and between the villages, provided the most employment for Hopis, and woodcutting and coal hauling were the only other regular means of earning a little money (Crane 1917: 25). Construction of the Bacavi Mennonite mission in 1913–17 and its subsequent operation provided another source of wage labor. Work of this nature was sporadic, but the cash income made goods accessible from stores in Oraibi and beyond.

Sheepherding was a significant pursuit for about half of Bacavi's able-bodied adult men, although only three had more than thirty head each (U.S. Government 10-30-1906).[5] One Bacavi man maintained a herd of cattle that he had run from Oraibi before 1906.

Four men kept horses, and two of these had more than one (three each). Most men kept at least one burro or mule, and usually two or more.[6] These were the routine beasts of burden, although they were being increasingly supplemented by wagons.

Wagons had been available in Oraibi prior to the split (see Chapter 4). In the early 1900s about ten wagons per year were sent for issue to Hopis who had performed extensive services for the agency (Burton 1-23-1903, 12-12-1903). The issue increased to twenty per year between 1911 and 1917 but then ceased, and Agent Crane (1919a:13) noted a chronic shortage in 1919. Although only a few men, probably no more than five, had their own wagons upon coming to Bacavi, this number increased through the years as greater involvement in the cash economy enabled purchases: at Hopi, a wagon outfit cost $125 in 1919 (Crane 1919a:13). Wagons persisted until they were gradually replaced by pickup trucks. They had largely become things of the past by the 1960s, although one older Bacavi man, who had never owned a pickup, continued to use his wagon regularly until the mid-1970s.

Though wagework was sporadic, involvement in the cash economy began with Mormon trading and continued at Thomas Keam's trading post established in the late 1870s (McNitt 1962:161). Work for the agency, including freighting and irregular labor, provided the largest source of cash income in the early 1900s:

During the year, the Indians have earned cash as follows:

Sale of wood	$1,834.00
Sale of beef	1,306.70
Freighting	2,004.37
Irregular labor	4,637.19
TOTAL	$9,782.26

(Burton 1902:520)

Trade for cash and credit was common practice by the early 1900s at the Oraibi trading post and Hopi-owned stores. At Bacavi it is not certain who operated the first store, since any man who had the resources would occasionally buy goods in Winslow and return to sell them from his house. Kewanimptewa himself was the first to do this on a consistent basis. In 1915 Walter Tsinampti from

Table 5.10. Economic Statistics of Bacavi Household Heads, 1922

Household Head (male except where noted)	Age	Marital Status	Children	Horses	Burros/Mules	Sheep	Cattle	Chickens	Corn (bushels)	Beans (bushels)	Melons/Squash (wagonloads)	Orchard	Additional Comments
1	32	M	2	4	...	...	...	5	30	1	3		[a]
2	53	M	5	3	...	30	...	...	20			+	Good orchard
3	78	M	2	...	...	200	...	10	20				
4	53	M	4	3	...	...	...	...	50	2		+	Fine orchard
5	53	M	3	3	...	...	...	...	50	3			
6	41	M	3	7	6	...	...	24	10 acres	3 acres		+	Small peach orchard, garden
7	53	M	2		5			"a no."	120			+	Small peach orchard
8	25	M	...	4	4		20	24	100	400 lbs.	+	+	Great many melons, small peach orchard
9	27	M	...	8	1				12 acres	2 acres	1 acre	+	Small peach orchard
10	23	M	2	2	1				10 acres	1 acre		+	Small orchard, good garden; employed as helper at Day School
11	26	M	1	1	4		5						
12	49	M	5	3	...	...	...	15	12	5			
13	59	M	1	4	...	...	...	15	30	10			
14	43	M	5	7		300			100	10	2	+	Excellent orchard of peaches and apricots
15 (female)	49	Wid	4	5		25	...	6	30	5	1		Son does farm work Daughter seamstress at Day School

HH	Age	Sex											Notes
16	74	S	…	…	…	…		20	5	+			Fine orchard of peaches and apricots, good garden of squash, melons, beans
17	57	M	…	…	…	…		10	…				100 melons
18	35	M	2	6	…	…		50	5	+			
19	31	M	2	4	…	50		50	2	2			
20	61	S	…	3	…	…		10	…				Corn only crop
21	49	M	4	3	…	…		35	…				
22	91	M	…	…	…	…	3	+	…				A little corn, no other crops
23	42	M	3	8	…	…		60	3	2			
24	29	M	3	8	…	20	25	60	5		+		Extra good peach orchard, plans to do some freighting next year
25	54	M	3	5			12	50	3	+			
26	27	M	3	4	…	…		30	2	+	+		A few melons, good orchard of apples, peaches, apricots
27	25	M	1	3	20	…	10	50	5	2	+		Orchard of apples, peaches, and apricots
28	30	M	2	3	50	…	20	40	+	+	+		Some beans, squash, melons, good orchard
29	45	M	2			340		10 acres	1 acre	1 acre (mel.)	+		An orchard
TOTAL			64	101	20	340	1015	45	179+	1460+[b]		[c]	[d]	16

SOURCE: *Industrial Survey of the Moqui Indian Reservation* (1922).

[a] Ellipses indicate a negative record (e.g., Household 1 had no sheep). Blank spaces indicate no information available (e.g., we do not know whether Household 6 had any sheep).
[b] 1 acre of corn = ten bushels, according to the survey.
[c] Beans harvested total 68 bushels + 7 acres + 400 lbs.
[d] Melons/squash harvested total 12 wagonloads + 2 acres + 100 + "a great many" + "a few" + "some."

Moencopi married into Bacavi and opened the first full-time store. When his wife died shortly thereafter, he returned to Moencopi. Other stores opened in the following years and were a popular enterprise: "They [the Hopis] are naturally traders. Paqavi, for instance, with a population of only one hundred and forty, has five Indian stores. The Navahos bring considerable trade to these stores, exchanging blankets, cattle, horses, and sheep, for corn, canned groceries, and dry goods" (Stauffer 1926:12). Outside traders seem to have had little involvement in Bacavi. In 1925 the Hubbell family bought Tsinampti's store (U.S. Senate 1932:9432), intending to use it as a branch of Hubbell's trading post. It never was so used and Hubbell sold the building back to the village in the 1930s.

Despite increasing involvement with a cash-based economy, the subsistence economy remained predominant throughout the 1920s. A 1920s agency survey (Industrial Survey of the Moqui Indian Reservation 1922) of Hopi households records information on which Table 5.10 is based. The nature of the data is variable, so the table should not be treated as absolutely indicative (for example, according to my consultants, several more men owned burros than are recorded here).

Although there was movement off the reservation as early as 1919 (U.S. Government 1919) to obtain employment, the numbers involved were very small indeed—fewer than five into the 1930s (see above). The 1930s saw a considerable expansion of employment opportunities at Hopi with the introduction of several federal programs to alleviate the depression. Although most Hopis were still intensively engaged in the subsistence economy, they were targets for "relief" also. Beginning in 1933 and for several years thereafter, the Civilian Conservation Corps employed many Hopi men on various road-building, well-digging, and dike-building projects (Leathers 1937:65).

A picture of the mixed economy of the 1930s emerges from a 1933 farm census of thirty Bacavi and Hotevilla households (Table 5.11). Using this data, Leathers (1937:68) emphasizes:

1. Nine families do not have a team. 2. Eighteen families do not have sheep. 3. Twenty-six families do not have cattle. 4. Six families do not have chickens. 5. Ten families do not have a plow. 6. Twenty-one families do

Table 5.11. Economic Census of the Seventh- and Eighth-Grade Class Members, Hotevilla-Bacabi Day School, 1935

Household	Number in Family	Horses	Mules	Burros	Sheep	Cattle	Goats	Chickens	Plows	Cultivators	Wagons	Corn (wagonloads)	Dried Fruit (24-lb. bags)	Cash Income
1	8	5	0	1	180	0	0	15	2	1	1	5	0	$112.75
2	4	3	1	0	0	0	0	17	1	0	2	5	0	193.30
3	7	0	0	0	0	0	0	14	0	0	0	3	0	106.50
4	6	10	0	0	223	0	38	0	0	1	1	4	0	196.10
5	5	7	4	0	0	64	0	4	2	2	1	2	0	214.10
6	8	0	0	2	0	0	0	13	0	0	0	5	8	173.35
7	7	0	1	0	24	0	5	4	1	0	1	4	1	41.25
8	5	3	1	3	0	1	0	0	1	0	1	2	0	116.90
9	6	0	1	2	0	0	2	16	1	0	0	3	0	179.00
10	7	7	2	0	200	0	60	5	1	0	2	4	0	49.00
11	3	2	1	0	0	12	10	21	0	0	2	3	0	96.10
12	5	2	3	0	0	0	0	13	0	1	1	7	0	53.40
13	6	2	2	1	26	0	10	14	1	0	1	8½	39	212.30
14	9	0	0	33	55	0	7	5	0	0	0	7	0	174.75
15	9	3	2	2	50	0	10	5	2	0	2	7	0	24.15
16	9	2	4	0	0	0	30	0	1	1	1	5	0	80.30
17	9	1	3	0	90	0	50	0	0	0	1	5	0	119.50
18	7	0	1	0	0	0	0	6	0	0	1	5	0	68.00
19	6	3	0	0	0	0	0	10	1	0	1	4	4	36.50
20	6	0	0	4	120	0	0	0	0	0	3	4	0	637.35
21	5	5	4	0	516	0	9	15	1	2	2	7	0	1048.21
22	6	0	0	0	22	0	1	11	1	0	1	8	4	75.75
23	8	0	0	0	0	0	10	15	1	0	1	3	6	42.10
24	5	0	0	1	0	0	0	26	1	0	1	7	0	80.05
25	7	2	0	1	0	0	0	4	1	0	1	1	7	81.00
26	7	5	0	0	6	0	0	24	1	0	1	5	0	41.05
27	8	6	2	0	0	32	0	11	1	2	1	12	1	150.20
28	5	3	1	0	0	0	0	0	1	1	1	2	1	133.75
29	5	2	3	0	0	0	0	13	1	1	2	13	2	468.10
30	3	4	0	0	0	0	0	8	0	0	1	3	0	102.25
TOTAL	191													$5507.60
												Dollars per person $		28.83

SOURCE: Leathers (1937:91).

not have a cultivator. The result of this census also shows that about 57 per cent of the annual income for 1935 was derived from the Public Works Administration. About 19½ per cent of the income came from the products of Indian Arts and Crafts and the remaining 23½ per cent was realized from crops, sheep, wool, and labor secured at the Day Schools.

It is also noteworthy that only four households lacked a wagon and every household was significantly engaged in agriculture.

Technological adaptations gradually increased. The 1930s mark the introduction of the first automobiles (mostly pickup trucks) in Bacavi, although only three men acquired them prior to the 1940s, when they really began to take hold.

The effects of World War II on the general Hopi economy were profound:

The war brought great changes in its wake; several hundred men served in the armed forces. Others, men and women alike, moved to the towns to work for the railroad and in other jobs as far distant as Barstow and Los Angeles. When they returned after the war they usually had savings. Others did not return to the reservation, but sought and obtained employment in the towns adjacent to it, along Highway 66, particularly Winslow and Flagstaff, although a large number of Hopi are regularly employed at Grand Canyon. (Kennard 1965:26)

The 1940s signal the great increase in off-reservation residence, with concomitantly radical economic changes for nonresidents. As noted earlier, the 1950s saw expanded changes in technology. Propane-fueled stoves gradually replaced the old wood/coal stoves that had come into use during the 1910s and 1920s. The number of trucks and cars in Bacavi grew; in 1959, Highway 264 was completed, greatly facilitating communication with other villages and with off-reservation towns:

One of the results of this ready accessibility and widespread ownership of cars is that the relative isolation of the villages has completely disappeared. Before the war all items handled by the traders had to be trucked in. Now, foodstuffs, daily newspapers, fresh meat, citrus fruits, and other items are delivered daily. The old trading post has been replaced by a sort of supermarket. Cash transactions have replaced the trade for goods on credit. (Kennard 1965:27)

This process led to the decline of stores in Bacavi. In 1981 there was no local store, nor has there been since the 1950s, although several households sell refreshments on ceremonial occasions. One household keeps a small supply of candy and soda pop for children and another maintains a pop machine. Hotevilla has a small store, but most Bacavi people do their shopping at the supermarket in Kykotsmovi or at supermarkets in Flagstaff, Tuba City, or Winslow.

In summary, Bacavi's economy has seen many changes since its origin, although a number of features have persisted. Despite a considerable decline in the subsistence economy, Bacavi maintains a more active involvement in subsistence agriculture and the decline has been rather slower than at most other Hopi villages. The reasons in part concern its long isolation from developing centers of employment at Hopi. This situation has diminished with the developments in transportation and the expansion of Tribal employment opportunities based in Kykotsmovi. Future changes in Hopi economy may be expected as a result of three other forms of change: government budget practices, the acquisition of significantly larger landholdings with the gradual opening of the Hopi Partitioned Lands as a result of the legislative settlement of the Hopi-Navajo land dispute, and long-term changes in the national and world economy, in which modern Hopi society is unquestionably enmeshed.

6
Kinship and Social Structure

In Chapter 3 I discussed kinship and social structure in turn-of-the-century Oraibi. Some features have remained more or less the same, whereas others have changed greatly. Changes can be linked both to economic change and to the decline of the religious societies (see Chapter 7); these two trends have certain mutually influential effects.

Still other "changes" reflect a different perspective on the meaning of kinship in anthropology. Since the 1940s, when the exemplar texts on Hopi social structure were written, analytical constructs in which kinship practices are cast have altered significantly. More radical attacks on kinship theory (e.g., Needham 1974; Schneider 1984) implicitly subvert the truth-claims of all ethnography couched in kinship-theory genre conventions. Although it is not my intent to thoroughly reexamine Hopi kinship and social structure diachronically, some aspects are subjected below to revisionist scrutiny in order to see exactly where the changes lie: in the institutions themselves, in the apprehension of them with newer ethnographic lenses, or both in various measures. Before considering specific changes in

Bacavi from nineteenth-century Oraibi, further comment is needed on some general properties of Hopi social structure.

The Sexual Division of Labor in Hopi Social Structure

Chapter 3 (see also Whiteley 1985b) mentioned that the practical arrangement of the economy in Oraibi departed significantly from the conventional accounts that stress the importance of clans and lineages as economic corporations. There was extensive variation in the organization of agriculture and herding labor and in usufruct rights in land: in practice, matrilineal descent rules did not keep people in puppet-like enslavement to the dictates of an inflexible social structure.

In addition, we must address the sexual division of labor.[1] This division is critical for an understanding of kinship in Bacavi and, by extension, for an understanding of kinship in pre-split Oraibi also.

Male involvement in the subsistence economy was devoted primarily to agriculture, herding, and hunting (although the last was comparatively minor). All three activities were practiced away from the village in fields, grazing, or hunting areas. The most valued role culturally for a male is as a cultivator: "A Hopi is first and foremost a farmer," as one consultant put it, an axiom expressing ethnic identity as much as economics. The most highly valued element culturally of the traditional economy was corn. The predominance of corn symbolism in Hopi religion bears this out; sheep or cattle motifs are virtually nonexistent. Economically, then, men are construed mainly as producers of the crops. But they do not own their produce. They cultivate (and herd and hunt) *away* from the village and bring the finished products *in* to the village to present to its rightful owners, the women.

Women's major economic activities are the processing, preparation, and distribution of the produce provided by men. In respect to its economic role, the women "own" the village, so to speak; they control the domestic domain through ownership of the economic produce and of the houses from which they distribute it. In the sense that the domestic economy is female-owned, largely female-organized, and female-articulated, the role of males as providers of the raw materials is conceptually subsidiary.

In ritual and politics, the other major contexts for an analysis of kinship, the pattern is converse. Men are the major ritual and political protagonists. The major loci of ritual action are kivas rather than households. Whereas a man's birth into a particular lineage segment in a household provides specific connections into the ritual and political orders, the actualization of his roles occurs largely in settings away from the household.

For the most part, women's ritual and political roles are subsidiary.[2] Apart from the three women's societies (which have male chief-priests as well as a principal woman), ritually women are largely providers of food for the male participants and for visitors to household feasts. Women have prominent roles in rituals centered in the household: those of birth, infant-naming, and marriage.

It is not my intention to espouse a full-blown Lévi-Straussian structuralist position, but in a general, descriptive sense there is some profit in dividing men and women into opposed conceptual domains. Men's economic role is outside and away from the village and is, in some ways, secondary to the major organization of the economy, which takes place inside the domestic domain of the household, within the village. This domestic domain is controlled by women. The sexual division of the economy can be expressed structurally as:

men : women :: fields(outside/periphery) : households(inside/center) :: laborers : managers

Ritually and politically, the arrangement is the obverse. In the ritual ordering of village space, the kivas (and the plaza, too) become the "centers" and the houses are on the "periphery":

men : women :: kivas(inside/center) : houses(outside/periphery) :: managers : laborers

Clearly, these oppositions can be broadly related to a conceptual dichotomy between men and women (with marks of dominance and subordination), which Sherry Ortner (1974) has argued is universal. But my characterization is intended specifically rather than comparatively. And, as I have stressed, the oppositions are reductions of general empirical tendencies rather than postulated deep-structural features in some pan-Hopi collective psyche. With these caveats, we can analytically combine our two equations:

men : women :: ritual : economy :: kivas : households

Since these are general tendencies, exceptions are plentiful, particularly on the female side. Some women, without male support, work in fields. In the past, especially, many women owned and tended garden plots with small quantities of various crops (I am unaware that Hopis divide crops themselves sexually). Likewise, women gather plants outside the village, although not usually as far away as the cornfields. Women, of course, have significant ritual roles in the women's societies, as well as in household-oriented ceremonies, although they do not have routine access to kivas. On the other hand, men have occasional roles as processors of food (such as in corn roasts in underground pits) and have much greater economic control over sheep and cattle.

Nevertheless, the division can be heuristic. If we grant that it shows that the most important culturally defined foci of men's and women's attention were the religious-political domain and the domestic-economic domain, respectively, this must have implications for other features of the social structure. Kinship relationships, for example, should have particular importance for men ritually and politically, for women economically.

Households

Nagata (1970:223–87) has extensively described kinship change at Moencopi. He argues that the cardinal economic unit has changed, for exogenous reasons, from a lineage or a lineage segment making up a matrilocal household to the nuclear-family household:

The prevalence of the nuclear family household type is a result of a recently increasing preference for neolocality and the feasibility of early "fission" of a young household as a result of participation in the modern economic conditions and the breakdown of the traditional agricultural society. (Nagata 1970:257)

*Table 6.1. Bacavi Household Composition
of Resident Populace, 1981*

Household Type	No. of Households	Percentage
Nuclear Family	22	34.9
Couple	11	17.5
Matrifocal Family	10	15.9
Matrilineage Segment	9	14.3
Single Individual	8	12.7
Siblings	2	3.2
Nuclear Family + Related Couple	1	1.6
TOTAL	63	100.0

More notable still is Nagata's conclusion that "the household structure of today's Moenkopi can be described as *bilaterally oriented*. Apart from the solidarity of mother and children, revealed at divorce, no salient matrilineal feature is present in the household group" (1970:269).

Contemporary household composition in Bacavi is shown in Table 6.1. Of the sixty-three households, nuclear families account for one-third. At least another third were originally nuclear families, the developmental cycle having transformed them into other categories. These figures are roughly commensurate with Nagata's figures for Moencopi: he shows a greater percentage of nuclear-family households (53.7 percent), but "when combined with two person households, [this] includes nearly sixty per cent of Moenkopi households" (1970:256).

Some clarificatory remarks are required on the meaning of the nuclear family in Bacavi. In contrast to Nagata's Moencopi, in Bacavi matrilineality is an enduring principle. A house is a woman's property. She has ultimate authority over the choice of its heir, who is usually a daughter—very often the youngest one, who has remained in the house to take care of aging parents, while her sisters have moved out (according to my consultants, this was the case in Oraibi, too). This means that over time the house appears as continuously owned within a lineage, although the actual proprietor at any given time is one woman. In a sense, then, the "nuclear family" is itself a two-generation matrilineage segment with an inmarried affine.

Kinship and Social Structure

Further, kinship behavior and friendship behavior in this close-knit community (where many friends are also kin) makes for a rather different pattern from isolated, urban, nuclear-family households. Thus although a child's "home base" is most likely in his/her mother's house, its proximity to other houses with close kin and friends, enables him/her to spend many nights under other roofs and days eating at other tables. Similarly, adult interaction and cooperation in a great many activities (particularly between women with close kin and affinal ties) vitiates the idea of rigidly separated, nuclear-family households. With one woman at the center of a household, the most frequent commensal and overnight residents are usually her husband and her children. But the intensity of daily interaction between houses, which may be separated by no more than a joint wall or a distance of a few yards, suggests that nuclear-family households are not strongly discrete integral units.

The data on Bacavi households comparable to Nagata's on Moencopi may ostensibly suggest that "changed" household compositions derive from similar economic changes. Economic conditions in Bacavi since 1960 have indeed followed a pattern in some ways parallel to Moencopi over a longer period. But I think the similarity of causes for household change ends there. My reasons concern the notion that there is any, or much, change from household composition in pre-split Oraibi. It is not possible to compute with absolute accuracy the number of households or household types in Bacavi's earliest years. Since the village was composed of fragmentary groups from Oraibi, the picture of household types which might be reconstructed would be rather distorted. It is more heuristic, then, to compare household composition in modern Bacavi with that of Oraibi prior to the split.

Chapter 3 presented a view of Oraibi households as typically composed of matrilineage segments: a woman, her husband, their daughters and their inmarried husbands, along with a third generation of the daughters' children, all residing together in a house or a set of adjoining rooms. But there are problems of household definition in the literature:

Identification of a household group has been a problem among several authorities on the Hopi. Titiev (1944) and Eggan (1950) put more emphasis on the lineage, while Beaglehole (1935) and Brainard (1935) saw in a biological family the basic form of a Hopi household. The former defined the form of a household as a matrilineally extended family of three generations (Titiev 1944:7,46; Eggan 1950:29) whose primary function was socialization or "primary orientation" (Eggan 1950:30). (Nagata 1970:246)

Both Beaglehole and Brainard in the 1930s "found that the biological family of father, mother, and children was the modal household group" (Nagata 1970:247). Particularly, Brainard's data for Hotevilla showed a possible maximum of 55 percent nuclear-family households.

Meyer Fortes (1958:3) has demonstrated the ethnographic flaw of examining household composition frozen at one phase of the developmental cycle:

> Two investigators can arrive at totally discrepant conclusions about the incidence of different "types" of residence in the same community though they use what seems to be the same census methods. In fact the source of the apparent discrepancies is the neglect by both investigators of the developmental dimension.... Residence patterns are the crystallization, at a given time, of the developmental process.

These remarks seem eminently applicable to the differences of modal household types identified by various Hopi ethnographers. Although a complete reanalysis of Hopi domestic groups from the cyclical perspective is much needed (in light of Fortes's and Goody's 1958 insights), this is beyond my present scope. It is more apropos to question the orthodox view of Hopi household composition in its own terms. Brainard and Beaglehole notwithstanding, the accepted version of household composition in anthropological discourse remains that of Titiev and Eggan.

Titiev's census data of Oraibi households prior to 1906 (Titiev n.d.) reveal a rather different perspective on household composition from the interpretations of his *Old Oraibi* (1944). Structural-functionalist predispositions may have been responsible for the prevailing lineage model of Hopi social structure and in particular of household groups. Titiev did not publish a statistical analysis of household composition types, but though his census notes (not untypical of any fieldnotes) are not wholly consistent in their organization of household composition data, they are, in general, quite clearly laid out and fairly easily susceptible of analysis. Table 6.2 shows household types for Oraibi based on my own analysis of

Kinship and Social Structure

Table 6.2. Oraibi Household Composition
of Pre-1906 Populace

Household Type	No. of Households	Percentage
Definite Nuclear Family	57	31.0
Likely Nuclear Family	27	14.7
Definite Matrilineage Segment	41	22.3
Likely Matrilineage Segment	9	4.9
Indistinguishable Nuclear Family/ Matrilineage Segment	27	14.7
Couple	9	4.9
Indefinite and Miscellaneous	14	7.6
TOTAL	184	100.1

SOURCE: Titiev (n.d.).

Titiev's notes. There is certainly room for error, but the figures are highly indicative. The figure for "definite nuclear families" is conservative: criteria for this category included (in conjunction with the household's list of occupants and their interrelationships) such marginal comments as "no one else lived here"; "no mother or sisters lived here"; "daughters moved out at marriage." I assumed that, unless otherwise stated, sons moved out at marriage. I denote definite nuclear-family households those instances in which a married daughter stayed with her husband in her mother's household for only a short period (as specified in the notes) before moving to a neolocal residence where she resided for the rest of her life or until Oraibi split.

Table 6.2 suggests that the nuclear-family household demands consideration as the modal, pre-Oraibi split, Third Mesa household type. Brainard's and Beaglehole's interpretations receive confirmation. Although Nagata (1970:274) considers prevalence of neolocal residence at Moencopi the result of atypical conditions, he also recognizes that "the preference for neolocality has long been recognized by writers on the Hopi" (1970:265), and "a simple biological family, housed in a single room of a pueblo, has long been known" (1970:248). The probability that this was the rule rather than the exception is further specifically suggested in Titiev's notes. Discussing the composition of a particular household, Don Talayesva (one of Titiev's principal consultants) pointed out:

The girls lived here with their mother for a while + then moved out. Don says this is the pattern (unsolicited). Mo. + dtrs. live together for a while and then the girls move out. They may move into any vacant house— (same clan or not) or they may purchase any house they like[3]—follow up on this lead. (Titiev n.d. 18)

The tendency toward traditional neolocality is clear in Talayesva's view. Indeed, in many cases of "definite matrilineage segments" in Table 6.2, movement out of the house by a majority of daughters was prevalent: in seventeen cases out of the total of forty-one (or 41.4 percent), only one daughter remained in the household after marriage. Nagata argues that, in Moencopi, access to wage labor with concomitant economic independence enables daughters to move out immediately upon marriage rather than remaining in the parents' household for a while (1970:274). This is a general pattern in Bacavi also (although there are exceptions). But this tendency to slightly earlier neolocality hardly indicates a radical change in long-term household composition.

In summary, the "orthodox" view of traditional Hopi household structure is inaccurate. Although a slightly greater proportion of nuclear-family households in Bacavi than in Oraibi may be inferred from Tables 6.1 and 6.2, this does not imply major change. Kinship behavior has changed in certain contexts (see below), but household composition appears to be an independent factor. In short, the structure of the household in modern Bacavi shows no apparent formal changes from pre-split Oraibi.

The household remains the primary economic unit for everyday purposes. Women, frequently lineage mates from separate households, prepare food together for ceremonial occasions or just social gatherings of a dispersed extended family. Also, the nature of the modern household economy reflects the gradual movement from subsistence agriculture to a cash-based system. But, despite the persistence of some interhousehold activities on the one hand, and the changes effected by absorption into the national economy on the other, the household retains its role as the primary economic unit.

In keeping with the conceptual male-female opposition described, households can be seen as more important ritually and politically for men and economically for women. Upon marriage, a man acquires membership in a second household, his wife's. The conventional accounts suggest that he is a "mere inseminator" (Nagata 1970:273) in his wife's household, of little economic import (Titiev 1944:43). At the same time, his major economic responsibilities switch from his natal to his affinal household (cf. Eggan 1950:55–56), so his economic role in the former is greatly diminished. Although there is an element of truth here, these suggestions are misleading. First, the contradiction that a male's economic responsibilities lie first to his wife's household, but that his role there is actually insignificant, results from a failure to adequately distinguish the conceptual context of the sexual division of labor. A man's seeming economic insignificance, I suggest, derives from cultural emphasis on his role as provider rather than manager. Second, though *conceptually* subordinate, his practical importance as provider of raw materials is nevertheless crucial for a nuclear family. If this was the modal household composition, obviously the interpretation of a male's role in his affinal household traditionally must change. Moreover, the apparent increase in a man's economic significance in contemporary nuclear-family households cannot have its cause in change in household types. Instead, I suggest that this increase derives from his position, culturally sanctioned by the mores of the national society, as "breadwinner" who is not required to turn over all his cash income to his wife; cash has not assumed the cultural status of productive (and, through matriliny, reproductive) resources as the property of women. Simultaneously, owing to decline in the ritual system—in which his natal household and lineage was more important—a man's possible roles as ritual protagonist have diminished (see Chapter 7). Thus although male household roles (in both natal and affinal household) have indeed changed, the reasons are more complex than a straightforward change in household type. The persistence of much female economic practice in households suggests that change has impacted less on women. A woman remains house-owner in most cases, inheritance is matrilineal, and she still manages much of the productive and reproductive economy. The influx of cash and commodities and decrease of subsistence products, though important, has mostly altered the content rather than the form of a woman's role in the household.

The importance of clan-houses has diminished, owing to clan and ritual decline. Establishment of clan-houses in Bacavi was complicated by the dispersal of clans formerly integral in Oraibi. In several ways clan-houses in Oraibi continued as the spiritual centers of particular clans, although many members had moved to new villages. This was less pronounced in Bacavi than in Moencopi, which (maintaining a close colony relationship with Oraibi) established no new clan-houses at all (Nagata 1970:244–45). In modern Bacavi there is a vestigial sense in which certain houses are regarded as clan-houses. Evidently, the Badger clan *wu'uya* were kept in Bacavi for a time, and as Kewanimptewa's wife's house held the Blue Flute sacra, its status as Spider clan-house had a traditional underpinning. In both these instances, the materials were passed to people in Hotevilla upon the death of their Bacavi trustees. Because of matrilineal inheritance, other Bacavi houses (particularly those around the *kiisonvi*) have come to be associated with particular clans. This runs counter to the situation Nagata records for Moencopi, where "the older house structures have long ceased to be objects of inheritance" and "the inheritance of houses remained and still remains undefined" (Nagata 1970:266). In contrast, house inheritance in Bacavi continues through matrilines. Houses, including older ones, have occasionally been sold to nonkin but the majority have remained in the same lineage since the village's beginnings. The decline in the role of particular houses as repositories of clan sacra is a formal change from the situation in Oraibi, deriving from changes in the ritual order.

Lineage, Clan, and Phratry

Bacavi's lineage, clan, and phratry composition diverge extensively from Oraibi's. The movements from Oraibi to Hotevilla and Bacavi did not for the most part involve entire lineages or clans. Thus Bacavi's original populace comprised a number of lineage and clan fragments; there were no instances of an entire lineage's relocating. Hotevilla appears to have had a total monopoly on the *Kookop* clan, but there are no parallel cases in Bacavi.

This original fragmentary composition of the village has had

Table 6.3. Bacavi's Phratries, Clans, and Lineages, 1981

Phratry	Clan	Number of Lineages	Number of Households	Population			
				F	M	Total	Percent of Total
I	Rabbit/Tobacco	1	1	2	1	3	0.8
II	Bear	2	5	21	17	38	10.4
	Spider	1	0	0	2	2	0.5
III	Snake	3	12	42	29	71	19.4
	Sand	1	1	4	3	7	1.9
IV	Eagle	1	1	2	5	7	1.9
	Sun	1	1	2	1	3	0.8
V	Greasewood	6	20	64	71	135	36.9
	Reed	2	10	25	17	42	11.5
VI	Coyote	4	6	7	12	19	5.2
VII	Badger	1	1	4	5	9	2.5
VIII	Corn	2	3	7	10	17	4.6
...	[No Clan]	...	3	7	6	13	3.6
TOTAL	12	25	64	187	179	366	100.0

lasting effects on its lineage, clan, and phratry complexion. Occasional virilocal marriages and occasional immigration of nuclear families from other villages have added other lineage segments, sometimes introducing a new clan contingent, to the village. Modern clan and lineage structure is not, then, merely an outgrowth of the original populace.

Lineages, clans, and phratries in modern Bacavi are shown in Table 6.3. Inmarried males from other villages, included in resident population figures (Chapter 5), are excluded here, but off-reservation residents who belong to Bacavi lineages are included. Whole lineages or lineage segments that have practically ceased to maintain active ties with the village are excluded. Further, one extra household, not normally resident, has been included, since it does periodically maintain a house in the village.

Lineages in the late twentieth century (at least) do not function as corporate economic units, owning land in common and laboring together. Similarly, inheritance of ritual office has ceased to be a factor in lineage differentiation, since there are no longer formal offices to inherit. Nevertheless, lineages are fairly easily identified genealogically. For men, lineages are mostly nexuses of association and identity, and in many cases it is questionable whether the identification of lineage membership is more than marginally meaningful. A man can still differentiate a closer (classificatory maternal) "uncle" from a distant one and is aware of the "pedigree" his lineage or lineage segment provides, especially if it was formerly associated with ritual office.

For women, on the other hand, lineages maintain a stronger grounding in everyday practices. For certain economic tasks, especially in cooking for ceremonial occasions, a woman cooperates with close lineage mates, and often lineage-related households combine to feast other relatives and friends on these occasions. Although women are increasingly taking active roles in the wage economy, most remain based in their households. Some of the more arduous tasks of food processing have been alleviated with technological innovations, but there is still no easy way to husk corn or shell beans. Women cooperate in these activities more to be sociable than for economic need. This is also the case with basket- and plaque-weaving, and sewing and quilting bees. Groups of women who work together are not always lineage mates or kin, but my impression is that such ties are common among them. Women thus maintain the opportunity to interact socially with close same-sex relatives more than do men. The major meeting place for male socializing was the kiva, which has ceased to have this function on a day-to-day basis.

Two sets of ceremonies that center in the household serve as important expressions of lineage unity among women: weddings and infant-namings (Voth 1900, 1905b, describes these in Oraibi). These are extended family rituals that mobilize women especially into lineage (and, by extension, clan) groups. Wedding ceremonies activate lineage ties, especially from the bride's clan, groom's clan, groom's father's clan, and groom's godfather's clan. Frequently, other relatives on the bride's side also contribute. Wedding ceremonies may well have become more elaborate in recent years; older people criticize the expansive gift-giving between parties to the conjugal bond, which stretches the capacity for proper reciprocity to excessive limits.

Infant-naming similarly mobilizes the woman of a lineage, who formally name a brother's child after their clan. On the naming day

Kinship and Social Structure

(traditionally twenty days after birth but in modern times often shortened to ten), each woman from the father's clan who chooses goes to the child's house at dawn and bestows a name. In the 1980s naming ceremonies remain common practice. Though technically any clanswomen can participate in a wedding or infant-naming, typically only close lineage mates are involved.

For both men and women, lineages remain important identity groups within a clan. Since Oraibi clans were dispersed with the split, the solidarity of intravillage clan sections has strengthened at some expense to Mesa-wide clan unity.

Lineages recorded in Table 6.3 are identified on the basis of common origins and perceived continuance of unitary identity, where this is known by the author or alluded to by consultants. "Common origins" refers to a variety of permutations. Bacavi's original populace was composed of nuclear-family households with dependent relatives. Because these groups were smaller than whole lineages and were physically separated from lineage mates, each fragment's descendants (where there are any) usually constitute one unitary lineage in modern Bacavi. There are exceptions, particularly involving older people with few close relatives in Bacavi but with lineage mates in Hotevilla.

Original lineage fragments (Table 6.4) are identified by reference to three sources: Titiev's census notes of Oraibi, a comprehensive genealogical survey of Oraibi lineages by Leslie White in 1931–32 (White n.d.), and my consultants' accounts. In two instances, original lineage fragments have split into separate lineages owing to disputes. In all, fourteen modern lineages derive from twelve of the original twenty-one fragments in Bacavi. Nine of the original fragments became extinct (in most cases because their original composition was entirely male). Eleven lineages, representing nine clans, from six villages of origin (two from Second Mesa, the rest from Third), have been introduced to the village since its earliest years through neolocal and virilocal marriages. (In addition, in Table 6.3 there are thirteen individuals without clans—i.e., children of a Bacavi father and a non-Hopi mother—or lineages.)

In sum, lineages are palpable segments of Third Mesa clans in modern Bacavi, although their distinctive features are not always clear. They appear as extended families organized on the basis of

Table 6.4. Bacavi's Clans and Lineage Fragments, 1910

Phratry	Clan		Lineage Fragments	Population			
	Titiev's Designations	Modern Designations		F	M	Total	Percent of Total
I	Rabbit	Rabbit/Tobacco	1	5	4	9	7.1
	Parrot	Parrot	1	0	1	1	0.8
	Crow	Kachina	1	0	1	1	0.8
II	Bear	Bear	1	5	3	8	6.3
	Spider	Spider	2	4	3	7	5.5
III	Sand	Sand	1	0	3	3	2.3
	Lizard	Snake	2	15	11	26	20.5
	Snake		0	0	1	1	0.8
IV	Eagle	Eagle	1	1	3	4	3.1
V	Greasewood	Greasewood	3	10	9	19	14.9
	Reed	Reed	1	7	6	13	10.2
VI	Coyote	Coyote	1	1	1	2	1.6
	Water Coyote		3	9	11	20	15.7
VII	Gray Badger	Badger	2	2	9	11	8.6
	Navajo Badger		1	1	1	2	1.6
TOTAL	15	12	21	60	67	127	99.9

matrilineal descent. A perceived unity of identity and a role as networks of mutual aid are their clearest functional features. Lineage roles economically and ritually have altered considerably. Thus, whereas women continue to work often in groups united by lineage ties, cooperative lineage labor among men has mostly ceased. Similarly, though certain aspects of some prime lineages' proprietary ritual rights persist (such as the formal care of clan sacra that remain in Oraibi clan-houses), most are gone. But we must also question the signifier: the equation of "lineages" in the conventional accounts with ritually and economically incorporative functions neglects their cultural role as affective identity groups. Thus a suggestion that, in Bacavi, lineages are greatly changed from a former status as corporations with joint estates to a current status as identity groups weakly unified by affective bonds would be simplistic and distortive. Economic and ritual corporateness was never so great (see Whiteley 1985b), and affective unity never so insignificant.

The consistency with which certain groups of relatives associate in households on ceremonial occasions makes lineage ties evident.

Agnatic relatives may attend feasts also, but they are usually invited "specially," whereas lineage mates are simply expected to appear. With extensive nonresidence, lineages usually convene in their entirety only for special occasions. But unlike in Moencopi (Nagata 1970:passim), a lineage or segment is still the primary structure of association in such settings, rather than a bilateral kindred.

Clans also continue to be strong emblems of social identity. Their ritual nuclei have mostly become historical traditions; the periodic reaffirmation in annual ceremony of a clan's mythological arrival at Oraibi (such as was represented traditionally by *Powamuy* for the Badger clan or by the Blue Flute ceremony for the Spider clan) no longer occurs in Bacavi and the more esoteric aspects of a clan's ritual knowledge are no longer extant. Nevertheless, knowledge of more general, distinctive clan traditions remains pervasive in the 1980s. These provide marks of distinction both positive (for members) and negative (for nonmembers). Criticism of members of other clans raises less flattering traditions of their clan association—X behaves that way (e.g., from excessive gossiping to culturally defined madness) because he is a member of clan Y, which is known for it. Such boundary-maintenance mechanisms continually reinforce clan differences. The *Piikyas-Patki* conflict (cf. Titiev 1944:201–2) is only one of many old clan rivalries. The Greasewood clan's rights to the *Tsa'akmongwi* position result from a dispute with the Reed clan. Because of arguments, a ritual competition was devised; each clan would try to maintain a better spring below Oraibi. After a time, the Reed clan's spring dried up, leaving Greasewood the winner (the spring, now in the village of Kykotsmovi, is still formally maintained in the 1980s). The Reed clan forfeited the *Tsa'akmongwi* position to the Greasewood clan, who have held it since. This is a Greasewood clan version, and undoubtedly the Reed version is different. But my point is that clan rivalries inhere in the clan system.

Clanship continues to give the individual a primary identity that supersedes village or Mesa membership or more general "Hopi" identity: "First, I am a *Kyarswungwa* (Parrot clan member), then I'm an Oraibi, then I'm a Hopi," as a Third Mesa man put it. The social identity of clanship, nonetheless, no longer provides such differentiated sociocultural roles as in the past.

In the late twentieth century younger village members often do not know the clan membership of others (cf. Nagata 1970:239), which suggests a major social change. Kinship terms have become much less significant in everyday discourse. One term of address and reference continues to be mandatory: *me'öwi*, for a woman married into one's clan. Use of personal names for this affine is still frowned upon. Few other interactional contexts demand the use of kinship terms. One involves ritual smoking. Every man who wishes to participate in a ceremony must go to the kiva and formally smoke with the sponsor and others present. As the pipe is passed, the recipient formally addresses the offerer by the correct kinship term; when it is passed to the next man he must be similarly addressed. Knowledge of the correct term for every man in the village (and there are very few for whom one has no term, via the channels of genealogy, ritual kinship, and affinity) involves a fairly comprehensive understanding of clanship and clan interrelations. Evidently, younger men often resort to a general cover term (*i'kwaatsi*, "my friend") since they do not know the kinship terms for other kiva members, which indicates a significant change in the social meaningfulness of kinship.

The most important modern function of clans is in regulating marriage. Clan and phratry exogamy are still strictly enforced in Bacavi. Two intraclan marriages and two intraphratry marriages have occurred, all since 1960, and two ended in divorce. None occurred between two previous village members, and one of the intraphratry marriages was with a clan not represented at Third Mesa. Even so, these marriages were contracted under the weight of great criticism, which did not totally subside after the weddings. With the decline of distinct clan roles, of the Hopi language, and of the transmission of traditional knowledge, it is possible that intraclan and intraphratry marriages will increase in the future.

Clanship remains, then, a strong emblem of social identity, a subject for personal pride, and the object of another's criticism. That the overt sociocultural roles of particular clans have to a large extent become a matter of history does not subvert their perceived importance in the ascription of identity.

Bacavi did not receive a full complement of Oraibi clans (see Tables 6.3 and 6.4); two phratries were entirely unrepresented (contra Titiev 1944:212, who shows only one missing). Clan groups in Bacavi, therefore, could not possibly have replicated the pattern in

Oraibi, where each clan had specific roles, ritual or otherwise, in the overall social structure. Bacavi clans continue to regard Oraibi as the cultural center from which their significances radiate. As the center of a long-established, sacred sociocosmological landscape, Oraibi was not easily replaceable. The very idioms of clan history and mythology are inextricable from this sacred geography. The exodus from Oraibi to found new villages did not alter this: no revisionist mythology has recast Hotevilla or Bacavi as the central locus of clan history.

Chapter 3 suggested that clan and ritual organization were more entrenched at Oraibi than at the other two Mesas. Thus although Eggan (1967) reports a reworked mythological legitimation of the Snake clan as providers of the *Kikmongwi* at Walpi (after the extinction of the Bear and Spider clans), a parallel situation has not occurred (as of the 1980s) at post-split Third Mesa villages. The term *Kikmongwi* has occasionally been used honorifically in Hotevilla and Bacavi, but Hotevilla has never succeeded in mythologically rationalizing a shift from traditional Bear clan ownership of this position to another clan. A history of wrangling among *Kookop*, Sun, Spider, and Squash clan representatives for titular prominence since Yukioma's death in 1929 reflects the inability to reproduce this role with no Bear clan representatives. Efforts in the early 1980s to proclaim a *Kookop* clan man *Kikmongwi* met with his own refusal. I shall argue in Chapter 8 that political processes at work in the Oraibi split prevented complete social restructuring along the old lines.

The descendants of Bacavi's founders now account for seven clans in the village. The other five in Table 6.3 have been either added (Sun and Corn) or reintroduced after extinction of early clan representatives (Badger, Eagle, and Sand). Corn (the translation Hopis usually give for *Piikyas*) is the only long-established accretion (dating from 1915).

The final point I wish to make about changes in the clan structure derives from clan names, particularly as these have come to be used in English (this section expands upon some observations in Whiteley 1986). Again, some changes are empirical; others reflect a need to modify the orthodox version of Hopi social structure. Table 6.4 lists both Titiev's designations and modern designations in Hopi English.

Let us take the differences phratry by phratry. In Phratry I, Nagata (1970:233)points out that although both Eggan and Titiev consider the Tobacco clan to have been long extinct in Oraibi, it is clearly represented as being separate from the Rabbit clan at Moencopi. He also notes that one woman in Moencopi claims to be both Kachina clan and Rabbit clan. In Bacavi, Rabbit and Tobacco are regarded as an inseparable clan. Similarly, although Bacavi Rabbit/Tobacco representatives do not claim also to be Kachina clan, they acknowledge that some people in Hotevilla claim all three simultaneously. In the same phratry, there is a similar overlapping of Parrot, Kachina, and Crow clans. Titiev (1944:212,n.d.:27) lists one man, Polingyaoma, as Parrot and Crow in different contexts. The female heads of two households are identified as Parrot and Crow, respectively (Titiev 1944:52–54), but are revealed in Titiev's (n.d.:27a) census notes to be genealogical sisters—a fact confirmed by White's (n.d.) genealogies. In a 1977 census all five of Polingyaoma's grandchildren separately listed their grandfather as Kachina clan (Bacavi Village Census 1977).

Several factors account for this differential attribution of clan names. Variation between self-designation and another's designation is frequent. Titiev (n.d.:27) cites a revealing quotation from his consultant, the Oraibi *Kikmongwi*, Tawaquaptewa, concerning Polingyaoma's close lineal kin: "call selves Gyash [Parrot] but really Crow." Clan identities, it will be recalled, have both positive and negative aspects; which aspect is emphasized depends upon the point of view of the speaker. If the latter is speaking of a member of another clan or of someone who subscribes to an opposing political viewpoint, frequently how he feels personally toward the individual under discussion is important. Hence, in Titiev's census notes, Tawaquaptewa often attributes clan names to members of the Hostile faction which highlight less flattering aspects of their clan affiliation. Conscious, personally motivated choice in the ascription of a descent-group name to a particular individual is thus an important factor.

Similarly, identification of one's own descent-group name when speaking to a nonmember is influenced by a number of considerations, both cultural and personal. Some clans have more prestige than others. Although humility is an important Hopi ideal, some people fall short of it. Thus, some individuals identify their clan affiliations humbly, declining a prestigious identity that may be clearly perceived by others; other individuals deliberately vaunt the most prestigious clan name in their phratry as their own. Individual motives are not exhausted by these two extremes, of course.

In addition, whereas certain clans in the same phratry have had clear, recognizable boundaries between them through time (e.g., Bear and Spider), others have not. Thus, particular lineages or lineage segments that control the clan's sacred objects and knowledge may be more identifiable as the "real" members of such-and-such a clan. Indeed, the term "real" is frequently applied to clans throughout Titiev's census notes; it appears to be a direct translation of *pas*, an emphatic prefix, often a superlative. The attribution of clan identities not in the prime lineage or lineage segment seems more subject to variation. The modern situation is still more fluid with the decline of the ritual order and the correlative absence of public proof that one lineage or segment is the *pas* segment of the clan.

This last factor is especially evident in Phratry III. The problem involves Snake and Lizard divisions. Snake is the more prestigious element here (conceptually equivalent to the *pas* demarcator). In the 1980s all Bacavi members of this phratry section list themselves as Snake, or Rattlesnake (the literally more accurate rendering of *tsu'a*). By Titiev's designations (and we may assume these are via Tawaquaptewa), all these people should be Lizard. Eggan reports only one Snake clan family at Oraibi in the late nineteenth century (see Nagata 1970:234). This "family" became extinct early in the twentieth century. However, for two brothers Titiev records as "real Snake," White (n.d.) shows close genealogical proximity to a subsequent Bacavi lineage.

To complicate matters still further, Voth, who clearly distinguishes between Snake and Lizard clans in his writings, lists several members of the Snake society (who were subsequent residents of Bacavi and who are related to all three modern Bacavi "Snake" lineages) as "Snake clan" (Voth 1903a:282). The two brothers referred to in Titiev's notes were leading members of the Snake society. Likewise, the individuals identified by Voth as Snake clan were prominent Snake society members (interestingly, all those referred to by Titiev as Lizard [and only one "Snake"] were Hostiles). It is as though participation, and especially high office, in the Snake society conferred more of a right to be considered Snake "clan," in contrast to relatives not initiated into the society.

Although we have different stem eponyms for the "clan" groups here (viz., *Tsuungyam* and *Kuukutsngyam*), the same principle seems to be operating as in the use of the term *pas* among other clans. As noted, members of this clan group in Bacavi cite "Snake" as their true clan. Sometimes nonmembers criticize them as "all Lizard," and say that there are no "real" Snake clan members left. Both practices may reflect the desuetude of the Snake society which entails an inability to publicly mark the "real" *Tsuungyam*.

Phratry VII best illuminates the problems of descent-group structure. Titiev (1944:passim) lists three separate Badger clans: "Real" Badger, Gray Badger, and Navajo Badger. The origins of the last two are subject to debate. According to Titiev's notes, the ancestress of the Navajo Badger clan was a Navajo woman who married a Hopi man. Other versions hold that a Badger clan woman was captured by Navajos and lived among them for several years before returning to Oraibi with her children. According to White's genealogies, the Gray Badger branch derives originally from Awatovi.

Queried about these divisions, a Badger clan man did recognize them but dismissed them as insignificant. He explained the differences in terms of relative prestige. "Real Badger," *Pashonanngyam*, is considered more prestigious than the other two, so members of a particular Badger lineage could attribute inferior status to another Badger clansman as a way of elevating themselves or denigrating him. A means of internal descent-group distinction is often sought when Hopis tease each other about this or that clan relative who is widely known for some infraction of social norms. A reply often follows the line, "Well, he's not really one of us *Pashonanngyam*, he's a *Masihonanwungwa* [Gray Badger individual]." The shallow depth of recognition of actual genealogical relationships renders such distinctions more susceptible of debate than in those societies in which genealogical accuracy is an important cultural concern.

A whole series of terms for categories of prestige, referring often

Kinship and Social Structure   183

to color when the name concerns an animal, are really or hypothetically recognized. Thus, with Badger there are several variations on *honanwunga* (Badger descent-group individual). Although there is some doubt at the top end, recognized prefixes, in order of relative prestige, are as follows: *kuwan-* (brightly colored, beautiful); *pavan-* (most important, best); *pas-* (real); *masi-* (gray); *petos-* (brown, dark-colored); *tasap-* (Navajo). The justification for considering these Badger branches as separate clans is doubtful. Although there are, for example, *Honanwungvasa* (Badger "clan-lands") in the Oraibi Valley, there are no separate *Masihonanwungvasa* (Gray Badger "clan-lands"), or *Tasaphonanwungvasa* (Navajo Badger "clan-lands"). Similar ascriptions occur with other descent groups, for example, Bear, Eagle, and Rabbit.

As mentioned in Chapter 3, Hopi clans situate people cosmologically as well as sociologically. In relation to the natural world, descent groups have conceptual rights over an ethnotaxonomic class of natural objects. Thus, Badger members have exclusive rights of symbolic identification in naming practices, for example, with Butterfly (recognized as a recently extinct descent-group designation), Porcupine, and certain medicinal plants (see Bradfield 1973:220–23). Therefore, it is conceivable that someone from the Badger clan could instigate a claim to being really "Porcupine descent group." If such a claim originated in the context of an ongoing social dispute, gradual establishment of "Porcupine" as a conceptually separate descent group might easily occur.

These variations in the pattern of descent-group membership demonstrate that the different clans and phratries identified by Titiev and Eggan are not isomorphic categories belonging to the same structural types. Clans are more distinct in some phratries than in others. In some cases it is doubtful that we can refer to them as separate "clans" at all. In short, ascription of descent-group names in Hopi is not an unambiguous convention: it is loaded with political and social considerations that have nothing to do with genealogy.

It has been suggested in the conventional accounts that, while Hopi has no terms for either "lineage" or "phratry," the terms *-ngyam* and *-wungwa* denote "clan." The issues discussed above make these glosses seem arbitrary. For instance, within the Badger "clan," *Honanngyam* could count either as a phratry term including several clan branches or, alternatively, as a single clan composed of smaller units—possibly Hopi "lineages." The notion that Hopi has no terms for "phratry" or "lineage" is really meaningless and reflects an inordinate bias toward the nominal categories of English-language anthropological usage. The fact that there are no precise terms corresponding to anthropological descent-group categories suggests that these categories may not fit the Hopi situation too well. Adherence to such abstract categories may, in fact, prevent us from identifying particular, concrete terms in Hopi for distinguishing supposedly unnamed categories.

I have elaborated disagreements with the conventional view of Hopi descent groups elsewhere (Whiteley 1985b,1986). The structural and functional variability of Hopi "clans" suggests that the neat, geometric model of isomorphic descent groups with ordered layers of inclusion is not a very precise representation of Hopi social structure. Actual Hopi social units, which have been treated as discrete, frequently shade into each other. Phratries definitely are distinct groupings, coinciding with the boundaries of kin-term usage. For smaller units, clans and lineages operate on a sort of sliding scale between precise differentiation (e.g., the Bear and Spider clans) and rather imprecise conflation (such as in Phratries I, III, and VII).

Phratries within and beyond Bacavi maintain significance in two respects: as the largest exogamic units and as the largest units of kin-term usage. Within Bacavi no phratry contains more than two clans, and four contain only one clan each. Further, in practical terms, only Phratry V contains two significant clan representations with long-term interrelationships in Bacavi. In Phratry II there is only one Spider clan representative. In Phratries III and IV, three clans—Sand, Eagle, and Sun—are recent (re)introductions and comprise single, nuclear families. These have no more than a nominal affiliation with their phratry cohorts in Bacavi. Since the ritual order has largely declined and economic security has considerably increased from the time when famine was a frequent threat, the "mutual aid" characteristic of phratry groupings has become somewhat irrelevant. As mentioned above, clan rivalries are frequently bitterest between phratry mates.

In sum, in modern times lineages, clans, and phratries all give the individual primary identities that orient him/her to the social world, within the village and within Hopi society generally. These identities have significant roots in historical traditions and continue to operate as points of articulation among the social groups they define. Descent groups persist in Bacavi as mutual-aid networks of potential cooperators for particular practices. The functional "corporateness" of clans and lineages, as units controlling land and/or ritual prerogatives, has changed somewhat with the decline of the subsistence economy and of the ritual order. But the conventional view of Hopi descent groups as solidary corporations reflects structural-functionalist theoretical bias. The insistence that lineages and clans constitute distinct groups centered upon corporate estates obscures the realities of Third Mesa Hopi society in pre-split Oraibi, as well as for the late twentieth century. That these descent-group levels are potentially observable is not denied. That they appear in isomorphic forms with parallel functions in the total structure is quite simply not the case. Some of the primary contexts of social action—ritual, politics, and economy—have changed significantly in the twentieth century; however, it seems doubtful that a rigid definition of corporateness was ever applicable to Oraibi descent groups, beyond the fact that they regulated marriage. Prescriptive exogamy marks out the major divisions—between "phratries"; within these groups, criteria of more narrow descent-group identity vary widely.

The descent-group system provides one (very important) kind of template for social action, but it is not incontrovertible, and Hopis seem never to have been troubled by infractions of matrilineal principles other than exogamy. Agnatic ties, especially between fathers and sons, and affinal ties, both between brothers-in-law and between fathers-in-law and sons-in-law, were (and are) often the basis for economic cooperation, religious-society membership, and even inheritance of high office.[4]

Kinship Behavior

With changes in descent-group significance, there have also been changes in kinship behavior. Titiev (1944:15–29) discusses the reciprocal behavior of kin in Oraibi. I shall not reiterate his account here but shall mention two examples of change. As Nagata (1970: 251) points out for Moencopi, fathers have generally become stricter and less indulgent with their children; correlatively, the disciplinary role of the mother's brother has diminished. From the model of the national society, the role of the father seems to have become more prominent. Fathers occasionally object when their brothers-in-law discipline their children. With the softening of traditional descent-group functions, especially for males, and the imposition of the national education system, the uncle's tutelary role has been deprived both of occasions for its practice and of some of its significance.

Nevertheless, when an individual takes a major role in a ceremony—as a sponsor, for example—close clan ties (which are otherwise mostly latent) emerge clearly. The sponsor receives considerable aid from lineage mates and will likely appoint close nephews to particular ritual roles. Thus although descent ties do not have as many occasions for ritual activation as formerly, they are still a vital force in Hopi social organization.

Another relationship has maintained a great deal of behavioral importance in everyday life and on ritual occasions: *kya'a-möyi* (father's sister-brother's son).[5] This relationship is perhaps the most common focus of social amusement. A male's "aunts" (in Hopi English) wash his hair at birth and name him after their clan. From the beginning of his life, they exercise a pretended proprietary sexual interest in him. Few opportunities for sexual banter are missed; the relationship clearly provides much sociable pleasure. When a man marries, his aunts descend upon their brother's (his father's) house, vociferously proclaiming their superior sexual skills, and engage in a mud-fight with the boy's female relatives. Their brother also comes in for a good deal of harassment for having "given away" their nephew to someone else. Though this behavior is largely symbolic, the emphasis on this relationship is maintained throughout life. When a man dies, his aunts wash his hair and prepare him for the world beyond.

Eggan (1950:39) has discussed the importance of this tie in general, but he does not emphasize its effect at the individual level on the entire social structure. Since Hopi kin categories are classificatory and cover whole phratries, as well as the phratries of ritual godfathers, the number of individuals of different descent groups who are involved in *kya'a-möyi* ties probably surpasses all other relationships. For a male, all women of his father's phratry and godfather's phratry are his "aunts." Even with distant aunts in other villages, the relationship is one of emphatic affection and jocularity. Other classificatory relationships seem to focus in practice on those who are genealogically close, but this is not the case with *kya'a-möyi*. Women who act in the ritual roles mentioned will usually be close relatives to the boy's father, but this is not always so. Both sexes are eager to maximize the number of potential aunts or nephews because of the pleasurable character of the relationship.

For the aunt, the range of individual males to whom she is *kya'a* is not limited by descent group. Every male born to every man in her phratry is her *möyi*. Since her male phratry relatives will be married into many other descent groups, the clan affiliations of her nephews are multiple. If we include those males to whom she is a ritual "aunt," the relationship is ramified more widely still.

One has only to witness the closing stages of a Social Dance to see these principles activated and to see them underscored by symbolic economic exchanges. For a Social Dance, a girl, who must be unmarried, chooses her partner from among all her "nephews"; the chosen man is often genealogically distant rather than close. The honored nephew provides her with gifts (minor household utensils are common), and at some later time she will reciprocate with basketry plaques and perhaps some cooked food. Toward the close of the dance, any woman from the audience, married or not, may push in front of the girl to dance with her *möyi*. She may pick any *möyi*, and frequently an elderly woman, much to the audience's amusement, will muscle in on several dance couples.

According to the conventional view of Hopi social structure, strong descent-group ties are seen as threatening integration and thus require mitigation by cross-cutting memberships in other (ritual) groups. But this ignores the structural consequences of formalized cross-sex relationships that unite individuals in *dyadic pairs* rather than in groups. The *kya'a-möyi* tie may give a woman formal, affectionate links with males of every clan outside her phratry. This, I think is a vital aspect of Hopi social structural integration that has been largely overlooked. It remains prominent in Bacavi and shows little modification from the pattern described for Oraibi.

Marriage Patterns

The general features of Bacavi's marriage patterns are shown in Tables 6.5–6.7. Table 6.5 lists marriages involving Bacavi spouses from 1910 to 1981. Though there are surely some omissions, I believe it is fairly complete (it is based on the population sources cited in Chapter 5, especially my own historical household census).

Table 6.5. *Bacavi Marriages, 1910–81*

Origin of Spouse	Number	Percent	Percent of Total
Third Mesa			
Bacavi (individual spouses)	48	22.43	
Hotevilla	44	20.56	
Kykotsmovi	23	10.75	65.0
Moencopi	16	7.48	
Old Oraibi	8	3.74	
Second Mesa			
Shongopavi	17	7.94	
Mishongnovi	4	1.87	11.7
Shipaulovi	4	1.87	
First Mesa			
Polacca[a]	11	5.14	5.1
Non-Hopi			
Navajo	7	3.27	
Apache	7	3.27	
Pima	5	2.33	
Papago	2	0.93	
Zuni	1	0.47	
Laguna	3	1.40	
Mohave	2	0.93	18.2
Shoshone	1	0.47	
Creek	1	0.47	
Omaha	1	0.47	
Anglo	4	1.87	
Hispano	2	0.93	
Non-Hopi unspecified	3	1.40	
TOTAL	214	99.99	100.0

[a]Third Mesa Hopis generally refer to the whole First Mesa area nowadays as "Polacca." They do make distinctions, especially between First Mesa Hopis and Hopi-Tewas, in discussing particular issues, but for purposes such as identification of a spouse's origin, these distinctions are largely ignored.

Table 6.6. Bacavi Marriages by Decade

Origin of Spouse	Age							Total
	20–30	30–40	40–50	50–60	60–70	70–80	80–90	
Females								
Bacavi	1	2	1	2	1	5	8	20
Hotevilla	...	4	4	1	3	1	...	13
Kykotsmovi	1	1	1	2	5	2	1	13
Moencopi	...	2	1	2	...	1	2	8
Old Oraibi	1	1	3	...	...	...	1	6
Shongopavi	4	3	1	3	...	...	...	11
Mishongnovi	1	...	2	...	...	...	...	3
Shipaulovi	...	...	...	1	...	1	...	2
Polacca	1	2	2	1	...	1	...	7
Non-Hopi	2	4	10	4	...	3	1	23
Approximate Decade of Marriage	1970s	1960s	1950s	1940s	1930s	1920s	1910s	106
Males								
Bacavi	1	2	1	2	1	5	8	20
Hotevilla	5	5	5	1	4	1	3	24
Kykotsmovi	...	1	1	4	2	1	1	10
Moencopi	...	...	...	1	2	1	1	5
Old Oraibi	...	...	...	1	...	...	...	1
Shongopavi	2	2	...	...	...	1	1	6
Mishongnovi	...	...	...	...	...	...	...	0
Shipaulovi	...	1	...	1	...	...	...	2
Polacca	...	1	1	1	1	...	...	4
Non-Hopi	1	3	3	4	2	1	1	15
Approximate Decade of Marriage	1970s	1960s	1950s	1940s	1930s	1920s	1910s	87

NOTE: Excludes marriages of those born before 1890, none of whom were living in 1981. The great majority of these were already married in Oraibi before coming to Bacavi. Their subsequent remarriages have not been included. These figures are also used in Table 5.7.

Table 6.7. Summary of Bacavi Marriages

Origin of Spouse	Number	Percent
Females		
Third Mesa	60	56.6
Second Mesa	16	15.1
First Mesa	7	6.6
Non-Hopi	23	21.7
TOTAL	106	100.0
Males		
Third Mesa	60	69.0
Second Mesa	8	9.2
First Mesa	4	4.6
Non-Hopi	15	17.2
TOTAL	87	100.0

An obvious inference is the significant preference for marriage within Third Mesa. From Titiev's census notes (n.d.) it appears that intermarriages between Oraibi people and outsiders at the turn of the century were extremely few. Consultants suggested that in the past parents advised their children against marriages with Second Mesa since "their customs are different from ours—they do everything differently over there." The advice was even stronger with First Mesa people, whose customs were seen (and are still by some) as radically different. The figures in general bear out these preferences, with 65 percent of all Bacavi marriages occurring within Third Mesa society, only 11.7 percent with Second Mesa, and still fewer with First Mesa—5.1 percent. But trends have changed through time and differ according to sex.

From 1910 to 1930 (Table 6.6), the propensity for marrying within Third Mesa, and especially within Bacavi, is high. After the 1920s, marriages within Bacavi diminish while those with Hotevilla and Kykotsmovi increase. Marriages with Second Mesa increase considerably in the 1940s and maintain frequency to the 1980s. Although the numbers are fewer, this pattern seems to apply with First Mesa also. The origin of spouses varies significantly by sex (Tables 6.6 and 6.7). Postmarital residence of those who stay on the reservation heavily favors village uxorilocality. Thus, for a woman marriage mostly does not alter involvement with her natal village: in this respect, her husband's village of origin is not important. For a man, on the other hand, which village he marries into significantly affects his ability to remain active in his natal village, where his personal, ritual, and political commitments are focused. With decreases in the complexity of religious responsibility (see Chapter 7), and with changing modes of transportation, this has become a less restrictive factor.

Tables 6.6 and 6.7 show that a significantly greater proportion of males has married within Third Mesa than females. The consistency with which men have married into Hotevilla is second to none and this has been the dominant pattern since the 1950s. Although women have a high level of marriages with Hotevilla also, it is much less marked. Marriages outside Third Mesa have been much more sporadic for men than for women. Marriage with non-Hopis forms the second largest class for both men and women, after Third Mesa. In a sense, this is a misleading class since it comprises those from a variety of origins; it achieves significance by comparison to intra-Hopi marriages. I have noted the economic reasons for off-reservation residence and they are also very likely related to the incidence of marriage with non-Hopis. Titiev's census notes indicate that Oraibi marriages with non-Hopis were extremely few; the great increase seems to be a twentieth-century phenomenon. The most obvious cause is the education system. Most Hopi teenagers go to off-reservation boarding schools, where they interact with students of other Indian backgrounds; opportunities for forming non-Hopi attachments are much greater than in the past. In this category, also, Bacavi women have married out more often than men.

In sum, Bacavi people have generally married within Third Mesa, especially within Bacavi, and secondly with Hotevilla. The strength of preference changes over time and is more marked for men than for women. Outmarriages with other Hopi villages beyond Third Mesa have increased, particularly for women, since the 1940s. Outmarriage with non-Hopis has been fairly consistent over time, though with significant increases (which subsequently fell off) in the 1940s and 1950s.

7
◨ Ritual, Politics, and Some Broader Contexts

Contemporary Ceremonial Patterns

For the most part, Bacavi's ceremonial practices in the 1980s are limited to Kachina and Social Dances. During the 1950s and 1960s, very few Kachina dances occurred, and the kivas fell into disuse. In the 1960s, this decline coincided with increased participation in the Mennonite church, while a rather zealous missionary family was in residence. The 1970s saw a great increase of interest in Kachina dances. An average of one night dance and one plaza dance have taken place every year since about 1972. This renewal of interest coincided with the departure of the missionaries, but it also reflects the resurgence of Native American traditionalism nationwide (McNickle 1973).

Bacavi's *Powamuy* (Bean Dance) in February consists of a slightly modified Kachina night dance. The grand pageantry of a traditional whipping-initiation *Powamuy* (as still practiced in the 1980s in Shongopavi and to a lesser extent in Hotevilla, Mishongnovi, and Walpi) is much attenuated, although there are rumors that parts may be revived. Despite the abbreviation, Bacavi's performance involves a serious commitment of time and energy by the participants. Beans are sprouted in the kivas, beginning roughly ten days before the public performances. Coal from the Peabody Coal Mine at Black Mesa is gathered in abundance for kiva supplies by parties of men.

Each kiva represents a different group of Kachinas. Shortly after dawn on the morning of the ceremony, several Kachinas emerge from the *katsinki* (Kachina resting place) or their kivas and distribute bean plants around the village to the women of every household, with Kachina dolls and small woven plaques for uninitiated girls and painted bows and arrows for uninitiated boys. The Kachinas then retire to their kivas, and the women add the bean plants to mutton and hominy for *haruqwivi* (bean stew), which is served from midday on to many relatives and friends. Should the whipping initiation be revived it will likely follow Hotevilla's pattern, involving an afternoon-long procession of multifarious Kachinas led by *Heehe'iwuuti*. At night the special *Powamuy* Kachinas (see Voth 1901) would perform in the kivas (unlike in the early 1980s; see below).

Toward midnight, a Kachina night dance takes place. Each group of Kachinas visits each kiva; sometimes a visiting group comes from another village. After the dances, for those being initiated—who tend to fall in the six–ten age range as formerly (although there may be older individuals also)—there follows the major period of instruction. Though less elaborate than a traditional whipping initiation, it serves as the rite of passage from the spiritual innocence of infancy to a deeper understanding of the significance of Kachinas.

Thus, though abbreviated, Bacavi's *Powamuy* is still an extended ritual occasion and constitutes the most important one of the year. During the 1960s there were very few *Powamuy* celebrations in Bacavi. Several Bacavi children were initiated in other villages for fear that there would be no further opportunity at home.

Next in importance to *Powamuy*, a modified *Niman* (Home Dance) is usually performed, although not every year. It is more important than other Kachina plaza dances, although its observable form is not very different. Without the traditional priests for more esoteric *Niman* rituals, there is no final blessing in the *tipkya* ("womb" of the village), as occurs at Hotevilla or at First Mesa and

Second Mesa. Nevertheless, Bacavi's *Niman* in 1980 displayed more traditional features than a usual Kachina dance. The Kachinas chosen for personation were *Angaktsinam* (Long Hair Kachinas), a type traditionally associated with *Niman* at Third Mesa. The sponsor insisted on the observance of other traditional customs, such as the quiet distribution of Hopi artifacts and foods to particular audience members. In contrast, most Kachina plaza dances at all villages in the 1980s include a melee during the last dance, with the random throwing of oranges, apples, carrots, cookies, candy, and so on, for which younger spectators noisily vie. The absence of this at Bacavi's 1980 Home Dance—and its concomitant higher seriousness—was much remarked upon, even meriting praise in the local newspaper (*Qua' Töqti* 8-7-1980).

Other ceremonial performances, more secular in nature, are regaining popularity. Social Dances in August or September are grand communal occasions that typically involve dance groups from other villages as well. Bacavi's Butterfly Dance in 1981, for example, was "raided" by groups from Upper Moencopi, Kykotsmovi, and Hotevilla. A raiding group passes into the *kiisonvi* while the home group is moving out. The singers compete with each other, trying to drown out the others and confuse their dancers. The result is a voluble and impressive cacophony.

As well as Kachina and Social Dances, there is some evidence that ceremonial revitalization is embracing other forms. In 1982, Bacavi put on a winter Buffalo Dance (similar to Rio Grande Pueblo game-animal dances), which, though not a masked or society performance, is thought of as more significant than the late-summer Social Dances. It was their first Buffalo Dance since 1938, from which some of the same songs were taken. In 1984, Bacavi men conducted a four-day rabbit hunt, after Hotevilla's *Soyalangw*-related *Qööqöqlöm* Kachina perfomance (Hotevilla men conducted a separate hunt). Bacavi then held a rabbit-stew feast in its Community Center. Though not significant ritually per se (no other elements of *Soyalangw* were enacted), the hunt represents an instance of traditional revival which originally had a ritual context. Again, in November 1985, Bacavi conducted an *Owaqöl* performance, or Basket Dance. This was an even more notable renewal, since in former times, the *Owaqölt* was a religious society requiring initiation, and since Bacavi's previous performance had been in the early 1920s. As with the Buffalo Dance, some of the same songs were taken from the previous performance, suggesting a remarkable persistence over time (and without ceremonial context) of oral literature in song.

Although my ordering of Hopi religious societies (Chapter 3) includes *Owaqölt* in the second order, Third Mesa performances in the 1980s (i.e., in Hotevilla) have been extensively secularized. Any woman or young girl (including some not yet Kachina-initiated) may participate; there is no initiation of members, no male or female priests, no altar, and therefore no society in the traditional sense. This contrasts markedly with the Hotevilla Snake and Antelope societies, for example, which maintained rigorously traditional observances until their demise in 1980. Thus, although Bacavi's *Owaqöl* suggests a noteworthy resurgence of a traditional form, the forms susceptible of resuscitation and the manner in which they may be resuscitated are limited. Basket Dances have a significant element of the communal sociability of Social Dances: large quantities of household goods are thrown at random by young *Owaqöl* women into a rambunctious crowd of male spectators who fight for them with great gusto. It seems inconceivable, within the prevailing ideology, that more serious ritual performances, such as the Flute, Snake, or those of any of the first-order societies could be reinvigorated.

Bacavi's ceremonial activities are not confined to performances within the village itself. Groups of performers from the village occasionally visit other villages (see below on intervillage relations). Further, Bacavi groups occasionally participate in nontraditional occasions (such as "Indian Day" at Hotevilla-Bacavi Community School, or the dedication of new buildings on the reservation) when Social Dances are held. A group of Bacavi women (with floating membership) is well known for such performances.

Ritual activities, particularly *Powamuy* and the Kachina performances, provide a critical benchmark for changing perceptions of cultural identity. Formerly, to become a fully adult Hopi, a man had to be initiated into one of the *Wuwtsim* societies.[1] Now that these societies have all but disappeared from Third Mesa, the question of cultural identity has shifted, so to speak, from what it means to be a fully adult Hopi, to what it means to be Hopi at all. This issue is pervasive in Hopi discourse. Perhaps the most critical issue is linguistic persistence. Most Bacavi residents over the age of twenty in the 1980s understand and speak at least some Hopi. Some frequently have difficulty with complexities of the language which their elders use on an everyday basis, and admit that their speaking knowledge of "street Hopi" is much lacking in the richness of their grandparents' idioms. For children and teenagers, the situation is more marked. Especially since the introduction of television around 1970, increasing numbers are monolingual in English. With television, storytelling in the winter months (a traditional form of entertainment during which much cultural knowledge was communicated to children in linguistically educational narrative forms) has practically ceased. Instructions to younger people participating in dances must frequently be translated into English, often to the chagrin of the ritual leaders, and not many younger voices are heard singing at the dances. The situation is slightly better at Hotevilla and Second Mesa, and elsewhere it is the same or even more marked: many First Mesa adults in their twenties cannot speak Hopi. The muted and shallow understanding of cultural traditions which results is keenly felt by many concerned to see their cultural heritage maintained.

It is against this background that Kachina performance and initiation has become a critical index of cultural identity. Many Third Mesa people welcomed the decline of the higher-order religious societies since they involved heavy responsibilities that curtailed freedom of action. *Wuwtsim* entailed the complete loss of spiritual innocence and concomitant exposure to dangerous supernatural forces. The uninitiated are regarded as "safe" from these dangers. Hence, the prophecies of religious decline (see Chapter 8) referred largely to the higher-order societies. There is a pervasive notion at Third Mesa (and it is present at the other Mesas also, though less markedly) that at some point all that would remain of the traditional religious cycle would be the Kachina ceremonies; in contrast to the higher-order societies, Kachinas are unambiguously beneficial and it is regarded as highly desirable that performances should persist.

Kooninkatsinam (Havasupai Kachinas), Bacavi, 1924. Photographer unknown, Special Collections, University of Arizona Library, Tucson.

Kachina ceremonies thus symbolize a "bottom line" of significant cultural identity, in spite of the fact that the seriousness of intent to procure vital blessings of rain for life-supporting crops is to a large extent lost on younger performers, who are mostly not involved in the subsistence economy or do not understand the words of the songs. They may be criticized by older cohorts for lack of comprehension and merely aesthetic participation motivated by vanity. To confirm this, older people remark on the increasing number of fast-paced dances with "a lot of action," including *Qa'ökatsinam* (Corn Dancers), *Kooninkatsinam* (Havasupai Kachinas), and *Navankatsinam* (Velvetshirts). In contrast, slower-paced, more low-key performances were prevalent in the past. Also, clown ceremonies, entertaining as they are, are felt by some older people to occur too often and to diminish the seriousness with which people should appreciate the Kachinas.

Thus although Kachina ceremonies are flourishing, their meaning has partially altered under the influences of other sociocultural changes. Their significance in the agricultural cycle remains strong in the minds of some participants, but for others they are mostly artistic performances rather than religious imperatives crucial to sustain the chain of life.

Bacavi's Changing Ceremonial Patterns

Bacavi originally had a fuller ceremonial calendar, although, contrary to Titiev's assumption (1944:212–13), there was no attempt to recreate the ceremonial cycle *in toto*, for reasons which will become clear in Chapter 8. During its early years, Bacavi had the following ceremonies: *Wuwtsim*, Blue Flute, *Powamuy*, *Niman*, *Owaqöl*. It never had a full *Soyalangw*, nor Snake-Antelope, Gray Flute, *Maraw*, or *Lakon* (though some vestigial observances by initiates were made at the appropriate times of the year, especially, for example, at *Soyalangw*, with the personation of *Qööqöqlöm* Kachinas and the making of prayer feathers).

The first Kachina dance (which featured *Soyohim*, Mixed Kachinas) was held at night around a bonfire (since no kiva was yet built), probably in early 1910. A short time after this, *Maamalom* (*Maalo* Kachinas) came from Shipaulovi, evidently to cheer up the Bacavi people on account of their miserable circumstances. The first *Powamuy* took place in 1911, and several children were initiated.

It is doubtful that the first *Wuwtsim* celebrations occurred before 1912. Poliikiva was originally built (between 1910 and 1912) for *Powamuy*. Its later role as the home of *Wuwtsim* was not part of the initial plan. *Wuwtsim*, it is said, was reinstituted (despite considerable dispute) not for the religious benefit of the community, but out of felt duty on the part of initiates and pride in parading the performative machinations of their "power." A rift occurred between Kewanimptewa, who opposed the resurrection of *Wuwtsim*, and some Badger clan men. The latter prevailed, but the ceremonies did not last long.

Wuwtsim took place in its complete form two or three times, and then began to be curtailed by the mid-1910s (since five of the more knowledgeable, older participants died before 1917 [U.S. Government 1910–1917:passim]). Abbreviated performances occurred into the mid-1920s, and one *kwaanitaqa* (One-Horn man) continued to make annual observations, alone, into the late 1930s.

Lomahongyoma was the head of Bacavi's *Wuwtsim*, and Poliikiva acquired the name Sakwalenvi, after Oraibi's chief kiva of

Ritual and Politics

Soyohim (Mixed) Kachinas in Bacavi, ca. 1911–15. Photograph by Emry Kopta, Museum of the American Indian, Heye Foundation, New York City.

which Lomahongyoma had been head, in honor of his position. Talaswuhioma (Badger) led the *Kwaakwant*, which met at Kwan kiva. There were two active *Taatawkyam*, who were siblings (neither assumed the title *Tawmongwi*, Singer Chief), who used either Poliikiva or a private house. Polingyaoma (Kachina clan) led the few *Aa'alt* who met at the hogan of Talashoyoma (Badger clan, and a Two-Horn man).[2]

The *Owaqölt* performed into the early 1920s. I am unable to determine whether it had priestly leaders and conducted esoteric rituals, or whether it had already assumed a more secular form.

Lomahongyoma was head of the Blue Flute society. The Oraibi altar was kept in his niece's (Kewanimptewa's wife's) house, which thereby assumed the status of *Kookyangwungwki* (Spider "clanhouse"). A *leenangwva* (Flute spring) was sacralized for the ceremony. Bacavi had several of Oraibi's Blue Flute officers (cf. Voth n.d.b). But curation of the altar was disputed by Lomayestewa, Lomahongyoma's brother at Hotevilla, who wanted to perform the ceremony there. Lomahongyoma held onto the altar, and Bacavi performed the ceremony, until his death in June 1919 (U.S. Government 1919). Bacavi, then, performed the ceremony three or four times, the last one probably in 1917. After Lomahongyoma's death, his son, Wishövioma, passed the altar to Lomayestewa and the ceremony moved to Hotevilla. Blue Flute was the only second-order society in Bacavi to initiate; approximately twenty youngsters were initiated, although no attempt was made to keep the society going after Lomahongyoma's death.

The full *Powamuy* continued until deaths of the principal priests, Nasiquaptewa (Badger) and Polingyaoma (Kachina) in the late 1940s. Neither priest passed on his office. *Powamuy* and *Niman* were well supplied with officiants, since six of the Badger clan contingent were *Powamuywiwimkyam* (*Powamuy* members). The last full *Niman* with *Hemiskatsinam* (Hemis Kachinas) was held in the early 1940s. Nasiquaptewa and Polingyaoma held important roles in *Niman* also, together with Pongyaquaptewa (Badger).

Historically, Bacavi's Kachina performances occasionally featured more esoteric, more "powerful" Kachinas than appear in modern times. At *Powamuy* the *Sooyoko* ("ogre") Kachinas appeared periodically. Third Mesa people say these were more dangerous at Third Mesa (some children actually died of fright, it is said) than at Second Mesa or First Mesa (where they still appear annually) and were summoned only rarely to punish incorrigible children. Further, although little of *Soyalangw* was observed, *Qöö-qöqlöm* (untranslatable) Kachinas—the first group of the year who "open" the kivas after *Soyalangw*—were personated into the 1930s.

Bacavi also conducted a *Saalako* performance in the mid-1920s. Hopi *Saalako* (distinctly different from Zuni) is an elaborate, seemingly ancient, and highly sacred Kachina performance, occurring roughly every ten years, in association with the *Niman* ceremony. The sponsor (a Greasewood clan man) married into Hotevilla, where he was initiated into the *Kwaakwant* in 1924; traditionally at Third Mesa, *Saalako* was periodically performed at *Niman* following *Wuwtsim* initiations the previous November. The Bow clan owned the *Saalako* at Oraibi but this clan was gradually dying out (there have been no living representatives since the 1960s). The sponsor's mother, Kewanquapnim, had inherited the *Saalako* sacra (Greasewood is a phratry cohort of Bow) and kept them in her

Ritual and Politics

house at Bacavi. *Saalako* was a rare event (no other performances have ever been recorded by outsiders at Third Mesa: Barton Wright, personal communication). It was revived at Shongopavi in 1939, the first performance there since the nineteenth century, and has been conducted there since then roughly every ten years, including in 1981.

Sopkyaoma, a fairly esoteric ritual drama connected with the harvest (see Titiev 1944:184–87), was performed twice by Bacavi people. The sponsor may well have been Lomanaksu (Parrot clan), who had been head of *Lalkont* at Oraibi, since *sopkyaoma* was connected with this society.

With the last appearances of the more sacred Kachina ceremonies connected with higher-order religious societies in the 1940s, the progressive secularization (from a Hopi perspective) of Bacavi had reached its final stages. For the most part, all that was left were ordinary Kachina ceremonies. The mechanics of this decline are fairly clear, its motivations more complex. First, no important ritual offices were passed on by their incumbents (who traditionally hold the right to refuse to do so). When they died, the ceremonies simply ceased or were maintained in much-abbreviated form. Second, no first-order society initiations were ever conducted in Bacavi, and although there were initiations into the second-order Blue Flute society, these do not involve such a demanding, lifelong commitment. The character of supernatural power invoked in the Blue Flute ceremony is unambiguously beneficial, specifically involving a purificatory purpose. *Wuwtsim* powers are more dangerous and thoroughly ambivalent. Older consultants regard the absence of *Wuwtsim* initiations in Bacavi as a deliberate policy of the priests.

It might be postulated that the absence of *Wuwtsim* initiations was owing to a lack of priests (with the necessary knowledge and authority). After all, as Table 7.1 shows, Bacavi's total male population over the age of sixteen amounted to only thirty-three individuals—considerably less than Hotevilla's or Oraibi's. The conclusion that there was a shortage of priests, however, could not be more incorrect.

When discussing the earliest founders of the village, older consultants repeatedly emphasized several as *pavansinom* (important,

Table 7.1. Bacavi's Clan and Ceremonial Groups, 1910

Phratry	Clan	Men[a]	Women[a]	Wuwtsim Sakwalenvi	Wuwtsim Hawiovi	Wuwtsim Tsu Kiva	Kwan	Al	Taw	Blue Flute	Snake	Antelope	Powamuy	Momtsit	Maraw	Owaqöl	Lakon
I	Rabbit	0	1														1
I	Parrot	1	0	1						1							1[b]
I	Kachina-Crow	1	0					1					1				
II	Bear	0	2							1							
II	Spider	2	1	2						2[c]		1		2			
III	Sand	3	0	1	1		1										
III	Lizard	6	6			2	1				3	1[c]		2	2	2	
III	Snake	1	0			1					1						
IV	Eagle	2	1	2		1	1			1	1	1		1	1	1	1
V	Greasewood	1	8	1								1[c]	1		4	6	2
V	Reed	3	2			1				1	1				2	0	
VI	Coyote	1	1												1	1	1
VI	Desert Fox	5	5	1	1		1		1	3	1				2	1	3
VII	Gray Badger	6	2	1				2	2				6[c]				
VII	Navajo Badger	1	0			1				1			1				
	TOTAL	33	29	9	2	6	4	3	3	10	7	4	9	5	12	11	9

NOTE: Compare with Titiev (1944:212). Ceremonial ties refer to affiliations while resident at Oraibi.
[a] These figures are discrepant with those in Table 5.3. "Adults" here includes those (roughly over 16 years old) who were initiated into higher-order societies.
[b] One man was in this society.
[c] One woman was in this society.

powerful people). The following statements (translated from Hopi) are illustrative:

[A]: Almost all of the ceremonies were observed in Bacavi. We had people who were initiated into all the societies and also many people who came here were extraordinary people, people who had extraordinary powers. Thus we know that they were able to carry out the full responsibilities of the religious societies.

[B]: There is another thing about which there is no doubt. Some of these people who came over here were really old. They were people who had complete belief in Hopi religion, and were able to grow a lot of corn, beans, and watermelons right around the village where it seemed like there was hardly any soil. This was because of their faith. . . . Right where the main village is now was all farmed and especially near the site of the Community Building. This was possible because these people had one heart and one mind: all their prayers were together and they had complete understanding of the religion. It is said that other villages were envious of what the people were able to do here with their farming.

[C]: I have to say that I admire and respect these older people who came here. I cannot overemphasize their dedication and their knowledge of the Hopi way. People from other villages came for their advice and assistance, because they realized this was indispensable.

Shortly after Bacavi was established, Mishongnovi sent a group of Kachinas to honor the new village. Bacavi reciprocated soon after, returning a group of Kachinas to dance at Mishongnovi. Older consultants interpret this exchange as particularly significant, since Mishongnovi has a Hopi-wide reputation as a supernaturally powerful village:

[A]: The people at Mishongnovi are known for their great powers. They were *popwaqt* [perhaps best translated here as "exceptional individuals with transformative supernatural knowledge"] and they had extraordinary abilities to control the forces of nature and the world. This was also the reputation of the Bacavi people. It was because of this relationship between the two villages that these dances were held. . . . Based on this comparison between the two villages, I am not exaggerating when I say that our old people were also extraordinarily powerful. They brought over the knowledge of these powers from Oraibi.

[B]: The knowledge and power of these old people explains why they settled here in a desolate, barren place. They had abilities to control the weather—to bring rain, to make it cold, or warm. We do not possess their abilities or their knowledge now, and for this reason it makes it hard to believe. Some of us even have genuine doubts that those people had such powers, especially nowadays, when we are living a completely different lifestyle. People today cannot really understand this.

My own reaction was initially doubtful. The view that Bacavi originally had a large and exceptional contingent of *pavansinom* probably derived, I thought, from a mixture of nostalgia and a current feeling of ritual inferiority toward Hotevilla, Bacavi's dominating neighbor. And if this were really the case, why had Bacavi not reconstituted an extensive ceremonial cycle? However, through the gradual compilation of names, clan identities, and religious-society offices of the founding members of the village—from consultants' memories, Titiev's (n.d.) census notes of Oraibi, and finally, annual government censuses of the village from 1910 on—my skepticism disappeared. *Pavansinom* characteristics of a number of individuals, disproportionate to village size, began to emerge. Let us examine some:

LOMAHONGYOMA had been (see Chapter 4) one of the most important leaders of the Oraibi Hostiles. He was rival *Kikmongwi* to Loololma, head of the Spider clan, head of Oraibi's chief kiva, leader of the Hostiles' *Soyalangw* after Loololma's ejection from the chief kiva, head of the Blue Flute society, and a prominent member of the Warriors' society (his mother's brother had been its head [Titiev 1944:73]).

LOMANAKSU (remembered in modern times as "Melooni"; he appears in government censuses as "Setalava") was the head of Oraibi's Parrot clan, chief-priest of the *Lalkont*, an officer in *Soyalangw*, a leading member of *Wuwtsim* at Sakwalenvi (the chief kiva), and a member of the Blue Flute society. According to Titiev (1944:245), he was also head of Oraibi's Taw kiva, although he was not a member of *Taatawkyam*. Lomanaksu was Loololma's *Wuwtsim* godfather, and gave the name "Loololma" after his clan (*loololma* means "beautiful" (pl.); the reference is to a design of parrot feathers). His selection as the (future) *Kikmongwi*'s godfather is an especially significant mark of his status, since the godfather is responsible for much ritual instruction. Early on, he had supported the Friendlies, but he later changed sides.

MASANGÖNTEWA was one of the Hostile leaders who confronted Cushing in 1882. He was chief-priest of the Snake society in the 1890s and may have been the head of the Snake clan (this is debatable—Titiev, probably from Friendly bias, lists him as Lizard clan, but see Voth 1903a:passim), chief-priest of *Wuwtsim* at the Snake kiva (one of four main branches of *Wuwtsim*), head of the Snake kiva, *qaleetaqa* (guardian) in *Soyalangw*, and a member of the Warriors' society.

NAA'USITEWA was a member of the Greasewood clan, an officer in the Blue Flute society (Voth 1912b:135,n.d.b), a member of *Wuwtsim* at Sakwalenvi, and a member of the Warriors' society. There may be other factors marking him as a *pavansino*, since my older consultants consistently emphasized him as such; I have been unable to determine them, however.

KEWANIMPTEWA was Bacavi's chief, Sand clan, and the emerging leader of the returned Hostiles in Oraibi. He was married to Lomahongyoma's sister's daughter and was initiated into *Kwaakwant*, the most exclusive and smallest of the *Wuwtsim* societies, regarded as conferring fearsome supernatural powers (cf. Titiev 1944:134; Nequatewa 1936:104 n. 10). Kewanimptewa is generally regarded throughout Hopi society as having been an exceptional man, a clairvoyant, and a *powaqa* (with both positive and negative connotations, depending on the speaker). As agency policeman in the 1910s, he was the object of much fear in Hotevilla (particularly concerning the rounding up of children for school)—despite intense political opposition— for his reputed supernatural power. His father, Naawungni'ima, had been Kachina clan head in Oraibi and Kachina chief in *Niman* and *Powamuy*. His two brothers, Qötsaquahu (see below) and Humiyestewa, both had prominent ritual roles: Humiyestewa was chief-priest of *Taatawkyam* in Hotevilla. Two close lineage mates (mother's sister's sons)—Qöyahöinewa and Naquaheptewa—were head of *Wuwtsimt* and *Kwaakwant*, respectively, in Hotevilla. His lineage was thus of considerable ritual importance, although I cannot specify exactly why, since there is very little information available about the next ascending generation.

NASINGAINEWA (a.k.a. Yooki) was a veteran of Alcatraz, the oldest to be sent there, although he lived into the 1920s. He was Eagle clan, one of the last three initiates into *tsutskut*, the Clown society, of which his brother, Qoyatpela, was chief-priest (suggesting that they were of the core Eagle lineage segment, since this was the Eagle clan's main ritual). He was a member of *Wuwtsim* at Sakwalenvi and was a major *tuuhikya* (medicine man), one of only three "old time doctors" in Oraibi, according to Tawaquaptewa (Titiev 1972:69).

TUUTUSPA was Masangöntewa's brother (Snake clan) and an officer in the Snake society. He was a member of *Wuwtsim* at Snake kiva and a member of the Warriors' society.

SUUKAOMA (Snake clan) was another leading officer in the Snake society (Voth 1903a:278); his brother, Kuktiwa, was chief-priest for a time (Voth 1903a:273). He belonged to *Wuwtsim* at Snake kiva.

LOMAMSAI'IMA (a.k.a. Dilko) was Coyote clan and a member of *Taatawkyam* and the Snake society. He is regarded as having been an important man, though I am unaware of any ritual offices.

QÖTSAQUAHU, Kewanimptewa's brother, is recorded by Titiev only as a member of *Wuwtsim* at Sakwalenvi. Older consultants (from Hotevilla and Bacavi) recall that he had a leading role in Oraibi's *Wuwtsim*. When Hotevilla wanted to reinstitute *Wuwtsim* initiations in the early 1920s, Qötsaquahu was requested to help (evidently by Yukioma, who repeatedly visited him at his field),[3] since he was regarded as the only man in either village with a full knowledge of *Wuwtsim* songs and rites from Oraibi's chief kiva. He also led a group of *patsavu* Kachinas from Bacavi to Hotevilla during the following *Powamuy*; this ceremony "seals" the *Wuwtsim* initiations of the previous November.

GYASHHONGNEWA was Lomahongyoma's brother (Spider). Voth (n.d.c) records that he had charge of the Blue Flute altar for a time in Oraibi. He was a member of Oraibi's Antelope society and later became head of Hotevilla's Antelope society (although he continued to live in Bacavi). He was a *tuuhikya* (medicine man) in Oraibi (Titiev n.d.:passim records a total of thirteen).

PONGYALETSTEWA (Coyote clan) belonged to *Wuwtsim* at Snake kiva. His father had been the Antelope society head. It was his Bear clan wife who died in Oraibi shortly before the second split.

Apart from these associations with *pavansino* status, he was widely recognized as an expert horticulturist who had supernatural abilities with particular cultigens. This special power is selectively hereditary. From Pongyaletstewa, it passed through a matriline and in the 1980s is "owned" by a Hotevilla man married into Bacavi.

In addition to these figures, Polingyaoma (Kachina clan) had enough ritual knowledge to install Bacavi's *kiisonvi pahoki* (plaza shrine) and was Oraibi's only lightning medicine man (Titiev 1972:22). Nasequaptewa (Badger) was one of five men who regularly served as Kachina father at Oraibi. Several other men had minor ritual offices and were associated by kinship or affinity with high-status clan segments.

Of Bacavi's founding women, a number likewise stand out as important, although the division of labor generally did not give women political or ritual importance of the same nature as men's. Women's social standing is often reflected in natal and affinal kin groups. My consultants indicated that those of higher social rank used to intermarry as much as possible (cf. Nagata 1970:44); for example, one woman from a *"sukavung"* (commoner) clan married to a Bear clan man emphasized that in former times such a union would have been most unusual. A few of Bacavi's *pavansino* women included:

KATSINMANA[4] (Eagle clan) had been married to Tuuvi, the early leader of Moencopi and intermediary with the Mormons. In her natal kin group, her father, Kelwistewa of the Cedar clan, had been Oraibi's *Kwanmongwi* (head of the One-Horn society).

KEWANHÖINIM was a leading officer in Oraibi's *Mamrawt*. She was married to Masangöntewa (see above).

TUWAMÖINIM (Reed clan) was an officer in *Mamrawt*. She had been married to Masangöntewa and later to Nasingainewa (above).

NASIMÖISI was of the core Greasewood clan segment that supplied the *Tsa'akmongwi* (Crier Chief) and owned the *Yaayat*, a now-defunct "Conjurers" society. She was married to Suukaoma (above); her sister, Jorsmöinim (who died before 1906), was married to Patupha, the early Hostile leader, and was female head of the *Lalkont*.

TAWANIMSI (Snake clan) was married to Talaswytewa upon coming to Bacavi. Her first husband had been Tuviyesva (Bear clan), who became head of *Soyalangw* (this office is shared among Bear members of the core segment, rather than always performed by the *Kikmongwi*) in the Friendly version after they were ejected from Sakwalenvi. He was killed by Navajos around 1900.

This array of important men and women was quite disproportionate to Bacavi's population size. It is impossible to ascertain definitively how disproportionate it was in comparison to Oraibi, Hotevilla, and Moencopi. Sources on Oraibi politico-religious officers in pre-1906 Oraibi are in several instances contradictory, so it is not feasible to construct a totally reliable list. I have chosen, then, to use just one source for the sake of consistency (and because it is probably the most complete): Titiev's census notes of Oraibi prior to the split. Tables 7.2 and 7.3, constructed from this source, indicate the post-split distribution of chief-priests in the religious societies and the extent of their representation relative to population size in the post-split villages.

I must stress several caveats with these tables. As noted in Chap-

Table 7.2. *Distribution of Third Mesa Politico-Religious Leaders (male only), 1906–9*

Society/ Ceremony	Pre-Split Oraibi, 1906	Post-Split Oraibi (+ Moencopi)	Hotevilla ca. 1907	Bacavi 1909	Bacavi's Percentage of Pre-Split Total	Bacavi's Percentage of Hostile Total
Soyalangw	3	2	...	1	33.3	100.0
Wuwtsim	4	2	...	2	50.0	100.0
Kwan	2	2	...	...	0	...
Al	2	1	1	...	0	0
Taw	2	2	...	...	0	...
Blue Flute	1	...	...	1	100.0	100.0
Gray Flute	1	1	...	...	0	...
Snake	2	...	1	1	50.0	50.0
Antelope	2	...	2	...	0	0
Powamuy	3	3	...	...	0	...
Maraw	1	1	...	...	0	...
Owaqöl	1	1	...	...	0	...
Lakon	1	...	...	1	100.0	100.0
TOTAL	25	15	4	6	24.0	60.0

SOURCE: Titiev (n.d.)

Table 7.3. Distribution of Third Mesa (male)
Politico-Religious Leaders in Relation to Population Size,
1906–9

Location	Population	Officers	Ratio of Officers to Total
Total Population			
Pre-Split Oraibi (including Moencopi)	863	25	1:34.5
Post-Split Oraibi (including Moencopi)	450	15	1:30
Hostiles, 1906	413	10	1:41.3
Bacavi, 1909	127	6	1:21.1
Adult Males			
Pre-Split Oraibi (including Moencopi)	336	25	1:13.4
Post-Split Oraibi (including Moencopi)	172	15	1:11.5
Hostiles, 1906	164	10	1:16.4
Bacavi, 1909	33	6	1:5.5

SOURCE: Titiev (n.d.).

ter 3, Titiev's main consultants for this census were Friendlies (specifically Tawaquaptewa: Fred Eggan, personal communication), who occasionally downgraded Hostile *pavansinom*.[5] This factor, I think, contributes significantly to the imbalance of officers in favor of the Friendlies. Other sources, including Voth's published and unpublished works, and Titiev's own *Old Oraibi*, list other individuals as chief-priests besides those mentioned in the census notes—none of these are included. The tables take no account of those who were not chief-priests but who were significant officers (such as Qötsaquahu, above). Neither do the tables include factional political leaders, such as Yukioma, Kewanimptewa, or other men consensually regarded as "powerful," such as Nasingainewa or Pongyaletstewa. I strongly believe that, if these and secondary ceremonial officers were included, the disproportion in Bacavi's favor would be greater still, but this must remain speculative since it cannot be conclusively demonstrated. Further, the proportional distribution incorporates an element of chance: only those who were still alive in 1906–9 (based on Titiev's notations) are included, so some offices feature more than one individual but others do not. The population distribution among the villages is difficult to establish with complete precision because of discrepant figures.[6] Finally, of course, we are dealing with such small figures that random variation could be invoked to statistically vitiate the tables' significance.

Despite all these caveats, the tables would generally confirm the thesis that Bacavi was more disproportionately peopled with *pavansinom* than any other village after the split. The demise of the religious societies in Bacavi cannot thus be attributed to an absence of those with the requisite knowledge. In fact, by this standard (and especially if we include individuals omitted from the tables) Bacavi was capable of recreating a far more complete cycle than Hotevilla. The reasons it did not do so are discussed in Chapter 8.

Political Structure

Bacavi's governmental history parallels changing ceremonial patterns. Modern governance is secularized, although religious overtones emerge periodically. The village is administered by an elected governor and Board of Directors, consisting of a lieutenant governor, treasurer, secretary, sergeant-at-arms, Tribal Council representative, and approximately four members-at-large. These are all unpaid positions except for the secretary and the Council representative (compensated by the Tribal Council), who sits on the Tribal Council in Kykotsmovi and acts as formal liaison between the village and the Council. In practice, a community development specialist (a federally funded position) frequently acts as an informal village representative because he/she is continuously available (for example, to plaintiffs from nearby Hotevilla who do not recognize the Tribal Council) at the Community Center. The governor (whose role is not executive, as he/she is simply titular head of the board) and Board of Directors largely have deliberative rather than legislative authority, and their decisions are often not enforceable by coercive resources. The board meets formally at irregular intervals, roughly every two to three weeks. Meetings are conducted mostly in Hopi and, where necessary, follow a procedural order based loosely on Tribal constitutional procedure and parliamentary rules of order. A draft village constitution and by-laws, based on those formally instituted in the villages of Kykotsmovi and Upper Moencopi (the latter is legally incorporated under Arizona state law), has not yet been officially adopted. Board meetings can be open or closed and raise issues of local import considered in ranked order—from the serious land dispute with Hotevilla to the writing of village history by a certain English ethnographer.

There is no village police force. Situations requiring coercive force depend on Bureau of Indian Affairs Hopi Tribal Police and, in extreme cases, upon the Federal Bureau of Investigation.

Disputes within the village have not caused prolonged village-wide factional rifts, as occurred in Oraibi or seem in the 1980s to be in progress in Hotevilla. A means of resolving at least some disputes, especially concerning land, is found in the Board of Directors. The usual practice is to persuade both parties toward consensus without strong juridical coercion. Land disputes are probably the most common. They typically have long histories, and cases are investigated in public meetings for which village elders are often called in to testify. The ideal is for a solution to be gradually hammered out. Occasionally, dissatisfied plaintiffs take their cases to the Hopi Tribal Court, a formal judicial body under the Bureau of Indian Affairs, for internal Hopi dispute settlement, or even to the Arizona state court. Some intravillage disputes persist without effective means of resolution other than withdrawal or avoidance by one or both parties. A 1970s dispute over a kiva resulted in the withdrawal of several kiva members. Passive responses of this nature (in order to avoid more serious threats to village integrity) seem to have been common in the past also (cf. Titiev 1972:passim).

Village support for the board tends to be largely tacit. Few people (mostly women) attend village meetings at which the board formally announces decisions, but in this small, face-to-face community such information is successfully communicated through less formal channels. Voter turnout at biennial elections is significantly higher (based on observation of two). Dissenters from board policy (such as on the introduction of plumbing facilities) are free to personally reject it if this does not jeopardize the rights of other villagers.

The Board of Directors grew in the 1970s from a smaller body comprising (in the 1960s) a governor and one or two untitled assistants (later named lieutenant governor and Tribal representative). The shift toward secular leadership has been gradual. Traditional criteria of *pavansinom* status have mostly ceased to operate with Bacavi's ceremonial decline, but vestiges are still evident. People occasionally express a preference for a Bear or Spider governor for traditionary reasons, and secular leaders occasionally have their authority questioned on the basis of traditional criteria in, for example, confrontations with Hotevilla.

Further, the term *pavansinom* has been adapted to changing circumstances. Older consultants were readily able to identify those presently of this status, although it no longer entails ritual prerogatives and so serves largely as an honorific. All those identified were older than seventy-five; prominent individuals in their sixties were excluded on account of relative youth. Those selected represented five clans. The men were or had been political leaders or ceremonially prominent; the women were highly respected "clan mothers" for their clan contingents in the village, although not all women who could claim such a role were included. Age alone was not a sufficient condition: several individuals over seventy-five were excluded.

Traditional roles that do persist continue to be sources of social status. Bacavi has a highly respected *tuuhikya* (medicine man) with numerous Hopi and Navajo clients. Kiva heads have some standing, although less than previously since kivas are used only for short ritual periods: kivas have ceased to function as multipurpose meeting places or men's clubs and have thus diminished in institutional significance. The Community Center, built in the 1970s, has become the primary meeting place. Nonetheless, a few individuals either "own" or "take care of" the particular kivas and are often chosen as "father" of the Kachinas (who leads the Kachinas into the plaza, reminds them when they reach particular points in songs, and generally acts as their "caretaker" while they are in the village). The role of Kachina father is a mark of social prestige and may be filled by one other than the kiva chiefs. Similarly, those chosen by the sponsor as *kukuynaqa* ("center man") in a line of Kachinas, who leads the songs, or as clown chief, who leads a troupe of sacred clowns in a two-day performance, also accrue prestige from these traditional roles. Anyone can sponsor a dance if he has the time and energy, and if his family or lineage segment has the necessary economic and ritual resources to devote to it, although typically a few individuals are repeatedly active in this role, which reciprocally reflects a measure of social standing in the community. Since the more important offices in the traditional politico-religious system have disappeared, these lesser roles have attained more significance as markers of status. None of them, however, confers overt formal authority outside a ritual context, and none is accompanied by differences in material wealth. These factors suggest continuity of the traditional system of distinctions.

Increasingly, women are participating in political affairs. Several women have served on Bacavi's board, although there has not yet been a female governor as of 1986. The Tribal Council also counts several female representatives, suggesting that this change is not restricted to Bacavi. Increased female involvement in public affairs receives some criticism from men, who see it as a breakdown of traditional gender roles. Nevertheless, this is clearly the most significant social change involving women. The reasons for it are several, but the demise of ritual leaders' control of the political order has definitely opened female access to a sphere from which women were formerly mostly excluded (notwithstanding popular accounts on the Hopi of traditional matriarchal tendencies). The number of women taking public roles (especially since 1970) suggests an interest and an eagerness to participate in decision making, despite some remaining cultural constraints.

Political History

Until his death in 1947, Kewanimptewa was the dominant force in Bacavi's political life. Since his role was not that of true *Kikmongwi*, formal relationships with religious society heads did not occur. He maintained a close relationship with his wife's uncle, Lomahongyoma, and with Sikyave'ima (Reed clan) and Nasiquaptewa (Badger, identified in 1910 as "sub-chief" of Bacavi [Lawshe 11-1-1910]) in particular.

Kewanimptewa was a powerful man at the other Third Mesa villages and exerted influence at the other Mesas. He had good relations with successive agency superintendents, and as sometime agency employee (variously "Judge," "Laborer," "Policeman"), he acted as an intermediary with several Hopi leaders. In January 1913 he was appointed Bacavi's agency policeman (Crane 12-20-1912). Duties included the controversial program of getting Hotevilla children into school, at which, owing to his fearsome supernatural reputation, he was very effective. This office lasted for a few years only, but he continued to identify with it by wearing the police uniform until the end of his life.

Kewanimptewa had particularly close ties with First Mesa, according to both Third Mesa and First Mesa people. Oliver La Farge (1937:n.p.) confirms this in a general account of Bacavi:

Pakabi was founded by Kiwanemtiwa who originally followed Yukeyouma to Hotevilla.... He then settled at Pakabi, and around him grew up a village of about 150 people. Consciously progressive, and with a selfmade chief who believes in cooperation with the Government, they have formed an extremely pleasant little group ... the chief is now in his fifties. He speaks no English but is none the less a reasonably open-minded man to deal with. He is careful always to emphasize the fact that he is not a true Kikmongwi since he is not Bear clan and lacks some of the sacred paraphernalia. He looks to his fathers the true chiefs for guidance—in practice mainly Kutka of Walpi.... He seems to be a real leader of his village, but this may partly be because he has a keen sense for the trend of public opinion and then knows how to get out in front.

Moreover, Kewanimptewa, as noted, was clairvoyant and a prophet.[7] These abilities (still recognized in the 1980s throughout Third Mesa's older population), combined with his reputation for fearlessness associated with membership of the One-Horn society, endowed Kewanimptewa with a far-reaching charismatic authority. He is remembered as a leader who took farsighted measures for change which would have been intimidating to most. Fear of group criticism is a generally effective restriction on radical action in Hopi society; those who can withstand this and promulgate radical policies are exceptional. Kewanimptewa was thus a *powaqa*—in the positive sense, as someone with extraordinary abilities to manipulate the course of events, to his supporters, and negatively, as a witch, to his detractors. The following are representative consultants' quotations:

Ritual and Politics

Even when they first settled in Hotevilla, Kewanimptewa began to talk about what he envisioned happening.

I can never understand how Kewanimptewa knew about the life today. How and from where did he know all this?

All of what people say about Kewanimptewa leads me to believe that he was indeed a *powaqa* [in the sense of clairvoyant].

One thing Kewanimptewa always said to me was that he was not afraid to admit he was a *powaqa*. He already understood the white man's way and that's why he was not afraid to visit or to live it.

Now we all talk about Kewanimptewa. He was a man of vision, an idealist, he knew prophecy, and he was not afraid.

That's how he was, he was not afraid and he carried things through.

As an intermediary with the government and as charismatic leader, Kewanimptewa developed a redoubtable power base. His home in Bacavi was a meeting place for other leaders, including Tawaquaptewa and Yukioma, who came to discuss issues of importance at night under cover of darkness (see Chapter 8). Initially, Kewanimptewa had great support in Bacavi since, though a young man in his thirties, he had provided effective leadership through the difficult period of transition from Oraibi to Bacavi. After the establishment of Bacavi, however, dissent arose over some of his radical ideas. His political stance remained unabashed, as the following public statement to a Senate meeting at the Hotevilla-Bacavi School suggests:

Since a long time ago, I have determined to follow instructions from Washington and to adhere to those instructions, and I have to this date kept my people under control and in peace. I have many people that have increased in number. I have in my heart their welfare always. (U.S. Senate 1932:9431)

Opposition came especially from the strong contingent of Badger-clan men. Pongyaquaptewa was a leading protagonist of this dissident group, and Titiev (n.d.:48a) records a struggle for leadership between the two during the 1930s, although Kewanimptewa was never dislodged.

In general, Kewanimptewa seems to have been an unusually strong leader and was astute in his dealings with other leaders and with the government. He molded a "founding philosophy" for

Bacavi which espoused cooperation with the government and eventual acceptance of Christianity, although he never personally converted and this goal has since fallen by the wayside. His conviction that Bacavi should adopt some American ways and abandon some important traditional Hopi practices is regarded as reflecting and fulfilling the plans for radical sociocultural change which were put into effect with the split of Oraibi.

Although not a formal *Kikmongwi*, Kewanimptewa was honorifically referred to as such and usually as "Chief" in English. At least from the 1930s he was occasionally referred to as "Governor" (e.g., Simmons 1942:368), and he was Bacavi's representative on the first Tribal Council, in 1936 (Hopi Tribal Council 1-18-1937). After his death, Bacavi's leadership lost connection with charismatic status and supernatural power. A successor was the subject of some debate. Titiev (1972:347) records that Kewanimptewa's son (presumably he means the older) refused the position of leadership, and that the office eventually fell to Howard Talayumptewa (Desert Fox, married into the Bear clan). According to my consultants, Ray Tawayesva (Badger) was Kewanimptewa's choice,—a fact which Tawayesva publicly affirmed in 1955:

As we lived here in this community, Kewanimptewa told me that if he was to ever go out of existence, certainly the people would propose to find another leader, and upon telling me this he also stated being a leader was a great obligation because the welfare of the people was at stake. Referring to that, he told me that I would be his successor. This gave me great thought and I was very reluctant in accepting this position, after the time came. If I had accepted this position, according to the custom it would naturally then be inherited by my brothers who would succeed me. (Hopi Hearings 1955:226–27)

Tawayesva is remembered (he passed away in the 1960s) as a "traditional." His interpretation of the position he was to succeed to, especially regarding subsequent inheritance, is clearly more associated with a traditional conception of Hopi leadership than with a purely secular governorship.

As "governor," Howard Talayumptewa remained in office through the 1950s. Quasi-traditionally (see Chapter 3 on traditional political offices), he was assisted by two brothers of the *Piikyas* clan. Subsequent governors, who included Kewanimptewa's son and his son's son, held office for shorter periods, until this became formalized into a two-year elected position in the late 1960s, since which time there have been numerous incumbents.

Impinging Institutions

The Missionary Effort

Involvement with the Mennonite church located within the environs of the village is fairly minimal in the 1980s; a number of people attend Hotevilla's church, which is run by a distinguished, older Hopi Mennonite. Bacavi's Sunday services are conducted by a lay minister from the village or from the larger Mennonite communities at Kykotsmovi and Moencopi; in 1980 the congregation was very small (fewer than ten people). Occasionally, small street-meetings are held in the village, with hymn singing (in Hopi) broadcast by loudspeakers; participants include converts from other villages, notably Kykotsmovi.

Hopi conversion to Christianity (to the exclusion of Hopi religious practices) is remarkably low—representing probably no more than 10 percent of the population—given the effort of various missionary sects since the 1850s. Among missionaries, the Hopi have achieved a degree of notoriety for their resistance to conversion: "the Hopi Indian is known to be one of the most reluctant of all Indians to accept the gospel" (Suderman n.d.:7). Perhaps because of early experience with the Franciscans and the general missionary denigration of Hopi religious practices, Hopis perceive a direct rivalry between the two religions. Several older consultants recalled (with a gleam in their eyes) that the man assigned to be Bacavi's missionary, who built the first church building, had a frightful encounter with a Hopi deity one night in the building, after which he moved back to the Oraibi mission and soon died.

In 1952 the missionary for Bacavi and Hotevilla, Walter Goossen (11-19-52), reported no converts at all. The following year, he brought over one older Bacavi man (who had been a member of Oraibi's Friendly faction and moved to Bacavi only upon marriage).

The late 1950s and the 1960s saw an upsurge of interest in the church. The paucity of Kachina dances may have created a felt gap

First Mennonite church building in Bacavi, with the village in the distance. Photograph ca. 1913–16, Evelyn Bentley Collection, Arizona Historical Society, Tucson.

in communal celebrations. From a young Bacavi Christian's point of view, there were other reasons:

> By 1960, Bacavi Mennonite Church began to experience growth in its church to include as many as fifteen families. Young Hopi men turned from Hopi religion because of actual spiritual visions about Jesus Christ in the kiva or working in the fields. These spiritual experiences brought changed men forward for baptism into the Mennonite church. Their wisdom and knowledge of the Bible grew rapidly over a year or two. They gave bible studies; their wives taught Sunday school. (Myron 1979:3)

Myron attributes the subsequent decline in church interest to the paternalistic attitude of the missionaries and their reluctance to hand over control of the church to Bacavi Christians. Growing frustration and dissatisfaction led to a diminished church membership and a split in the congregation in 1969. One group left the Bacavi church to congregate in an unused mission building in Hotevilla. The others remained in Bacavi, but both groups dwindled to three or four families (Myron 1979:4). By the time the General Conference of Mennonites officially transferred control to Hopi Christians in 1977, "for the Bacavi group it was too good to be true as well as a bit late. The men had long since left the church.

Three women remained to keep the church sewing circle going" (Myron 1979:4). The sewing circle has persisted, with about a dozen participants, but it is more of a social than a religious group.

An ongoing dispute between the village and the Mennonite Church over the land it occupies came to a head in the early 1980s. The original agreement between the Church and the Department of the Interior granted twelve acres for "temporary use and occupancy" as long as it was used for missionary purposes (Meritt 1-9-1914). Since the land is no longer used as pasture for the early mission's milk cow, and since early plans to build an orphanage never came to fruition, the Board of Directors wants the land returned to village jurisdiction. The Church has been unwilling to give up its lease (despite the legal tenuousness of its position) and in 1982 began to place white Mennonite lay workers in the church buildings to substantiate its claim for continued missionary need. After a fire in an outbuilding in 1983, a new one was built and the church was renovated, again suggesting the reassertion of Church occupancy.

The nature of Hopi Christian practice is somewhat idiosyncratic. Not a few Hopi Christians have been regarded with suspicion, by non-Christians and other Christians (in a way which suggests the persistence of indigenous beliefs) alike, as witches, both before and after their conversion. Further, the extent of conversion is frequently much tailored to Hopi religious and philosophical tenets. Hopi beliefs are deeply rooted in the local environment and in agricultural practices. Hopis were not slow to notice that, despite the white man's technological superiority, his attempts at agriculture in the desert were often less impressive. The "portable" Christian cosmology, with its lack of telluric grounding and its inattention to human ecology, appeared correlatively impractical—the pudding of the proof, as it were. Thus Hopi Christians who are still involved in subsistence agriculture often syncretically maintain decidedly Hopi beliefs about this aspect of their lives.

One Christian event is regularly celebrated: Christmas. Since construction of the Community Center in 1968, a large Christmas revue—attracting people from other villages, too—has been held there every year. A children's nativity play is a central feature. There are skits, Christmas carols (in Hopi and English), and other musical events. A Santa Claus (who shares performative features of Hopi ritual clowning) distributes gifts to the children and humorous "gifts" to some adults. Before the Community Center was built, well-attended Christmas gatherings occurred in the churches in both Bacavi and Hotevilla and at the school, and these also continue (except for the one in Bacavi's church). Many Hopis who otherwise have nothing to do with Christianity attend for the festivity—not unlike Christmas in the larger U.S. society. Christmas at Third Mesa as a regular event goes back to Voth's first celebration in 1894 (Voth 1895:62). Household celebrations of Christmas, involving the display of a tree, a Christmas dinner, and gift-giving, began to occur in Bacavi in the 1950s and have become pervasive.

Thus, although Hopis have mostly been averse to full-scale acceptance of Mennonite Christian teaching,[8] they are quite willing to participate in communally entertaining festivals of the Christian tradition and to recite its positive moral doctrines. A fairly clear cultural choice has been made in what has been accepted and what rejected of the "white man's religion."

Historically, the church in Bacavi was the outgrowth of the Oraibi mission, which underwent extensive reorganization as a result of the tripartite split of Oraibi. Government approval for a new mission at Bacavi was sought at least as early as 1913 (Duerksen 6-30-1913). Visits to the village since 1909 had been infrequent, although regular Sunday meetings were held (C. J. Frey 9-30-1913). In October 1913 J. B. Frey moved over from the mission at Moencopi to live in a newly constructed barn and became the first official missionary at Bacavi (the barn builder was C. J. Frey, a cousin). The missionary divided his time among visits to Bacavi and Hotevilla, Sunday services and Sunday-school classes in Bacavi, and translating the Bible (J. B. Frey 11-17-1913). He was also allowed to preach in the Day School (see below).

There were several changes of missionary personnel over the next few years. The Bacavi mission chapel was built in the fall of 1916 (Duerksen 7-5-1917), and J. R. and Susanna Duerksen took over in January 1917 (Schirmer 1-12-1917). From 1919 until 1929 or 1930, both Bacavi and Hotevilla were under their jurisdiction. As noted, their missionary efforts were not very successful:

The two villages have about 540 inhabitants together, Hotevilla being the larger with 400. Not one is a Christian and as far as we can see none cares to be one. They come to the mission for anything and everything except for the Word. This we bring them in the home in the house to house visitations and twice a week in each village on the street. . . . The people of Paqavi are friendly toward the government and send their children to school willingly. As to the attitude towards the Gospel there is no difference: To a stranger the Paqavis may seem more friendly toward the missionary, but that is only as far as personal matters go, because they have more respect for the white man. (Duerksen and Duerksen 1923:12–14)

According to missionary correspondence, the Mennonite General Conference seriously considered abandoning the Hopi missions altogether on several occasions. Between 1929 and 1953, the Bacavi and Hotevilla missions were in the charge of J. P. Suderman, who was based at the Moencopi mission, forty-five miles away, and consequently spent little time at Bacavi (*The Mennonite Encyclopedia* 1956,2:819). The decrease in missionary presence clearly reflected a lack of results. From 1953 to 1972, three more missionary families ran the Bacavi mission, with desultory success. As noted earlier, the mission was then neglected for a decade and subsequently occupied by lay personnel.

Schools

In the 1980s, schooling of Bacavi children in the vicinity takes a variety of forms. In the 1970s the Hotevilla-Bacavi Day School—located equidistant between the two villages—underwent some radical policy changes. In 1970 the first Hopi principal was appointed and in 1974 the school elected to change its name to the Hotevilla-Bacavi Community School. From that time, the school began to redefine its educational goals to cater to a Hopi cultural orientation. In 1978, under provisions of the Indian Self-Determination Act, an innovative School Board decided to contract the school's services via the Hopi Tribal Council, and control by the Bureau of Indian Affairs ceased. The school developed thoroughgoing bilingual, "bicultural" programs that were very successful for a few years. The teaching faculty became increasingly Hopi-dominated. Many Bacavi parents actively supported the changes and some served on the School Board. But the changes also generated controversy, some people suggesting that Hopi practices should be reserved for the home. In 1983 the innovations were dropped, the school went back under the BIA, more non-Hopi teachers were hired, and a vigorous emphasis on standard, three-r's teaching was reinstituted. A number of parents withdrew their children, sending them either to the Kykotsmovi Day School or the Mennonite Mission school (also in Kykotsmovi). A small group opened an alternative school in Bacavi supported by private funding.

The Hotevilla-Bacavi School is a major locus of community action. Its facilities—library, gymnasium, track, for example—are used by community members, and periodic fairs (such as "Indian Day") and movies attract many. Until 1986, there was no high school on the Reservation, and children mostly had to attend Indian boarding schools in Phoenix or Stewart (Nevada), or commute to high schools in Winslow, Flagstaff, or Tuba City. The new Hopi High School—opened in 1986—between First Mesa and Keam's Canyon will undoubtedly have profound sociocultural effects.

The Bacabi Day School in the canyon below the village was built in 1910–11 and opened in 1912 (Crane 3-7-1912;4-10-1912). Bacavi children, ironically, had for the most part simply not attended school since they left Oraibi in 1909. Hotevilla children, by contrast, were forcibly kept at the Keam's Canyon Boarding School. Thus when the Bacabi Day School opened, its students were entirely Bacavi children; the school closed in the spring of 1916 (Bacabi Day School Quarterly Reports 1913–16). It was replaced by the Hotevilla-Bacabi Day School, which took children from both villages; this school opened in October 1916 (Hotevilla-Bacabi Day School Quarterly Report 12-31-1916).

The Bacabi Day School exerted considerable influence toward acculturating children in some respects, though not much in others. Noting the "filthy condition" of children in Hotevilla, Superintendent Leo Crane recorded:

In strong contrast to the Hotevilla children were the pupils from the Bacabi Indian School . . . [who] were very neat and clean in corduroy clothing and well laundered shirts and good shoes; whereas the majority of the Hotevilla children of the village were dirty, long haired, and only scantily clothed if clothed at all. (Crane 6-12-1912)

Many of the Bacavi children remained in first grade (there were three grades altogether) for the four years they went to school there (Bacabi Day School Quarterly Reports 1913–16). Older school alumni report experiencing great difficulties with the English language when, after seven years of schooling in the day schools (i.e., the other three years at Hotevilla-Bacabi), they were sent to off-reservation Indian boarding schools in Phoenix, Riverside, or Albuquerque. The persistence of Hopi as the first language (especially among those over the age of twenty-five in the 1980s) suggests that the school's rigid insistence on the use of English (pupils were beaten for speaking Hopi) was not the success the government had hoped. In earlier years, the school followed the rather draconian educational policies of BIA schools in general (cf. Rhodes 1982; Szasz 1974).

Nevertheless, the school's role as the predominant instrument of acculturation has been continuous and has increasingly inculcated generations of Bacavi children with Anglo-American paradigms of knowledge. Awareness and understanding of Hopi traditions has reciprocally become more self-conscious. The conflicting cognitive schemes have resulted in the "compartmentalization" (Spicer 1961; Dozier 1961) of each, with a concomitant marking of "Hopi" practices and values as emblems of cultural identity over and above their intrinsic qualities.

Intervillage Relations at Third Mesa and the "Traditional"—"Progressive" Question

The Oraibi split gave rise to the immediate or eventual formation of five new villages on, or attached to, Third Mesa: Kykotsmovi, Bacavi, Hotevilla, Upper Moencopi, and Lower Moencopi. This dispersal had a dramatic effect on Third Mesa social relations, not least in the political sphere. Since its initial developmental period in the mid-1930s and more properly since its active resuscitation in 1950–51 (cf. Clemmer 1978:61), the BIA-organized Tribal Council has become a dominant issue in Hopi politics. Villages that have generally supported the council since its beginnings have tended to become political allies, as have, on the other side, its opponents.

These alliances are most clearly seen at Third Mesa since the alignment of villages there has been almost continuous (it has varied considerably at First Mesa and Second Mesa). Bacavi has, in general terms, been an enduring supporter of the council, as have Kykotsmovi and Upper Moencopi. Hotevilla, Old Oraibi, and Lower Moencopi have for the most part rejected the Tribal Council. The former group are known as "progressive" villages and the latter as "traditional" or conservative.

In reality, of course, Bacavi's relations with other Third Mesa villages are rather more complex than this division suggests. Similarly, the designations "traditional" and "progressive" serve more as labels for expressing political divisions than as reflections of actual commitment to "Hopi traditional ways" on the one hand, or "the white man's way" on the other. Nagata (1970:92–96) discusses factional divisions at Moencopi and the applicability of the designations "traditional" and "progressive": "I have not heard the anti-council activists of the tribe speak of their antagonists as 'progressives' but always as 'council.' Some of them explicitly denied that their antagonists are in any way 'progressive'" (Nagata 1970:93).

Nagata cites some Hopi terms for the two parties (1970:93), noting that the contrast they provide is between Hopis and whites. The terms "traditionals" and "progressives" are in use in English in modern times though this may be a reflexive response to Anglo usage. The Hopi terms most frequently given to me differ a little from those cited by Nagata, but they retain the notions of factional difference operative in the Oraibi split, namely, *Pahannaanawaknaqam* and *Qapahannaanawaknaqam*. The literal translations are "white-man–likers," from *pahaana* ("white man") and *naawakna* ("to want, like, or love"), and its opposite, "white-man–dislikers," by addition of the prefix *qa-* ("not"). The semantic import has been interpreted to me as "those who want the white man's ways" versus "those who want to remain strictly Hopi."

The council, then, has become a focus for expressing more deeply rooted political issues and a nexus of alliances and oppositions. The alliance between Bacavi, Kykotsmovi, and Upper Moencopi is also apparent in the greater frequency with which these villages cooperate on ceremonial and other occasions. Cooperation consists in sending a group of performers to participate in another village's ceremonies or in inviting a man from another village to serve as Kachina father. In that the latter practice does not involve a village group but a single individual invited by the family that sponsors the dance, it is somewhat easier to arrange. Bacavi cooperates most frequently with Kykotsmovi in this respect, although the "traffic" is usually one way—Kachina fathers are invited from Bacavi to Kykotsmovi. Bacavi occasionally invites a Kachina father from Hotevilla; one well-respected Hotevilla "progressive" has often served in this capacity in Bacavi and occasionally in Kykotsmovi.

Bacavi and Kykotsmovi's ceremonial cooperation is regarded as having a historic deliberacy. Older consultants say that Kewanimptewa told Bacavi people that if they were to cooperate with another village, it should be with Kykotsmovi, since both were *sukavung* villages, that is, lacking the religious societies and having similarly diminished involvements with supernatural power. Bacavi's ceremonial ties are closer with Kykotsmovi for these historically ordained reasons than with Upper Moencopi, which also lacks religious societies, but which came into existence as a separate village only in the late 1930s and 1940s.

Ceremonial exchanges of this nature also occur between Bacavi and other villages (and also between Kykotsmovi and other villages). Bacavi is the only Third Mesa village that occasionally has a group of visiting dancers from Hotevilla, especially from the "progressive" group at Hotevilla's Kwan kiva. More seldom, a Second Mesa group comes over. Exchanges between Bacavi and First Mesa groups are probably rarer, although they do occur. Such visits are usually reciprocated by a group of Bacavi performers some time thereafter.

Reciprocal ceremonial visits do not occur at all between Bacavi and both Oraibi and Lower Moencopi. Bacavi has little or no contact with these villages *qua* villages. From being a wholly "Friendly" village after the two splits had expelled all the Hostiles, Oraibi turned about face. Its leadership (since Tawaquaptewa died in 1960) under Mina Lansa was aligned politically with the Hotevilla "traditional" viewpoint (see Clemmer 1978). After her death in 1979, Stanley Bahnimptewa, her successor, has generally followed a policy of nonalignment. Oraibi's population has hovered around 120 since the 1930s (Titiev 1972:327), and it has long been regarded at Hopi as a decaying village. It is hardly flourishing in the 1980s, though it shows no signs of absolute decline and abandonment. Titiev (1944:94–95) records the process of increasing emigration from Old Oraibi to Kykotsmovi and Moencopi. After his return from Sherman Institute, Riverside (in 1909), Tawaquaptewa "exhibited a quality of character which served to irritate his people and to cause them to drift away from the pueblo" (1944:94). It is widely believed that Tawaquaptewa wished to fulfill prophecies on the abandonment of Oraibi by gradually driving everyone away, so that the village itself would die with his own death. In line with this, he drove out those who converted to Christianity to Kykotsmovi, and prevented those who wanted to Americanize their lifestyles in other ways from doing so in Oraibi. The latter mostly moved to Moencopi or Kykotsmovi (Titiev 1944:95).

These movements led to Kykotsmovi's becoming the most "progressive" village and to the gradual transformation of Moencopi from a farming colony to a separate village. Moencopi maintained its colonial status, though, in terms of its religious dependence upon Oraibi: all its men returned to Oraibi to perform their ceremonies (except for Kachina and Social Dances), no local shrines were consecrated, and no clan-houses were built as repositories of clan sacra (Nagata 1970:13–14).

In time Moencopi became economically independent of Oraibi while remaining politically and religiously dependent (see Nagata 1970). When Moencopi itself divided into Lower and Upper villages, Lower Moencopi maintained dependency, but Upper Moencopi gradually broke it (Nagata 1970:42–97). Nagata regards Upper Moencopi as the "most Americanized village of all." Although "religious" dependence has ceased to have much meaning between Lower Moencopi and Oraibi today, owing to the virtual absence of any ceremonies at the latter village (except highly abbreviated *Soyalangw* observances, *Powamuy*, and very occasional Kachina and Social Dances), it does persist to some extent: during a plaza Kachina dance in Oraibi in June 1981 a troupe of clowns and Warrior Kachinas came from Lower Moencopi. Political dependence has less meaning since the death of Tawaquaptewa, but both villages are generally "traditional" and anti-Tribal Council. In this respect they share political views with Hotevilla, but this is about as far as such ties go. There is no ceremonial cooperation at all between Hotevilla and either Oraibi or Lower Moencopi (cf. Nagata 1970:67).

Bacavi's most important ties are with Kykotsmovi and Upper Moencopi on the one hand, and with Hotevilla on the other. Relations with Hotevilla are the most complex, since they unite and oppose the two villages in different contexts. Although Hotevilla and Bacavi are generally opposed politically and specifically over land claims, Hotevilla is nevertheless the village with which Bacavi individuals interact most on a daily and continuing basis. Since Hotevilla is always characterized as *the* traditional Third Mesa village and Bacavi is reckoned to be progressive, and since both spring from the original "Hostile" faction in Oraibi, the nature of their interrelations is quite illuminating of Hopi politics generally.

Hotevilla has always been a larger village than Bacavi—roughly three times the population size. It is also by far the closest to Bacavi, lying but a mile away; indeed the outskirts of both villages intersect. In contrast, Kykotsmovi is six miles away by road, Oraibi is four, and Moencopi is forty-five. So the situational reasons for greater interaction between Bacavi and Hotevilla are obvious. These physical reasons have been somewhat mitigated with the introduction of metalled roads and the widespread use of cars and pickups since 1950, but still the bulk of Bacavi's intervillage interactions is with Hotevilla.

Two prominent institutions have joint participation by both villages: the Hotevilla-Bacavi Community School and the Hotevilla post office. Both are located between the two villages, roughly on the boundary line (as it is perceived by Bacavi people).[9] During its innovative phase, the school tried to effect a rapprochement between the villages, and it served as an expanded nexus of joint activity between both communities. Since the complete about-face in its educational philosophy, this unifying role seems to have considerably diminished. The Hotevilla post office serves as a kind of neutral ground where people from both villages, especially older individuals, meet and converse.

In these two institutional settings, village members *qua* village members (as contrasted with their other roles) have a bridge between the two communities upon which to meet and discuss intervillage matters. Otherwise, the channels for communicating politically between the two villages as wholes are often deadlocked. Land disputes are a pertinent example. In 1984, for example, over an issue concerning an individual's right to install electricity in a home near the village boundary, the recently formed Hotevilla Village Board (a "progressive" group within Hotevilla, but opposed to Bacavi in this instance) imposed a moratorium on new construction in a large area disputed by the two villages. The boards of both villages presented their cases before the Tribal Council, and though no formal action was taken, support for Bacavi's position was apparent (the merits of the case were clearly in Bacavi's favor). Hotevilla's community development specialist, a leading proponent of the moratorium, had the funding for his position cut, and Bacavi has pointedly ignored the ban.

Since pre-split Oraibi did not have to deal much with intervillage boundaries,[10] the basis for discussion between newer villages in dispute has no clear precedent. Modern disputes between Bacavi and Hotevilla have a variety of bases on which claims can be made or, alternately, refuted, including the following (see also note 9): individual ownership of particular areas according to traditional claims to ascendants' fields, orchards, and so on; the occasional invocation of U.S. property laws, such as "squatters' rights"; the likewise occasional notion that since this is a reservation, the federal government is the real "owner" of the land, and therefore village title must be sought through the government; and, a powerful traditional dimension, that *Maasaw* is the only "owner" of the land, over which human beings can have no really proprietary control.

These alternative bases for argument also reflect the different kinds of political systems in the two villages. Bacavi supports the Tribal Council form of political practice. Its governing body coordinates itself with Tribal structures and has no traditional Hopi offices. The village as a whole has been reasonably supportive of this political system. Although a number of villagers disagree with this system, do not cooperate with edicts that affect them personally, and tend to align themselves with Hotevilla "traditionals," these dissidents are too few to constitute an identifiable "faction," since their general position is one of noninvolvement and passive resistance. A large proportion of Hotevilla, by contrast, does not recognize the Tribal Council, and the village does not send Tribal representatives. But a group representing a "progressive" element in the village has organized a Village Council that wants Tribal Council representation. They have been in active opposition against the "traditionals," reflecting a definite factionalization of Hotevilla.

Use of the terms "traditionals," "traditional village," "Traditionalists," "progressives," and "progressive village"—common in the literature (e.g., Clemmer 1978) and in the discourse of many younger Anglo-Americans supportive of the (largely mis-) perceived aims of the former—requires some clarification. Hotevilla is regarded as a "traditional village" composed of many "traditionals," that is, people oriented toward "Hopi traditions." This gloss generally conforms to *qapahannaanawaknaqam*, "those not wanting the white man's ways." I discuss below some of the cultural implications of such "traditionalism." "Traditionalists," which I capitalize following other writers (e.g., Clemmer 1978), refers to an active political group (perhaps equatable with a party) in demonstrative opposition to the Tribal Council. This group receives considerable support from sympathetic individuals and organizations in the larger U.S. society and Europe, to whom Traditionalist leaders make frequent appeals by means of lecture tours, participation in such conventions as the Russell Tribunal, and an effective use of the media (see, for example, the 1985 documentary film "Broken Rainbow").

"Traditionalists" and "traditionals" overlap, and the former receive their Hopi support from some, though by no means all, of the latter, but the two terms should not be regarded as synonymous. Much general Hopi (i.e., including both "traditionals" and "progressives") criticism of *both* the Tribal Council *and* the Traditionalists focuses upon their intermediary roles with American society. The Tribal Council is perceived as frequently estranged from the Hopi people, because of its constant tailoring of Hopi needs to a federal bureaucracy that has little awareness, let alone concern, for the specific Hopi context of its enactments. The Traditionalists, on the other hand, are similarly estranged, in that their appeals for support beyond the Hopi community often entail dire misrepresentation of Hopi society and culture to an audience whose interest is mostly informed by stereotypical images of Indians. The images—and their concomitant reflections of interest—seem to have two basic sources of inspiration: first, an updated noble-savagism that depicts Hopis as idyllic preservers of arcadian lifestyles (especially popular in Germany, where the Hopi are the subject of wide interest); and second, a perceived empathy for aims simplistically construed as "anti-Establishment" (prevalent especially among younger, white, disaffected groups in the United States which owe their origins primarily to the 1960s counterculture).

"Progressives" and "progressive village" in Hopi terms are basically *pahannaanawaknaqam* ("those wanting the white man's ways"). The term "Progressivists" is not in use; those who are active in this camp are Tribal Council supporters, or just "council."

During the mounting publicity over the Relocation Act (to settle the Hopi-Navajo land dispute), opponents of the Act have repeatedly drawn a hopelessly misconceived picture of Hopi political allegiances. They (in, for example, the film "Broken Rainbow") depict "traditional religious leaders" and "Kikmongwis" as representative of the great Hopi majority that, it is alleged, actively opposes relocation. Conversely, the Tribal Council is portrayed as a wholly unrepresentative body, puppets of the government, with no support in Hopi society. In brief, this is an appallingly naive understanding of internal Hopi politics. On balance, although the Tribal Council continually wrestles with the problem of representativeness and is unceasingly criticized by many of its active supporters (as well as everybody else), it has become the de facto political forum for the majority of Hopi people.

With the gradual decline of the religious structure at Third Mesa, there are no clearly ordained and universally recognized politico-religious officers of a traditional nature at Hotevilla. From the 1930s until his death in 1972, Yukioma's son Dan Qötshongva served as a powerful leader. However, he was not chosen as Yukioma's successor, but rather maneuvered himself into the position; the heir-apparent, James Pongyayaoma, left the village in 1967 (for more on Hotevilla's leadership, see Clemmer 1978:36; Waters 1963:326–37). After Qötshongva's death, some efforts were made to have Pongyayaoma, who had returned to Hotevilla, stand as a recognized *Kikmongwi*, but he refused. David Monongye, who was closely connected with Qötshongva, is an eloquent and persuasive speaker who has been very active on and off the reservation in the "Traditionalist" movement and who acts as a political focus for some Hotevilla people. However, both his advanced age and his guru-like status to many young white visitors to Hotevilla, to whom he is "Grandfather David," weaken his appeal within the community. In short, traditional leadership in Hotevilla has dissipated and no viable substitute with wide support has yet emerged.

Political negotiations between Bacavi and Hotevilla which would be fully bilaterally representative are, then, practically impossible. On the one hand, a large part of Hotevilla does not recognize the Bacavi Board of Directors as a legitimate governing body, since it is aligned with the Tribal Council and is a "white-man's way" of governing. On the other hand, the Hotevilla Village Board, which could stand as a viable negotiating body and which has already had several fruitful meetings with the Bacavi Board, is likewise not regarded by a large number of Hotevilla people as their representative. Agreements made between the two boards meet with extensive noncompliance. In short, there are so many potential cross-purposes involved in any intervillage political discussions that they have usually had only fragmentary meaning.

Beyond the level of relations between Bacavi and Hotevilla considered as separate political configurations lies another and perhaps ultimately more significant dimension: individual interrelations. Out of a total of 214 marriages for Bacavi (see Chapter 6) since its inception until 1981, 44 have been with Hotevilla—almost as many as those internal to Bacavi (48). The large number of intermarriages means that the most extended families in Bacavi have personal ties with one or several Hotevilla families. Several virilocal marriages between the villages have led to "Hotevilla lineages" residing in Bacavi, though having most of their close relatives in Hotevilla, and vice versa. Also, the residence site of Bacavi-Hotevilla marriages serves less to diminish contact between the spouses and their natal families than in other intervillage marriages, owing to the mutual proximity of Bacavi and Hotevilla—one can sleep in the former but conduct much of one's daily business in the latter, or vice versa.

Furthermore, with the exception of the Bear clan, every Bacavi clan has close and historic lineage ties with Hotevilla clans. Although clan ties cut across the Mesas, they are much closer within each Mesa's set of villages. At Third Mesa, Hotevilla and Bacavi clan ties are especially close, owing to their common history as well as to their proximity, which allows for more frequent reaffirmation. As some older people put it, "We are, after all, the same people who split off from Oraibi."

The formation of the other new Third Mesa villages diverges greatly from the pattern of village formation represented by Hotevilla and Bacavi. Moencopi began as a "Friendly" Oraibi colony, gradually growing in populace, partially attaining the status of an independent village, and then splitting into two villages. Kykotsmovi was formed by gradual attrition from Oraibi after the split, and only after many years did it attain the status of a "true" village—with a plaza, kivas, and so on. Neither Lower nor Upper Moencopi nor Kykotsmovi ever practiced much of the ceremonial cycle or had traditional forms of village government.[11] Only Hotevilla and Bacavi resulted from the Hostile exodus from Oraibi, and although there was periodic talk that Hotevilla people would move on to their prophesied destination of Kawestima (see Chapter 8), within a very few years they had become ensconced as a new village at the present site. When the Hostile subfaction left Oraibi for the second time they did so with the clear intention of founding a new, integrated, and independent village at Bacavi.

Thus although Bacavi is divided from Hotevilla politically (and it should not be denied that feelings often run deep), it is united at the individual level by a great deal of intermarriage, common clanship ties, and a common original history. Though Bacavi is united with Kykotsmovi and Upper Moencopi politically and also by extensive intermarriage (though not as extensive as with Hotevilla), it is divided from them by a history more traditionally Hopi than theirs. If Hotevilla is the most "traditional" of the Third Mesa "traditional" villages, Bacavi may be considered the most "traditional" of the "progressives," as it were.

The practical effect upon lifestyle of the distinction between traditional and progressive is largely a relative matter in modern times: prominent members of the Traditionalist faction use pickups, farm machinery, and many other consumer goods. Though the attempt by the BIA to extend electricity lines into Hotevilla was vigorously resisted (cf. Clemmer 1978:73–76) in 1968, many Hotevilla people enjoy watching TVs hooked up to their pickup truck batteries. There is similar resistance to Public Health Service plans for water and sewage lines into the village, but the past few years have seen the digging of several "pirate" lines with a number of spigots throughout the village. Again, the use of propane (for light as well as cooking here) is as ubiquitous as in the other Hopi villages.

So while Hotevilla does not, as Bacavi does, have a metalled road into the village, the use of a formal system of electricity lines, telephone lines or much indoor plumbing, individuals have managed to introduce a level of amenities not far behind Bacavi's and a long way from the situation Titiev (1972:346) describes for the 1930s. The cardinal distinction Hotevilla people make is that they want full individual control of these amenities, rather than being at the potential mercy of a white-run corporation, public or private: it is not so much that the conveniences and other economic changes themselves are not desired. Other changes in the traditional economy of sheepherding and farming are also nearly parallel between the two villages (see Chapter 5).

Similarly, if the criterion of adherence to the ritual order is used to distinguish a "traditional" village, we also run into problems. It is true that Hotevilla has retained more of the ceremonial cycle than any other Third Mesa village, but this is a relative matter. In the 1980s, Hotevilla has active performances only by the third-order societies (see Chapter 8 for a fuller account). In contrast, Shongopavi at Second Mesa maintains most of the ceremonial cycle in flourishing form. By this criterion, then, it is far more "traditional" than Hotevilla. Nevertheless, although Shongopavi also includes a strong contingent of the Traditionalist faction, Hotevilla is stronger in this regard. The fact, for example, that Shongopavi has been unwilling and unable to prevent the intrusion of power lines into large areas of the village is regarded as a measure of Hotevilla's greater "traditionalism" in this respect.

The relationship between "traditionalism" and ritual activity is not, then, straightforward. Some of those characterized as "progressive" in Shongopavi and who have worked actively with the

Tribal Council are at the same time holders of high offices in the religious societies. In an article on the Hopi-Navajo land dispute, one of these so-called "progressives," a man of advanced age who had been the chief-priest of the Two-Horn society, specifically took issue with the term "traditionalist": "Viets Lomaheftewa, the 90-year-old-man who spoke in his stone house in Shongopavi, had little use for the self-proclaimed traditionalists. *'We are all traditionalists,'* he said" (*Albuquerque Journal* 4-12-1981:B4, my emphasis). Similarly, Hotevilla "progressives" who are initiated into higher-order socities are sincerely committed to their traditional religious responsibilities.

The point I am concerned to make is that the traditional-progressive opposition is primarily political.[12] As with opposing parties of many governmental systems, specific political principles and points of issue are susceptible of change over time: they are not readily identifiable with any fixed criteria for measuring sociocultural "conservatism/traditionalism" or "progressivism." It should also be pointed out that a large number, probably even the majority, of Hopis are active supporters of neither group, preferring to tread a middle ground and simply to observe political activities from afar without becoming involved. Although Bacavi has been characterized as a "progressive" village (e.g., Clemmer 1978:58), the reality is that most people are not involved politically much at all.[13] There is a good deal of criticism of both the Tribal Council and the Traditionalists. In a discussion of the political complexion of Bacavi, the perceived existence of *three* (informal) basic groups was pointed out by a consultant: "those who want the white man's way," the "traditionals," and the "in-betweens"; in 1981 probably the majority of Bacavi people fell into the last category. When under pressure from their numerically more powerful and more assertive "traditional" neighbor (Hotevilla), this majority tends to look to its governing body and to the Tribal Council for political protection. Here we touch on a reason why the less traditional villages have supported the Tribal Council, and thus on the meaning the council holds for these villages.

In trying to marshal support for the idea of the Tribal Council in the mid-1930s, Oliver La Farge, author of the Tribal Constitution, used a mixture of threat and cajolery. The threats concerned the might of the U.S. government. One consultant emphasized that La Farge concluded several public discussions with: "If you Hopi people cannot govern yourselves according to this Tribal Constitution, then we have something *much* harder for you." Threats, based on might, to implement alien cultural dominion had never proven very effective at Hopi since the Spanish period. With the cajoling, on the other hand, La Farge hit upon an argument with greater appeal. He recommended that, as well as a Tribal Council, each of the new villages which had branched off from Oraibi should establish a chartered government with its own constitution. The consultant recalled his persuasion: "For only with this kind of government will you be able to be stronger than these traditionalists. For this kind of government will have authority in the white man's way and you will then have power over these traditionalists."

Despite a general notion of village autonomy and the decline of the Third Mesa ritual order, leaders basing their authority on traditional politico-religious power continued to exert their presence in the less traditional villages. As mentioned in Chapter 3, "power" in this sense has dangerous supernatural, as well as secular, underpinnings. Authority in the traditional system was partly maintained through the inculcation of fear of the supernatural power of the politico-religious officials. This fear is embodied in the idea of *maqastutavo*, a pervasive religious and moral doctrine. It involves the doctrine (*tutavo*) that people should adhere to Hopi norms for fear of provoking inevitable, negative, supernatural repercussions against themselves or members of their families. To the extent that individual control over some supernatural power ensues from *Wuwtsim* initiation, this gives the initiated a powerful psychological weapon over the uninitiated in situations of personal and/or political confrontation. Although Hotevilla has not performed *Wuwtsim* initiations for a long time, some "traditionals" are older men who were initiated when Hotevilla still did conduct initiations.

Furthermore, there is the allied notion that political authority is conditional upon ritual status. Without *Wuwtsim* initiation, therefore, the individual has not even a basis to claim political office, from this standpoint, but is eternally a *sukavungsino* (commoner) with no access to power.

The effects of these pervasive attitudes on the intervillage political context at Third Mesa generally, and between Bacavi and Hotevilla specifically, are profound. From the "traditional" standpoint, those villages that never initiated anyone into *Wuwtsim* have no legitimate power base *nor even a single legitimate claim to authority* (even in internal affairs). Thus, in political meetings, noninitiated officials in "progressive" villages are frequently confronted by traditionally oriented individuals who question their authority. Such questions prove difficult to answer for two reasons. First, the fact of hierarchy and secrecy in the distribution of ritual knowledge is such an axiomatic Hopi principle that it is almost impossible for the noninitiate to plausibly reject the knowledge/power of *wiimi* (religious practices and beliefs) through skepticism, critical analysis, or access to some superior form of wisdom: he would have no audience. Second, the general precepts of *maqastutavo* contribute greatly to even the nontraditional individual's unwillingness to openly challenge the power of the initiated.

Thus La Farge's proposals for giving "progressive" villages a totally new power base, by means of a Tribal Council supported by the U.S. government, had great political appeal to those villages "disenfranchised" in the traditional system. This may go some way toward explaining why Bacavi, Upper Moencopi, and Kykotsmovi have, in general, supported the Tribal Council from the beginning. This is also the reason why the council is such an important focus for political relations between villages and, significantly, between Bacavi and Hotevilla.

Many of the specific political issues have changed greatly from those in turn-of-the-century Oraibi. Nevertheless, the general character of political relations between two polarized factions, which identify themselves with the same reference terms used in Oraibi, remains remarkably similar. Only the Third Mesa context has changed dramatically: from the pre-1906 situation when the setting was a single, integral polity, to the modern situation of six dispersed villages. However, the recent common origins of these newer villages in turn-of-the-century Oraibi, the predominant intra-Mesa marriage patterns, close kinship ties, and a shared Third Mesa identity[14] all attest to the necessity of considering the total Third Mesa context in any discussion of just one of the villages.

While they no longer form a single polity, in many ways they are not completely independent either.

Bacavi's Changes: Points of Emphasis

I would like to underscore three major issues of sociocultural and social structural change that have emerged from Chapters 5, 6, and 7. The first concerns the different ways change has impacted upon the sexes. In many respects, change has affected men much more than women. Men's roles, especially with regard to the abandonment of the traditional ritual order and the activities associated with it, have altered greatly from the Oraibi system outlined in Chapter 3. The traditional roles and statuses emanating from positions in the ritual order pervaded the entire social fabric, interweaving with politics and kinship. The decline in importance of kinship roles for men (which is by no means absolute) derives quite directly from the ritual decline.

For women, on the other hand, changes in social roles have been considerably less profound. Women are still the owners of houses and the managers of the productive and reproductive economy in the domestic domain. They remain the processors, preparers, and distributors of food, though some of the techniques have changed, and the raisers of children (with strong conceptual intergenerational ties through matriliny). Ritual activities centered in the domestic domain—concerning marriage and childbirth, especially—continue to flourish, with little but technical changes from former practices. These activities also highlight the meaning of lineage and clan ties and interrelationships among women, and here again the importance of the traditional kinship system seems to have changed little. The only major changes concern, first, the abandonment of the three women's religious societies, which do not seem to have had such a proportionally important place in women's lives as the men's societies did in men's lives, and second, the new involvement in village and Tribal politics. Women are also going to work in the wage economy in increasing numbers, but this new phenomenon has yet to replace their role as managers of the domestic economy.

Second, with the social structural changes noted in Bacavi from the system in Oraibi, the *meaning* of formal aspects of the traditional structure which persist has in large part changed. This also relates to another set of changes I want to underscore: namely, shifting anthropological perspectives. Thus, lineages, clans, subsistence economic activities, ceremonies, and other features have been discussed as markers of cultural and intracultural identity. This obviously represents a considerably changed perspective from what I have characterized as the "conventional view" of Hopi society, which treats these institutional features as integrative mechanisms conducing to the equilibrated functioning of the social structure. What, then, has changed—Hopi society or the anthropological interpretation of it? The answer, of course, is both. In Bacavi, traditional forms of Hopi social organization have in many instances dissipated, and there is a definite feeling on the part of older people that village life is less integrated than it used to be. That this is more than mere nostalgia is attested by the kinds of examples given. These involve the fact that the traditional authority system, which was largely upheld by respect and fear of the leaders' supernatural powers, has for the most part become inoperative. A classic difference perceived between today's society and formerly is that communal work parties, on a kinship or village-wide basis, used to be a regular feature of village life. Since the authoritative sanctions of traditional leadership have evaporated, the complaint is that it is no longer possible to mobilize large groups of people (especially men) for communal work. Here again, the contexts for mobilization of kinship ties have changed the most for men, to whom they have in many respects ceased to have functional significance on a daily basis.

Nevertheless, descent groups as structural units continue to be prominently recognized as identity groups and still function for the regulation of marriage ties that serve to perpetuate distinct group identities. As Louise Lamphere (1977) has persuasively demonstrated for the Copper Canyon Navajo, the functional unity of kin groups is significantly active as a basis for regular cooperation for certain tasks or through which an individual can call upon a network of potential cooperators. This view does not necessitate rigidly conceived modes of stereotypical status/role behavior ordained by the mandates of an all-pervasive and superordinate descent-group system. The resultant, more flexible picture of the ebb and flow of social behavior is applicable to modern Bacavi matrilineal kin networks also.

In sum, units of Hopi society have changed in many of their functional attributes, especially for men. However, the perception of such units according to their classic functional definitions (e.g., as landholding corporations) has changed in anthropology, too. No longer is the primary analytical aim to seek for groups and institutions functionally welded together into a symmetrical whole. The representation of modern Bacavi society as a loosely ordered organization of identity groups with different bases, which can be drawn upon to instigate types of social action, contrasts significantly with the picture of Oraibi society as an integrated weave of structural elements. But the pictures reflect changed canvases as well as changes in the landscape. Nevertheless, it is abundantly clear that modern Bacavi is much changed from turn-of-the-century Oraibi. Some changes proceed from various forms of acculturative influence. Others significantly result from conscious choices to change features of the traditional system.

One final point remains to be emphasized. We have noted that, despite the much-attenuated ritual order in modern times, Bacavi's original populace contained a disproportionate number of people with a great deal of ritual knowledge. It is difficult to translate the cultural significance of this from a Hopi perspective. Perhaps the most trenchant statement I heard on the matter came, in English, from an older Hotevilla man with close ties to Bacavi: "If you want my view, Bacavi was founded by the intellectuals."

III
INTERPRETATIONS

8
᚛ Hopi Analysis and Anthropological Analysis

> As in many revolutions, the decisive subversion of the system was a work of the people in power: an abuse of power.
> —*Marshall Sahlins (1981:45)*

We now have a picture of social and cultural change in Third Mesa Hopi society over roughly a century. The picture has been constructed to demonstrate that the changes were neither isolated events occurring willy-nilly in a cultural vacuum, nor simple reflex responses to just one set of stimuli, such as changing material conditions. The stimuli and responses to them were multiple and multifaceted.

How are we to "explain" these changes, from turn-of-the-century Oraibi society to Bacavi in the 1980s? Clearly, they occur, at one contextual level, in a situation of conflict between a dominant, imperial polity and a subjugated indigenous minority. Can we then account for them with an acculturationist model? If so, how do we explain the persistence of some cultural traditions and not others—at some villages and not others? Why, for example, in 1986 does Shongopavi—a village of fewer than two hundred people in the late nineteenth century—have a virtually complete ceremonial cycle, whereas Third Mesa's has virtually disintegrated?

My concern in this chapter is to assess different explanations of change in twentieth-century Third Mesa society and, specifically, to promote a Hopi, or what I shall call "ethnosociological," analysis as indispensable to a thoroughgoing interpretation. My focal point is the Oraibi split. This is *the* critical event instigating the most significant changes. Without it, Bacavi would not exist, and the patterns of social and cultural change would have been very different. The persistence of Oraibi's social system was contingent upon its continued societal integrity. The split was no casual "budding off" of a self-regulating system with no damage to the main stalk. Simply, the split shattered the axis upon which the Oraibi world pivoted. Let me begin, then, by examining some prior analyses of the split.

Anthropological Analyses of the Oraibi Split

Previous analyses of the split have been, in one way or another, determinist. They have sought its causes in circumstances external to society or in a predisposed incapacity of the society to respond effectively to external change. In either case, Oraibi is depicted as falling apart at the seams when certain external pressures were brought to bear.

As noted earlier, accounts of the split reach double figures (see Laird 1977), and I shall not deal with all of them here. I specifically exclude published Hopi accounts from this section, since they are important for the presentation of the ethnosociological analysis below. I also exclude several accounts that derive from Titiev's analysis (1944:69–95) and largely reiterate either his conclusions or those of the other two major arguments discussed below. The reader is referred to Eisenberg (1968) for a useful summary of such derivative accounts. I am concerned here with those analyses offering distinctive interpretations of the split's causes.

Sociological Determinism

Titiev's account is the most comprehensive of all. He regards internal social structural weaknesses as responsible for the split: that is, his determinism is sociological. For Titiev, Hopi social structure is intrinsically fragile:

> Such a social system rests on unstable foundations, for the more firmly people adhere to clan lines, the weaker must be their village ties. A Hopi pueblo is like an object with a thin outer shell which holds together a number of firm, distinct segments—should the shell be cracked, the segments would fall apart. (1944:69)

This, he holds, is precisely what happened to Oraibi—"a modern instance of a pueblo that fell apart when its outer shell was cracked" (1944:70). Internal strength of the clans operating against each other as corporate units was conjoined (rather contradictorily) with other sociological ties in the events leading to the split:

> I should say that the division of Oraibi proceeded somewhat as follows. First, the chiefs of the Bear and Spider clans, finding their phratry affiliations too weak to hold them together in the face of disputes over land and other strong differences of opinion, began a struggle for control of the pueblo. Second, the members of their own clans quickly sided with their leaders. Third, the men of the conflicting clans brought into their respective parties their wives and children, thus emphasizing household ties and beginning to break up clan cohesion. The most important results of this step were to link the Masau'u clan with the influence of Lololoma's wife; and to join the Water Coyote and the Spider clans on the basis of Lomahongyoma's marriage to a Water Coyote woman. Another notable consequence of conjugal fidelity was the addition of the Kokop clan to the conservative faction. Fourth, the women of the five leading clans in the struggle generally induced their husbands and other household relatives to join their cause, thus breaking down clan ties still more. Fifth, those men who were not closely related to the leaders either through descent or marriage made their choice of sides on the basis of their most cherished ceremonial connections; for with the establishment by the Hostiles of a full ceremonial cycle to rival that of the Friendlies, all the villagers were forced to declare themselves unequivocally on one side or the other. Sixth, when this stage was reached the original clash between Hostiles and Friendlies resolved itself into a struggle between the participants in the Spider-led ceremonies and those in the Bear-controlled rituals. Seventh, wives and unmarried children tended to follow the leads of husbands and fathers. Eighth, after the entire populace had been divided, a climax occurred when the Friendlies expelled the Hostiles from Oraibi on September 7, 1906. (1944:92–93)

And (finally) in summarizing causes, he stresses that "in reality there was a strong sociological aspect to the quarrel between the Bear and Spider leaders . . . the primary division of the village resulted from the splitting of the weak phratry tie that held two strong clans together" (1944:75).

I have suggested elsewhere (Whiteley 1986) that Titiev's representation of clans and phratries as respectively isomorphic structural units—a necessary feature of his explanation of the split—is empirically inaccurate. Instead, I suggest that Hopi descent groups operate more on a sliding scale of inclusiveness, coming together for a variety of purposes (even the temporarily expedient), rather than as discrete groups incorporated about definable estates of some kind. In short, the perceived social structural weakness at the heart of Titiev's explanation of the split is predicated upon an insufficient analysis of Hopi descent groups.

Further, there are several inaccuracies, inconsistencies, and contradictions in his eight-fold summary. Items 2, 3, and 7 seem mutually contradictory: either clans are the solidary units, or they are not and households are. If the latter is the case, the principle of the unity of clan cohorts is meaningless. The supposed peripheral status of a man in his wife's household, another necessary feature of the superordinate principle of clan solidarity, seems vitiated in items 3 and 7. Titiev's assertion that the "Water Coyote" (Desert Fox) and *Kookop* clans joined the Spider clan's part (item 3) because of Lomahongyoma's wife requires an overarching importance for Lomahongyoma that is not historically justified. The basis of *Kookop* clan involvement as deriving from the strength of its phratry tie with the Desert Fox clan, which in turn was involved because of one affinal tie with the Spider clan, seems to push a sociological argument beyond reasonable bounds; we are led to believe that, whereas clan ties were a basic source of alliance in other instances, here they were simply overridden by a stronger phratry-cum-affinal tie. The prominence of *Kookop* clan men (two of whom—Patupha and Heevi'ima—are documented as Hostile leaders long before Lomahongyoma's name appears in the records) rested surely on more than a tie of affinity that did not include them personally anyway (Titiev 1944:92 n. 173). The fact that Lomahongyoma's role as leader had largely ceased before the split casts further doubt on this assumption.

The supposed complete division of the *Kookop* and *Maasaw* clans as Hostiles and Friendlies, respectively, is also questionable. In contrast to Titiev's claims that these are entirely separate clans (1944:49), White's (n.d.) thorough genealogical research of 1932 treats them as a unitary clan. I have emphasized the muddy lines between many "clans" (see also Whiteley 1986)—these are two of them—and the common claims to joint clan membership. It seems eminently possible that the separation of these "clans" in Tawaquaptewa's identifications for Titiev's census notes is a post hoc rationalization, emphasizing a distinction between those who remained loyal to his part and those who did not.[1]

Although the Spider clan is clearly identifiable as separate from the Bear clan and all of the former were Hostiles, one Bear clan segment (see Chapter 6) was Hostile and there were bitter feelings between this segment and the others. Further, the idea that Lomahongyoma's wife was a link between Spider and "Water Coyote" clans is undermined by Titiev's own indication (1944:87) that fully one-third of this populous clan (16 out of 45) remained Friendly.

Item 5 contains a significant inaccuracy (see Chapter 4)—that is, that two full ceremonial cycles developed at the turn of the century.

I am not contesting the general idea that sociological factors had a role in the Oraibi split: clearly they did. But the emphasis upon these as *the* motivating forces is questionable. It depends upon a flawed characterization of Hopi social structure and ignores the actualities of Hopi political processes. It also neglects some vital historical contexts of the division and the ensuing results of political action.

Material Determinism

The next major type of explanation I call "material-determinist." Its most thorough proponent (others include Goldfrank 1948 and Alvarado 1968) is R. M. Bradfield (1971). Bradfield's argument is that population pressure on limited resources reached a critical point before 1906 and the split occurred in direct response. Central to his thesis is the idea that downcutting of the Oraibi Wash rapidly destroyed prime farmlands in the Oraibi Valley. Initially he suggested that this occurred between 1901 and 1906:

> The immediate, precipitating cause [of the split] was economic. In the space of five years some 800 acres of the best farmland in the valley was lost: a third of the total. And this land belonged to the traditionally dominant lineages in the village, those that were responsible for initiating and carrying through the principal ceremonies in the annual liturgy; at a blow, the economic ground of their leadership was undermined. Had there been a ready supply of alternative land to turn to, the split might yet have been averted. (1971:23)

Just prior to publication, however, Bradfield discovered that two older Hopis remembered the dissection of the wash as occurring after the split rather than before. This invalidated his conclusion. So he footnoted an alternative:

> The climatic sequence of the latter nineteenth century was, I still hold, the ultimate cause of the splitting of the village in 1906. By 1891 the old pueblo had reached the limit of its field resources; the thirteen lean years from 1892 to 1904, by reducing the yield from the cultivated land, put an increasing economic strain on its inhabitants; this strain was reflected in the dissensions which rent the community during those years, and which led directly to the schism of 1906. (1971:45)

There is no question that economic conditions were an important aspect of Oraibi factionalism. My older consultants cite population pressure as one of the elements in the split and refer to a mythological ordination that, once a certain line was crossed in the northeastward expansion of Oraibi's dwellings, the people would have to be dispersed. They also stress that the water supply in Oraibi's main spring had slowed to a trickle, requiring women to wait for hours while their containers slowly filled. Nevertheless, Bradfield's exclusive emphasis upon demographic and ecological factors as either the immediate precipitating cause or the ultimate cause, is, I believe, misconceived. Since his first argument—that arroyo-cutting was the immediate cause of the split—is central to his monograph, the postscripted footnote has had only a marginal effect on its refutation; the former argument still proves popular with southwestern archaeologists of a materialist persuasion (personal communications beyond number). Both positions, then, still require scrutiny.

The "immediate-cause" argument contains false premises. Elsewhere (Whiteley 1985b,1986), I have questioned the assumed relationship between political leadership, descent groups, and control of arable land. Leadership, I suggest, was based on control over ritual knowledge rather than over a land base: the supposed "economic ground" of their leadership was thus not susceptible to undermining.

Bradfield's analysis of the economic situation is basically inadequate. He argues that a four-mile radius from the village was the optimal expanse for agricultural fields and that anything beyond would "have precluded the use of any considerable acreage of farmland" (1971:22). This, I presume, is his reasoning that there was no "ready supply of alternative land," but it is simply incorrect. First, there was an extensive field system at Oraibi's colony at Moencopi, which was increasingly absorbing elements of Oraibi's population; by 1900, eighty-five people were in permanent residence (U.S. Government 1900). Moencopi (literally, "continuously flowing water place") had the advantage of a permanent water supply. Since the 1870s Mormon settlers had developed this into an irrigation system, which was also used by Moencopi Hopis. Also, there was extensive agricultural commerce between Moencopi and Oraibi: Moencopi fields represented a secondary source of produce when Oraibi harvests were poor. Further, other lands, north and west of Oraibi and around the Dinnebito Wash, were already under cultivation by 1893 (Mayhugh 2-14-1893). The eastern side of the Dinnebito Valley especially provided a good supply of land (the western side may have been occupied by Navajos at this point). Moreover, according to my consultants, the area around No-Trail Mesa, to the southwest of Oraibi, was farmed before the split. These areas were indeed farther from Oraibi than the prime land in the Oraibi Valley, but they clearly comprise readily available alternatives that were in fact being used.

In part, the reason for the availability of these alternative lands was the introduction of wagons. Bradfield represents the indigenous economy of the 1890s and early 1900s as pristine and self-contained. In reality, various agencies of Anglo-American society had begun to provide not only significant economic alternatives to aspects of the traditional system, but also direct aid in times of acute hardship. Bradfield's "four-mile limit" is predicated on the assumption that haulage technology was limited to human and burro backs. Mayhugh (2-19-1894) notes the presence of some wagons at Oraibi in 1894, and by 1899, when forty were distributed among the villages by the agency, wagons had become part of the government's annual issue of goods—to promote "civilizing influences" (Hazylett 1899:158). In addition, the availability of wage work at the agency, at the Oraibi mission, and elsewhere was a significant alternative. In a year of almost total harvest failure in 1902, for example, the Oraibis were not completely destitute: "during August many of them had gone to the Mormon settlement, about fifty miles west from here [Tuba City], to earn something during harvest" (*The Mennonite* 12-11-1902). Access to commodities at the Oraibi store provided palpable supplements to the subsistence economy by the late 1890s. In Chapter 4, I also noted the government's continual attempts to disperse the villages to single-family farm sites, even offering the inducement to build tin-roofed houses (several of which were built for Oraibi families in the 1890s) for those willing to move.

In short, other possibilities were available for dealing with population pressure on a limited economic base. The base was not as limited as Bradfield suggests and was considerably broadened by the introduction of both supplementary economic alternatives and new haulage technology. Acceptance or rejection of these new alternatives was a cultural and political matter, but the point is that the traditional economy was not the pristine isolate Bradfield would have us believe.

My third quarrel with the immediate-cause argument concerns Bradfield's premise that prior to 1865 the land base restricted maximum population to 720, and that actual population was likely never higher than 660 (1971:22,29); it was an increase to about 880 in 1905–6 (1971:63) that caused additional pressure on land. Bradfield's use of population figures is rather selective: earlier estimates with which he disagrees he simply says are "much too high" (1971:61)—without citing any. It is likely that some earlier figures were too high, but to assume that all were requires a substantive treatment of specifics. Every single figure cited in Chapter 2, with one egregious exception,[2] is considerably higher than Bradfield's maximum. Moreover, Dobyns's work (e.g., 1983) suggests strongly that conventional assumptions of low Native American population size at earlier periods are thoroughly erroneous.

Bradfield's second argument—that economic pressure was the *ultimate* cause—tells us nothing of political or cultural significance. For example, that nine prominent Hostiles spent up to eighteen months in jail in 1890–92, or that nineteen languished in Alcatraz for almost a year in 1895, or long after the split, that Yukioma continued to be imprisoned (even for a three–year term in 1916–19 [Crane 1925:186]) seem to me matters that demand greater explanation than ultimate causes in economic stress. The cultural point applies to both Bradfield's arguments. Implicitly the split is represented as a reflex response to economic conditions that surpassed the Oraibi leaders' grasp. Yet climate and economy are matters of critical religious and political concern which receive constant, minute attention in the annual cycle of ritual works. It seems reasonable to infer that Hopis in the 1890s were at least as acutely aware of the significance of ecological conditions as they are in the 1980s. The material-determinist position ignores this cultural reality. Instead, we have a black-box behaviorist implication that the mindless Hopis, uncomprehending of the conditions of their existence, responded like laboratory rats to randomly changed stimuli. All they could do in a last-ditch situation was divide their population and disperse its use of resources. They are thus attributed collectively with little capacity for deliberate action, little understanding of their environment, and little credit for having probably maintained a large integral community in this fragile ecosystem for the preceding several hundred years, which were, we must assume, free from serious economic threats. In sum, this perspective treats the Oraibi split not as a sociocultural phenomenon but as a biological one.

Acculturative Pressure

The third major explanation of the split seeks its cause in pressure to acculturate from the dominant society. Of several proponents of this viewpoint, none stands out as main exemplar. The idea of intercultural friction is of course implicit in the terms "Friendly" and "Hostile" and these reflect the primary interpretation of the

Hegemony in action. A group of Arizona politicians photographed in front of a line of *Tasapkatsinam* (Navajo Kachinas), Sichomovi, ca. 1915. The stars-and-stripes flutters above a house behind. Photograph by Wesley Bradfield, courtesy Museum of New Mexico, Neg. No. 130372.

factional division in American society at the time. But as we saw in Chapter 4, use of these terms was relative: the Hostiles had white allies and the Friendlies were not unequivocally acquiescent. The terms are significant only in relation to the government and its policies, particularly the controversial education program.

Hargrave summarizes well the acculturative-pressure argument:

> Many of the Oraibians still resented the Government order to send their children to school at Keam's Canyon and again rebelled against the plans of the agency. Others adopted a more liberal attitude toward civilization. Since neither side would concede its principles a settlement by means of a tug-o-war was agreed upon, the losing side to leave the village. (Hargrave 1932:7)

Titiev also pays tribute to this argument, despite his basic commitment to sociological causes. Like some Hopi versions of the split, he suggests that Loololma's visit to Washington led to a reversal in his attitude toward the education program: "Lololoma's change of policy immediately caused a violent reaction among his people.

Some of them favored the new attitude, but a large part of Oraibi's populace was ultra-conservative and vigorously condemned the Village Chief's change of heart" (1944:73). The idea that Loololma's "change of heart" generated the factional division requires that his visit occurred prior to the first reports of factional troubles. Cushing's account of 1882 (Chapter 4) describes a serious rift almost eight years before Loololma's visit to Washington and five years before the education program affected Oraibi at all.

Elsie Parsons also propounds the acculturative-pressure cause: "the Oraibi split was a consequence of friction with white culture" (Fewkes 1922:283). More recently, Richard Clemmer suggests that the split came about "after a quarter-century of tension and conflict resulting from the immediate ideological issue of U.S. Government interference in Hopi life ... [which] ... set up a dichotomy between those who favored the government and those who did not" (Clemmer 1978:58).

As with the other major arguments, there are elements of truth here also. Many Hopis assuredly aligned themselves with factional leaders on the basis of acceptance or rejection of the government and perceived this as the immediate ideological issue. But this tells us little of the actual sociocultural processes at work in Oraibi or why these culminated in the dramatic split of the village. Unless we assume, rather rashly it would seem in view of the history recounted in Chapter 2, that Oraibi had never faced an ideological issue of equivalent magnitude, this does not so much explain the split as explain it away.

John Golden's argument (1951) does suggest some internal political processes behind the split, although he also uses a variation on the acculturative-pressure theme. Golden identifies a tripartite ideological division between leading clans. The Spider clan, he maintains, tried to wrest control from the Bear clan for leadership of the village and authority over land. The Bear clan saw its only hope of victory as lying in an alliance with the government. But the price was acquiescence to acculturation, and here the *Kookop* clan, as guardians of the traditional Hopi way, protested and allied with the Spider clan. With the subsequent split, the Spider and *Kookop* allies also divided, resulting in the two new villages.

The notion of clan blocs facing off against each other is simply not the way Hopi politics works. Although support for political leaders may come from fellow clan members, this does not entail clearly differentiated political clan groups like parties in a parliamentary system. First, cross-clan ties and institutional modes of interrelationship were multiplex. Second, nearly all important decision making was conducted in private by a relatively few leaders consulting together rather than by whole clan groups. I argue below that ideological opposition was largely a catalyst exploited by political leaders to mobilize commoners into clearly opposed camps. It was the perception of the resulting alignments (symptoms, then, rather than cause) by outsiders which led to this view of straightforward ideological division. But such a view completely ignores the subtleties and complexities of Hopi social structure and political action. Again we are left with an analysis in which the split is mechanically played out among (misconceived) abstract units of social structure, and in which the empirical context of actual Hopi practice is occluded.

In sum, each of these major arguments indicates some important contextual considerations of the split. But each appeals to abstract explanatory models that neglect crucial cultural and historical detail. None provides an adequate explanation of why the particular response to the problems perceived by each analyst variously as fundamental was the split, in lieu of other possible solutions. In short, each explanation is teleological and each is underpinned (in differing degrees) by monistic determinism. Thus we are still left with the problem "why the split?" and what exactly its consequences were, long-term as well as immediate. If we examine a Hopi interpretation, we shall see a more comprehensive interlinking of cause and consequence.

Hopi Analyses of the Split

There is no single Hopi "orthodox version" of the split and this should be expected with an event of such tumultuous significance. Individual Hopi representations of historical events, although perhaps not as "deeply perspectival" as those of Ilongots (Rosaldo 1980:20), in that they must conform when publicly expressed to collective standards of truth evaluation, are nevertheless politically charged statements. Moreover, knowledge of history is not a free commodity in Hopi society. It is a primary medium of prestige and rank, and the more esoteric the knowledge, the more closely guarded it is. This has changed somewhat during the twentieth century, but it is by no means obsolete.

Hopinavoti is the general category of Hopi ideation that provides thoroughgoing analyses that are comparable to anthropological analyses, in that they stem from a demarcated tradition of interpretation that is specialized, restricted, and "expert." *Navoti* indicates a system of knowledge that includes philosophy, science, and theology and incorporates conceptual models for explaining the past and predicting, or "prophesying," future events (for those convinced that Hopi is a "timeless language," see Malotki's 1982 critique of Whorf's view): in short, it is a sort of Hopi hermeneutics. The predictive element and the temporal connection between cause and effect mean that present conditions can be explained by reference to past predictions and that future events will in some way reflect contemporary "prophecy"—a term used for *navoti* in Hopi English ("theory" is another).

The nature and depth of understanding of *Hopinavoti* differs. *Sukavungsinom* are regarded as having a shallower understanding than *pavansinom*. With regard to ritual symbolism, for example, discrete layers of meaning are recognized by the more knowledgeable, who can and do identify the more profound layers in appropriate circumstances. An obvious parallel in western society is between the knowledge claimed by the academic community and the intelligentsia in general over the meanings and functioning of phenomena, and the "common-sense" understandings of the "general public." However, the structure of knowledge distribution in Hopi society departs from this parallel and is more aptly compared to established ecclesiastical structures differentiating a clerical hierarchy from a laity. The boundaries separating a *navotiytaqa* (literally, a "man of knowledge"—a common term for distinguishing the validity of an interpretation's source) from others are maintained by strict controls on access to knowledge. We might portray the sociology of Hopi knowledge as a series of concentric rings marking boundaries of secrecy between circles of knowledge or, as

Barth (1975:passim) suggests for the Baktaman, as an assemblage of Chinese boxes.

The Hopi analysis of the split of most interest comes from numerous accounts by older Hopis of their experience of the events and/or the interpretations and analyses recounted to them by participants. It derives from those people who represent, or whose knowledge is derived from, the *pavansinom* class, and I shall treat it as more sophisticated than some other Hopi analyses. Criteria for judging ethnographically whether a particular interpretation was more or less sophisticated were mostly based upon its explanatory adequacy, coupled with the (vestigial) social rank of the consultant or quoted source. In time, a dialogic pattern emerged, wherein reference to a particular interpretation was greeted with remarks to the effect, "That's just the superficial view: the real meaning. . . ." If I could substantiate by reference to other oral sources and archivally that the latter explained more and did so more incisively, then I would accept it as a more sophisticated analysis.

At the time of the split, knowledge of the more profound analysis was restricted. Those who discussed it with me, however, emphasized that with the passage of time, and as the effects of the split became increasingly entrenched, those privy to this interpretation explicitly intended that it be made public. I doubt that any older Third Mesa Hopis would find anything unfamiliar in the present account. Although the information was once esoteric, it is no longer.

Wiimit orayvi yukilti—Oraibi's religion is terminated.

Now, the ceremonies and what goes into them goes back to what we did in Oraibi. The ritualism, all the songs, the ritual prayers and the knowledge were ritually destined to be forgotten. No one will possess these ever again. This is what was done at the time Oraibi split. They instructed the people who left Oraibi that as they went into the future, their prayers and their faith should be through the cornmeal alone, that they should not let this cornmeal go, for this was the most fundamental sacrament of all. Kewanimptewa used to tell me that *wiimi*, as it was in Oraibi, had ended with the split. We used to have arguments over this point with him. I asked him, "How can it end, these ceremonies, when we find doing even Kachina dances enjoyable and when we even continue to talk some ritual language during our smoking down at the kiva?" All the old man would say in reply was, "This was what was decided in Oraibi at the time of the split."

It was even said that any village established after the split is a *sukavungki* [commoner village]—Kykotsmovi, Hotevilla, Bacavi, Moencopi. It was said that not even kivas were supposed to be built in those villages. These were the words they exchanged and left each other with. Tawaquaptewa's followers had in fact chosen to live the white man's way. After the people went to Hotevilla and later to Bacavi, they went ahead and did the *Wuwtsim* ceremonies again, because it was simply a part of them, being Hopis. This is how we both got to building our kivas again.

These are Bacavi versions. Substantively the same story was related by consultants from Hotevilla, Lower Moencopi, and Old Oraibi. An Old Oraibi version:

Now *wiimi*, that was ended at Oraibi in 1906. They purposefully destroyed it. All the head priests at Oraibi decided that no one should carry it on. Even the people who went away [the Hostiles] made a vow not to practice it. This is what was agreed upon. It was ended. . . . The split was carried out based on *navoti*. Using this they planned the destruction of the ceremonies. But after they sat down and really talked about it, they saw that they could fulfil the prophecy [on the destruction of Oraibi] easily by taking into consideration that Oraibi was overpopulated, water was scarce, and good farming land was depleted. So the old chiefs pondered and talked about this situation of hardship. It was decided that the only way for the people to survive was to split up. All the chiefs agreed and it was decided on in good faith and with no ill feelings toward each other. Yukioma agreed to lead one group out of Oraibi, and in this way he would fulfill his clan's prophecy of return to their ruins at Kawestima. . . . But Yukioma had a change of heart: he refused to go on his own and carry out his promise. . . . Some of us who knew little of the plan between Loololma, Tawaquaptewa, and Yukioma saw the bitterness as real. We *sukavungsinom* started the real fighting and were truly bitter toward each other—it was not supposed to go this far.

The abolition of the ritual order must be seen not only in its religious aspect, but also in the ramifications it had for the rest of the social structure—politically, economically, and in terms of kinship. The ending of the ritual order meant the demise of traditional priestly office—in short, the end of the *pavansinom-sukavungsinom* division—of ritual clan-lands (such as these were), and of significant intraclan ritual knowledge.

According to these versions, those who left Oraibi were supposed to go to Kawestima (generally thought to be Keet Seel in Tsegi Canyon, although this is debated[3]). When they reached Kawestima, they might have reconstituted the ceremonial cycle, but they forfeited the right to do so when they returned to Oraibi. As we saw in Chapter 7, most of the Hostile priests did indeed go back to Oraibi. Yukioma himself is regarded as vacillating on the issue (contemporary documents show that he did not want to leave Oraibi and, after he had left, wanted to return and have Tawaquaptewa's faction put out of the village [U.S. Government 1906–10: passim]). The following was pointed out by an older Hotevilla consultant:

Those claiming authority in Hotevilla, or anywhere else on Third Mesa, by their religious offices, don't really have it. Everyone nowadays is just a commoner; the religious leaders who led the people to Hotevilla lost all their authority the moment they turned to go back to Oraibi.... So it was by virtue of their going back to Oraibi that the *pavansinom* lost their power, or did not have to be listened to any more. This and the split itself involved making everyone equal as commoners, so there were to be no chiefs who would be superior to anyone else.

It is important to emphasize that the notion of ritual abolition is widespread across Third Mesa and is not just confined to the descendants of the Bacavi faction. It is equally important to stress that the above account is that of an older Hotevilla man, who by traditional ritual standards has a powerful claim to high status. The viewpoint is not, then, motivated by political aims. It is particularly significant that the view is shared in Hotevilla, because this was the village that did reconstitute most of the ceremonial cycle during its earlier years. The fact that *any* ritual performances by the higher-order religious societies were conducted after the split must be accounted for, and I shall return to this below. First, however, the argument presented here as the sophisticated Hopi analysis needs additional corroboration; after all, my consultants could all be aberrant!

Published Hopi Accounts

The only published Hopi account of the split I have found which does *not* treat it as a deliberate plot or as the fulfillment of prophecy is Don Talayesva's *Sun Chief* (Simmons 1942). The two-page account (109–10) is straightforwardly descriptive, and where causes are referred to elsewhere they are attributed to the education issue.

Every other account (e.g., Nequatewa 1936:passim [see below]; Hopi Hearings 1955:passim; Qoyawayma 1964:13–48, passim; H. Sekaquaptewa 1969:passim; E. Sekaquaptewa 1972:247–48; Yava 1978:111–15,150) mentions either the conspiratorial or the prophetic aspects of the split or both.

Edmund Nequatewa's treatment (1936) is the earliest. He explicitly distinguishes between the superficial version—"the one believed by most of the Hopi" (1936:131 n. 47)—and the more exclusive "true story." Nequatewa's "true story" is a First Mesa version (although Nequatewa himself was from Second Mesa), which assigns original impetus for the split to the Washington visit of 1890. I quote this account at length because it provides an excellent example of the recounting of the flow of events in a Hopi frame of reference:

When they reached Washington, they were asked to try to bring their people down off their mesas and advised to get them to spread about and form other small communities in the country nearby. At this time the Navajo were beginning to press into Hopi country and occupy their lands and it was thought that if the Hopi could be induced to spread out they could lay claim to more land and check the Navajo advance. It is not known whose idea this was, but it is unlikely that it had its origin in Washington.

Each chief, or representative, was asked to choose sites for the proposed colonies. . . . Lololama was the only one of the party to think out a plan to move his people and he worked this out in his mind on the way home. Of course, he knew very well that just asking his people to move out would not be enough to get them started. They would have to have some strong reason, like a quarrel or a disagreement among themselves. Now Lololama knew that this was a traditional plan or "theory" among his people and that it always had worked. When the leaders found that for some reason it was desirable for their people, either the whole village, or a part thereof, to move away and found a new establishment, they would deliberately get together and plan to foment a quarrel. This would be invariably carried out in such a clever way by the leaders that the people themselves would never suspect the plot, and eventually the separation or move would occur just as it had been planned.

However, after such a conspiracy these leaders always considered themselves guilty because of the trouble and distress they had brought upon their people in the process of working out a plan which was to benefit these same people eventually. They often "sacrificed" themselves deliberately, in atonement for the distress caused their people in this process and any misfortune befalling them after such an act, even though for the good of their people, was considered right and just punishment. . . . So Lololama and Youkioma made an agreement and Youkioma was to lead his people just a little way off from the village—"Just to take them a few steps away from Oraibi," as the Hopi say. Then he was to ask them whether they were really his faithful followers or whether they were doubtful about following him wherever he might lead them. If they felt doubtful, he would say that they could go back to Oraibi, or make up with the chief there, or do whatever they wished. By doing this Youkioma thought that he would "start an argument" which would result in breaking up the people into still smaller groups. It would seem that he actually tried this.

Later Lomahungeoma and Kiwanimptiwa (whom it is believed were in the conspiracy with the two chiefs, and who were related to each other) broke away from Youkioma's people and Lomahungeoma started out to lead a group of people away to find another home. On the way, it is said, he lost his nerve (for he was thinking of the Navajo that were now pressing in around the Hopi and of what might happen to his people) so Kiwanimptiwa stepped in and took over the leadership and they finally settled at Bakabi. (Nequatewa 1936:132–33 n. 47)

Certain points of Nequatewa's account are at minor variance with the events described in Chapter 4 and in this chapter (Navajo encroachment as the original cause is surely too narrow, for example). But he highlights several important features of the Hopi analysis: the conspiracy of political leadership; the established practice of leaders manipulating the people to unwittingly fulfill clandestine plans; and the element of self-sacrifice on the leaders' part—in effect, planning their own demise or the demise of their positions of authority.

Emory Sekaquaptewa's account (1972) is also worth quoting at length since it ties together a number of the threads we have been pursuing. Because of the closeness of Sekaquaptewa's account with the version I have presented above, I should stress that I did not read his article until my main period of field research was complete:

The Oraibi split of 1906 is said to be the result of controversy between two factions in the village over this agreement [of 1890 in Washington]. Yukeoma, the leader of the conservative faction, openly accused the faction under Lololma of betraying his trust as a Hopi chief. This agreement was considered by Yukeoma and his faction as a rejection of the Hopi way of life. On the other hand, Lololma saw himself as the last traditionally ordained chief at Oraibi, fulfilling the prophecy that all *wii wimi* (broadly interpreted by some Hopis to mean cultural practices, but more narrowly by others to mean only religious practices) would be "put to rest" at Oraibi. He saw his agreement with the government as the alternative by which the Hopi people would accept the white man's way of life. This prophecy warned against transplanting of the *wii wimi* to any other place, with the exception of *katcina* practices.

The more sophisticated view is that the division itself was the substance of the prophecy, in that it was designed in deliberation or, in Hopi terms, *diingavi*. It held that such a division was necessary to the survival of the Hopis as a people, in that establishment of another Hopi community would secure to the Hopis the lands between it and Oraibi. It also held that the sanctity of the religious authorities had become subject to more and more abuse as Oraibi grew in size and social complexity so that ritualism began to serve personal edification more than it served communal spiritual needs. It was said that much of the ritualism in traditional practices took on the character of sorcery which "preyed" on people to the detriment of natural population growth, and it was said that a new community would encourage increase in population when it existed without these corruptive devices. The division was said to be the fulfillment of prophecy taught by a religious ceremony in which an act in finale by the participants was a declaration in unison that "this is the way we shall go to Kawestima." The participants would make this declaration just as they left the kiva, after having wrapped up their altars and put them over their shoulders. Presumably, this commemorates the prophecy that the Hopi people will return and reclaim the ancestral home of Kawestima, which name was said to belong to the kikmongwi of that ancient village. Yukeoma and his followers were to seek and resettle Kawestima after their ejectment from Oraibi. Thus the Lololma agreement with Wasendo [Washington] was said to be merely an instrument to dramatize the conflict and to represent it as a political one. Hopi historians say that dramatization was necessary in order to generate high emotions on both sides, which would evoke greater determination and dedication to their respective causes tending to lessen the difficulty of those who had to uproot their homes and families, and also promoting their adjustment to harsh conditions of living wherever they resettled. (E. Sekaquaptewa 1972:247–48)[4]

Further supportive context for the Hopi analysis appears in accounts of the destruction or abandonment of previous villages. Several of these follow a parallel mode of representation. Signs of decadence and corruption, frequently in the form of immoral and antisocial behavior, are noticed by village leaders. After warnings to improve behavior fail, they plot to destroy the village and many of the people with it. Examples of villages (and even the previous world below) destroyed in this way are numerous (e.g., Voth 1905a: 16–26, 241–46; Nequatewa 1936:7–23, 85–102). One of the most recent, and assuredly one of the most powerful cases in Hopi oral literature, is the destruction of Awatovi. Several published versions (see Laird 1977) follow the pattern alluded to. Because of decadence in the Hopi way (some versions specifically include the fact that Awatovi allowed the Franciscans to reestablish a mission), the *Kikmongwi* organized a scheme with the chiefs of other villages whereby Awatovi would be attacked and utterly destroyed. One of the better versions was told to H. R. Voth (1905a:246–53) by Tangakhoyoma, an Oraibi man, before the split. It features the chief's desire that his village, including himself and his family, be immolated; secret plotting with the chiefs of other villages to this end; and the realization of the plot after the Awatovi people are fooled into a position of weakness by the chief. If Tangakhoyoma's version was tailored to contemporary significances (providing, as Malinowski [e.g. 1948] would have it, a "charter for social action"), he may well have been subtextually adumbrating the situation of Oraibi. Similarly, around the same time, Yukioma presented a version of the emergence myth:

> A very long time ago they were living down below. Everything was good there at that time. That way of living was good down there. Everything was good, everything grew well; it rained all the time, everything was blossoming. That is the way it was, but by and by it became different. The chiefs commenced to do bad. Then it stopped raining and they only had very small crops and the winds began to blow. People became sick. By and by it was like it is here now, and at last the people participated in this. They, too, began to talk bad and to be bad. And then those who have not a single heart, the sorcerers, that are very bad, began to increase and became more and more. The people began to live the way we are living now, in constant contentions. Thus they were living. Nobody would listen any more. They became very bad. They would take the wives of the chiefs. The chiefs hereupon became angry and they planned to do something to the people, to take revenge on them. They began to think of escaping. So a few of the chiefs met once and thought and talked about the matter. (Voth 1905a:16)

Though Yukioma seems to place more blame on the chiefs than on the people, the paradigm is similar, and it would be hard to find a stronger subtextual prediction of the events to come in Oraibi.

A final example of this pattern appears in another tale from Oraibi:

Hopi and Anthropological Analysis

One time the children (people) of the chief in Oraibi were very bad and the chief concluded that he would punish them. So he went over to the warrior chief in Walpi. He sat down and they first smoked, then the warrior chief asked him what his object in coming was. "Yes," he said, "my children are very bad and I have come to see what you think about it. After some days we will come by here to attack Walpi. You must then be ready and come to meet us in the valley, and when my children return and run, you must kill them." (Voth 1905a:255)

After the chief tricks his people into attacking Walpi, many are killed on the return journey. The narrative concludes:

This is the way chiefs often punished their children (people) when they became "bewitched." That is one reason there are so many ruins all over the country. Many people were killed in that way because their chiefs became angry and invited some chief or inhabitant from other villages [*sic*] to destroy their people. (Voth 1905a:256)

My point is that the analysis presented of the Oraibi split is not a unique interpretative pattern: it conforms to a historical paradigm with ample precedents.

Documentary Sources

Contemporary documents are in general not terribly sensitive to ethnographic detail, but some do reveal opinions that go beyond the common view that the problem hinged solely on intercultural relations. Chapter 4 has cited some observers' doubts about the purported friendliness of the Friendlies and about prophetic aspects of the split. One of the outsiders present during the split reported:

From all I can learn from the Hopis the dispute has to do with their religion and nothing to do with the U.S. School as most people think. It appears that the Unfriendly's [*sic*] are against the School because the Friendlies favor it and the Friendlies favor it because they think it gives them the support of the Government. (Woodgate n.d.)

Missionary Epp's report of the split gives more detail. He notes that upon his arrival in 1901:

The principal question seemed to be the school, very likely because this was before them 10 months of the year, and affected every family with children.

The men of the "hostile" party, with few exceptions, wore partly or entirely "white-man's" clothes, about which the "friendlies" would constantly tease them. Then the "hostiles" continually blamed the "friendlies" of being the ones who called in the school, the policemen, and everything else belonging to the "white-man", which the "hostiles" do not want. So there is among these "hostiles" less feeling against the Government; such feeling is rather against their "friendly" neighbors.

The "friendlies" *hate* the others—as they say—because they are not friendly to the "white-man". This I could never understand, because to my observation the "friendlies" were and are friendly only for the Dollar and for the conveniences derived from being thus friendly. And therefore I could never get to a satisfactory conclusion by debating this question with the "friendlies". I have, therefore, been suspecting among these "friendlies" a different cause for disliking the "hostiles". I find so far, that the "friendlies" *begrudge* the "hostiles" of every benefit they get from the "white-man" (some have wagons; haul freight etc.; many work a great deal for white people). These benefits are detracted from the "friendlies"—of course. I have seldom—lately *very* seldom—heard a "friendly" speak of the school as a *benefit*, but as an obligation. . . . I find in 9 cases out of 10 the Hopi giving me either a wrong reason or else a secondary reason for his actions—in fact very seldom does he (the Hopi) state the real reason for any of his actions, to a "white-man". . . .

Anyone acquainted with the Indians knows that they have more *traditional* reasons than any "white-man" ever finds out, for actions of the kind that transpired at Oraibi on Sept. 7th inst., as well as for smaller deeds. (Epp 9-20-1906, emphases in original)

Contemporary accounts also show that, despite Titiev's (1944: 87) assertion that both factions were "about equal," the Hostiles were in fact considerably more numerous and could, had they wished, have put up a much stronger fight on the day of the split. According to Elizabeth Stanley (9-18-1906:4), the school principal, one-third of the village carried out the other two-thirds: "I do not understand why the Hostiles did not resist more, unless they are fatalists, as some think." Superintendent Lemmon (9-9-1906:5) rode through the Hostile camp on 8 September and corrected his original estimate of four hundred Hostiles to "nearer six hundred." According to a census of the Hostile camp recorded on 30 October, there were 539, including about 52 from Second Mesa (U.S. Government 10-30-1906). As Lemmon remarks:

Half a dozen estimates are that from two-thirds to three-fourths of the village were taken out of their houses and pushed out of the village by the remaining one-third or one-fourth and yet nobody hurt except an epileptic woman. Mr. Epp and Mrs. Gates believe this and believe that the arms captured from the unfriendlies without a shot being fired or an arrow being sped was because of the prowess of the friendlies. I fought some of these people [i.e., the Hostiles] when they were in fighting mood and know this is the veriest rot under the sun. Those people were shrewd enough to seduce the friendlies into an attack and then yielded. Two ladies who saw the whole thing today expressed wonder at the fact that on the faces of most of the unfriendlies was a smile during the whole of the contest. They went simply and solely because the superstitions drilled into them by some twenty-five old mental mummies who ought to be in prison made them afraid not to obey their infernal orders. (Lemmon 9-9-1906;5-6)

After Commissioner Leupp gathered eyewitness accounts of the split, he commented:

Just how far the attitude of either party was due originally to its hatred or tolerance of Caucasian ideals is open to question. It is believed by not a few persons who know these Indians well that their division grew wholly out of the internal political dissensions of the tribe. (Leupp 1907:118)

In addition, some documents refer to the contemporary citing of prophecy (cf. Leupp 1907:124). For example, two days after the split, Tawaquaptewa and other Friendlies told Lemmon

that it was a Hopi prophesy that all this would come about and that whichever party was vanquished must leave the village and the Hopi country for ever. That they must go far to the north to the land of Ka-weis-ti-ma, told of in their religious songs; that nobody knows where this is or when it will be reached but the initiated have such a description of it that they will recognize it when they reach it. (Lemmon 9-9-1906)

Lemmon heard the same from the Hostiles and attempted to convince them that there was no land to the north where whites were not already moving in.

The Interpretive Context

The Nature of Political Decision Making

Since knowledge in Hopi society is the currency of power and is closely guarded in secrecy, it follows that the political decision-making process—the actions of knowledge-holders—is a secretive, conspiratorial affair. Political meetings were typically held by leading men in secret, under the cover of darkness. Formal occasions during which the events of the following year were discussed and planned (such as in the chief kiva during *Soyalangw*) were generally known about, but more ad hoc meetings would usually occur clandestinely in a house at night.[5] What occurs during such meetings is referred to as *pasiuni*, or "ritualized planning." *Pasiuni* can refer to the planning of a ceremony, although *tiingavi* is usually used for this meaning. *Pasiuni*, according to my consultants, more properly means a "planning of destiny." Above, Sekaquaptewa uses *tiingavi* for the deliberate planning of the Oraibi split, but since my consultants consistently used *pasiuni*, I shall use the term also.

In a political context, *pasiuni* refers to the process of decision making. Decisions are ritually agreed upon and "sealed" in such a way that their planned consequences are ineluctable: "once something is planned that way, it *has* to happen." These ideas inhabit a cosmology far from the western conception of an intentionless arrangement of material phenomena in which events often occur at random. Rather, the Hopi universe is filled with intentional forces, of which mankind is a part. *Pavansinom* have the capacity to tap these intentional forces to affect the course of events. Thus political actions are construed to relate not merely to social conditions narrowly considered, but also to climate, ecology, and "man in nature." The planning of a bountiful harvest or conversely of adverse weather conditions is, because of the effects on the life of man, a political as well as a ritual act. Ecological events are often explained as the results of intentional acts by the *pavansinom*, and are interpreted as a reward or punishment for collective behavior.

An informative analogy to the process of secret planning was offered by an older consultant:

Hopis are like clowns and Kachinas—they plot what's going to happen; they plan out life. This is what the chief priests do in real life as well. . . . Remember, in the Hopi way everything is done through *pasiuni* by the chiefs—once planned, once the wheels have been set in motion, the ends *have* to occur. This is how Hopi politics and society works.

This analogy refers to a segment of the two-day clown ceremony. It involves the bargaining by the clown chief (*tsukumongwi*) with the chief of a disciplinary group of Warrior Kachinas. Toward the end of the first day, the clowns are approached by Warrior Kachinas and warned about their excessive, outrageous behavior. The clown chief tries to persuade the Warrior Kachina chief (usually a *mongwu*, or Great Horned Owl Kachina) to spare his people (i.e., his fellow clowns) from dreadful punishment, including the threat of death. At various junctures during the remainder of the ceremony, the clown chief is seen squatting down to one side of the plaza in discussion with the Warrior Kachina chief. He is rebuked for his failure to produce an improvement in the clowns' behavior and so offers increasingly persuasive blandishments to plead mercy for the clowns, finally presenting a turquoise necklace as a sort of mortgage on their lives (although in the ceremonial context the outcome is never a foregone conclusion). During the last of the four negotiations, especially, the other clowns look on suspiciously at what they take—quite rightly—to be a conspiracy about their own destiny between their leader (whose role represents the *Kikmongwi*) and the Warrior Kachina chief.

The analogy, then, indicates that political decision making is secret and has a conspiratorial character, the destiny of the people is planned by leaders, and the ritual sealing of decisions (e.g., with the turquoise necklace) renders their realization inevitable.

Edward Kennard (1972:469–70) further illuminates the concept of *pasiuni*:

> The fundamental idea underlying their cosmology, their assumptions about the universe, their obligations as Hopi, and what they perceive as threats to their individual and collective lives is that everything is predetermined. Every December, during Soyalangwu, the complete sequence of events for the coming year is laid out: each ceremony, each dance, the time for planting are magically enacted in advance, in the hope that these performances will determine their success and prosperity throughout the coming year. The Hopi word for magically predetermining such future events is *pasiwna*. In Hopi belief, once this has been done in the kiva during the Soyalangwu, what is devoutly hoped for must also be manifested at the appropriate time in the year that follows. In the same sense of *pasiwna*, the destiny of the Hopi was determined from the Beginning, and is still being unfolded generation by generation.

This places the concept in a universal context. More concretely, and stressing the significance of deliberate human intention, one consultant phrased it this way: "*Tunatya. Pasiuni. Okiw antani.* This is the cornerstone of the Hopi way." Not uncharacteristically, he explained this metaphorically by reference to the maize cycle.

Tunatya refers to the initial idea, the "seed of thought" concerning the desired future event.[6] *Pasiuni*, in this processual context, refers to bringing together all the necessary elements to germinate and nurture the seed into a viable program of action. *Okiw antani* ("Now let it be this way," addressed to larger supernatural forces) expresses consecration of the plan; it pronounces the will and hope that the seed will bear fruit.

As I emphasized in Chapter 3, the respect and even awe of the politico-religious leaders, which was used to maintain structures of dominance, rested on the depth of belief in their supernatural power to plan the future course of events. Moreover, in contrast to Kennard's somewhat idealized view, events planned were not always overtly beneficial to the people: epidemics, famine, plagues of crop pests, and other forms of misfortune were often interpreted as the results of political decisions. Such misfortunes were invoked to redress perceived natural or social disharmony caused by the collectivity's lack of adherence to sociocultural norms.

It is also important to emphasize that, in the absence of coercive mechanisms for enforcing political decisions, methods of psychological manipulation were subtle and effective (as not a few Euro-American antagonists found, to their cost). Aware that standard Anglo interpretations of individual and group behavior are often based on rationalist assumptions about the pursuit of goals, some consultants repeatedly stressed, "Hopi psychology is very powerful." Thus, in order to actualize a plan, the *sukavungsinom* might be mobilized with entirely misleading ostensible aims, which would nevertheless realize the primary goal as a seemingly coincidental consequence. One consultant put it in English: "*pasiuni* is called 'ritual planning,' but it's really faking it for the *sukavungsinom*." An apt example is the second split of Oraibi in 1909. Tawaquaptewa and Kewanimptewa, it is said, had already agreed in private that the latter would lead the returned Hostiles out of Oraibi to found a new settlement. But they needed to generate a sufficiently antagonistic climax between the two parties so that the soundness of this solution would be apparent to all. So they hatched a plan to confront each other during a public meeting and get into a physical fight. Such hot-headed displays of aggression are extremely rare in Hopi society and between leading men are utter anathema. The gravity of discord would then be played out for all to behold, so that a second departure would be reckoned inevitable and desirable. In this instance, the drama was interrupted:

When the argument got really heated, one of Kewanimptewa's followers said aloud to him, "Why are we staying here? Don't you already have a place picked out for us to move to? Isn't it in your plans for us to move out anyway?" ... So, this man, by pressuring Kewanimptewa in public, revealed a plan which was supposed to have been kept secret.

The Prophecy

It is impossible to recreate fully the interpretations that Oraibis in the late nineteenth century, either *pavansinom* or *sukavungsinom*, were making of the events surrounding their lives. As we have seen, the basic idea of the ethnosociological analysis was that the split was a deliberate plan and that one of its most significant aims was to bring the ritual order to an end, in part because of decadence and corruption. Purity of intention (a "pure heart") and conduct (including fasting and sexual abstinence) is mandatory for the successful consummation of ritual action. At some point during Loololma's tenure as *Kikmongwi*, certain severe transgressions of ritual propriety occurred. Loololma's responsibilities as *Kikmongwi* included maintaining general religious harmony within the village. These improprieties (which are still too sensitive to discuss in print, but for confirmation, see E. Sekaquaptewa 1972:247–48)—deliberately plotted by certain priests—partly involved a direct attempt to undermine Loololma's religious duties.

Such corruption is regarded as critical to the desire to bring the ritual order to an end. The world had ripened to where events signaled fulfillment of the prophecy on the destruction of the central axis of Oraibi society, its *wiiwimi* or ritual matrix. This prophecy held that after Oraibi's division the ejected party would return to destroy the village completely. The attack was supposed to be launched from the ruined village of Huk'ovi, about two miles to the northwest of Oraibi, which is where the departing Hostiles should have gone first. After destroying Oraibi, they would return to Kawestima, making three stops on the way[7]; they would rest at each stop for four years (the archetypal measure in Hopi sacred narrative is four units)—time to raise enough corn for the journey to the next resting place.

At Kawestima they would reconstitute *wiiwimi* (particularly the first-order societies) on the lines of Oraibi, but this should not be done at any of the temporary settlements. Meanwhile, if Oraibi was not completely destroyed, it would gradually decay anyway into a ghost town. Sometime in the future, after renewed nomadic migrations with no permanent homes (similar to the period after the Hopi emerged from the world below), people will return to Oraibi, crawling on their hands and knees. After this, Oraibi will rise again to be a flourishing community.

An important additional prophecy concerns the return to Hopi of the elder white brother, Pahaana.[8] After emergence into the present fourth world, Pahaana had departed for the east, agreeing to return at some future point to share his acquired knowledge with the Hopi and to adjudicate between those who had sincerely adhered to the Hopi way and those who had departed from it. Those who had strayed—the *popwaqt* (witches)—would have their heads cut off. The one sure way that Pahaana would be recognized was by his possession of a missing corner to one of several sacred tablets in the hands of Oraibi leaders. On numerous occasions since the late nineteenth century, this tablet has been presented to various Anglo-Americans to see if they were Pahaana.[9]

It seems there was considerable debate over whether Anglo-Americans were truly Pahaana, even though none could supply the missing piece. Apparently at least some of the Friendlies regarded them as such (the term is now in general use for a white person), although the Hostiles had doubts. In several encounters with Anglo-Americans, Hostile leaders demanded that troops should be sent to Oraibi, apparently to adjudicate disputes as to who had departed from the Hopi way and who had adhered to it. This occurred during Cushing's visit in 1882, and with Captain Williams in 1894 (see Chapter 4). During an interview with H. R. Voth in 1905, Yukioma urged:

Now you take this writing to the east and hand it to our elder brother, to the one who has not had his head washed [i.e., is not a Christian], and then when he will hear about us here and find out about our trouble maybe he will come here and when he comes he will cut the heads off of those who are bad. He lives somewhere near the ocean where the sun rises. He does not wear his hair the way we do and he is not dressed the way we are, but is dressed like the white men and he has not been baptised. For him we are waiting. . . . And when he comes here he will ask who the chief is here, and then undoubtedly a great many will say, "We are the chiefs". "Very well," he will say, "then it is on your account that these Hopis are living so unhappily here," and he will then cut off their heads. Then he will ask, "Who is it that wrote it to me, that wants to go the old road, the road of the ancestors? Who is it that has not responded to the demands of the Americans, because the old manner of living is still sacred to him?" Our old village and this land here are sacred to me, but if our elder brother then finds that I am one of the powakas too, very well, I shall be without a head also. Whatever that one says it will be so. If I am to be chief, very well. If not, very well too. After he has cut off the heads of the popwaktu, I shall show him my writing [the stone tablet] and then when he looks at it he will say, "Well here is your village, here are your fields, here is your mesa, this belongs to the Masauwu." Then he will probably say that I shall be the chief because I represent the Masauwu. (Voth n.d.a:2–3)

A corollary of Pahaana's return is that it will coincide with a stage when the Hopi way of life has become corrupt and decadent: *koyaanisqatsi* (corrupt life). The intent of much Hopi ritualism is to ensure beneficial natural and social conditions. Chapter 4's reconstruction of various events in Oraibi at the turn of the century reveals ecological and social near-chaos. These events can reasonably be assumed to have been interpreted as ample proof that something indeed was rotten in the state of Oraibi. At one point, Titiev (n.d.:47) reports, Lomahongyoma and Yukioma specifically leveled the accusation that Loololma was unable to "bring rain and couldn't take care of his people."

Pahaana did not appear, however, or at least no one who matched the expectation. Thus it was resolved to bring the corrupt way of life in Oraibi to an end—especially the axis of the system, the *Wuwtsim* societies, where the corruption was deemed to be based. By splitting the village, the leaders could simultaneously solve the symptoms of corrupt ritualism—that is, the land, water, and population problems, of which they were very well aware. For such a drastic course, they realized they would have to divide the *sukavungsinom* into antagonistic camps. The education program and the general issue of acceptance or rejection of the white man's ways were chosen as the necessary catalyst. The leaders could move toward their ultimate aim unbeknown to the common people, who were, nevertheless, unwittingly carrying out the plans. However, the leaders could not bring matters to a sufficient peak without additional assistance, and so it was decided to invite leaders from other villages into the plot: the result was the movement to Oraibi of the Second Mesa Hostiles:

There was a lot of fighting in Shongopavi by the Spider clan [the speaker is including Bluebird clan under this rubric] and so they were driven to Shipaulovi. Then some of them under the leadership of Tawahongnewa and supported by Yukioma had a fight in Shongopavi. They then came over here to Oraibi adding to the strength of the Oraibi Spider clan. . . . After that relocation, that's when the feuding really started to build up. Originally Tawaquaptewa only wanted to drive out the Shongopavis, but the Coyote clan, who had a lot of influence over him, wanted to drive out everyone who was a traditionalist.

Post-Split Third Mesa Society and the Hopi Analysis

In some ways, Hopi analyses have as much secondary elaboration as their anthropological counterparts: it is apparent that historical interpretation gives events more order than the experience of them. The suggestion that all decisions were reached consensually is surely an idealization: political rivalry is clearly a part of the picture, as Yukioma's stated interest in becoming chief (above) shows. Similarly, Superintendent Lemmon's remark that Tawaquaptewa was manipulated into an attack on the Hostiles who were "shrewder" than he and the prevalent Hopi idea that Tawaquaptewa was chosen over his older brothers to succeed Loololma because of inexperience and greater manipulability by older leaders indicate that the leaders were wheeling and dealing with each other as well as with the common people. Further, the education program that forcibly separated children from their parents was genuinely a matter of profound concern. Political oppression by the government was not a sham dreamed up by Oraibi leaders; it was very real.

In spite of such discrepancies, let me examine what this Hopi analysis can tell us about twentieth-century Third Mesa society.

Bacavi

Anthropological interpretations of the split generally pay little or no attention to its longer-term sociocultural consequences. By contrast, the Hopi analysis addresses long-term changes as explicit results of the split's program. Many of the changes in twentieth-century Bacavi society, especially those involving economy and technology, are obviously linked to the acculturative influence of American society. But a substantial proportion, especially those affecting social structure, can be seen to derive from decline of the politico-religious system. Disappearance of the higher-order societies entails the absence of a traditional system of offices and the perceived elimination of powerful supernatural forces that animated the meta-dynamics of all Hopi social action. The main component of *pavansinom* status was inherited ritual knowledge and its attendant transformative power, the demise of which has left everyone nowadays *sukavungsinom*. In short, the Oraibi split as social "revolution" effectively abolished the Third Mesa "class system." The terms of distinction are still applied on the basis of general criteria such as clan affiliation or official incumbency in the modern political system. But this usage no longer connotes possession of extraordinary powers.

The decline of control over supernatural power is accompanied by decline of *maqastutavo*, the powerful ethical system that includes supernatural sanctions for breaches of societal norms. Consultants compared *maqastutavo* to a legal system as a means of maintaining social order. Older Hopis remark on its decline, together with that of the ritual order, as specific causes of the disintegration of social solidarity in community life. The complete lack of *wimvaavasa* (ritual farmlands) at Bacavi symbolically underscores social structural changes deriving from ritual abolition. The content of kinship relationships has changed, particularly for men. Traditionally, a primary feature of clan and lineage membership concerned rights and duties in the ceremonial system, which in turn served to periodically reenact the mythico-historical prerogatives of particular descent groups. With no ceremonial system, this important nexus of a man's kinship network has virtually dissolved.

Kinship relationships are still important in those ceremonial occasions that remain, but their scope and prominence in a man's life have greatly diminished. The increase in patrilineal inheritance of fields may also be associated with this structural change. Since women's involvement in ritual was largely secondary, ceremonial decline has not impacted upon women's kinship relationships in the same way or to the same extent.

In Chapter 7 the dynamics of ceremonial decline in Bacavi were seen to involve the refusal to pass on offices and to initiate young men into the *Wuwtsim* societies. The only societies that did initiate were the Blue Flute, Kachina, and *Powamuy*. These three effectively ceased operations, at least concerning esoteric ritual practice, with the passing of their chief priests: in 1919 for the Blue Flute, and in the late 1940s for the two third-order societies.

Refusal to initiate and to pass on ritual office were deliberate policies with consciously intended results. Without exception, and as a straightforward matter of fact, the reason offered by older Bacavi people was that this had been decided at Oraibi and was put into effect with the split. Why then were there any ceremonial observances at all in the earlier years? The answer concerns the felt religious responsibility of individual initiates and sheer pride in their status-giving knowledge: "neither Bacavi nor Hotevilla was supposed to put on ceremonies—both Kewanimptewa and Yukioma were against it—but after a while *qwiiqwivit* [proud people] started to do them again." Nevertheless, all performances conducted after the split are regarded, from this point of view, as merely formal, aesthetic representations, lacking in ritual power (previously their very essence) to produce effects in the world. I shall return to this idea below.

If Bacavi's development conforms to the explanatory contours of the ethnosociological analysis of the split, what of the other villages? Those requiring examination are Oraibi and Hotevilla. Lower Moencopi maintained ceremonial dependence on Oraibi. When it separated from Lower in the 1930s, Upper Moencopi practiced only Kachina and Social Dances. Likewise, Kykotsmovi, which only gradually became a village rather than an aggregation of houses, has never attempted anything more esoteric than third-order ceremonies.

Oraibi

As we saw with Bacavi, a ceremony's decline is usually not an abrupt, cut-and-dried affair. Minor, individual observances may continue long after the main public performance has ceased. The dates cited below, then, concern major public performances.

Oraibi's last *Wuwtsim* initiations were held in 1909, the year of the second split.[10] Evidently, after his return from Riverside in the summer of 1909, Tawaquaptewa wanted to hold one more *nat'nga* (*Wuwtsim* initiation) in Oraibi as a final gesture. This was directly connected with the second split, although exactly how is disputed. The "Friendly" version is that Tawaquaptewa wanted all the returned Hostiles out of the village, where they could not interfere. But a Butterfly song (recalled by many people) composed by Kewanimptewa shortly after the second split has Tawaquaptewa pleading for the departed Hostiles' return, since he needed their priestly help with *nat'nga*. Whichever is correct, it is clear that some of the immediate factional trouble of November 1909 concerned these initiations.

The more general *Wuwtsim* ceremonies seem to have declined gradually. Parsons (1922:291) records only the *Wuwtsim* society proper and the Singers society as still active in 1920; both the Two-Horn and One-Horn had lapsed within the previous few years. Titiev (1972:338) wrote in 1972 that the *Wuwtsim* ceremonies had not been performed "for over half a century." Inferably, *Wuwtsim* functionally ceased in the 1920s.

Oraibi's 1908 Snake ceremonies were mentioned in Chapter 4. There were no Antelope society participants, and the Snake performers are regarded as having put on the ceremony "just to show they could do it," after most of the society's members had gone to Hotevilla or were among the returned Hostiles (who did not take part). Forrest (1929:139) records the unserious, burlesque-like nature of the performance. The last Oraibi Snake Dance occurred in 1918 (Crane 1925:269). In 1916 (with anthropologist Robert Lowie present [Parsons 1922:289 n. 14]), there were again no Antelope performers, and it is very likely this had been the case since 1908.

The returned Hostiles performed the Blue Flute ceremony under

Lomahongyoma in 1907. The Gray Flute society, controlled by the Friendlies but ritually subordinate to the Blue Flute society, did not perform in 1907 at all (Forrest 1929:317).[11] In 1909 the situation was reversed. Tawaquaptewa was vigorously opposed (in absentia) to the 1907 Blue Flute performance under his old rival (Titiev 1944:250), and it seems likely that his return deterred a repetition. Talayesva (Simmons 1942:141–42) mentions the Gray Flute performance in 1909, and Forrest (1929:348) records a performance in 1913. Parsons's record of societies active in Oraibi in 1920 makes no mention of the Gray Flute and by implication—that is, that the "former Gray Flute chief's" descendants had converted to Christianity (1922:290)—it had ceased to function by this time.

Parsons (1922:291) notes that the *Maraw* society had also become defunct by 1920. The *Owaqöl* ceremony was still active, "but it has become generalized, so to speak; it may be performed by anybody, at any season" (Parsons 1922:291). I am doubtful the season was so flexible, but its "generalization," involving a lack of priestly roles and esoteric ritual practice, was also true in Bacavi and Hotevilla. The *Lakon* society apparently had ceased to function in Oraibi even before the split (Titiev 1944:81 n. 116).

The *Soyalangw* and *Powamuy* societies continued, though in gradual decline until their functional demise in the 1950s (Titiev 1972:338–42). As head of *Soyalangw* from the 1930s, Tawaquaptewa apparently wanted to bring the ceremony to a gradual close, culminating in his own death. By the 1930s, it was already greatly attenuated, and it "virtually disappeared" two decades later (Titiev 1972:338). In the last years of his life, Tawaquaptewa had the *Soyalangw* altar on public display in his house which, it was suggested to me, signified his intention to terminate the ceremony. When he died in 1960, the *Soyalangw* sacra were buried with him. Vestigial observances of both *Soyalangw* and *Powamuy* still persist in Oraibi but apparently are greatly diminished in ritual content.

It is generally believed that Tawaquaptewa wanted to bring Oraibi to its final end during his lifetime. After the split the population dwindled rapidly, comprising only 112 people in 1933. Many of those moving away are said to have been pressured to leave by Tawaquaptewa (cf. Titiev 1944:94). In 1911 he seriously considered "selling" Oraibi to the government for a national monument

Hopi and Anthropological Analysis

(this is recalled by consultants and is recorded by Agent Lawshe [6-13-1911]). Harry James (1974:143), his long-time acquaintance, remarks that Tawaquaptewa "became increasingly convinced that it was his destiny to serve as *Kikmongwi* of Old Oraibi until it ceased to exist as a viable community." Titiev elucidates this further:

> According to Tawaquaptewa, the time is quickly approaching when he will lose his entire following and will remain alone at Oraibi with his ceremony (Soyal). All other rites, dances, and prayers will be given up, and there will come a great famine, after which the full ceremonial calendar will be revived. Such does Tawaquaptewa regard Old Oraibi's destiny to be, and complacently he awaits its fulfillment. (Titiev 1944:95)

In short, a good deal of Oraibi's ceremonial cycle had come to an end by 1920 and that which remained gradually passed in the same fashion as at Bacavi. Although Tawaquaptewa initiated a few men into *Soyalangw* in the 1930s, this was severely criticized by other authoritative village members (Titiev n.d.:53a). After his death, there was some confusion over the position of *Kikmongwi*, but he is generally regarded as having reneged on his occasional designations of various successors (Oraibi no longer had any Bear clan members) and refused to formally pass on the office. Subsequent titular heads in Oraibi have been referred to by the term *Kikmongwi*, but this has been largely honorific.

Oraibi, then, also bears witness to the plan for abandonment of the ceremonial cycle, together with its multiple social and cultural ramifications. The importance of these effects is underscored by Titiev: "All informants agree that the collapse of the ceremonial calendar is the most drastic aspect of culture change at Old Oraibi" (Titiev 1972:337).

Hotevilla

Although the cycle was never fully reconstituted, Hotevilla has been ritually the most active village on Third Mesa since the split. It no longer has *Wuwtsim*, although initiations into the four *Wuwtsim* societies were conducted three times: in 1924, 1932, and 1939.[12] The *Wuwtsim* societies ceased public performances in the mid-1950s. *Soyalangw* still has some vestigial observances, although without many *Wuwtsimwiwimkyam* (*Wuwtsim* initiates) left, these are much attenuated. Thus, what were traditionally the most important organizations in the religious structure have practically disappeared and are regarded as irretrievable.

The Snake and Antelope societies were still active in 1980, although the public performances then were very likely the last ones. The Antelope society initiated five young members in 1980, but the chief Snake priest and his assistant had apparently refused to initiate anyone for a long time. For years each performance brought predictions it would be the last, since it is widely assumed that the Snake chief will refuse to pass on his office (he was already very elderly in the 1980s). Since there were no performances in 1982, 1984, or 1986, this probably means that the ceremonies have ceased. As the Antelope society is functionally dependent on the Snake society for their joint performances, the demise of the latter has incapacitated the former.

The Blue Flute society, which most likely did not get underway in Hotevilla until after Lomahongyoma's death in 1919, when the Blue Flute sacra were transferred to Hotevilla from Bacavi, ceased performing probably in the 1940s. The Gray Flute society was never active there, since the majority of its members had remained in Oraibi. The major Kachina ceremonies—*Powamuy* and *Niman*—are still celebrated fairly extensively. Of the women's ceremonies, *Owaqöl* is still operative, albeit in the secularized form noted above. *Lakon* was probably never held in Hotevilla (consultants differed); if it was, performances ceased in the 1910s or 1920s at the latest. The *Maraw* society continued to perform until 1980, although the extent of ritual practice had evidently been diminishing over a long period. The chief priestess passed away in 1981, leaving instructions that no one should inherit her office and that the society should cease to function. This was her explicit prerogative, and it conforms to the pattern.

The 1980s demise of Snake-Antelope and *Maraw* has for most purposes reduced Hotevilla to a *sukavungki* (commoner village) with few traditional officers. The remaining observances of *Soyalangw*, *Powamuy*, and *Niman* involve conceptual ties to the more sacred *wiiwimi* of the first-order societies, but such ties are greatly diminished. The pattern of decline is the same noted for Bacavi:

refusal to initiate new members and to pass on ceremonial office. Both reflect deliberate decisions on the part of priestly incumbents. Still, the recency of decline, and the fact that there were active *Wuwtsim* societies for many years after the split, requires some accounting for if the Hopi analysis presented above is to be treated as an adequate explanatory scheme.

According to *navoti* (see above), none of the more sacred ritual practices was to be reconstituted until the Hostiles reached Kawestima (indeed if then—there is some variation, as we shall see). That the possibility of moving on toward Kawestima was perceived as real for several years after the split is attested to in missionary correspondence as well as consultants' recollections. The Mennonites did not seek to build a permanent mission (they established a temporary one in 1907) at Hotevilla because they were unsure whether people would stay there or move on (e.g., Epp 7-1-1908).

Although a Snake Dance was held in 1908, *Wuwtsim* ceremonies evidently did not begin until 1914 (according to a consultant's personal record). After ongoing debate in the village over whether to move toward Kawestima, there was much argument over the resumption of *Wuwtsim*. According to my consultants, Yukioma himself was not in favor but bowed to popular demand. This finds confirmation in a 1974 article in the Hopi newspaper *Qua' Töqti*:

According to Benjamin Wytewa, Sr., whose father was a Spider Clansman, and one of the lieutenants of Yukioma, the chieftain told Wytewa's father in his presence (Wytewa's) that the ceremonial cycle and ritual cycle had ended with the split at Oraibi, and that he did not want it revived in the new village (Hotevilla). However, at the insistence of former members of the various priesthood societies at Oraibi, he relented and gave his consent. But he predicted that it would not last, since it was not meant to be, Wytewa said. (*Qua' Töqti* 9-12-1974, cited in Yava 1978:150 n. 59)

According to my consultants, a formal count was taken: all those in favor of resuming the ceremonies at Hotevilla should gather at one spot, and those opposed a short distance away. Somewhat more than half were in favor and carried the day. In effect, this signaled a decision to keep their settlement in Hotevilla, although movement toward Kawestima was debated for many years thereafter and continues to be raised periodically. One of the modern Hotevilla factions has plans to build a new village in the Hopi

Partitioned Lands when they become available, and only half-jokingly, the story is that it will be called "Kawestima."

Thus the establishment of Hotevilla's ceremonial cycle was by no means an immediate affair. The Snake-Antelope ceremonies were performed without interruption and *Powamuy* may have been reinstituted in 1908 after the men had been released from prison during the previous year, but *Wuwtsim* and probably *Maraw* did not take place until several years after. The Blue Flute ceremony was probably not performed until after its cessation in Bacavi around 1917. Only three full *nat'nga* (*Wuwtsim* initiation) rites were conducted. In order to put these on, Yukioma had to persuade certain Bacavi people, most notably Kewanimptewa's brother Qötsaquahu, to help, since Hotevilla had no one with the requisite knowledge. But if the split was to terminate the ritual order and the social order it upheld, why did Hotevilla people start it up again, and why did Bacavi help them? Let us return to the Hopi analysis.[13]

It will be recalled that the plotting of the split concealed the true motives from the *sukavungsinom*. Evidently a good many were very bitter when they later learned of the conspiracy:

When my grandfather learned about the plot and the real reasons behind it, he vowed to have nothing more to do with the leaders and pay no attention to their directives. You see, on the day of the split, he had been lying on a roof with an old shotgun and other weapons at the ready. He was quite prepared to do battle and kill people—even his own relatives. So when he learned that it was really just a big hoax, he was very angry at those leaders who had plotted it.

The great majority of *pavansinom* in the Hostile party—that is, those who understood the true motives and had a part in the conspiracy—returned to Oraibi and later founded Bacavi. Hotevilla's original populace consisted largely of *sukavungsinom*, and the *Wuwtsim* ceremonies were reinstituted "by popular vote" rather than by priestly decision. The plan to terminate the religious structure of Oraibi was, it is held, unknown to many Hotevilla people, neither were they privy to esoteric ritual knowledge. In time, as more of those who assumed ritual office in Hotevilla became aware of the reasons for the plot and of the aptness of ending the ritual order in view of the changing state of the world, they decided to bring their ceremonies to a close, in the same gradual manner as in Bacavi. Meanwhile, as Hotevilla persisted with ceremonies, it was subject to the derision of other Third Mesa people. Another Butterfly song (these have an occasional tendency to sociopolitical commentary[14]) composed in the 1910s predicts that despite Bacavi's progressivism and Hotevilla's conservatism (which is mocked), a point will come in the future when Hotevilla will leap in front of Bacavi in this trend, in the manner that a male Buffalo Dancer leaps in front of his female partner at a certain point of the dance.

I noted above that those individuals with access to more esoteric knowledge make a distinction between ritual form and content. It is the content, its religious basis and essential power, which, it is maintained, were put to rest at the split. From this perspective, as with Bacavi, those ceremonies reestablished in Hotevilla consisted only of the aesthetic forms—the inner power had been irrevocably destroyed (cf. Wytewa's remarks quoted above). This distinction was made to me most emphatically by an older Hotevilla consultant (in English):

There are two aspects to the *wiimi*: religious and cultural. It was only the cultural part that was revived in Hotevilla. . . . Yukioma used to go and see Qötsaquahu a lot in Bacavi, particularly with regard to starting the *Wuwtsim* ceremonies again. Yukioma wasn't personally in favor of it, but the people wanted to, so he agreed to go along with it. However, he knew that those things had lost their power with the destruction of Oraibi.

Thus it was that Qötsaquahu was persuaded to help Hotevilla reestablish *Wuwtsim*. But he (and others) knew that it was impossible to recuperate the magico-religious core. Some consultants even suggest that this was a large-scale Hopi joke. Certainly other instances of such practical jokes, with rather serious material, occurred between villages. For example, uninvited, a group of Bacavi Kachina dancers would occasionally go to Hotevilla in the early years for a night dance. They made a point of taking some piece of technology with them, such as a kerosene lantern, to poke fun at Hotevilla's conservatism; this was much resented by Hotevilla people, who were nevertheless constrained from protesting by the ritual context.[15]

I think it is clear that Hotevilla people were very genuine in their desire to maintain tradition. Even when they became aware of the plot, they considered that it had been made by those—either Oraibi Friendlies or Bacavi Hostiles—who were inimical to their cause and who had, as it were, sold them a bill of goods. Why should they heed such antagonists? Maintaining their ritual order was, so to speak, a "slap in the eye" against those who had tricked them: a return ruse consistent with intervillage rivalry. Bacavi's joke on Hotevilla, then, backfired somewhat. As mentioned in Chapter 7, the fearsome aspect attributed to *Wuwtsim* initiates has occasionally been used in later years as a tool of dominance by Hotevilla people against the uninitiated in Bacavi. Although the early Bacavi *pavansinom* were secure in their underlying knowledge, much of this has not passed to members of the younger generations, who are sometimes intimidated by what they take to be superior ritual status and knowledge.

Hotevilla obviously presents some anomalies to the ethnosociological analysis of the split. These anomalies are explicable if one accepts the premises of the analysis and the practical reality of their consequences. The interpretation presented of Hotevilla ceremonialism is in many, though not all, cases exogenous to the village. In acknowledging the possibility of politically motivated consultant bias, let me reemphasize three features. First, in modern times the issues involved are still the subject of considerable intervillage sensitivity, and new disputes are often couched in the discourse of historical antagonisms. For those to whom Hotevilla's greater adherence to traditional forms is a lever of power, open concession to a position undermining its effectiveness would be counterproductive (even foolish). Notwithstanding this, the view is not wholly exogenous to the village. Several Hotevilla people, well respected throughout Third Mesa society as well as within their village, acknowledge it also. Second, the redistribution of *pavansinom* after the two splits left very few traditional politico-religious leaders, who knew of the conspiracy, in Hotevilla. Those who desired to reestablish the ritual order lacked the knowledge to restore the central element, and those who agreed to help them with it may not have been without ulterior motives. Third, the decline of Hotevilla's ritual order is quite close to the pattern exhibited in Bacavi and Oraibi: it was simply longer in the making. Neither can this decline be attributed solely to acculturative pressure, both by comparison with the extensive maintenance of the ritual order at villages on other Mesas (especially Shongopavi), and because throughout the twentieth century Hotevilla has been the most fiercely resistant of all Hopi villages to such pressure in other respects.

The Hopi Analysis: Synopsis

The Hopi analysis of the Oraibi split, which I have offered as that made by the more knowledgeable sector of society, concentrates on a set of features:

1. The split was a deliberate plot, brought into operation by Oraibi's active *pavansinom*, or politico-religious leaders, via the subtle machinations of Hopi political action.
2. The split was foretold in a body of prophecies, recorded in ritual narrative and song, and the years prior to the split were recognized as fulfilling the conditions set forth in the prophecies as appropriate for the destruction of the village.
3. The split's primary purpose was radical change in the structure of society.
4. Such radical change was directed particularly toward the politico-religious order, which was regarded as the central axis of the social system.

This analysis does not seek for unitary, deterministic causes. Its emphasis on the above features as primary by no means excludes other factors in the split's background, including internal political struggle, population pressure upon waning resources, and powerful acculturative pressure. What distinguishes the Hopi analysis is its emphasis upon processes of Hopi political and social action within their cultural and historical contexts. A crucial difference between this and the anthropological analyses is the injection of a deliberate, decision-making element with specifiable sociocultural consequences. By contrast, the anthropological analyses, in their various ways, all imply an unwitting reflex response by an unintelligent social organism to uncomprehended forces of change.

A consideration of the Hopi analysis allows us to interpret the dynamics of subsequent sociocultural change at Third Mesa in a consistent fashion and with an explanatory adequacy more comprehensive than those of alternative analyses. It is, in fact, the analysis that explains not only hypothesized causes of the split, but its long-term sociocultural effects as well. Of all those considered, it is the most predictive, relatively nonteleological, and open-ended.

9
ᛟ Intentional Actors and Sociocultural Interpretation

Throughout this consideration of Hopi history and social structure, I have emphasized a number of issues. First, Oraibi society had a long history of negotiation with Euro-American regimes. The documentary record offers extensive evidence for the development of a sophisticated political modus operandi. Second, this modus operandi was articulated through definite, hierarchical political structures inherent in the ritual order: Hopi society in Oraibi was not a random egalitarian mishmash. Third, the forces behind the Oraibi split were multiple, complex, and deeply rooted; it was not an impulsive, social reflex-response to poorly comprehended events, but a deliberate political act. Fourth, its consequences as a deliberate act are clearly discernible in the patterns of twentieth-century social change and are particularly manifest with my primary case, Bacavi.

I have argued for the utility of taking a Hopi, or ethnosociological, analysis of social and historical processes in explaining Third Mesa sociocultural change over a roughly one-hundred-year period. The rubric such an analysis would ordinarily be placed under in anthropological discourse is "folk models," but this term perpetuates the notion that "we" (scientific experts, authoritative cultural interpreters, what you will) have a corner on the market of high-quality truth, while "they," the "folk," have "native" interpretations that are cognitively and explanatorily inferior. At worst, folk models have been treated as concatenations of misconceived interpretations which result from an inferior cultural capacity to think critically (yes, even recently: see, e.g., Hallpike 1979). Evans-Pritchard's famous remarks on Zande thought as a "closed" system, which allows for no tradition of critical scrutiny, have become almost axiomatic in anthropological thinking (which is, conversely, an "open" system, in Popper's sense [e.g., 1972]): "In this web of belief every strand depends on every other strand, and a Zande cannot get out of its meshes because it is the only world he knows. The web is not an external structure in which he is enclosed. It is the texture of his thought and he cannot think that his thought is wrong" (Evans-Pritchard 1937:194–95). Arguments both for and against this view of "primitive thought" have been numerous (see, e.g., Wilson 1970:passim; Horton and Finnegan 1973:passim) and have spawned a whole field of anthropological debate between "rationalism" and "relativism." The debate continues (see, e.g., Hollis and Lukes 1982; Geertz 1984; Overing 1985; Gellner 1985), and nonwestern cultures must still fight for the cognitive validity of their own perspectives:

Implicitly, members of society are seen as being, by and large, ignorant of the causes and consequences of their activities, as being able to formulate models which are merely justificatory and not explanatory, and moreover contingent and not general enough, while anthropologists are, on all these counts, better. . . . The net result is that people's explanations are either similar to the anthropologist's explanations, but being more naive and less complete, they should be discarded and replaced by anthropologists' models; or they are different, which means untrue, and should be discarded again. (Holy and Stuchlik 1981:9)

Moreover, the "folk models" perspective tends to lump all native accounts into a potpourri of uniform quality. Yet, as "professional" analysts of social forms, anthropologists place their interpretations above those of "common sense" analysts in their own society. Such a social division, on the basis of access to expertise, is thoroughly appropriate for Hopi society, too: here it is even more strongly marked as a device of social distinction. The ethnographic problem of deciding which or whose account to accept as authoritative and more explanatorily adequate is, to be sure, demanding and difficult. If canonicity is a thorny problem in the interpretation of written texts, so much more is this the case with the fleeting representations of oral narrative (cf. Grele 1985). But this does not absolve ethnographers from the necessity of prosecuting such investigation as far as possible. The Hopi analysis discussed derives from that sector of society generally recognized throughout Hopi society as having superior access to knowledge, the "theorists," so to speak.

Thus, for the intrinsically prejudicial "folk model," I prefer to substitute "ethnosociological analysis," in acknowledgment of a serious aim for a truly "dialogical" anthropology (cf. Tedlock 1979). Anthropologists cannot plausibly maintain that Hopi society is a pristine isolate removed from the audience to which ethnographic texts are mostly addressed. Hopis know (perhaps all too well) what anthropologists are up to. Many have read the accounts, and there are numerous points of disagreement as well as accord. But they resent the intellectual apartheid of such "experts," who rarely even pay lip service to Hopi analytical thought. Especially in view of the turmoil of sociocultural change since the late nineteenth century, many Hopis continually subject their society to critical analysis, with depths of cultural insight far more penetrating than most anthropological accounts reveal. In the present work, I have attempted to demonstrate the power of such analyses for the elucidation of Hopi social structural dynamics and sociocultural change.

A great deal has been written of American Indian culture change in the form of "acculturation studies" (e.g., Linton 1940; Spicer 1961). Yet the present investigation of culture change in Third Mesa Hopi society has, of necessity, simultaneously been a study of social structure through time. I have criticized the "orthodox" view of Hopi social structure, and the modifications I suggest emerge directly from the treatment of Hopi social structure as process, rather than as a static pattern of abstract institutional forms in fixed functional relation. Thus, I wholeheartedly applaud Robert

Murphy's suggestion (1964: 853) that we do away with the term "acculturation":

It has long been recognized that the purpose of acculturation studies is to analyze processes. But we miss the point when we see these as acculturative processes, for the situation of change is the ideal one for the analysis of general processes of change and for the analysis of social structure itself. The latter study is concerned with relationships between variables, and these are best seen when the variables change.

Previous anthropological analyses of Hopi social structure have neglected the ritual order as its key articulating principle. Though the ritual order has certainly been treated as important, in general "kinship" has been the vantage point from which all else is seen to flow. But discussions of change using a kinship-based model of social structure (e.g., Titiev 1944; Bradfield 1971) have proven insufficient. By showing how the destruction of the ritual order ramified directly into many other fields of sociocultural change, the ethnosociological analysis identified a structural axis with greater explanatory implications.

Further, the acculturation perspective tends to reify cultures and their bearers into passive respondents to stressful forces emanating from outside society. In a classic article Anthony F. C. Wallace (1956:269) identifies various types of stress as causes of radical cultural change: "climatic, floral and faunal change; military defeat; political subordination; extreme pressure toward acculturation resulting in internal cultural conflict; economic distress; epidemics; and so on." It should by now be evident that, in one way or another, *all* these agencies were present in Oraibi between 1890 and 1906. Nevertheless, the critical emphasis introduced by the ethnosociological analysis is that, from a Hopi perspective, the sources of stress were not simply external forces. Rather, they emanated from a universal order of which human society is an intrinsic part, not a separate system unto itself opposed—as "culture" to "nature"—by the rest of the universe.

According to the general western world-view, events often occur at random. Hopi world-view is very different in this respect. Events are seen not as chance emanations from an intentionless void, but as the products of an intention-filled universe that suffuses the social system. Instead of society perceived as an object upon which random stresses impinge from extrinsic sources, stresses are predictable (and indeed predicted by *navoti*) and inextricable from the political administration of society. Now this view may entitle us to criticize Hopi historical analyses as conspiracy theories. But at the same time and, I feel, more importantly, it should draw our attention to the ineluctable fact that society consists of intentional actors, operating significantly within "webs of meaning" (pace Clifford Geertz 1973), not passive automata mindlessly fulfilling the preordained mandates of superordinate social institutions (Mary Douglas [1979,1982] registers a similar complaint). The Hopi analysis promotes a view of human beings not only as objects undergoing change but as subjective agents of change. Such a view is hardly novel in western thought, at least since Marx, but it has scarcely penetrated the anthropological treatment of nonwestern, "primitive" societies. Anthropological emphases upon "actor-oriented" approaches have gained some currency since the 1960s (e.g., F. G. Bailey 1969; Geertz 1974; Kapferer 1976). Since the 1970s, and taking their inspiration most notably from Pierre Bourdieu (1977), some of the "practice" theorists (see Ortner 1984 for a good synopsis) have focused upon the actor as intentional agent of social process as well as recipient and embodiment of structure. Still, "although actors' intentions are accorded central place in the [practice] model, yet major social change does not for the most part come about as an *intended* consequence of action. Change is largely a by-product, an *un*intended consequence of action, however rational action may have been" (Ortner 1984:157).

The Oraibi split was a radical upheaval of the social order, which, by comparison with larger-scale societies, is legitimately considered a "revolution": supposedly an impossibility in a society of this nature. The politico-religious leaders effectively destroyed Oraibi, via destruction of the very axis upon which the social structure was built—the ritual order: change in the rest of the social structure followed inevitably, as I have tried to demonstrate in the development of Bacavi society. In other words, radical social change was a direct consequence, not a by-product, of intentional action. To be sure, this revolution occurred under the impact of particular historical, ecological, and political forces—but don't they all?

It may be objected that the Hopi explanatory paradigm requires acceptance of some philosophical premises that are either false, irrational, or both—specifically, the notion of an intentional universe and the ultimate predestination of all important historical changes. But if these "basic statements" of Hopi theory prove uncomfortable, all we in fact need to accept is the proximate idea that the split was a deliberate plan that had as a primary purpose the ending of the ritual order. Since the ritual order did indeed disintegrate at Third Mesa in a rapid, systematic manner (for the most part), the evidence would seem to corroborate the hypothesis rather well.

This brings me to my final point, which foregrounds the concern with cultural relativism that has so far been largely implicit. A growing body of critical thought in the philosophy of science questions whether "the scientist" is any more open-minded about his cultural axioms than any other kind of "native." Thomas Kuhn's benchmark study (1962) addresses this problem, and on the same subject, Karl Polanyi (1958:286) remarks:

Our most deeply ingrained convictions are determined by the idiom in which we interpret our experience and in terms of which we erect our articulate systems. Our formally declared beliefs can be held to be true in the last resort only because of our logically anterior acceptance of a particular set of terms, from which all our references to reality are constructed.

With scientistic biases, anthropologists have too often prejudged "native" interpretations of sociocultural processes and practices as inconsequential. Such preconceptions, deriving from intellectually exalted aims, no doubt, in effect are ethnocentrisms of the culture of western academia: they merely stereotype "other" societies by qualities opposed to "ours"—with the same symbolic domination Edward Said (1978) describes in *Orientalism*. As a result, ethnographic description is too often underpinned by a sort of cognitive hegemony that reproduces at an intellectual level the political dominance of the culture under discussion by the anthropologist's society of origin.

Hopis view their society as composed of intentional beings who construe their experience into meaningful interpretations and engage in deliberate actions with purposive consequences. In the words of an older consultant:

Intentional Actors and Socioculture

I can only look upon our life now as a destiny we are fulfilling on behalf of our *momngwit* (leaders). It all comes down to those people, those priests and chiefs who planned this all out for us.

Surely this is not too radical a notion for our dialogue?

IV

REFERENCE MATERIAL

Appendix 1

Commissioner Leupp's Program for Dealing with the Existing Hopi Troubles (from "Oraiba Troubles," file 2. Record Group 75, National Archives, Washington, D.C.

(1) That the Shimopovi immigrants, who appear to have caused all the trouble, be ordered to go back to their own village and leave the Oraibis alone;

(2) That the *Oraibi* Hostiles, except Yu-ke-o-wa and To-wa-hong-ni-wa, be permitted to return *for the winter* to Oraibi, on their pledge to behave themselves peaceably, and a like pledge from the Friendlies to treat them peaceably; this to be with the understanding that it is a temporary arrangement, merely to avoid suffering for the old and weak during the bad weather, and that before spring the rest of the program will be worked out by the Government;

(3) That Yu-ke-o-ma and To-wa-hong-ni-wa be given their personal effects from Oraibi, including their season's crops, and permitted to give these to their families for subsistence purposes, but themselves be notified that as disturbers and inciters of their people to resistance against the Government they must leave that part of the country—the Hopi country—at once; their refusal, or their return after going, to be punished by imprisonment—this time without any pleasant accompaniments but on prison fare and at hard labor;

(4) That Ta-wa-quap-te-wa be required to learn English and thus fit

himself for the good citizenship and official position to which he aspires; and that he be given his choice between going to a local school or a non-reservation school for this purpose;

(5) That Ta-wa-quap-te-wa be deposed from chiefship, though allowed to retain his priestly orders, until he has fitted himself, by acquiring enough knowledge of English to be able to speak and understand fairly the language of the Government, for the headship of his people which he assumes to undertake;

(6) That the old Friendly Judge [Qoyangainewa] whom I met last summer, and whose name has escaped me for the moment; and a Judge chosen from the Hostile side by the Superintendent or the inspecting officer who may be in charge of the reservation when this program is put into operation; and the Teacher in charge of the Oraibi school, shall constitute a commission for the temporary government of the pueblo—the Teacher presiding of course—until a new order of things is established, or in any event till the coming spring;

(7) That the ringleaders of the rioters who resisted arrest or otherwise interfered violently with the police in discharge of their duty at Shimopovi last spring (or whenever that riot occurred) be removed under arrest and imprisoned in a military prison or prisons, on prison fare and at hard labor, for such terms, not under one year, as their respective bad conduct seems to justify;

(8) That any others besides the Hostile chiefs already mentioned and the Shimopovi ringleaders, who may, on later investigation ordered by the Indian Office, be proved to be a trouble-making element, shall be banished or imprisoned;

(9) That regular troops be sent to Oraibi to preserve order while these arrangements are in progress and to make arrests as indicated here or as directed by the Superintendent or inspecting officer in charge:

(10) That the whole Oraibi populace be notified that the Government intends to have their children sent to school somewhere, just as white people are required by their governments to send their children to school somewhere, till they have learned enough to take care of themselves properly and to start them on the road to citizenship; that they be given a free choice between sending them to the day school, or sending them to Keams Canyon; that when they have decided this point, their decision be properly attested and then that they be compelled to stand by their decision, so that the children shall not be shifting about;

(11) That the same notice be given, and the same option extended, at Shimopovi;

(12) That at both villages the parents who refuse to send their children to the day school shall be considered as electing in favor of Keams Canyon; but that the officer who carries out this work of obtaining their decisions shall *not* be anyone connected regularly with Keams Canyon School, as this whole business must be kept as free as possible from even a *suspicion* of unfairness—the only compulsory feature of it anywhere being the demand that the children *shall* be given a schooling *in one place or another*;

(13) That especial pains be taken to make the Indians understand that the Government has reached the limit of its patience with the old way of handling all these matters among the Indians, and that hereafter the Indians will conduct themselves reasonably like white men or be treated as white people treat those of their own number who are forever quarrelling and fighting among themselves;

(14) That steps be taken at once to examine the law as to the land ownership of the Hopi Indians, and, if there be no obstacle, their lands be allotted by the usual process; or, if more legislation be required, that the necessary items be prepared for action by the Congress at its coming session;

(15) That in announcing the decree of the Government to Yu-ke-o-ma, he be reminded that I reasoned with him last summer at the night council on the plaza of Oraibi, and tried to show him the folly of his course, and that his only response was an insolent defiance; that I reminded him then of the kindness of the Government towards his people, and its effort to raise them out of their ignorance and helplessness by giving them a school where their children could go and come every day, by protecting them from the intruding adventurer and by averting taxation from them; and that in now looking to this Government for help, when he has always treated it with contempt, he is acting the part of a coward instead of a manly man.

September 29, 1906

Appendix 2

Letter from Reuben J. Perry to the
Commissioner of Indian Affairs, 11-17-1906
(from "Oraiba Troubles," file 3.
Record Group 75, National Archives,
Washington, D.C.)

DEPARTMENT OF THE INTERIOR,
UNITED STATES INDIAN SERVICE,
Keams Canon, Arizona,
November 17, 1906.

The Honorable
The Commissioner of Indian Affairs
Washington, D.C.

Sir:
   Referring to Office letter of the 4th ultimo giving outline of work to be accomplished in an endeavor to settle trouble existing between the Friendly and Hostile factions at this place and to Office message of the 13th instant instructing me to report what had been accomplished to date, I have the honor to report that an effort has been made to carry out your orders and to state briefly below what has been done, following your outline as closely as possible in making this report.
   1. The Shimopovi Indians were returned to their village on the third as

reported in my letter of the 5th instant. Their children have all been placed in school, excepting one young man who is held for work on the roads on account of his refusal to attend school as directed to do.

2. All Oraibi "Hostiles" who have agreed to obey the orders of the Government in the future have been permitted to return to the village for the winter, but with the understanding that they will be moved out in the spring and have new homes of their own building. The "Friendlies" have promised to live in peace with the returned Hostiles and most of them will not object to building houses down on the level.

3. Yu-ke-o-ma and Ta-wa-hong-ni-wa were arrested October 28th and the former deposed from chiefship, both were notified that they would never be permitted to return to the Hopi Country. Their crops and personal effects are being disposed of in accordance with your instructions and their desire. Peter Staufer, General Mechanic, being instructed to ascertain the desire of these and the other prisoners with regard to their property and to carry same into effect. Mr. Staufer is well acquainted with these Indians, and inasmuch as Supt. Lemmon has resigned and will leave the reservation soon, I believed him to be the best qualified employee to look after the disposition of said property. The arrest of these two men and 26 others was reported to the Office in letter under date of October 29th.

4. Ta-wa-quap-te-wa, the chief of the "Friendly" faction, on learning that you desired him to go to school for three years or more for the purpose of learning English and fitting himself for the position of leader among his people, readily consented to go to the Riverside school for a term of three years and left on the 15th instant with his family and 22 pupils from the Oraibi day school, the consent of parents and pupils being obtained largely through his influence.

More of the "Friendly" children will go to Riverside in a few days and some of the "Hostiles" to Phoenix.

5. The requirements of this section of your program; viz: the deposing of Ta-wa-quap-te-wa from chiefship was carried out by effecting his transfer as stated in the first preceding section and by establishing a board of control to govern the village as hereinafter reported.

6. The establishing of a temporary government for the pueblo, as required by section six of your outline, has been effected by having the Indians of both factions understand that the teacher in charge of the day school, the "Friendly" Judge Quoing-in-iwa and Ke-wan-imp-te-wa, a bright young man selected by me from the "Hostiles," are to form a Board of Control for the village.

Letter from Reuben J. Perry 301

The position of judge or labor (*sic*) at $7.00 per month should be created and this young man appointed to same. Paying him something will have the effect of showing him and his people that he is treated as well as the "Friendly" judge and he will be impressed with the fact that he has become a part of the government machinery. I recommend that the Superintendent be instructed to take this man up on his agency rolls.

In this connection, I desire to add that the new government seems to be running smoothly. The only suggestions I saw fit to make were that the judges consult the teacher frequently, keep the children in school and arrange to have all ceremonies take place on Saturdays so as not to interfere with school or the Sunday service of the Missionary.

7. The arrest of the parties who violently interfered with the police at Shimopovi last spring was consummated on the 28th ultimo and said prisoners with the Oraibi ringleaders in opposition to the Government left here on the 14th instant for Fort Wingate, to be disposed of in accordance with your order and by the War Department.

8. You state "That any others besides the Hostile chiefs already mentioned and the Shimopovi ringleaders, who may, on later investigation ordered by the Office, be proved to be a trouble-making element, shall be banished or imprisoned."

This has been partially carried into effect by placing under arrest 70 Oraibi men who hold out in opposition to the Government, they to be required to work on roads, etc. for a term of ninety days or longer if they do not change their attitude. These men remain stubborn and passively defiant. They receive the message that the government desires to help them and wants only obedience about as the Chief Yu-ke-o-ma received your advice when you visited this place, however, it is believed that in time they will change.

9. The two regular troops, under command of Capt. Lucius R. Holbrook assisted by Lieutenant Lewis arrived Saturday, October 27th and greatly assisted in all of the work. Captain Holbrook is a kindly disposed man and did all in his power to convince the Indians that they were in the wrong and that the government could not tolerate their attitude and tried to persuade them to desist in their opposition to the government and schools. His services aside from commanding the troops were very beneficial.

One troop returned to Keams Canon on the 5th with the 28 prisoners, being under command of Lieutenant Lewis. This troop and Officer rendered satisfactory service in making arrests, collecting children and guarding prisoners.

In this connection I would respectfully suggest that the War Department be informed of the satisfactory service of Officers and troops.

10. All of the people of Oraibi have been informed of the intention of the Government to have their children attend some school and to have them behave themselves as white people are required to do. They were given their choice but all excepting a few rejected all schools, therefore, most of the children were sent to the Keams Canon school but the small ones belonging to parents who afterwards agreed to keep them in school are being returned to the day school. The children whose parents will not agree to keep them in school anywhere, if there be any such by vacation time, should not be allowed to go home for vacation but should be kept in the boarding school the entire year.

11. All of the Shimopovi children are in the day school at second mesa or Keams Canon, excepting one young man who promised to enter the boarding school after helping his folks to return their belongings to their village, but he refused to do so and is held for road work. None of the Shimopovis have or will agree to keep their children in school, however, they made no resistance when the teacher demanded the children who were returned from Oraibi for school and they have been in regular attendance since.

12. Your requirements relative to allowing the parents to elect between the day and boarding school has been carried out by permitting those who would agree to keep their children in school to select the school. Only a few selected and their selection was the day school where their children were placed. All other pupils were sent to Keams Canon under my order, but as stated in section 10, some of these pupils are being returned to the day school. No one connected with the boarding school has been permitted to suggest or solicit pupils for said school.

13. I have taken especial pains to have the Indians understand that the Government has reached the limit of its patience and have endeavored to have them understand just what is expected of them in the future.

In this effort my work has been partially successful only, and the 70 men held for road work are as far from obedience and reform seemingly as their people ever have been. They believe they will be released in ten days or two weeks and are encouraging each other to hold out in disobedience for awhile and say they will be allowed to go without any reform or promise. Yukeoma, the hostile chief, has encouraged all the prisoners in the belief that this affair will terminate as their troubles have in the past. That is, they will be kept in prison for a short time and then allowed to return to the reservation. He told his people that I was not telling the truth when I informed him and them that he and Ta-wa-hong-ni-wa would

Letter from Reuben J. Perry

never be allowed to return to the Hopi country. The Office order requiring him to leave the Hopi country forever is a good one and should be strictly adhered to.

14. I have presumed that the Office will examine the laws relative to allotting the land in severalty. I have told the Indians that their lands are to be allotted and there seems to be but little or no objections to such action.

15. In council and before his arrest, I told Yukeoma the way you tried to reason with him and all that you suggested that should be said to him and have from time to time explained to these Indians what you have suggested and what the Government intends to require of them. It is my opinion that they will believe when they learn the facts to be true and this knowledge will necessarily have to come from cold, hard experience. They seem to hold the Government schools and all white people in contempt and, as they put it, will live by the traditions of their forefathers and in the old "Hopi Way."

This problem is not yet settled but there is no further need for troops; but if the Government obtains obedience, it will be by compelling these 70 men now held to work or remain in prison until they change their way.

Relative to the Moen Copis disobeying their Agent by sending armed men to assist the Oraibis I have before reported that this matter has been disposed of to the Satisfaction of Superintendent Murphy by requiring Frank Si-emp-ti-wa, the prospective chief, and his family to attend school for a term of three years. They left on the fifteenth for Riverside, California.

November 19, 1906.

I spent the day yesterday talking with the prisoners and explaining why things must be done as the Government desires and that their disobedience must be punished in order to convince them of the power and right of the Government over them. I did this by separating a few of the men from the entire number, talking with them and getting them to repeat the conversation of the others. This was the first time any interest has been shown in the idea of building a new village. I was encouraged to believe that these men are beginning to think seriously about their condition and to believe that the mental change so much desired is beginning to come. They seemed to think that ninety days rather a long time to work for their disobedience. I told them that I would suggest that the time of the men who work well and assure us that they will be obedient in the future be shortened a little and the time of those who do not so conduct themselves be extended.

The organization of the police has been completed and the time of the prisoners began today.

In order to enable the police to handle so many and to prevent the necessity of any being injured in case of an effort being made to escape, I have locked them together in twos. They will be separated as soon as we believe it can be safely done.

The Hostiles have had many sympathizers among the residents and visitors to the reservation but these people have been able to see the justice of the stand taken by the Government. Some of these parties have been invited to talk to the Indians and assist me in getting them to see that they are in the wrong. In all such cases, the white parties have been convinced of the stubbornness of these people and that any reform must, at least, be started by force.

The Hostiles who remain in the camp have built comfortable homes, have harvested or are harvesting their crops, are near wood and water and will pass the winter as comfortably as they would in the village.

A site for a new village should be selected and the water supply ascertained. The village for the Hostiles should be some distance from Oraibi so the range for the stock of the two factions will not be so burdened and for the further reason that they will live more in peace if separated some little distance.

I shall in the near future examine what are considered desirable locations and submit recommendations concerning same, and I recommend that the Superintendent be instructed to ascertain the quantity and quality of water for domestic use.

Of course the foregoing plan would contemplate the building of a new day school for the Hostiles and it seems to me that it would be well to have the two day schools and reduce the capacity of the one at Oraibi.

I further recommend that the Government furnish doors, windows, lumber for floors and door and window casings and roofing for the new houses. Of course the houses should be built of stone or adobe and laid up in adobe mud. Similar houses were built some years ago by a number of the Friendlies and they seem to be very comfortable and the owners seem to take good care of them.

I wish to suggest that all Indian houses should have fire places and chimneys. The fire place furnishes the most satisfactory method for ventilating an Indian house for the reason that the doors and windows are generally not used for the purpose.

In the foregoing, I may have gone beyond what the Office desires in the way of recommendations, but I have stated what I believe to be the best for these Indians.

Letter from Reuben J. Perry

The Indians from the Hostile Camp have been disposed of as follows

Sent to Fort Wingate by soldiers:	28 men,	
Kept prisoners, Keams Canon:	70　"	98
Returned to Shimopovi:	3 men,	
	19 women,	
(Placed in Second Mesa school)	4 school girls,	
Do	2　"　　"	
(Under school age)	11 children	39
Returned to Oraibi:	41 men,	
	42 women,	
(Placed in day school)	14 boys	
Do	27 girls,	
(Under school age)	25 children	
(Excused from school on account poor health)	2 boys,	151
Keams Canon school:	48 boys,	
	40 girls	88
Yet in Hostile Camp:	7 men,	
	63 women,	
(Under school age)	21 children,	91
	Total	467

It is next to impossible to get a correct count of the Hostile camp for the reason some are out harvesting crops and the Indians there will not furnish any information. I think there are a few more belonging to the camp than this shows but this is not far from correct.

Complying with instructions contained in Office letter "Education 94378" of October 29th asking for recommendations for increasing the capacity at the Oraibi and other day schools so as to furnish accommodations for all children of school age, I have the honor to state that about 20 more pupils will be transferred to nonreservation schools.

I then recommend that forty of the Oraibi pupils now at Keams Canon be returned to the Oraibi day school and placed with parents if possible; if not possible, that they be entered as boarding pupils. I believe in two or three weeks' time the forty pupils can be placed with their parents who have and who will return to the village and I have directed that they be returned as fast as possible. In case it becomes necessary to have boarders at the day school, one or two more employees will be required and it will be necessary to rent two Indian houses and fit them for dormitories or store the school goods in them and use the store rooms for dormitories.

In case the pupils are disposed of as above suggested, the schools on the reservation will have enrollments about as follows:

Boarding school, 180; First Mesa day school, 55;
Second Mesa day, 111, Oraibi day school 155 to 160.

Very respectfully submitted,
Reuben Perry,
Supervisor.

Appendix 3

Agreement Signed by Hostiles Returning to Oraibi (from "Oraiba Troubles," file 3. Record Group 75, National Archives, Washington, D.C.)

WE, THE ORAIBI MEN AND HEADS OF FAMILIES OF THE FACTION USUALLY CALLED HOSTILES, each for himself and family, hereby agree and promise, as follows, to-wit:

1st. That, if our families are allowed to return to the Oraibi village for the winter, we will live in peace and harmony with the faction known as Friendlys, during the time our families are allowed to remain in the village;

2nd. That we will place all of our children of school age in school and keep them in school until they reach the age of 20 years unless excused from attendance by order of the Superintendent of the Reservation;

3rd. That we will go to work, when directed so to do by the Superintendent or other representative of the government, and build houses for our families at such place or places as the Commissioner of Indian Affairs or his representative may direct;

4th. That, in the future, we will obey any and all orders of the Commissioner of Indian Affairs or his representative;

5th. That we will submit to and obey the orders of the parties named by the Superintendent or Inspecting Official to control and govern the village during our temporary stay and to any orders of the superintendent of the reservation;

6th. That our new homes, villages and conduct shall be governed in accordance with the desire of the Commissioner of Indian Affairs;

7th. That we agree, each for himself and family, to do whatever work may be required by the field matron toward keeping the village and houses in a clean and healthful condition.

8th. That we agree to accept, hold and cultivate whatever lands may be given us by the allotting agent who may allot the Hopi lands at some future time;

9th. That we agree to assist in carrying out the foregoing and in apprehending and bringing to justice any Hopi who does not obey the same.

| Names | Marks. | Names | Marks. |

⌐ Appendix 4
Letter from Horton H. Miller to the
Commissioner of Indian Affairs, 11-12-1909
(from "Oraiba Troubles," file 5.
Record Group 75, National Archives,
Washington, D.C.)

DEPARTMENT OF THE INTERIOR,
UNITED STATES INDIAN SERVICE,
Moqui Agency, Keams Canon, Arizona
Nov. 12, 1909.

Subject:
Oraibi situation.

The Honorable
Commissioner of Indian Affairs,
Washington, D.C.

Sir:
This will confirm my telegram of the 11th instant, as follows:
"Oraibi situation is being adjusted. Letter giving details will follow."
I have the honor to refer to my letters of October 30 and November 3, and to report that I reached Oraibi on the evening of the 4th instant. Upon my arrival, the Principal Teacher told me that affairs appeared to be a little easier than they had been a few days before. He said Rev. Epp had

inquired for me a short time before I arrived, but had gone up into the village to spend the night, preparatory to getting an early start the next morning for Moencopi, a Hopi village near Tuba, Arizona, where the Mennonites have a mission. On the morning of the 5th, at about 8:30, a messenger gave me a note from Mr. Epp, in which he stated, "We are on our way to Moencopi, and may not return for a long time. The entire situation on the reservation is unsafe. Herewith, all our mission property is placed in your care. There are cows and chickens who need attention. The rest, you know."

The messenger gave me a key, which he said was to Mr. Epp's mission. I went to the mission and found an old Hopi man who had been left there to care for the chickens and to look after the place while Mr. Epp and family were away, presumably for three or four days. We had the two cows removed to the day school and the principal teacher agreed to take care of them. The chickens were left in the care of the old man, who is, I understand, the only convert the mission has among the Hopis.

I learned from Quo-you-wy-ma, who delivered Mr. Epp's note, that Tewaquaptewa's followers held a council in the kiva early on the morning of the 5th, and that Rev. Epp, Quo-you-wy-ma and his brother were present. He says the Chief asked him if he wanted Mr. Epp to stay around here, and that he answered, "you are the chief, and it is for you to say whether you want him or not." The chief's uncle, Te-lash-quap-tewa, the ruling priest of the Bear Clan, of which the chief is a member, said he did not want Mr. Epp around there. Quo-you-wy-ma says he told Tewaquaptewa, "You are the chief; we are willing to do as you want us to do."

Quo-you-wy-ma has been working for Mr. Epp, and it appears some of the Tewaquaptewa faction want to deprive him of his standing in their faction and class him as a Hostile.

The old friendly judge is also in bad standing with the Tewaquaptewa faction, and they have heaped ridicule and insult upon him and his family for several years, because he has been too progressive for them. He called upon me on the evening of the 6th, and stated that he was very sorry because he and his family were to be driven from their homes. He said he did not know that he or any of his family had done any serious wrong, that they had tried to live as the Government wanted them to live, and were willing to any thing the Government people wanted them to do.

I told the old judge that he and his people did not have to leave their homes, and that, if any one should attack them and do them any harm, that one would be punished according to the injury he did. After this assurance of support, the old judge retired.

Kewanimptewa, the young judge, who became leader of the returned

Letter from Horton H. Miller

Hostiles when they agreed to recognize the Government's authority over them, was present when the old judge stated his case, and, after the old judge retired, stated that he was very sure the Tewaquaptewa faction would drive them out again and that his people did not want to be treated as they were three years ago. I explained to him that when his people returned to the village of Oraibi three years ago, it was a part of a temporary plan the Government had arranged, whereby those of the Hostile faction, who would agree to certain conditions, might return to Oraibi for the winter, in order that their families might have comfortable quarters during the cold weather. I read the agreement to him and also the names of the fifty-three men who signed it, and explained that we did not know what they would decide to do when spring came, neither did we care how long they remained in Oraibi if they could live there in peace, but the plan for their return was only to furnish shelter for their families for the winter.

I told him that Tewaquaptewa told me that he (Kewanimptewa) had said to him on the morning of October 27, 1909, that, since the two factions could not live together, at Oraibi, in harmony, it would be better for his faction (the returned Hostiles) to select a new location, build new homes and move there quietly as soon as possible after the houses were finished, and Tewaquaptewa told me that he replied, "It would be well for them to do that way."

Kewanimptewa said he was mad when he made that statement to Tewaquaptewa, but if I wanted them to move, he and his people would leave Oraibi. I told him I did not want them to move, but if they could not live at Oraibi in harmony with the other faction, it would probably be a good thing for them to move out and build comfortable homes for themselves in a new location where they could live as they desired without having neighbors to quarrel at them. He asked, "If we move to another location, will I be allowed to remain in the position of judge, (His present position is laborer at $10 per month.) and if any thing happens to my people, will the Government help them and protect them?"

I told him the Government tried to help and protect all of the Indians without regard to their tribal misunderstandings, that all of their trouble had been on account of their ceremonies and that the Government would take no part in this controversy, unless someone did bodily harm to another, or the conditions were such that some one would be injured unless protected by Government authority.

He said if I would select a location for them, they would begin preparation for the construction of their new houses at once. I told him I would not make the selection, but would go with him any time he might state. He said he would go in two days and show me a place they had talked of where there was plenty of water. He said if they moved to this new location, they would like for the Government to build a school at that place for their children, who were now attending the Oraibi Day School, because the distance would be too great for their children to go to Oraibi to School. They would also like for the Government to furnish them tools to work with and, if possible, some doors and windows for their new houses. I told him we had tools that could be issued to them, that I would recommend the establishment of a day school for them and would ask for authority to purchase doors and windows for their new houses. He said the place they had in mind was about a mile from Hotevilla, that he had many friends in that village, that some of their children might want to attend the new school and that it was possible some of the Hotevilla people might want to build homes in the new village.

He said he had talked the matter over with his people, and they now understood that the Government was trying to help them, and they were willing to do any thing the Government wanted them to do, that they would like to have lands allotted to them before lands were allotted to the Oraibis and they wanted me to ask Mr. Murphy to allot them first.

He said they wanted to build a village nicer than any of the other Hopi villages, and they would be glad if I would help them to plan the new village.

I told him we were pleased to have any of the Indians build comfortable homes for their families, and would be glad if some of the Hotevilla people would join them in their support of the Government's plan to put all of the Hopi children in school, that I would ask Mr. Murphy to allot their lands as soon as possible, and would give them such advice as I could in regard to the construction of their new homes.

On the morning of the 8th instant, I went with Kewanimptewa and Secavama, a head man of his faction, to look at the location they had selected. I found it to be a very desirable site for a village because of the bountiful supply of good pure water. There are five springs on the side of the mesa and it is one of the few places in the Hopi Country where I have seen running water.

After I had inspected the springs, Kewanimptewa gave me thirty-two beans representing the number of children of their faction now attending the Oraibi School and asked that I recommend the establishment of a school at Bä-cä-bi (this being the name of the spring where their new village is to be located), for these pupils and such others as would attend from the village of Hotevilla which is located across the mesa about one mile distant.

Letter from Horton H. Miller 313

He also gave me twenty-four beans which represented the number of young married women (heads of families) who would build houses at the new village, and stated there would also be old men and women who would come with their sons and daughters to this village.

On the morning of the 9th instant, I sent a messenger to ask Tewaquaptewa, and any of his head men who desired, to come to the Oraibi Day School in order that I might talk to them. Tewaquaptewa came and I explained the plan for the Kewanimptewa faction to leave Oraibi, as follows:

(1) The Kewanimptewa faction have decided to leave Oraibi, and will begin work to-day preparatory to constructing new homes at Bacabi, the place they have selected for their new village.

(2) They will leave their families and personal effects in Oraibi until their new homes are ready for occupancy.

(3) They are to have such timbers as they want out of the houses they now occupy and from the houses vacated by the hostile faction when that party left Oraibi.

(4) The members of the Kewanimptewa faction are not to be molested in any way, but are to be permitted to come and go, to and from Oraibi, at will, during the time they are building their new homes and are to be allowed to move their personal effects as well as any part of their present houses whenever it pleases them.

(5) After they leave Oraibi, they are to be permitted to return, to visit such friends as they may have in that village, without hurt or hindrance.

(6) Old Judge Quoinginiwa and his family, Quoyouwyma and his family, and all other persons living off the mesa are not to be disturbed in any way, but are to be allowed to remain in the homes they have built off the mesa and go about their affairs without molestation, and that old man Wickeywy, who was baptized some time ago and who is now staying at the mission, must not be troubled in any way.

I further explained to Tewaquaptewa that Rev. J. B. Epp had gone from Oraibi and had placed all of the mission property, including the chapel and mission buildings, in our care, and that it would be protected as Government property while it was under our care, that, when a representative of the mission society came to take it over, it would be returned to the society. I also explained to him that it was good for them to have a licensed trader who would buy their products and sell them such supplies as they wanted to buy from him, that I had found the two Indian stores closed nearly all day on the previous day, and that it was a convenience for the people to have a white trader who kept his store open during business hours on business days, and that Mr. Armijo was there for that purpose, that he was in no way responsible for their misunderstandings and ought not mix in their village affairs. Finally, I told him that if any harm was done to any one connected with Kewanimptewa's faction, old Judge Quoinginiwa's family, the missionary's family, the trader's family or any other person, or the property belonging to, or in the keeping of, any of the people named, the one inflicting the injury or harming the property would be punished under the law, according to the nature and extent of the offense.

The chief said he would tell his people what I said.

The following persons were present when this plan was presented to the chief: Mr. Gossett, principal teacher in charge of the Oraibi Day School, Frank Jenkins, policeman, and Harold Youkti, official interpreter.

In order that the Office may understand the situation, copies of letters relative thereto are submitted, as follows:

From Principal C. A. Gossett, Oct. 29, Nov. 1, and 3. Rev. J. B. Epp, Nov. 1, 5, and 8, and my letter of Nov. 5 to Rev. Epp.

I have asked Tewaquaptewa to tell his brother Bert Frederick when he comes to Oraibi that he was acting like a rattle-brain, and needed some good advice, and that I wanted to see him and give it to him before he got into serious trouble. I will try and quiet him down when I see him.

In conclusion, I have the honor to recommend that a day school be established at Bacabi for the children of the Kewanimptewa faction, and such of the Hotevilla children as would attend it; that lands be allotted to the Kewanimptewa faction without delay, and, if possible, doors and windows be furnished for issue to them to use in the construction of their new homes.

It is possible there may be some difficulty in working out the plan, and I shall be very greatful for any suggestion or instruction the Office may offer to guide me in the adjustment of the Oraibi situation, or any other matters that must be dealt with among these queer people.

Very respectfully,
Horton H. Miller
Superintendent.

7 Inclosures.
HHM(AB)

Appendix 5

Telegram from Horton H. Miller to the Commissioner of Indian Affairs, 12-4-1909 (from "Oraiba Troubles," file 5. Record Group 75, National Archives, Washington, D.C.)

Keams, Canon, Ariz., Dec. 4, 1909. rec'd Dec., 8.
Commissioner Indian Affairs,
Washington, D.C.

Kewanimptewas faction voluntarily moved to New location two weeks ago. Men women and children are constructing homes no disturbances or rumors of trouble since my report of Nov. twelfth.

Miller,
Supt.

Notes to the Chapters

1. Introduction: The Question and Its Context

1. No single orthographic usage is followed throughout the present work, for several reasons. First, many Hopi names, referring to both persons and places, have been written for so long that it would be futile to attempt changes. For example, according to current Third Mesa orthographies established largely by Emory Sekaquaptewa and Ekkehart Malotki, working independently, "Oraibi" may be more accurately rendered as *orayvi*, "Shongopavi" as *songoopavi*, "Bacavi" as *paaqavi*, and so forth. Second, when Hopi preferences for spellings are well known and conventional—for example, "Bacavi," "Kewanimptewa," "Moencopi"—they are maintained. Quotations from written sources adhere to the spellings they contain. Otherwise, I have attempted to follow Sekaquaptewa's and Malotki's orthographic conventions (the former unpublished, the latter in Malotki 1978:201–2), which provide a simple, pragmatic means of rendering Hopi phonemes in Roman script.

2. Currents of History

1. For the different names and spellings applied to the Hopi, who were generally referred to as "Moqui" into the early twentieth century, see Connelly (1979:550–53).

2. "Olalla" is clearly identical with Oraibi (Luxán 1929:102 n. 118). This is the first time Oraibi is mentioned by name in the historical record.

3. The multiplier of six people per household I derive from Governor de Anza's statement in 1780 that this is the "usual rule" (Thomas 1932:236).

4. *Risueño* is perhaps better rendered as "smile." Coues (1900:390 n. 22) says he changes the sense for satirical effect, but the original may have been more appropriate. It seems eminently possible, judging by other forms of Hopi humor, that the Oraibis, while refusing Garcés the priest all succor, may nevertheless have been amused at Garcés the man spending two nights in a street with only his mule to preach to.

5. The actual date of Tuuvi's conversion is difficult to establish. His certificate of baptism in the St. George (Utah) baptismal records is dated 25 March 1876 (a copy was shown to me by Arizona historian P. T. Reilly). Yet a Mormon diary records that he was "ordained a priest" on 12 February 1876 (Brown 1875–77).

6. Several general ethnographic accounts of Hopi appear in the Latter-Day Saints' Historian's Office Journal History of the Church (especially 10-30-1869; 3-12-1870; 12-21-1880). Since these do not focus specifically upon Oraibi politics (I have found no mention of factions), I have omitted mention of them in the text.

7. Mateer (1878:8) gives Oraibi's population as "at least 650."

3. Oraibi Society in the Late Nineteenth Century

1. Eggan (1950:65–66) lists the clan contingents for Walpi, Mishongnovi, Shongopavi, and Oraibi. They are, respectively: sixteen (in ten phratries), fourteen (in eight phratries), nine (in four phratries), and twenty-nine (in nine phratries).

2. Hopi kinship terminology is discussed in detail by Eggan (1950:19–29) and Titiev (1944:7–14), among others.

3. *Poaka*, or *powaqa* (pl. *popwaqt*) following contemporary orthography, is in fact a noun referring to an individual user of supernatural power, rather than to the power itself.

4. I have never heard this term used. Other fieldworkers at Third Mesa agree that *pavansinom* is generally the category opposed to *sukavungsinom* (S. Nagata, E. Malotki, personal communications). Nequatewa (1936:125 n. 1) refers to all three terms, treating *mongsinom* as superior to *pavansinom*. However, his characterization of these two as "First Class" and "Middle Class," respectively, and *sukavungsinom* as "Low Class," is, I think, greatly oversimplified.

5. The English translation I have been given for the term is simply

"ruling people" or even "royal family." Many times when speaking to me, an Englishman, Hopis compared their system to the British monarchy.

6. *Momngwit* is plural of *mongwi*, usually rendered "chief." *Pavan* has been explained in the text in the discussion of *pavansinom*. *Wim-* is from *wiimi*, meaning, roughly, "religious practices."

7. This suggests "Friendly" bias: the head of *Momtsit*, who according to my information was the *Qaletaqmongwi*, was traditionally from the *Kookop* or Spider clan (cf. Titiev 1944:156).

4. From Oraibi to Bacavi

1. Thomas Keam, a trader who had been established in Keam's Canyon since the 1870s (McNitt 1962), noted in an 1890 letter to the Commissioner of Indian Affairs that "none of this tribe has ever been East of Albuquerque, New Mexico" (Keam 1-13-1890). This is particularly indicative, since the argument for an earlier visit states that Keam arranged it.

2. Contrary to Parsons's title *Oraibi in 1883* and her editorial note on the date (Cushing 1922:253,259), Cushing's visit was from 19 to 25 December 1882 (Bureau of Ethnology 1886:xxxix–xl), quite possibly during *Soyalangw*. His purpose was to collect Hopi artifacts for the Bureau of Ethnology, under the direction of Victor Mindeleff, who had been at Hopi since August 1882 (Bureau of Ethnology 1886:xxxix) but who did not accompany Cushing to Oraibi.

3. All the available evidence indicates that Patupha is the individual referred to as a leader of the Hostiles in the early 1890s and as the "great medicine-man of all the Moquis" (Donaldson 1893:passim). Stephen (1936:723) records only one other living initiate into *Porswimkyam*, from Mishongnovi; even at First Mesa (Stephen's residence), Patupha was regarded as a powerful man. He is pictured in several photographs of Oraibi Hostiles, including the first two photographs in this chapter.

4. Duvewuhioma is probably pictured in Voth (1903b:plate cxcvii). In this photograph of the two chief Antelope priests in 1896, he would be the one to the right. The other priest, Duvengötewa, was his brother and another important Hostile. Duvewuhioma also appears in the second photograph of this chapter.

5. Parsons (Cushing 1922:267 n. 15) misidentifies Heevi'ima as Hoveima, a member of the Snake society in 1896 (Voth 1903b:282). Voth (1903b: passim) repeatedly refers to Hoveima as a young boy, the youngest of the society, and so forth, so there is no possibility this is the same individual. Heevi'ima is pictured in the first two photographs in this chapter.

6. Masangöntewa is pictured in Voth (1903b: plate cl).

7. Parsons identifies "Kui-ian-ai-ni-wa" as the "War Chief in 1893 and later" (Cushing 1922:267 n. 14). This is Quoyangainewa, who held the role of *qaleetaqa* (warrior, guard) in Loololma's *Soyalangw* ceremony in the 1890s (Dorsey and Voth 1901:12). If this is the same individual, which is possible (I have a hunch Cushing interrupted *Soyalangw* at Sakwalenvi), he must have changed sides later. In 1900 he was appointed Indian Judge at Oraibi (Miller 2-13-1907) and was regarded as one of the most outspoken adherents to the progovernment line. It is also possible that "Kui-ian-ai-ni-wa," whom Cushing lists first, was the main "Hostile" leader who recited the creation myth, identifying himself as a "wizard," "master priest" (in Cushing's translations—n.d.:20), and member of the Spider clan. If so, my best guess is that "Kui-ian-ai-ni-wa" may have been another name for Talai'ima, whom Titiev (n.d.: 1a) identifies as head of the Spider clan, chief-priest of *Momtsit*, and Lomahongyoma's (see below in the text) mother's brother.

8. The original of this petition (in the National Anthropological Archives, Smithsonian Institution) identifies signatories by village.

9. Scott (Donaldson 1893:56) states this occurred on 2 October rather than 2 November; the rest of his account shows this is a misprint.

10. Scott (Donaldson 1893:57–59) gives a more detailed account of these events.

11. Titiev (1944:76 n. 73) thinks this man was Patupha. Since Patupha was the renowned medicine man (see note 3), it is more likely he was the second individual arrested.

12. Agent Mateer recommended in 1878 that the Hopi be relocated along the Little Colorado River; he listed seven reasons, including "a great tendency to Americanize these Indians, by encouraging them to open up separate farms along the river and to abandon their superstitious modes of life and dress" (1878:8). The same sentiments are voiced repeatedly in annual reports of the Commissioner of Indian Affairs over the next thirty years. In 1912 Superintendent Leo Crane recommended that all the people of First Mesa be removed to the valley below and the mesa top made uninhabitable by dynamiting the villages (Crane 10-24-1912).

13. *Pöökong* and *Palengawhoya* have associations with both the *Kookop* clan and the Snake clan. For the former, they are associated with the chiefship of the *Momtsit* or Warriors' society; in other records of confrontation in the 1890s, Heevi'ima represented *Pöökong* as the *Qaletaqmongwi*. For the Snake clan, the twin deities are prominent images in the Snake society. Since this was an occasion of war ritual, I am unable to determine why the deities were not personated by *Kookop* clan members—if Titiev's information is correct on this score. It is curious that

Heevi'ima and two other *Kookop* clan members (who, I would have thought, were more likely candidates to represent these deities) were imprisoned in the aftermath of these events, along with Patupha, Lomahongyoma, and several others (see note 14), but that Talasyestewa and Puhuwaitewa, Titiev's (1944:78) suggested War Twin personators, were not among them.

14. Accounts vary as to the number arrested—from seven (Donaldson 1893:39) to eleven (Donaldson 1893:38). The photograph of the prisoners at Fort Wingate shows nine, which accords with the Indian Affairs figure (U.S. Government 1892:585). Names of the five identifiable figures are from a list recorded in Mayhugh (1894; the information was recorded in 1892) compared to other photographs in which they appear. In addition, Mayhugh (1894) records three others: Qötswistewa (Rabbit clan), Puhu'ima (Sun clan), and Talangainewa (*Kookop* clan). One remains unidentified.

15. Stephen (1936:37) reports hearing, on 15 December 1892, that they had just returned from Fort Wingate. Heevi'ima was one of them (Mayhugh 2-14-1893:3) and Patupha another (U.S. Government 1892:585).

16. That they were Friendlies was determined by comparing the names with Titiev's census notes (Titiev n.d.), in which he indicates factional allegiances.

17. Cases of priests withdrawing from ceremonies, because of personal or family difficulties entailing mental or emotional turmoil, are common. Voth (1903b:273–74), for example, records successive withdrawals of three chief-priests of the Snake society.

18. Acting Agent Plummer, after a visit to Oraibi, suggested, "It appears that in addition to the other means being employed to get rid of the Indians the settlers are trying to create a disturbance between the two factions of the Oraibas, who are bitter enemies" (9-29-1894:2).

19. Mormon John D. Lee may have introduced the planting of wheat (in the fall) at Moencopi (see Chapter 2).

20. The Hostile leaders had said the same to Cushing: "Washington must come before this moon is gone, with all his soldiers, to kill the Oraibi and sit on their heads. We would like to see him do it" (Cushing 1922: 264). I shall return to this in Chapter 8.

21. The photograph of this group at Alcatraz also appears in James (1974:115) and Dockstader (1979:527). Unfortunately, in both publications ten of the prisoners are misidentified (the same in each). A correct list is contained in Williams (11-29-1894:4), which is confirmed by a letter to the prisoners from H. R. Voth (9-2-1895), in which he discusses the welfare of each prisoner's family. The date of release is cited by Dock-

stader (1979:527) as 7 August 1895. This, however, was when release was *authorized* (U.S. Government 1896:97). By 29 August, they were still at Alcatraz (Williams 8-29-1895). They were formally released at Fort Defiance on 29 September (Williams 9-29-1895), so presumably left Alcatraz a few days earlier.

22. This receives confirmation from the fact that after the split, Oraibi could no longer perform certain ceremonies, and Hotevilla and Bacavi certain others, for want of the requisite priests.

23. I can find no documentary evidence to support Helen Sekaquaptewa's intriguing suggestion (personal communication) that Oraibi was spared the disease owing to earlier vaccinations by Mormons.

24. Burton's description, hardly a model of ethnographic accuracy, probably refers to Kachina initiation, an important rite of passage.

25. Maasaw (the *Kookop* clan *wu'uya*) is mythologically regarded as the first occupant and "owner" of the Oraibi domain.

26. The text of Yukioma's statement runs as follows:

The night after the Chief of the Spider Clan yielded to the Government, the people had a council and made Ukeoma Chief. The next day Mr. Kempmire [*sic*], the Principal of the Oraibi Day School, came in and told them some things, asking that the children be sent to school. Ukeoma refused. Mr. Kempmire took hold of Ukeoma and pulled him out of the house and threw him down from the second story. They then walked him away to where the other Government employees, and Mr. Voth, the Missionary were. Mr. Voth and the Navajo Police held him while Mr. Kempmire clipped off his hair. . . . The doctor came and vaccinated Ukeoma and the children. Then they took Ukeoma and the children to Keam's Canyon, and put Ukeoma to work on the road for three months, after which time he returned home. Three other men were imprisoned at the same time. (Scott 12-5-1911:9–10)

27. Titiev (1944:83) states that Loololma died "about a decade" after 1891. A photograph in the National Anthropological Archives depicts Loololma in December 1903. Don Talayesva (Simmons 1942:109) reports Loololma died "about a year" before the summer of 1906.

28. Despite Titiev's argument (1944:84 n. 133) that this took place in 1904, Nequatewa's date (1936:64–65) of 1906 finds clear and abundant support in the official correspondence (cf. Staufer 9-18-1906; Lemmon 9-9-1906).

29. Perry states (11-17-1906:9; Appendix 2) that seventy prisoners were kept in Keam's Canyon. It seems more advisable to follow Lemmon's figure (11-13-1906) of seventy-two, since he gives details of his receipt of these prisoners. Six were released on 15 March 1907 after agreeing to cooperate and send their children to school; they returned to Oraibi to live with the other returned Hostiles (Miller 5-14-1907). The remainder were

released on 3 April 1907 and returned to Hotevilla (Perry 4-5-1907) to build a new village; their children were detained in Keam's Canyon and not allowed to return home for several years (H. Sekaquaptewa 1969:passim). Of those sent to Fort Huachuca, one was released on 23 June 1907, suffering from "nervous dementia"; the remaining sixteen were released on 17 October 1907 (Miller 5-25-1908). The latter included Yukioma and Tawahongnewa, who, the government (1906–10:passim) had repeatedly stated to other Hopis, were to have been banished for life. Those sent to Carlisle, several of whom were married with families, were kept there for five years, returning in July 1912 (Keam's Canyon Office Diary 7-3-1912); several of their wives had remarried.

5. Demography, Human Geography, and Economy

1. I have not computed annual growth rates of the whole Third Mesa population for this time period—an awesome task, because of the nature of the data. From a general source on annual Hopi growth rates, the estimated annual increase between 1901 and 1930 was 1.38 percent per year, and for 1874–1901, the growth rate was negative (Kunitz 1973:4). The study cited, however, is not very thorough for this period and may contain errors. It may nevertheless partially confirm that the disproportionately high number of individuals under twenty years old in Bacavi's original population cannot be attributed to any generally high birth rates during the 1890–1910 period. The situation is, then, quite different from that depicted in Table 5.7, in which the high proportion of young people is attributable to a high birthrate (and, presumably, a lower infant mortality rate) during the 1950s and 1960s.

2. District Six was originally a grazing district reserved for exclusive Hopi use in the 1930s as part of the Department of Agriculture's stock-reduction program. This area came to functionally delimit the Hopi Reservation, since Navajos prevented access to the rest of the 1882 Executive Order Moqui Reservation. Ensuing legislation reparative to original Hopi claims has been greatly protracted and is still in process in the 1980s, after extensive opposition to the Congressional Relocation Act of the 1970s.

3. The "Tribe" or the "Hopi Tribe" has connotations of place as well as of politics (see Chapter 7 on the latter). It is used to refer to the various branches of the Tribal Council headquartered near Kykotsmovi. Speaking from Bacavi, up on the mesa, one can go "down to the Tribe" or, from anywhere, discuss events "over at the Tribe," and so forth.

4. The discrepancy between Murphy's figure and that cited above in

the text for Bacavi's founding population (127) is due to the fact, also noted, that several people moved back and forth between villages for a while, before deciding which village to settle in.

5. Early stock figures are very sketchy. Probably the most accurate were recorded by Vandever (1890), working with A. M. Stephen, the Scottish ethnologist who had been living at First Mesa and Keam's Canyon. Vandever (1890:170) records 18,000 sheep, 4,300 goats, 1,200 horses, 3,000 burros, and 800 cattle. Twenty years later, Agent Lawshe (4-29-1911) recorded 12,000 sheep, 600 horses, and 1,100 cattle. In 1917 Agent Crane (1917:20) recorded 25,000 sheep and 8,000 cattle; either the latter had dramatically increased (and the documentary record does suggest that certain Hopi entrepreneurs, notably Tom Pavatea from First Mesa, had greatly increased their cattle holdings during this period) or Crane's figure is an overestimate.

6. These stock figures are taken from the census of Hostiles in Hotevilla in October 1906 (U.S. Government 10-30-1906). They were cross-checked against Titiev's census notes (n.d.), which record active individual herders at Oraibi; the similarity between Titiev's record of Hostile herders (he does not include stock figures) and the government census is great. My consultants' recollections of active herders also served as a cross-check; these also did not include stock figures.

6. Kinship and Social Structure

1. Alice Schlegel (1977) presents a rather different analysis of male-female relationships in Hopi society, although there are points of similarity.

2. For ceremonies, women mostly provide food, which is not symmetrically equivalent to the "raw materials" men provide for the domestic economy. In a sense, however, the circle of reciprocity can be extended, since the intent of much ritual action is to produce beneficial conditions for the crops—which eventually become these "raw materials." I am not proposing a direct exchange between males and females, considered as in dialectically opposed camps with different needs (such as in the "meat for sex" arguments, e.g., Siskind 1973). Hopi male-female reciprocities are more of a balance for the benefit of the entire community: although rituals create productive conditions for the crops, women are obviously not the sole beneficiaries, and though women distribute and prepare food, men are likewise not the only ones to benefit.

3. My interpretation of this is that each daughter moves into a separate house. Though it might be argued from the phrasing that this passage

implies all daughters move into one house *together*, such an interpretation is actually absurd: if that were the case, why move at all? The general context makes it clear that this possible ambiguity is the result of notes quickly taken on the scene.

4. Of seventy high officers listed in Titiev's Appendix 2 (1944:242–43), seven (10 percent) obtained their positions through patrilateral ties, and at least two, and probably four (5.7 percent), through affinal ties.

5. *Möyi* is also the term for a grandchild, but *kya'a-möyi* is recognized as a distinct dyad in Hopi practice.

7. Ritual, Politics, and Some Broader Contexts

1. For women, initiation into the *Mamrawt* (an approximate equivalent to the *Wuwtsim* society) was an important mark of adult female identity, but not the only one. Many women were not initiated into this society, and their adulthood status was achieved through such means as marriage, reproduction, and for some, roles in other religious societies (there are female roles in *Soyalangw*, the Antelope society, Blue Flute society, etc.). In the last case, responsibilities were sometimes regarded as sufficiently demanding to preclude initiation into other religious societies.

2. This is contrary to Titiev's assertion (1944:213) that the Two-Horn society met at Nasiwunka's house. None of my consultants agreed with this, and all concurred on the use of the hogan.

3. Qötsaquahu is also regarded as having been one of Yukioma's close associates in Oraibi. After the splits, they established fields next to each other in the Bacavi Valley, and some suggest that this was a pretext for ongoing conspiratorial consultations.

4. "Katsinmana" (Kachina girl) was a nickname. Her real name is debated. Helen Sekaquaptewa (1969:237, and personal communication), Katsinmana's sister's daughter's daughter, regards it as "Talasnimka." Several Mormon diaries (e.g., Gibbons 1878:20) record it as "Puhunimka." I have kept "Katsinmana" to avoid confusion.

5. Heevi'ima is a pertinent example. I discussed his prominent role as War Chief in Chapter 4. Titiev's notes give him no office at all.

6. Population figures used in Table 7.2 are based on Titiev's figures (1944:passim, especially 87). His total population figure is 863, of which 622 were "adults." "Adults" are presumably roughly over age sixteen, since some of those in his tables (especially Charts VIII and IX) are known to be below the age of twenty. Thus the "33" adult males attributed to Bacavi in Table 7.2 reflects the figure in Table 6.7 (it includes 6 males between sixteen and twenty), rather than those in Table 5.3.

Titiev's division of Friendlies and Hostiles into roughly equal numbers is undermined by contemporary documentary accounts. However, since I have used his figures on ritual leaders, it is only consistent to use his population figures here also.

7. Kewanimptewa is known for numerous supernatural feats. A commonly cited instance is that as a child he carved the outline of a railroad engine—long before he could have seen one—on a rock near Oraibi (it is still visible).

8. The choice is also clear with regard to the Mormon Christian tradition. Mormons have periodically conducted missionary activities throughout the twentieth century (cf. Sekaquaptewa 1969:238–44), and, as of the 1980s, still operate churches in Kykotsmovi and Polacca. For a short period in the 1960s, a Mormon Hopi who had married into Bacavi set up a church in a village house, but it received little or no village support.

9. The boundary is a matter of continuing dispute. Generally, Hotevilla's position is that Bacavi has no land except that on which the village nucleus is built, which was allegedly acquired with Hotevilla's permission when the village was first established. This view is compounded by the belief of younger Hotevilla people that in its earlier years Bacavi was surrounded by a barbed-wire fence. There is no evidence to substantiate this notion, and older Bacavi people regard it as entirely fictional. Older Bacavi consultants refer to a line between the two villages agreed upon as a boundary by Kewanimptewa, Lomahongyoma, and Yukioma. This boundary runs roughly north-northeast to south-southwest, passing through a midpoint approximately equidistant between the plazas of the villages. It starts from Laputsqavö (cedar-thicket pond) at the north-northeast, and goes through Pusukinva (drum springs), Owaskyavi (rocky ridge), and Qöyawöitöiqa (the name of a particular rocky outcrop), to Wisoqvösö (buzzard rincon) at the south-southwest.

10. The only village boundary Oraibi was concerned with was the one between it and Shongopavi in the Oraibi Valley. Since most Shongopavi farming took place to the south of Second Mesa, this boundary did not generate extensive disputes.

11. Although Moencopi did follow a more traditional pattern of village leadership (Nagata 1970:69), its colony relationship to Oraibi precluded the replication of major leadership roles.

12. For more details on these factional divisions in Hopi society, see Clemmer (1978, 1982) and Nagata (1968a, 1968b, 1978). I am in substantial disagreement with some of Clemmer's interpretations, but he does offer a trenchant critique of the literature on factionalism and of the

applicability of the term to the Hopi situation. For the Traditionalists, he prefers "movement." Nagata's idea that Hopi political groups are "opposed in principle"—that is, the political basis itself of opponents' positions is denied—is also good grounds for dispensing with the term "factions." Neither author, however, offers referentially useful alternatives for both groups. I use the term "factions" here for want of a better, more explanatorily adequate one.

13. Again, in contrast with Kykotsmovi and Upper Moencopi, Bacavi has been slow to develop its nontraditional government. Contrary to Titiev's assertion (1972:347) that "since 1959, Bacavi's affairs have been run by a council," the council system only really came to the fore in the 1970s (see text above). In contrast, Kykotsmovi (or New Oraibi, as it then styled itself) has had a Village Council since at least the 1920s (e.g., Daniel 4-17-1923). Its longtime early leader, Otto Lomavitu, one of the earliest Mennonite converts, began trying to organize a council (on which he wanted to have pan-Hopi representation) as early as 1916 (Keam's Canyon Office Diary 5-1-1916). Upper Moencopi had a Village Council by the 1930s (Nagata 1970:52–53) and in 1959 adopted its own constitution (Nagata 1970:62). Although efforts have been made, Bacavi, on the other hand, is still (in the early 1980s) without a constitution and bylaws for either the village or its Board of Directors.

14. When speaking to Hopis from other Mesas, a Third Mesa speaker, no matter which village he/she is from, often refers to himself/herself as "an Oraibi" and is easily distinguished by his/her dialect.

8. Hopi Analysis and Anthropological Analysis

1. References in the documentary record suggest that the *Kookop* and *Maasaw* clans were very close. Patupha seems to have referred to himself as *Maasaw* (Collins 3-18-1892) and in a claim to ownership of Oraibi, cited below in the text, Yukioma says, "I represent the old Masauwu" (Voth n.d.a:1) This close identification with *Maasaw* as their clan *wu'uya* (ancestral emblem) renders doubtful the notion that there was a rigid separation between *Masngyam* and *Kookopngyam*. In a long presentation of his viewpoint to Colonel Hugh Scott, Yukioma makes a distinction between the "Ghost" (i.e., *Maasaw*) and the "Ghost and Bird" (i.e., *Kookop*) clans: "In the ghost clan were two parties: one was known as the Ghost and Bird, and the other the Ghost clan proper. Ukeoma's clan was the Ghost and Bird clan" (Scott 12-5-1911). The nature of this division seems to accord with the notion of negotiable clan identity outlined in Chapter 6. It may be that the division of Oraibi provided the primary

criterion for absolute distinction of these two "clans." Again, clanship in Hopi society is not purely based upon genealogy but is subject to modification by changing social and political realities.

2. This is Governor Anza's estimate of 798 total Hopis in 1780. In Chapter 2 I cited Brew's observation that this figure is "ridiculous."

3. "Kawestima" may not be originally a Hopi word; "ka," as contrasted with "qa," is not, according to Malotki (n.d.), a word-initial Hopi syllable. E. Sekaquaptewa (1972:248, see below in the text) suggests the name derived from the former Village Chief's name. It may also derive from the Keresan term for a northern sacred mountain (spelled "Kawestima" by White 1942:83). Possible confirmation of the latter is found in Hopi oral traditions that locate Keresan-speaking peoples in the general Navajo Mountain area prehistorically.

4. Gordon Krutz (1973) takes Sekaquaptewa's argument and emphasizes the importance of "*diingavi*" in the Oraibi split. Although a rather superficial analysis of the Hopi point of view, Krutz's emphasis is consistent with the present aims. Richard Clemmer (1978:55) lambasts "the *diingavi* hypothesis" as not really an indigenous analysis but "a product of the mythic process, which provides destiny for action, and endless circles of dialectical evolution in Hopi perception." Clemmer's critique depends upon skepticism that the analysis was current at the time of the split; he sees it as a post hoc rationalization years after the event. Documentary sources, which I cite in the text, vitiate this argument.

5. Lest is be thought that this is an apocryphal tale of nonparticipants (like a witchcraft story), let me note that older consultants gave specific examples of waking up as children to see hushed, fireside discussions among supposedly rivalrous leaders—in particular, Tawaquaptewa, Yukioma, and Kewanimptewa.

6. Whorf (1956:61–62) presents some trenchant observations on *tunatya*:

The word is really a term which crystallizes the Hopi philosophy of the universe in respect to its grand dualism of objective and subjective; it is the Hopi term for SUBJECTIVE. It refers to the state of the subjective, unmanifest, vital and causal aspect of the Cosmos, and the fermenting activity toward fruition and manifestation with which it seethes—an action of HOPING; i.e. mental-causal activity, which is forever pressing upon and into the manifested realm.

7. The particular places are the subject of some disagreement: some say that Huk'ovi was supposed to be the first place, others Hotevilla, and others a place named Kaukwitsnayavu west of the Dinnebito Wash. According to the latter view, the next place, whose name I do not know, was a little to the north of Blue Canyon, and the last place just south of

Wakasva (Cow Springs). From here, they would be in striking distance of Kawestima, their fourth and final stop.

8. This idea is widespread among the Pueblos (cf. Parmentier 1979) and is commensurate with the Aztec expectation of Quetzalcoatl. There are numerous recorded Hopi versions, the first detailed one recorded by Cushing (1923) in 1882. The earliest reference I have found appears with the arrival of Jacob Hamblin in 1858 (Peterson 1971:183), although this version has some different twists. The idea is still current at Hopi in the 1980s, and although Anglos are referred to in general as *pahaanam* (pl.), there is a distinction made between them and "the true Pahaana."

9. Cushing (n.d. 38–39) was told about two "magic stones" in his 1882 confrontation with Hostile leaders. In spite of his repeated requests, he was refused a look at them, on the grounds that the time was not yet right. Fewkes (1922:277) records that those arrested in 1891 presented Colonel Corbin with a flat stone that was circulated among the officers and then returned. In 1911 Yukioma presented two flat stones to the Commissioner of Indian Affairs during his visit to Washington (U.S. Government 3-28-1911).

10. The dating of this last *nat'nga* was given by an elderly Oraibi consultant who was to have been initiated but was withdrawn by his uncles shortly beforehand because they feared for his safety (ugly rumors were evidently rife). This date receives confirmation in missionary correspondence concerning the troubles in Oraibi immediately before the second split (J.B. Frey 11-19-1909). Titiev (1944:133) suggests that the last *nat'nga* was in 1912, but his census notes reveal this to be an approximation; he also states that Don Talayesva was initiated at this time (1972: 73). Talayesva's autobiography (Simmons 1942:131–55) makes it clear that 1909 was the year.

11. Forrest's presence and photographs (1929, 1:315, 2:185) confirm that the Blue Flutes performed alone in 1907, but he mistakenly gives the reason for the absence of the Gray Flutes as owing to the relocation of most of their members to Hotevilla. They did not perform, in fact, because most of them were Friendly, and the ritual activities of Friendlies and returned Hostiles in Oraibi were kept rigorously distinct.

12. On two other occasions, the second in the early 1950s, a few individuals were initiated into the *Kwaakwant* (One-Horn society). These initiations generated considerable controversy in the village, especially the later one, in which one man was initiated by his father. Neither ceremony was regarded as a full-fledged *nat'nga* (*Wuutsim* initiation).

13. I should emphasize that not all Hopis share especially this part of the analysis: probably most younger-generation Hotevilla people do not.

Nevertheless, this version is subscribed to by knowledgeable, older Third Mesa people from all villages, and their presentation of it seems to be genuinely historical rather than overly clouded by political motives.

14. Song is a powerful way of communicating ideas in Hopi society. Two songs composed prior to the split (one a *Mastop* Kachina song, the other a *Wuwtsim* song)—some people still knew them by heart in the 1980s—foretold the split in metaphor, again suggesting its deliberacy. Immediately after the split, Tawaquaptewa sponsored a Butterfly Dance in Oraibi, which featured a song he had composed ridiculing the departure of the Hostiles.

15. Another instance of this form of "joking" is suggested in Nequatewa's account of the split: "The Hotevilla people would have become Christians if they had reached Kawishtima, a canyon near Navajo Mountain. This right-about-face would have been considered a 'joke' on Tewaquoptiwa's people" (Nequatewa 1936:132).

References Cited

Abbreviations

CHO: Church Historian's Office, Church of Jesus Christ of Latter-Day Saints, Salt Lake City, Utah
FDL: Fort Defiance Letterbooks, Record Group 75, National Archives, Laguna Niguel, California
KCL: Keam's Canyon Letterbooks, Hopi Indian Agency, Keam's Canyon, Arizona
MCF: Missionary Correspondence Files, Mennonite Library and Archives, Bethel College, North Newton, Kansas

Abbott, F. H.
 11-12-1909 Telegram to Reuben Perry. In "Oraiba Troubles," File 5. Record Group 75, National Archives. Washington, D.C.
Abel, Annie Heloise, ed.
 1915 *The Official Correspondence of James S. Calhoun, While Indian Agent at Santa Fe and Superintendent of Indian Affairs in New Mexico.* Washington, D.C.: U.S. Government Printing Office.
Adams, Eleanor B.
 1954 *Bishop Tamaron's Visitation of New Mexico, 1760.* Albuquerque: Historical Society of New Mexico, Publications in History 15.

1963 Fray Silvestre and the Obstinate Hopi. *New Mexico Historical Review* 28(2):97–138.
Adams, Eleanor B., and Fray Angelico Chávez, eds.
1956 *The Missions of New Mexico, 1776: A Description By Fray Francisco Atanasio Domínguez with Other Contemporary Documents*. Albuquerque: University of New Mexico Press.
Aitken, Barbara
1931 Folk-History and Its Raw Material: White Men's Raids on the Hopi Villages. *New Mexico Historical Review* 6(4):376–82.
Albuquerque Journal
4-12-1981 Navajo-Hopi Land Dispute Builds to Tense Final Act.
Alvarado, Anita
1968 Hopi Political Structure: A Response to a Marginal Agricultural Environment. *Southwestern Anthropology Association Newsletter* 10(3):7–13.
Arizona Miner
4-25-1866 Moqui Indians.
7-23-1870 The Moquis Indians.
Babbitt, Bruce E.
1973 *Color and Light: The Southwest Canvases of Louis Akin*. Flagstaff, Arizona: Northland Press.
Bacabi Day School Quarterly Reports
1913–16 Record Group 75, National Archives. Washington, D.C.
Bacavi Village Census
1977 Bacavi Community Center.
Bailey, F. G.
1969 *Stratagems and Spoils: A Social Anthropology of Politics*. New York: Schocken Books.
Bailey, Lynn R.
1966 *Indian Slave Trade in the Southwest: A Study of Slave-taking and the Traffic of Indian Captives*. Los Angeles: Westernlore Press.
Bailey, Paul
1948 *Jacob Hamblin: Buckskin Apostle*. Salt Lake City: Bookcraft.
Bancroft, Hubert Howe
1889 *History of Arizona and New Mexico, 1530–1888* (*The Works of Hubert Howe Bancroft*, vol. 17). San Francisco: The History Company.
Bandelier, Adolph Francis Alphonse
1892 *Final Report of Investigations Among the Indians of the Southwestern United States, Carried on Mainly in the Years from 1880 to*

References Cited 333

1885: *Part II*. Cambridge, Mass.: John Wilson and Son, University Press.

Bannister, Bryant; William J. Robinson; and Richard L. Warren
 1967 *Tree Ring Dates From Arizona J: Hopi Mesas Area*. Tucson: Laboratory of Tree Ring Research, University of Arizona.

Barth, Fredrik
 1975 *Ritual and Knowledge Among the Baktaman of New Guinea*. New Haven: Yale University Press.

Beaglehole, Ernest
 1937 Notes on Hopi Economic Life. *Yale University Publications in Anthropology* 15. New Haven.

Beaglehole, Pearl
 1935 Census Data from Two Hopi Villages. *American Anthropologist* 37 (1, pt. 1):41–54.

Benavides, Alonso de
 1945 *Fray Alonso de Benavides' Revised Memorial of 1634*, F. W. Hodge, G. P. Hammond, and A. Rey, trans. and eds. Albuquerque: University of New Mexico Press.

Bloom, Lansing B., ed.
 1931 A Campaign Against the Moqui Pueblos Under Governor Phelix Martinez, 1716. *New Mexico Historical Review* 6(2):158–226.
 1934 Bourke on the Southwest. *New Mexico Historical Review* 10(1):1–35.

Bourdieu, Pierre
 1977 *Outline of a Theory of Practice*. Cambridge: Cambridge University Press.

Bourke, John Gregory
 1884 *The Snake Dance of the Moquis of Arizona*. New York: Charles Scribner's Sons.
 1891 *On the Border with Crook*. New York: Charles Scribner's Sons.

Bowman, John H.
 9-27-1884 Letter to the Commissioner of Indian Affairs. FDL.

Bradfield, Richard Maitland
 1971 *The Changing Pattern of Hopi Agriculture*. London: Royal Anthropological Institute, Occasional Paper, no. 30.
 1973 *A Natural History of Associations: A Study in the Meaning of Community*, Vol. 2. London: Duckworth.

Brainard, Margaret
 1935 The Hopi Indian Family: A Study of the Changes Represented in Its Present Structure and Functions. Ph.D. Dissertation, University of Chicago.

Brandt, Elizabeth A.

√ 1977 The Role of Secrecy in a Pueblo Society. In *Flowers in the Wind: Papers on Ritual, Myth, and Symbolism in California and the Southwest*, Thomas C. Blackburn, ed., pp. 1–28. Ballena Press Anthropological Papers, no. 8. Socorro, New Mexico: Ballena Press.

1980 On Secrecy and the Control of Knowledge. In *Secrecy: A Crosscultural Perspective*, Stanton Tefft, ed., pp. 123–46. New York: Human Sciences Press.

1985 Internal Stratification in Pueblo Communities. Paper presented at the annual meeting of the American Anthropological Association, Washington, D.C.

Brandt, Richard

1954 *Hopi Ethics: A Theoretical Analysis*. Chicago: University of Chicago Press.

Brew, J. O.

1979 Hopi Prehistory and History to 1850. In *Handbook of North American Indians*. Vol. 9, *The Southwest*, Alfonso Ortiz, ed., pp. 514–23. Washington, D.C.: U.S. Government Printing Office.

Brooks, Juanita

1942 *Dudley Leavitt: Pioneer to Southern Utah*. No publisher listed. Copy at Special Collections, Brigham Young Univerity, Provo, Utah.

Brooks, Juanita, ed.

1944 Journal of Thales H. Haskell. *Utah Historical Quarterly* 12(1): 69–98.

Brown, James S.

1875–77 Journal of James S. Brown. George S. Tanner Collection. Special Collections Library, Northern Arizona University, Flagstaff.

Brugge, David M.

1964 Vizcarra's Navajo Campaign of 1822. *Arizona and the West* 6(1): 223–44.

Bureau of Ethnology

1886 *Fourth Annual Report, 1882–1883*. Washington, D.C.: U.S. Government Printing Office.

Bureau of Indian Affairs, Branch of Land Operations

1964 *Map-Atlas: Soil and Range Inventory of the Hopi District Six Area*. Bureau of Indian Affairs, Washington, D.C.

Bureau of Indian Affairs, Branch of Land Operations, Hopi Agency

1974 *Summary Report: Soil and Range Inventory of the Hopi District Six Area, Arizona*. Hopi Indian Agency, Keam's Canyon, Arizona.

Burton, Charles E.
1899   Report of School at Keam's Canyon, Ariz. In *Annual Reports of the Department of the Interior for the Fiscal Year ended 1899. Indian Affairs, Pt. 1*, pp. 382–84. Washington, D.C.: U.S. Government Printing Office.
9-11-1899   Letter to the Commissioner of Indian Affairs. KCL.
1900   Report of School at Keam's Canyon, Ariz. In *Annual Reports of the Department of the Interior for the Fiscal Year ending June 30th 1900. Indian Affairs: Report of the Commissioner and Appendices*, pp. 473–76. Washington, D.C.: U.S. Government Printing Office.
2-20-1900   Letter to the Commissioner of Indian Affairs. KCL.
3-7-1900   Letter to the Commissioner of Indian Affairs. KCL.
9-10-1900   Letter to the Commissioner of Indian Affairs. KCL.
9-15-1900   Letter to the Commissioner of Indian Affairs. KCL.
10-19-1900   Letter to the Commissioner of Indian Affairs. KCL.
1901   Report of School at Keam's Canyon, Arizona. In *Annual Reports of the Department of the Interior for the Fiscal Year ending June 30th 1901. Indian Affairs, Pt. 1. Report of the Commissioner and Appendices*, pp. 517–21. Washington, D.C.: U.S. Government Printing Office.
1-8-1901   Letter to the Commissioner of Indian Affairs. KCL.
3-24-1901   Letter to the Commissioner of Indian Affairs. KCL.
4-2-1901   Letter to the Commissioner of Indian Affairs. KCL.
1902   Report of School Superintendent in Charge of Moqui. In *Annual Reports of the Department of the Interior for the Fiscal Year ended June 30th 1902. Indian Affairs, Pt. 1. Report of the Commissioner and Appendixes* (1903), pp. 151–54. Washington, D.C.: U.S. Government Printing Office.
1-27-1902   Letter to the Commissioner of Indian Affairs. KCL (1901–1902, microfilm copy).
6-25-1902   Letter to the Commissioner of Indian Affairs. KCL.
1903   Report of School Superintendent in Charge of Hopi (Moqui). In *Annual Reports of the Department of the Interior for the Fiscal Year ended June 30th 1903. Indian Affairs, Pt. 1. Report of the Commissioner and Appendixes* (1904), pp. 122–24. Washington, D.C.: U.S. Government Printing Office.
1-23-1903   Letter to the Commissioner of Indian Affairs. KCL.
1-26-1903   Letter to the Commissioner of Indian Affairs. KCL.
2-9-1903   Letter to the Commissioner of Indian Affairs. KCL.
7-10-1903   Annual Report of the Moqui Reservation addressed to the

Commissioner of Indian Affairs. Manuscript in Richard Van Valkenburgh Collection, Arizona Historical Society, Tucson. (*Note*: The published report, U.S. Government 1904:122–24, omits a large section entitled "The Gates Incident," which appears in the manuscript.)

11-23-1903 Letter to the Commissioner of Indian Affairs. KCL.
12-12-1903 Letter to the Commissioner of Indian Affairs. KCL.
6-25-1904 Letter to the Commissioner of Indian Affairs. KCL.
7-28-1904 Letter to the Commissioner of Indian Affairs. KCL.
10-6-1904 Letter to the Commissioner of Indian Affairs. KCL.
11-10-1904 Letter to the Commissioner of Indian Affairs. KCL.

Christensen, Christian Lingo
   1877–85 Diary. Special Collections, Brigham Young University, Provo, Utah.

Clemmer, Richard Ora
   1978 *Continuities of Hopi Culture Change.* Ramona, California: Acoma Books.
   1982 The Rise of the Traditionalists and the New Politics. Paper presented at the School of American Research Advanced Seminar: "The Hopi Indians." School of American Research, Santa Fe, New Mexico.

Clifford, James
   1983 On Ethnographic Authority. *Representations* 1(2):118–46.

Code, W. H. (Chief Engineer, U.S. Office of Indian Affairs)
   12-16-1910 Letter to the Secretary of the Interior. Record Group 75, National Archives. Washington, D.C.

Collins, Ralph P.
   1891 Report of Moqui School, Keam's Canyon, Ariz. In *Sixtieth Annual Report of the Commissioner of Indian Affairs to the Secretary of the Interior for the Year 1891*, pp. 552–53. Washington, D.C.: U.S. Government Printing Office.
   3-18-1892 Letter to the Commissioner of Indian Affairs. Record Group 75, National Archives. Washington, D.C.

Connelly, John C.
   1979 Hopi Social Organization. In *Handbook of North American Indians.* Vol. 9, *The Southwest*, Alfonso Ortiz, ed., pp. 539–53. Washington, D.C.: U.S. Government Printing Office.

Coues, Elliott
   1900 *On the Trail of a Spanish Pioneer: The Diary and Itinerary of Francisco Garces (Missionary Priest) in His Travels Through So-*

nora, Arizona, and California, 1775–1776. New York: Francis P. Harper.
Crane, Leo
3-7-1912 Letter to the Commissioner of Indian Affairs. Record Group 75, National Archives. Washington, D.C.
4-10-1912 Letter to Thomas C. Lannan, Teacher at Bacabi Day School. KCL (microfilm copy).
6-12-1912 Letter to the Commissioner of Indian Affairs. Record Group 75, National Archives. Washington, D.C.
10-24-1912 Letter to the Commissioner of Indian Affairs. Richard Van Valkenburgh Collection, Arizona Historical Society, Tucson.
12-20-1912 Letter to Harriet E. Livesay, Bacabi Day School. KCL (microfilm copy).
1917 Annual Report of the Superintendent of the Moqui Indian Reservation, Arizona. Mimeograph. Museum of Northern Arizona, Flagstaff.
1919a Annual Report of the Superintendent of the Moqui Indian Reservation. Mimeograph. Museum of Northern Arizona, Flagstaff.
1919b Memorandum History of the Moqui Reservation and Schools, Compiled from the Annual Reports of the Commissioners of Indian Affairs, from 1886 to 1906. Manuscript Collection, Museum of Northern Arizona, Flagstaff.
1925 *Indians of the Enchanted Desert.* Boston: Little, Brown.
Crothers, W. D.
1871 Annual Report of the Moqui Pueblo Indians. In *Annual Report of the Commissioner of Indian Affairs, 1871,* pp. 703–7. Washington, D.C.: U.S. Government Printing Office.
1872 Annual Report of the Moqui Pueblo Indians. In *Annual Report of the Commissioner of Indian Affairs, 1872,* pp. 324–25. Washington, D.C.: U.S. Government Printing Office.
Curtis, Edward S.
1922 *The North American Indian.* Vol. 12, *The Hopi.* Cambridge, Mass.: University Press.
Cushing, Frank H.
1922 Oraibi in 1883. In "Contributions to Hopi History," E.C. Parsons, ed., pp. 253–68, *American Anthropologist* 24(3):253–98.
1923 Origin Myth from Oraibi. *Journal of American Folklore* 36(140): 163–70.
n.d. Report on Oraibi. Manuscript. National Anthropological Archives. Washington, D.C.

Daniel, Robert E. L. (Superintendent of Hopi Indian Agency)
   4-17-1923   Letter to the Commissioner of Indian Affairs. Record Group 75, National Archives. Washington, D.C.

Darwin, Charles
   1859   *The Origin of Species by Means of Natural Selection.* London: John Murray.

Day, E. Vance (Range Supervisor)
   1946   Range Management Plan for District 6—Hopi Reservation—Arizona. Hopi Agency, Keam's Canyon, Arizona.

Deloria, Vine, Jr.
   1969   *Custer Died for Your Sins: An Indian Manifesto.* New York: Macmillan.

Denevan, William, ed.
   1976   *The Native Population of the Americas in 1492.* Madison: University of Wisconsin Press.

Deseret Evening News
   1-21-1853   Letter to the Editor from Parley P. Pratt. Journal History of the Church. CHO.

Dobyns, Henry
   1966   Estimating Aboriginal American Population: An Appraisal of Techniques with a New Hemispheric Estimate. *Current Anthropology* 7(4):395–416.
   1983   *Their Number Become Thinned: Native American Population Dynamics in Eastern North America.* Knoxville: University of Tennessee Press.

Dockstader, Frederick J.
   1954   *The Kachina and the White Man: A Study of the Influences of White Culture on the Hopi Kachina Cult.* Bloomfield Hills, Michigan: Cranbrook Institute of Science Bulletin 35.
   1979   Hopi History, 1850–1940. In *Handbook of North American Indians.* Vol. 9, *The Southwest,* Alfonso Ortiz, ed., pp. 524–32. Washington, D.C.: U.S. Government Printing Office.

Donaldson, Thomas
   1893   *Moqui Pueblo Indians of Arizona and Pueblo Indians of New Mexico: Extra Census Bulletin.* Washington, D.C.: U.S. Census Printing Office.

Dorsey, George A., and H. R. Voth
   1901   *The Oraibi Soyal Ceremony.* Chicago: Field Columbian Museum, Publication 55, Anthropological Series 3(1).

Douglas, Mary T.
   1979   Passive Voice Theories in Religious Sociology. *Review of Religious Research* 21(1):51–61.

1982 *In the Active Voice*. London: Routledge and Kegan Paul.
Dozier, Edward
   1961   Rio Grande Pueblos. In *Perspectives in American Indian Culture Change*, E. Spicer, ed., 94–186. Chicago: University of Chicago Press.
Duerksen, J. R.
   6-30-1913   Letter to the Board of Foreign Missions, Mennonite General Conference. MCF. [In German]
   7-5-1917   Letter to the Board of Foreign Missions, Mennonite General Conference. MCF. [In German]
Duerksen, J. R., and Susanna Duerksen
   1923   The Paqavi Mission. *The Mennonite* 38(15):12, 14.
Eggan, Fred
   1949   The Hopi and the Lineage Principle. In *Social Structure: Studies Presented to A. R. Radcliffe-Brown*, Meyer Fortes, ed., pp. 121–44. New York: Russell and Russell.
   1950   *Social Organization of the Western Pueblos*. Chicago: University of Chicago Press.
   1964   Alliance and Descent in Western Pueblo Society. In *Process and Pattern in Culture*, Robert A. Manners, ed., pp. 175–84. Chicago: Aldine.
   1967   From History to Myth: A Hopi Example. In *Studies in Southwestern Ethnolinguistics: Meaning and History in the Languages of the American Southwest*, Dell Hymes and William Bittle, eds., pp. 33–53. The Hague: Mouton.
   1979   H. R. Voth, Ethnologist. In *Hopi Material Culture*, Barton Wright, ed., pp. 1–7. Flagstaff, Arizona: Northland Press; Phoenix: Heard Museum
Eisenberg, Leonard A.
   1968   Oraibi: An Example of Pueblo Fission. M. A. Thesis, University of Arizona, Tucson.
Epp, Rev. J. B.
   9-20-1906   "Report" to Superintendent Matthew M. Murphy. In "Oraiba Troubles," File 1. Record Group 75, National Archives. Washington, D.C.
   4-1-1907   Quarterly Report of the Oraibi Mission, to the Board of Foreign Missions, Mennonite General Conference. MCF. [In German]
   7-1-1908   Letter to the Board of Foreign Missions, Mennonite General Conference. MCF. [In German]
   12-8-1908   Letter to the Board of Foreign Missions, Mennonite General Conference. MCF. [In German]

11-1-1909   Letter to Superintendent H. Miller. In "Oraiba Troubles," File 5. Record Group 75, National Archives. Washington, D.C.
11-5-1909   Letter to Superintendent H. Miller. In "Oraiba Troubles," File 5. Record Group 75, National Archives. Washington, D.C.
9-28-1910   Letter to the Board of Foreign Missions, Mennonite General Conference. MCF. [In German]

Espinosa, J. Manuel
  1940   *First Expedition of Vargas into New Mexico, 1692.* Albuquerque: University of New Mexico Press.

Evans-Pritchard, Sir Edward E.
  1937   *Witchcraft, Oracles, and Magic Among the Azande.* London: Oxford University Press.
  1940   *The Nuer.* New York: Oxford University Press.

Fewkes, Jesse Walter
  1898   Archaeological Expedition into Arizona in 1895. In *Seventeenth Annual Report of the Bureau of American Ethnology, for the Years 1895–1896,* Pt. 2, pp. 519–742. Washington, D.C.: U.S. Government Printing Office.
  1900   Tusayan Migration Traditions. In *Nineteenth Annual Report of the Bureau of American Ethnology,* pp. 573–633. Washington, D.C.: U.S. Government Printing Office.
  1922   Oraibi in 1890. In "Contributions to Hopi History," E. C. Parsons, ed., pp. 268–83, *American Anthropologist* 24(3):253–98.

Flake, David K.
  1965   A History of Mormon Missionary Work with the Hopi, Navaho, and Zuni Indians. M.A. Thesis, Brigham Young University.

Forde, C. Daryll
  1931   Hopi Agriculture and Land Ownership. *Journal of the Royal Anthropological Institute* 41(4):357–405.

Forrest, Earle R.
  1929   *Missions and Pueblos of the Old Southwest.* 2 vols. Cleveland: Arthur H. Clark.
  1961   *The Snake Dance of the Hopi Indians.* Los Angeles: Westernlore Press.

Fortes, Meyer
  1958   Introduction. In *The Developmental Cycle in Domestic Groups,* Jack Goody, ed., pp. 1–14. Cambridge: Cambridge University Press.

Fowler, Don D., and Catherine S. Fowler, eds.
  1971   *Anthropology of the Numa: John Wesley Powell's Manuscripts on the Numic Peoples of Western North America, 1868–1880.* Smithsonian Contributions to Anthropology, 14.

Fowler, Loretta
  1982 Arapahoe Politics, 1851–1978: Symbols in Crises of Authority. Lincoln: University of Nebraska Press.
Frey, C. J.
  9-30-1913 Letter to the Board of Foreign Missions, Mennonite General Conference. MCF. [In German]
Frey, J. B.
  10-22-1907 Letter to H. R. Voth. MCF. [In German]
  11-19-1909 Letter to the Board of Foreign Missions, Mennonite General Conference. MCF. [In German]
  10-22-1913 Letter to the Board of Foreign missions, Mennonite General Conference. MCF. [In German]
  11-17-1913 Letter to the Board of Foreign Missions, Mennonite General Conference. MCF. [In German]
  1915 Among the Hopis of Arizona. In *A Review of the Rise and Progress of the Mission Activities of the General Conference of Mennonites of North America*, Gustav Harder, ed., pp. 19–26. North Newton, Kansas: Board of Foreign Missions.
Frigout, Arlette
  1979 Hopi Ceremonial Organization. In *Handbook of North American Indians*. Vol. 9, *The Southwest*, Alfonso Ortiz, ed., pp. 564–76. Washington, D.C.: U.S. Government Printing Office.
Gates, Gertrude Lewis
  4-21-1903 Letter to Charles F. Lummis. Gates Correspondence. Southwest Museum, Los Angeles.
  10-25-1906 Concerning the Separation at Oraibi Arizona, September 7th, 1906. In "Oraiba Troubles," File 1. Record Group 75, National Archives. Washington, D.C.
Geertz, Clifford
  1973 Thick Description: Toward an Interpretive Theory of Culture. In *The Interpretation of Cultures*, pp. 3–30. New York: Basic Books.
  1974 "From the Native's Point of View": On the Nature of Anthropological Understanding. *Bulletin of the American Academy of Arts and Sciences* 28(1).
  1980 *Negara: The Theatre State in Nineteenth-Century Bali*. Princeton: Princeton University Press.
  1984 Anti-anti-relativism. *American Anthropologist* 86(2):263–78.
Gellner, Ernest
  1973 The Savage and the Modern Mind. In *Modes of Thought*, Robin Horton and Ruth Finnegan, eds., pp. 162–81. London: Faber and Faber.

1985   *Relativism and the Social Sciences*. New York: Cambridge University Press.
Gibbons, Andrew Smith
   1858   Diary. CHO.
   1877, 1878   Diary. CHO.
Golden, John
   1951   Political Factions Among American Indian Tribes: The Hopi, Klamath-Modoc, and Fox. M.A. Thesis, University of Chicago.
Goldfrank, Esther S.
   1948   The Impact of Situation and Personality on Four Hopi Emergence Myths. *Southwestern Journal of Anthropology* 4(3):241–62.
Goodman, C. W.
   1894   Report of School Among Moquis Pueblos, Arizona. Appendix in *Sixty-Second Annual Report of the Commissioner of Indian Affairs to the Secretary of the Interior for 1893*, pp. 997–98. Washington, D.C.: U.S. Government Printing Office.
Goody, Jack, ed.
   1958   *The Developmental Cycle in Domestic Groups*. Cambridge: Cambridge University Press.
Goossen, Walter J.
   11-19-1952   Letter to John Thiessen, General Secretary of the Board of [Mennonite] Missions. MCF.
   4-3-1953   Letter to the Board of Foreign Missions, General Conference of Mennonites. MCF.
Gossett, C. A.
   10-29-1909   Letter to Superintendent, Moqui School. In "Oraibi Troubles," File 5. Record Group 75, National Archives. Washington, D.C.
   11-1-1909   Letter to Superintendent, Moqui School. In "Oraibi Troubles," File 5. Record Group 75, National Archives. Washington, D.C.
   11-3-1909   Letter to Superintendent, Moqui School. In "Oraibi Troubles," File 5, Record Group 75, National Archives. Washington, D.C.
Grant, Heber J.
   1896   Visit to the Moquis. *The Contributor* 17(4):203–6.
Gregory, Herbert E.
   1916   *The Navajo Country: A Geographical and Hydrographic Reconnaissance of Parts of Arizona, New Mexico, and Utah*. Washington, D.C.: U.S. Government Printing Office.

Grele, Ronald J., ed.
1985 *Envelopes of Sound: The Art of Oral History*, revised edition. Chicago: Precedent.
Gunderson, Carl (Supervisor of Allotting Agents)
3-24-1910 Letter to the Commissioner of Indian Affairs. Record Group 75, National Archives. Washington, D.C.
Hackett, Charles Wilson
1937 *Historical Documents Relating to New Mexico, Nueva Vizcaya, and Approaches Thereto, to 1773*, Vol. 3. Washington, D.C.: Carnegie Institution.
Hackett, Charles Wilson, and Charmion Clair Shelby
1942 *Revolt of the Pueblo Indians of New Mexico and Otermin's Attempted Reconquest, 1680–1682*. Albuquerque: University of New Mexico Press.
Hallpike, C. R.
1979 *The Foundations of Primitive Thought*. New York: Oxford University Press.
Hammond, George Peter
1957 Navajo-Hopi Relations, 1540–1956. 3 vols. Mimeograph. Special Collections, University of New Mexico Library, Albuquerque.
Hammond, George Peter, and Agapito Rey
1953 *Don Juan de Oñate, Colonizer of New Mexico, 1595–1628*. 2 vols. Albuquerque: University of New Mexico Press.
Hargrave, Lyndon Lane
1930 Shungopovi. *Museum Notes* (Museum of Northern Arizona) 2(10):1–4.
1932 Oraibi: A Brief History of the Oldest Inhabited Town in the United States. *Museum Notes* (Museum of Northern Arizona) 4(7):1–8.
Harrington, Isis L.
1931 "The Good-Bringing": A Tale from the Hopi Pueblo of Oraibi. *New Mexico Historical Review* 6(2):227–30.
Harris, Llewellyn
1879 Miraculous Healing Among the Zunis. *The Juvenile Instructor* 14:160–61.
Harvey, Byron III
1979 Introduction. In *Hopi Material Culture*, by Barton Wright, xiii–xiv. Flagstaff, Arizona: Northland Press; Phoenix: Heard Museum.

Hazylett, G. W.
  1899 Moqui Indians. In *Annual Report of the Department of the Interior for the Fiscal Year ending June 30th 1899. Indian Affairs,* Pt. 1, pp. 158–89. Washington, D.C.: U.S. Government Printing Office.
  4-18-1899 Letter to the Commissioner of Indian Affairs. FDL.
  5-8-1899 Letter to the Commissioner of Indian Affairs. FDL.
  6-6-1899 Letter to the Commissioner of Indian Affairs. FDL.
  9-4-1899 Letter to the Commissioner of Indian Affairs. FDL.
Hieb, Louis A.
  1972 The Hopi Ritual Clown: Life as It Should Not Be. Ph.D. Dissertation, Princeton University.
  1979 Hopi World View. In *Handbook of North American Indians.* Vol. 9, *The Southwest,* Alfonso Ortiz, ed., pp. 577–80. Washington, D.C.: U.S. Government Printing Office.
Hollis, M., and S. V. Lukes, eds.
  1982 *Rationality and Relativism.* Oxford: Blackwell.
Holy, Ladislav, and Milan Stuchlik, eds.
  1981 *The Structure of Folk Models.* Association of Social Anthropologists Monograph 20. London: Academic Press.
Hopi Agency
  1944 Livestock Record, Hopi Reservation. Hopi Indian Agency, Keam's Canyon, Arizona.
  1949 Sheep Bands on Third Mesa with Owners Listed in Each Band. Hopi Indian Agency, Keam's Canyon, Arizona.
  1960 Hopi Livestock Record. Hopi Indian Agency, Keam's Canyon, Arizona.
Hopi Agency Branch of Land Operations
  1981 Farm Plot Survey. Mimeograph. Hopi Indian Agency, Keam's Canyon, Arizona.
Hopi Hearings
  1955 Mimeograph. Bureau of Indian Affairs, Phoenix Area Office, Hopi Agency.
Hopi Indian Agency
  1950 Census of Bacabi.
  1968 Hopi Indian Reservation [Guide for New Employees]. Mimeograph. Hopi Indian Agency, Keam's Canyon, Arizona.
Hopi Tribal Council
  1-18-1937 Record of [the First] Meeting of the Hopi Tribal Council. Record Group 75, National Archives. Washington, D.C.
  1970 *Hopi Tribal Council Report, July 1969–December 1970.* Mimeograph. Hopi Tribal Headquarters, Kykotsmovi, Arizona.

Horton, Robin, and Ruth Finnegan, eds.
1973   *Modes of Thought*. London: Faber and Faber.
Hotevilla-Bacabi Day School Quarterly Report
12-31-1916   [The First]. Record Group 75, National Archives. Washington, D.C.
Huxley, Thomas H.
1863   *Evidences as to Man's Place in Nature*. London: Williams and Norgate.
Industrial Survey of the Moqui Indian Reservation
1922   Microfilm of Hopi Agency records.
Irvine, Alex G.
1877   Report Upon the Condition of the Moqui Pueblos. In *Annual Report of the Commissioner of Indian Affairs, 1877*, p. 160. Washington, D.C.: U.S. Government Printing Office.
Ives, Joseph Christmas
1861   *Report Upon the Colorado River of the West, Explored in 1857 and 1858*. Washington, D.C.: U.S. Government Printing Office (36th Congress, 1st Session, House Executive Document 90).
Ivins, Anthony W.
1875   Journal. CHO.
James, Harry Clebourne
1974   *Pages from Hopi History*. Tucson: University of Arizona Press.
Journal History of the Church
12-18-1856   Governor Brigham Young's Message to the Legislative Assembly of the Territory of Utah. CHO.
12-31-1858   Bishop Robert Duchey Covington's Account of Jacob Hamblin's Visit to the Moquis. CHO.
11-30-1859   Letter to George A. Smith from Marion J. Shelton. CHO.
1-8-1863   Letter to George A. Smith from John Steele. CHO.
2-4-1863   From Wilford Woodruff's Journal. CHO.
2-15-1863   Letter to Erastus Snow from George A. Smith. CHO.
10-30-1869   From the *Deseret News* 18:476. CHO.
3-12-1870   A Narrative of the Traditions, Manners and Customs of the Moquis Indians. From the *Deseret Evening News*. CHO.
12-21-1880   Peculiar People. From the *Salt Lake Herald*. CHO.
Kampmeier, Herman
1901   Report of Teacher of Oraibi School. In *Annual Reports of the Department of the Interior for the Fiscal Year ending June 30th 1901. Indian Affairs, Pt. 1. Report of the Commissioner and Appendices* (1902), pp. 522–23. Washington, D.C.: U.S. Government Printing Office.

1902   Report of Teacher of Oraibi School. In *Annual Reports of the Department of the Interior for the Fiscal Year ended June 30th 1902. Indian Affairs, Pt. 1. Report of the Commissioner and Appendixes* (1903), p. 155. Washington, D.C.: U.S. Government Printing Office.

Kapferer, Bruce
1976   *Transaction and Meaning: Directions in the Anthropology of Exchange and Human Behavior.* Philadelphia: ISHI Publications.

Keam, Thomas Varker
1-13-1890   Letter to the Commissioner of Indian Affairs. Record Group 75, National Archives. Washington, D.C.

Keam's Canyon Office Diary
1912–16   Record Group 75, National Archives. Laguna Niguel, California.

Keith, Miltona M.
1904   Report of Field Matron at Oraibi. In *Annual Reports of the Department of the Interior for the Fiscal Year ended June 30 1904. Indian Affairs, Pt. 1. Report of the Commissioner and Appendixes* (1905), p. 140. Washington, D.C.: U.S. Government Printing Office.
9-16-1906   Letter to Superintendent Matthew M. Murphy. In "Oraiba Troubles," File 1. Record Group 75, National Archives. Washington, D.C.

Kelly, Charles
1948–49   Journal of Walter Clement Powell. *Utah Historical Quarterly* 16–17:457–78.

Kennard, Edward A.
1965   Post-War Economic Changes Among the Hopi. In *Essays in Economic Anthropology*, Proceedings of the 1965 Annual Spring Meeting of the American Ethnological Society, June Helm, ed., pp. 24–32. Seattle: University of Washington Press.
1972   Metaphor and Magic: Key Concepts in Hopi Culture and Their Linguistic Forms. In *Studies in Linguistics in Honor of George L. Trager*, M. Estellie Smith, ed., pp. 468–73. The Hague: Mouton.
1979   Hopi Economy and Subsistence. In *Handbook of North American Indians.* Vol. 9, *The Southwest*, Alfonso Ortiz, ed., pp. 554–63. Washington, D.C.: U.S. Government Printing Office.

Krehbiel, Christian
1938   *History of the Mennonite General Conference*, Vol. 2. Indiana. No publisher listed.

Krutz, Gordon V.
1973   The Native's Point of View as an Important Factor in Under-

References Cited

standing the Dynamics of the Oraibi Split. *Ethnohistory* 20(1):77–89.
Kuhn, Thomas
    1962 *The Structure of Scientific Revolutions*. Chicago: University of Chicago Press.
Kunitz, Stephen J.
    1973 Demographic Change Among the Hopi and Navajo Indians. Lake Powell Research Project Bulletin, no. 2, National Science Foundation.
La Farge, Oliver
    1937 Notes for Hopi Administrators. Record Group 75, National Archives, Washington, D.C.
Laird, W. David
    1977 *Hopi Bibliography: Comprehensive and Annotated*. Tucson: University of Arizona Press.
Lamphere, Louise
    1977 *To Run After Them: Cultural and Social Bases of Cooperation in a Navajo Community*. Tucson: University of Arizona Press.
Land Management Unit No. 6
    1937 Land Planning Report, by Study Group "C," W. R. McKinney, Chief of Party. Hopi Indian Agency, Keam's Canyon, Arizona.
Larrabee, C. F.
    10-5-1906 Letter to the Secretary of the Interior. In "Oraiba Troubles," File 2. Record Group 75, National Archives. Washington, D.C.
Lawshe, A. L.
    11-1-1910 Names of Hopi Chiefs and Leading Men, Furnished by Sup't Miller Oct. 31, 1910. KCL.
    12-19-1910 Letter to the Commissioner of Indian Affairs. KCL.
    4-22-1911 Letter to the Commissioner of Indian Affairs. KCL.
    4-29-1911 Letter to Supervisor Bascom Johnson, Flagstaff, Arizona. KCL.
    6-13-1911 Letter to W. E. Freeland, Principal Teacher, Oraibi Day School. KCL.
    7-11-1911 Annual Report of the Moqui Indian Reservation. Mimeograph. Museum of Northern Arizona, Flagstaff.
Leach, Edmund
    1954 *Political Systems of Highland Burma*. London: Bell.
Leathers, Nezzie Lee
    1937 The Hopi Indians and Their Relations with the United States Government to 1906. M.A. Thesis, University of Oklahoma.

Lee, John D.
1955   A Mormon Chronicle: The Diaries of John D. Lee, 1848–1876.
2 vols. R. G. Cleland and J. Brooks, eds. San Marino, California: Huntington Library Publications.
Lemmon, Theodore G.
1905   Correspondence. KCL.
1-26-1905   Letter to A. H. Viets. KCL.
2-14-1905   Letter to A. H. Viets. KCL.
3-2-1905   Letter to Indian Traders, Moqui Reservation. Richard Van Valkenburgh Collection, Arizona Historical Society, Tucson.
7-23-1905   Letter to the Commissioner of Indian Affairs. KCL.
4-20-1906   Original Official Report of the "Scrap" with the Rebellious Hopis at Second Mesa. Manuscript. Los Angeles County Museum of Natural History, Los Angeles.
6-16-1906   Letter to the Commissioner of Indian Affairs. KCL.
8-20-1906   Letter to the Commissioner of Indian Affairs. KCL.
8-30-1906   Letter to the Commissioner of Indian Affairs. KCL.
9-8-1906   Telegram to the Commissioner of Indian Affairs. In "Oraiba Troubles," File 1. Record Group 75, National Archives, Washington, D.C.
9-9-1906   Letter to the Commissioner of Indian Affairs. In "Oraiba Troubles," File 1. Record Group 75, National Archives, Washington, D.C.
9-20-1906   Letter to the Commissioner of Indian Affairs. KCL.
11-13-1906   Letter to the Commissioner of Indian Affairs. KCL.
Leupp, Francis E.
9-29-1906   Program for Dealing with the Existing Hopi Troubles. In "Oraiba Troubles," File 2. Record Group 75, National Archives. Washington, D.C.
12-5-1906   Letter to Reuben Perry. In "Oraiba Troubles," File 3. Record Group 75, National Archives. Washington, D.C.
1907   Disturbances Among the Hopi. In *Annual Reports of the Department of the Interior, 1906. Indian Affairs* (1907), pp. 118–25. Washington, D.C.: U.S. Government Printing Office.
Lévi-Strauss, Claude
1962   Le totémisme aujourd'hui. Paris: Presses Universitaires de France.
1966   The Savage Mind. Chicago: University of Chicago Press.
Linton, Ralph, ed.
1940   *Acculturation in Seven American Indian Tribes.* New York: D. Appleton-Century.

Los Angeles Herald
  11-23-1909 Uprising of Hopi Indians Expected
Lowie, Robert H.
  1929 Notes on Hopi Clans. *Anthropological Papers of the American Museum of Natural History* 30(6):303–60.
Lummis, Charles F.
  1968 Bullying the Moqui. Prescott, Arizona: Prescott College Press.
Luxán, Diego Perez de
  1929 Expedition into New Mexico Made by Antonio Espejo, 1582–1583, as Revealed in the Journal of Diego Pérez de Luxán, a Member of the Party. G. P. Hammond and A. Rey, trans. and eds. Los Angeles: Quivira Society.
McCluskey, Stephen C.
  1980 Evangelists, Educators, Ethnographers, and the Establishment of the Hopi Reservation. *Journal of Arizona History* 21(4):363–90.
McGuire, Randall H.
  1980 The Mesoamerican Connection in the Southwest. *The Kiva* 46(1–2):3–38.
McNickle, D'arcy
  1973 *Native American Tribalism: Indian Survivals and Renewals.* New York: Oxford University Press.
McNitt, Frank
  1962 The Indian Traders. Norman: University of Oklahoma Press.
Malinowski, Bronislaw
  1948 Myth in Primitive Psychology. In *Magic, Science and Religion and Other Essays,* by B. Malinowski. Boston: Beacon Press.
Malotki, Ekkehart
  1978 *Hopitutuwutsi-Hopi Tales: A Bilingual Collection of Hopi Indian Stories.* Flagstaff: Museum of Northern Arizona Press.
  1982 *Hopi Time: A Linguistic Analysis of the Temporal Concepts in the Hopi Language.* The Hague: De Gruyter and Mouton.
  n.d. Hopiikwa Pangqawu'u—Say It in Hopi. Paper presented at the School of American Research Advanced Seminar: "The Hopi Indians." School of American Research, Santa Fe, New Mexico.
Marcus, George E., and Michael M. J. Fischer
  1986 *Anthropology as Cultural Critique: An Experimental Moment in the Human Sciences.* Chicago: University of Chicago Press.
Mateer, William R.
  1878 Annual Report of the Moquis Pueblo Indian Agency, Arizona. In *Annual Report of the Commissioner of Indian Affairs to the Secretary of the Interior, for the Year 1878,* pp. 8–10. Washington, D.C.: U.S. Government Printing Office.

Mathien, Frances Joan
  1981   Economic Exchange Systems in the San Juan Basin. Ph.D. Dissertation, University of New Mexico.
Mayhugh, John S.
  6-9-1892   Letter to the Commissioner of Indian Affairs. Record Group 75, National Archives. Washington, D.C.
  2-14-1893   Letter to the Commissioner of Indian Affairs. Record Group 75, National Archives. Washington, D.C.
  7-12-1893   Letter to the Commissioner of Indian Affairs. Record Group 75, National Archives. Washington, D.C.
  9-19-1893   Letter to the Commissioner of Indian Affairs. Record Group 75, National Archives. Washington, D.C.
  1894   "Moqui Allotment Schedules and Related Papers, 1894," including "List of Orabis Who Refuse to Take Their Allotments." Record Group 75, National Archives. Washington, D.C.
  2-19-1894   Final Report, Moqui Indian Reservation [to the Commissioner of Indian Affairs]. Record Group 75, National Archives. Washington, D.C.
Mennonite, The
  9-1894   From Our Moqui Mission. 9(12):94.
  1-1896   From Our Mission at Oraibe, Arizona. 11(4):5.
  9-1900   From Oraibi Arizona: Extract from a Report of Missionary H. R. Voth. 15(12):93.
  4-24-1902   Bright Arizona Prospects. 17(12):5–6.
  12-11-1902   From Oraibi, Arizona. 18(2):5.
Mennonite Encyclopedia, The
  1954–59   4 vols. Scottdale, Pennsylvania: Mennonite Publishing House.
Meritt, E. B. (Assistant Commissioner of Indian Affairs)
  1-9-1914   Letter to the Secretary of the Interior (Through the Commissioner of the General Land Office). Bacavi Village Community Building, Bacavi, Arizona.
Millennial Star, The
  1853   Strange Inhabitants of the Great Basin of North America. 16:167–68.
Miller, Horton H.
  2-13-1907   Letter to the Commissioner of Indian Affairs. KCL.
  5-14-1907   Letter to the Commissioner of Indian Affairs. In "Oraiba Troubles," File 3. Record Group 75, National Archives. Washington, D.C.
  5-25-1908   Letter to the Commissioner of Indian Affairs. KCL.
  11-21-1908   Annual Report of the Moqui Agency. KCL.

10-30-1909   Letter to the Commissioner of Indian Affairs. KCL.
11-12-1909   Letter to the Commissioner of Indian Affairs. In "Oraiba Troubles," File 5. Record Group 75, National Archives. Washington, D.C.
12-4-1909   Telegram to the Commissioner of Indian Affairs. In "Oraiba Troubles," File 5. Record Group 75, National Archives. Washington, D.C.
2-19-1910   Letter to the Commissioner of Indian Affairs. KCL.
8-15-1910   Annual Report of Moqui Agency. KCL.

Mindeleff, Cosmos
   1900   Localization of Tusayan Clans. *Nineteenth Annual Report of the Bureau of American Ethnology, for the Years 1897–1898*, pp. 635–53. Washington, D.C.: U.S. Government Printing Office.

Montgomery, Ross Gordon; Watson Smith; and J. O. Brew
   1949   *Franciscan Awatovi: The Excavation and Conjectural Reconstruction of a Seventeenth-Century Spanish Mission Establishment at a Hopi Indian Town in Northeastern Arizona*. Peabody Museum of American Archaeology and Ethnology Papers, 36.

Morgan, T. J.
   3-8-1890   Letter to C. E. Vandever. Record Group 75, National Archives. Washington, D.C.

Murphy, Matthew M.
   1905   Report of Superintendent in Charge of Western Navaho. In *Annual Reports of the Department of the Interior for the Fiscal Year ended June 30th 1905. Indian Affairs, Pt. 1* (1906), pp. 179–80. Washington, D.C.: U.S. Government Printing Office.
   9-20-1906   Letter to the Commissioner of Indian Affairs. In "Oraiba Troubles," File 1. Record Group 75, National Archives. Washington, D.C.
   9-1-1907   Letter to J. L. Singleton, Disciplinarian, Sherman Institute (addressed to Oraibi, Arizona). Tuba City Letterbooks. Record Group 75, National Archives. Laguna Niguel, California.
   2-12-1910   Letter to the Commissioner of Indian Affairs. In "Oraiba Troubles," File 5. Record Group 75, National Archives. Washington, D.C.
   4-18-1910   Letter to the Commissioner of Indian Affairs. Record Group 75, National Archives. Washington, D.C.
   11-23-1910   Letter to the Commissioner of Indian Affairs. Record Group 75, National Archives. Washington, D.C.

Murphy, Robert F.
   1964   Social Change and Acculturation. *Transactions of the New York Academy of Sciences*, Series II, 26(7):845–54.

Myron, Nadenia F.
  1979   The Early Mennonite Missionary's Approach and Attitude to the Hopi Indians and the Effects Upon the Mission Work. Manuscript. Mennonite Library and Archives. Bethel College, North Newton, Kansas.
Nagata, Shuichi
  1968a   Accommodative Context of Moenkopi Factionalism. Paper presented at the Joint Meeting of the Central States Anthropological Society and the American Ethnological Society, 1968. Copy at Museum of Northern Arizona Library, Flagstaff.
  1968b   Political Socialization of the Hopi "Traditional" Faction. Paper presented at the 8th Annual Meeting of the Northeastern Anthropological Association. Copy at Museum of Northern Arizona Library, Flagstaff.
  1970   *Modern Transformations of Moenkopi Pueblo.* Urbana, Ill.: University of Illinois Press.
  1978   Dan Kochhongva's Message: Myth, Ideology, and Political Action Among the Contemporary Hopi. In *The Yearbook of Symbolic Anthropology*, Erik Schwimmer, ed., pp. 73–87. London: C. Hurst.
Needham, Rodney
  1974   *Remarks and Inventions: Skeptical Essays About Kinship.* London; Tavistock.
Nequatewa, Edmund
  1936   *Truth of a Hopi: Stories Relating to the Origin, Myths and Clan Histories of the Hopi.* Flagstaff, Arizona: Northland Press.
  1944   A Mexican Raid on the Hopi Pueblo of Oraibi. *Plateau* 16(3):44–52.
Norris, Joe H. (Inspector, Department of the Interior)
  5-19-1910   General Investigation of Conditions at the Moqui Agency Schools and Indian Reservation under the Supervision of the Superintendent at Keam's Canon, Arizona: Section 6, Allotment. Record Group 48, Inspection Division. National Archives. Washington, D.C.
Office of Indian Affairs
  6-30-1890   Moquies Chiefs' Conference with the Commissioner of Indian Affairs, June 27th 1890. Museum of Northern Arizona, Flagstaff.
Ortner, Sherry B.
  1974   Is Female to Male as Nature Is to Culture? In *Woman, Culture, and Society*, M. Z. Rosaldo and L. Lamphere, eds., pp. 67–88. Stanford: Stanford University Press.

References Cited

1984 Theory in Anthropology Since the Sixties. *Comparative Studies in Society and History* 26:126–66.
Overing, Joanna, ed.
1985 *Reason and Morality*. New York: Tavistock.
Parmentier, Richard J.
1979 The Mythological Triangle: Poseyemu, Montezuma, and Jesus in the Pueblos. In *Handbook of North American Indians*. Vol. 9, *The Southwest*, Alfonso Ortiz, ed., pp. 609–22. Washington, D.C.: U.S. Government Printing Office.
Parsons, Elsie Clews
1922 Oraibi in 1920. In "Contributions to Hopi History," E. C. Parsons, ed., pp. 283–98, *American Anthropologist* 24(3):253–98.
1933 *Hopi and Zuni Ceremonialism*. Menasha, Wisconsin: American Anthropological Association Memoirs, no. 39.
Patterson, S. S.
1887 Annual Report Concerning Moqui Pueblo Indians. In *Annual Report of the Commissioner of Indian Affairs to the Secretary of the Interior for 1887*, pp. 177–78. Washington, D.C.: U.S. Government Printing Office.
Pattie, James O.
1905 [1831] *The Personal Narrative of James O. Pattie of Kentucky During an Expedition from St. Louis, Through the Vast Regions Between that Place and the Pacific Ocean...*, Timothy Flint, ed. Cincinnati: E. H. Flint.
Perry, Reuben
10-24-1906 Telegram to the Commissioner of Indian Affairs. In "Oraiba Troubles," File 2. Record Group 75, National Archives. Washington, D.C.
10-25-1906 Letter to the Commissioner of Indian Affairs. In "Oraiba Troubles," File 2. Record Group 75, National Archives. Washington, D.C.
10-29-1906 Letter to the Commissioner of Indian Affairs. In "Oraiba Troubles," File 2. Record Group 75, National Archives. Washington, D.C.
10-30-1906 Telegram to the Commissioner of Indian Affairs. In "Oraiba Troubles," File 2. Record Group 75, National Archives. Washington, D.C.
11-5-1906 Letter to the Commissioner of Indian Affairs. In "Oraiba Troubles," File 3. Record Group 75, National Archives. Washington, D.C.

11-7-1906   Telegram to the Commissioner of Indian Affairs. In "Oraiba Troubles," File 3. Record Group 75, National Archives. Washington, D.C.

11-10-1906   Letter to the Commissioner of Indian Affairs. In "Oraiba Troubles," File 3. Record Group 75, National Archives. Washington, D.C.

11-17-1906   Letter to the Commissioner of Indian Affairs. In "Oraiba Troubles," File 3. Record Group 75, National Archives. Washington, D.C.

1-17-1907   Letter to the Commissioner of Indian Affairs. In "Oraiba Troubles," File 4. Record Group 75, National Archives. Washington, D.C.

1-30-1907   Letter to the Commissioner of Indian Affairs. In "Oraiba Troubles," File 4. Record Group 75, National Archives. Washington, D.C.

4-5-1907   Letter to the Commissioner of Indian Affairs. In "Oraiba Troubles," File 4. Record Group 75, National Archives. Washington, D.C.

Peterson, Charles S.
   1971   The Hopis and the Mormons, 1858–1873. *Utah Historical Quarterly* 39(2):179–94.

Plummer, E. H.
   1894   Annual Report—Moquis. In *Annual Report of the Commissioner of Indian Affairs, 1894* (1895), 100–101. Washington, D.C.: U.S. Government Printing Office.
   4-10-1894   Letter to the Commissioner of Indian Affairs. FDL.
   9-29-1894   Letter to the Commissioner of Indian Affairs. FDL.

Polanyi, Michael
   1958   *Personal Knowledge: Towards a Post-Critical Philosophy.* Chicago: University of Chicago Press.

Popper, Karl
   1972   *Objective Knowledge: An Evolutionary Approach.* Oxford: Clarendon Press.

Posten, Charles D.
   1864   Report of the Arizona Superintendency. In *Annual Report of the Commissioner of Indian Affairs, 1864*, pp. 150–68. Washington, D.C.: U.S. Government Printing Office.

Powell, John Wesley
   1895   *Canyons of the Colorado.* Meadville, Pennsylvania: Flood and Vincent.
   1972   *The Hopi Villages: The Ancient Province of Tusayan.* Palmer

Lake, Colorado: Filter Press. Reprinted from *Scribner's Monthly*, Dec. 1875.

Powell, Walter Clement
   1949   W. C. Powell's Account of the Hopi Towns. *Utah Historical Quarterly* 16 and 17:479–90.

Price, Richard
   1983   *First-Time: The Historical Vision of an Afro-American People*. Baltimore: Johns Hopkins University Press.

Qoyawayma, Polingaysi (Elizabeth White)
   1964   *No Turning Back*. Albuquerque: University of New Mexico Press.

Qua' Töqti ("The Eagle's Call")
   8-7-1980   Letters to the Editor, 2. Kykotsmovi, Arizona.

Reed, Eric K.
   1942   Kawaika-a in the Historic Period. *American Antiquity* 8(1): 119–20.

Rhodes, Robert
   1982   Developments in Education: Hotevilla-Bacavi Community School. Paper presented at the School of American Research Advanced Seminar: "The Hopi Indians." School of American Research, Santa Fe, New Mexico.

Robinson, H. F. (Superintendent of Irrigation, U.S. Office of Indian Affairs)
   12-12-1910   Letter to W. H. Code, Chief Engineer, U.S. Indian Service. Record Group 75, National Archives. Washington, D.C.

Rosaldo, Renato
   1980   *Ilongot Head-hunting, 1883–1974: A Study in Society and History*. Stanford: Stanford University Press.

Sahlins, Marshall B.
   1981   *Historical Metaphors and Mythical Realities: Structure in the Early History of the Sandwich Islands Kingdom*. Ann Arbor: University of Michigan press.
   1985   *Islands of History*. Chicago: University of Chicago Press.

Said, Edward
   1978   *Orientalism*. New York: Random House.

Schirmer, Maria
   1-12-1917   Letter to the Board of Foreign Missions, Mennonite General Conference. MCF. [In German]
   4-1-1918   Letter to the Board of Foreign Missions, Mennonite General Conference. MCF.

Schlegel, Alice
    1977   Male and Female in Hopi Thought and Action. In *Sexual Stratification*, A. Schlegel, ed., pp. 245–69. New York: Columbia University Press.

Schneider, David M.
    1984   *A Critique of the Study of Kinship*. Ann Arbor: University of Michigan Press.

Scholes, France V.
    1929   Documents for the History of the New Mexican Missions in the Seventeenth Century. *New Mexico Historical Review* 4(1):45–58 and 4(2):195–201.
    1937   Troublous Times in New Mexico, 1659–1670. *New Mexico Historical Review* 12(2):134–74.

Schoolcraft, Henry Rowe
    1853–1857   *Information Respecting the History, Condition and Prospects of the Indian Tribes of the United States*.... 6 vols. Philadelphia: Lippincott, Grambo.

Scott, Col. Hugh L.
    12-5-1911   Letter to the Secretary of the Interior, including enclosure: "The Story of Ukeoma, Chief of the Hotivillos, a Village of the Hopi." In File "Re: Delegation of Moqui Indians Coming to Washington." Record Group 75, National Archives. Washington, D.C.

Sekaquaptewa, Emory
    1972   Preserving the Good Things of Hopi Life. In *Plural Society in the Southwest*, E. M. Spicer and R. H. Thompson, eds., pp. 239–60. Albuquerque: University of New Mexico Press.

Sekaquaptewa, Helen
    1969   *Me and Mine*, Louise Udall, ed. Tucson: University of Arizona Press.

Shipley, David L.
    7-6-1891   Letter to the Commissioner of Indian Affairs. FDL.
    1892   Report of Moqui Subagency. In *Sixty-First Annual Report of the Commissioner of Indian Affairs to the Secretary of the Interior, for the Year 1892*, pp. 211–12. Washington, D.C.: U.S. Government Printing Office.

Siemens, Alfred
    1962   Christ and Culture in the Mission Field. *Mennonite Life*, April 1962.

Simmons, Leo W., ed.
    1942   *Sun Chief: The Autobiography of a Hopi Indian*. New Haven: Yale University Press.

Siskind, Janet
  1973   *To Hunt in the Morning*. New York: Oxford University Press.
Solomon, William H.
  1873–74   Diary of the Arizona Mission. Manuscript. Special Collections, Brigham Young University, Provo, Utah.
Spicer, Edward H., ed.
  1961   *Perspectives in American Indian Culture Change*. Chicago: University of Chicago Press.
Stanley, Elizabeth C.
  9-18-1906   Letter to Commissioner F. E. Leupp. In "Oraiba Troubles," File 1. Record Group 75, National Archives. Washington, D.C.
Staufer, Peter
  9-18-1906   Letter to Superintendent Matthew M. Murphy. In "Oraiba Troubles," File 1. Record Group 75, National Archives. Washington, D.C.
Stauffer, Anna G.
  1926   *Mennonite Mission Study Course, Part II: Hopi Mission Field*. Newton, Kansas: Herald.
Stephen, Alexander M.
  1936   *Hopi Journal*, E. C. Parsons, ed. 2 vols. New York: Columbia University Press.
Suderman, Mrs. John P.
  n.d.   *Our Mission Among the Hopi Indians*. No publisher listed, and no date of publication. References in the text suggest 1944 or 1945. Mennonite Library and Archives. Bethel College, North Newton, Kansas.
Szasz, Margaret
  1974   *Education and the American Indian*. Albuquerque: University of New Mexico Press.
Tamarón y Romeral, Pedro
  1954   *Bishop Tamarón's Visitation of New Mexico, 1760*. Eleanor B. Adams, ed. (New Mexico Historical Society Publications in History 15). Albuquerque: University of New Mexico Press.
Tedlock, Dennis
  1979   The Analogical Tradition and the Emergence of a Dialogical Anthropology. *Journal of Anthropological Research* 35(4):387–400.
Thomas, Alfred Barnaby
  1932   *Forgotten Frontiers: A Study of the Spanish Indian Policy of Don Juan Bautista de Anza, Governor of New Mexico, 1777–1780*. Norman: University of Oklahoma Press.

1941 *Teodoro de Croix and the Northern Frontier of New Spain, 1776–1783*. Norman: University of Oklahoma Press.
Thomas, Diane H.
1978 *The Southwestern Indian Detours*. Phoenix: Hunter.
Thompson, Laura
1950 *Culture in Crisis: A Study of the Hopi Indians*. New York: Harper and Brothers.
Titiev, Mischa
1944 *Old Oraibi: A Study of the Hopi Indians of Third Mesa*. Peabody Museum of American Archaeology and Ethnology Papers, 2(1).
1972 *The Hopi Indians of Old Oraibi: Change and Continuity*. Ann Arbor: University of Michigan Press.
n.d. Census Notes from Old Oraibi. Manuscript, Peabody Museum of Archaeology and Ethnology. President and Fellows of Harvard College.
Turner, Victor W.
1957 *Schism and Continuity in an African Society*. Manchester: Manchester University Press.
1982 Social Dramas and Stories About Them. In *From Ritual to Theatre*, by V. W. Turner. New York: Performing Arts.
Twitchell, Ralph Emerson
1911 *The Leading Facts of New Mexican History*, Vol. 1. Cedar Rapids, Iowa: Torch Press.
1917 *The Leading Facts of New Mexican History*, Vol. 3. Cedar Rapids, Iowa: Torch Press.
Upham, Steadman
1982 *Polities and Power: A Social and Economic History of the Western Pueblo*. New York: Academic Press.
U.S. Government
1867 *Annual Report of the Commissioner of Indian Affairs*. Washington, D.C.: U.S. Government Printing Office.
1869 *Annual Report of the Commissioner of Indian Affairs*. Washington, D.C.: U.S. Government Printing Office.
1886 *Annual Report of the Commissioner of Indian Affairs to the Secretary of the Interior for the Year 1886*. Washington, D.C.: U.S. Government Printing Office.
1892 *Sixty-First Annual Report of the Commissioner of Indian Affairs to the Secretary of the Interior, for the Year 1892*. Washington, D.C.: U.S. Government Printing Office.
1895 *Annual Report of the Commissioner of Indian Affairs, 1894*. Washington, D.C.: U.S. Government Printing Office.

References Cited

1896 *Annual Report of the Commissioner of Indian Affairs*. Washington, D.C.: U.S. Government Printing Office.

1900 *Twelvth Census of the United States: Schedule No. 1. Population: Indian Population.* Washington, D.C.: U.S. Government Census Office.

1904 *Annual Reports of the Department of the Interior for the Fiscal Year ended June 30th 1903. Indian Affairs, Pt. 1. Report of the Commissioner and Appendixes.* Washington, D.C.: U.S. Government Printing Office.

1906–10 Oraiba Troubles. Correspondence Relating to Trouble between Factions of the Hopi Indians: "Friendlies" and "Hostiles." Files 1–5. Record Group 75, National Archives. Washington, D.C.

1906–14 Indian Census Rolls 1888–1940, no. 268, Moqui. Microfilm Group M595, National Archives. Washington, D.C.

10-30-1906 Census of Hostile Camp. On Indian Census Roll no. 268, Moqui 1906. Microfilm Group M595, National Archives. Washington, D.C.

1910–1917 Annual Censuses of Bacabi Village, Indian Census Rolls 1888–1940, no. 270, Moqui. Microfilm Group M595, National Archives, Washington, D.C.

3-28-1911 "Conference Between the Commissioner of Indian Affairs and Yukeoma, Hopi Indian." In File "Re: Delegation of Moqui Indians Coming to Washington." Record Group 75, National Archives. Washington, D.C.

1919 Census of Bacabi Village. Indian Census Rolls 1888–1940, no. 270, Moqui. Microfilm Group M595, National Archives. Washington, D.C.

1935 Census of the Hopi Reservation, 1935. Indian Census Rolls. Bacavi Community Center Offices.

1937 Census of the Hopi Reservation, 1937. Indian Census Rolls. Museum of Northern Arizona, Flagstaff.

U.S. Government, Department of the Interior

1903–4 Miscellaneous Correspondence re: Mrs. P. G. Gates in Oraibi. In Indian Division Inspection Reports, 1901–1907, Moqui and Keam's Canyon. Record Group 48, National Archives. Washington, D.C.

U.S. Senate

1932 *Survey of Indian Conditions Throughout the United States: Hearings Before a Subcommittee of the Committee on Indian Affairs.* U.S. Senate, 71st Congress, 3rd Session, Part 18: Navajos in Arizona and New Mexico, 8901–9840. Washington, D.C.: U.S. Government Printing Office.

Valentine, R. G. (Commissioner of Indian Affairs)
4-17-1911 Letter to the Commissioner of the General Land Office. Record Group 75, National Archives. Washington, D.C.

Vandever, C. E.
1889 Report of Agent for Moqui Pueblos. In *Fifty-Eighth Annual Report of the Commissioner of Indian Affairs to the Secretary of the Interior, for the Year 1889*, pp. 261–62. Washington, D.C.: U.S. Government Printing Office.
1890 Report of Moqui Pueblo Indians, Navajo Agency. In *Fifty-Ninth Annual Report of the Commissioner of Indian Affairs to the Secretary of the Interior, 1890*, pp. 167–72. Washington, D.C.: U.S. Government Printing Office.
6-4-1890 Telegram to the Commissioner of Indian Affairs. Record Group 75, National Archives. Washington, D.C.

Voegelin, Carl, and Florence Voegelin
1957 Hopi Domains: A Lexical Approach to the Problem of Selection. *International Journal of American Linguistics, Memoirs*, no. 14.
1970 Hopi Names and No Names. In *Languages and Cultures of Western North America*, Earl H. Swanson, Jr., ed. pp. 47–53. Pocatello: Idaho State University Press.

Voth, H. R.
1895 From the Moqui Mission. *The Mennonite* 10(8):62.
7-8-1895 Letter to Col. Francis L. Guenther, Commanding Officer, Alcatraz. Mennonite Library and Archives. Bethel College, North Newton, Kansas.
9-2-1895 Letter to Lomahongyouma, Alcatraz. Mennonite Library and Archives. Bethel College, North Newton, Kansas.
1900 Oraibi Marriage Customs. *American Anthropologist* 2(2): 238–46.
1901 *The Oraibi Powamu Ceremony*. Chicago: Field Columbian Museum, Publication 61, Anthropological Series 3(2).
1903a *The Oraibi Summer Snake Ceremony*. Chicago: Field Columbian Museum, Publication 83, Anthropological Series 3(4).
1903b *The Oraibi Oáqöl Ceremony*. Chicago: Field Columbian Museum, Publication 84, Anthropological Series 6(1).
1905a *The Traditions of the Hopi*. Chicago: Field Columbian Museum, Publication 96, Anthropological Series 8.
1905b *Oraibi Natal Customs and Ceremonies*. Chicago: Field Columbian Museum, Publication 97, Anthropological Series 6(2).
1912a *The Oraibi Marau Ceremony*. Chicago: Field Columbian Museum, Publication 156, Anthropological Series 11(1).

1912b   Brief Miscellaneous Hopi Papers. Chicago: Field Columbian Museum, Publication 157, Anthropological Series 1(2).
n.d.a   Interview with Yukioma. Mennonite Library and Archives. Bethel College, North Newton, Kansas.
n.d.b   Notes on the Hopi Blue Flute Ceremony. H. R. Voth Collection, Box 23, Mennonite Library and Archives. Bethel College, North Newton, Kansas.
n.d.c   Those in Charge of Altars in Oraibi. In Notebook on Hopi Religious Terminology. H. R. Voth Collection, Box 22, Mennonite Library and Archives. Bethel College, North Newton, Kansas.

Wallace, Anthony F. C.
1956   Revitalization Movements. *American Anthropologist* 58:264–80.

Waters, Frank
1963   *Book of the Hopi.* New York: Viking Press.
1969   *Pumpkin Seed Point.* Chicago: Sage Books.

Whipple, A. W.
1855   Report Upon the Indian Tribes: Explorations and Surveys for a Railroad Route from the Mississippi River to the Pacific Ocean, Vol. 3. Washington, D.C.: U.S. Government Printing Office.

White, Leslie A.
1942   *The Pueblo of Santa Ana, New Mexico.* Memoirs of the American Anthropological Association no. 60.
n.d.   Kinship System Charts of the Hopi (Oraibi) [by clan and lineage], noted by the 1932 Field Training Course. Manuscript. Laboratory of Anthropology, Santa Fe, New Mexico.

Whiteley, Peter M.
1983   Third Mesa Hopi Social Structural Dynamics and Sociocultural Change: The View from Bacavi. Ph.D. Dissertation, University of New Mexico.
1985a   Ceremony and Politics: Towards a Model of Power Among the Hopi. Paper presented to the symposium "Inequality in Native North America: Continuity and Change" at the 45th International Congress of Americanists, Bogotá.
1985b   Unpacking Hopi "Clans": Another Vintage Model Out of Africa? *Journal of Anthropological Research* 41(4):359–74.
1986   Unpacking Hopi "Clans" II: Further Questions About Hopi Descent Groups. *Journal of Anthropological Research* 42(1):69–79.

Whiting, Alfred F.
1939   *Ethnobotany of the Hopi.* Museum of Northern Arizona Bulletin 15. Flagstaff.

Whorf, Benjamin Lee
- 1956 *Language, Thought, and Reality: Selected Writings of Benjamin Lee Whorf.* Cambridge, Mass.: Massachusetts Institute of Technology Press.

Williams, Constant
- 11-15-1894a Letter to the Commissioner of Indian Affairs. FDL.
- 11-15-1894b Telegram to Commanding General, Department of the Colorado. FDL.
- 11-29-1894 Letter to the Commissioner of Indian Affairs. FDL.
- 8-29-1895 Annual Report of Moqui Indians. FDL.
- 9-29-1895 Letter to Ralph P. Collins, Superintendent, U.S. Indian School, Keam's Canyon. FDL.
- 1896 Report of Navajo Agency: Moqui Indians. In *Annual Report of the Commissioner of Indian Affairs, 1896,* p. 113. Washington, D.C.: U.S. Government Printing Office.
- 1898 Report of Navajo Agency: Moqui Indians. In *Annual Reports of the Department of the Interior for the Fiscal Year ending June 30th 1898. Indian Affairs,* pp. 123–24. Washington, D.C.: U.S. Government Printing Office.
- 10-12-1906 Letter to Reuben Perry. In "Oraiba Troubles," File 2. Record Group 75, National Archives. Washington, D.C.

Wilson, Bryan, ed.
- 1970 *Rationality.* Oxford: Blackwell.

Winship, George Parker
- 1896 The Coronado Expedition, 1540–1542. *Bureau of American Ethnology Annual Report* 14, for the years 1892–1893.

Witherspoon, Gary
- 1977 *Language and Art in the Navajo Universe.* Ann Arbor: University of Michigan Press.

Woodgate, A.M.
- n.d. [Personal report of the Oraibi split, probably to the Commissioner of Indian Affairs, though not addressed. Date likely September 1906.] In "Oraiba Troubles," File 1. Record Group 75, National Archives. Washington, D.C.

Woods, Thomas
- 1969 Demographic Characteristics: Hopi Indian Reservation, Arizona. Mimeograph. Bureau of Indian Affairs, Phoenix Area Office.

Wright, Margaret
- 1972 *Hopi Silver: The History and Hallmarks of Hopi Silversmithing.* Flagstaff, Arizona: Northland Press.

Yava, Albert
- 1978 *Big Falling Snow: A Tewa-Hopi's Life and Times and the His-

tory and Traditions of His People. Edited and annotated by Harold Courlander. New York: Crown.

Yount, George C.

1942 A Sketch of the Hopi in 1828 (presented by Robert F. Heizer). *The Masterkey* 16(6):193–99.

1966 *George C. Yount and His Chronicles of the West*, Charles L. Camp, ed. Denver: Old West.

Zeh, William E.

1930 General Report Covering the Grazing Situation on the Navajo Indian Reservation. In *General Report of the Southwest (Indian Reservations)*. U.S. Department of Agriculture, Soil Conservation Service Report.

Index

Aa'alt, 57, 59, 60, 126. *See also* Two-Horn society
Acculturation, 251–54, 282–83, 287–88
Agriculture, 56, 138, 139–41, 154, 156–57, 159, 160, 233. *See also* Horticulture
Aitken, Barbara, 29–30
Akin, Louis, 97
Alcatraz, imprisonment at, 88, 206, 251, 321–22n.21
Allotment, 6, 75, 76–83, 111, 118, 151–54, 297, 303, 307, 312, 314
Alvarado, Anita, 247
Antelope society, 72–73, 89, 195, 206, 275, 278, 280, 319n.4, 325n.1. *See also* Tsöötsöpt
Anza, Juan Bautista de (Governor of New Mexico), 26–27, 318n.3 (chap. 2), 328n.2
Apache Indians. *See* Indians (non-Hopi), Apache
Armijo, Antonio (trader), 103, 123, 313–14
Awatovi, 14, 15, 16, 18, 19, 20–21, 182, 262

Bacavi, 5, 121–239, 257, 258, 317n.1 (chap. 1), 322n.22, 323n.3, 326n.8; demography, 127–37 (*see also* Population, Bacavi); founding of, 6, 117–18, 121–26, 260, 312–14; human geography, 122–29, 130–34, 149–50; kinship, 162–91; land base, 150–54; politics, 210–17, 327n.13; relations with Hotevilla, 210, 211, 212, 227–33, 281, 326n.9; sociocultural change, 237–39, 273–74, 276, 277, 278–79, 280–81, 282, 285
Bacavi Valley, 121, 122, 150, 325n.3 (chap. 7)
Badger clan, 51, 125, 151, 172, 177, 182–84, 198, 199, 200, 207, 213, 215, 216
Bahnimptewa, Stanley, 226
Bancroft, Hubert Howe, 18, 20, 22
Bandelier, Adolph, 19
Barth, Fredrik, 256
Basket Dance, 194–95. *See also* Lakon; Owaqöl
Beaglehole, Ernest, 55, 56
Beaglehole, Pearl, 167–69

365

Bear clan, 52, 53, 66, 117, 179, 183, 207, 214, 246, 247, 253, 310; at Bacavi, 125, 141, 212, 216, 232
Benavides Memorial, 16–17
Bluebird clan, 103–4
Blue Flute ceremony/society, 58, 88, 177, 204, 205, 325n.1; at Bacavi, 125, 172, 198, 199–200, 201, 274; at Hotevilla, 278, 280; at Oraibi, 73, 89, 116, 206, 275–76, 329n.11. See also *Sakwalelent;* Gray Flute ceremony/society
Book of the Hopi, 2. *See also* Waters, Frank
Bourdieu, Pierre, 289
Bourke, John G., 34, 42, 93
Bow clan, 52, 55
Bradfield, R. Maitland, 52, 54, 57, 139–40, 247–51
Brainard, Margaret, 167–69
Brandt, Richard, 65–66
Brett, Lieutenant L.M., 78–79
Brew, J.O., 13, 22–23, 26, 27, 29, 328n.2
Broken Rainbow, 229, 230
Bureau of Indian Affairs, 211, 221–22, 223, 233. *See also* U.S. Government.
Burton, Charles E. (Agency Superintendent), 91–97, 102, 103, 322n.24

Calhoun, James S. (Superintendent of Indian Affairs, New Mexico), 30–31
Cardenas, Garcia Lopez de, 14
Carson, Kit, 38–39
Castañeda, Pedro de, 14–15, 16
Cattle. *See* Livestock
Ceremonial cycle. *See* Ritual order
Clans, 46, 47–48, 49, 51–53, 55, 56, 57, 60, 62, 63, 64, 237, 245, 246, 273, 318n.1, 327–28n.1; at Bacavi, 125, 172–84, 202, 212, 244, 245, 47, 51, 125, 172, 199, 226; clan-lands, 56, 151, 183, 257. *See also* Kinship; Lineages; Phratries; *and under individual clan names*
Clemmer, Richard O., 230, 253, 326–27n.12, 328n.4
Clown ceremonies, 2, 58, 197, 266
Collins, Ralph P. (School Superintendent), 76, 77, 79, 80
Connelly, John C., 46, 54
Corbin, Colonel H. C., 79–80, 329n.9
Coronado expedition, 13–15
Coyote clan, 55, 206, 207
Crane, Leo (Agency Superintendent), 1, 142, 155, 222–23, 320n.12, 324n.5

Crook, General George, 42
Crow clan, 180
Cubero, Pedro Rodriguez (Governor of New Mexico), 19, 20, 21
Curtis, Edward S., 29
Cushing, Frank H., 42, 71, 72, 81, 205, 270, 319n.2, 320n.7, 321n.20, 329nn.8, 9

Darwin, Charles, 34
Desert Fox clan, 55
De Vargas, Diego, 18–19
Dinnebito Valley, 5, 121, 139, 150, 249, 328n.7
District Six, 3, 139, 143, 148. *See also* Hopi Reservation
Dobyns, Henry, 15, 251
Dockstader, Frederick J., 29, 321n.21
Donaldson, Thomas, 39–40, 78
Dorsey, George A., 92
Douglas, Mary T., 289
Drought, 23, 26–27, 97–99, 140. *See also* Water supply
Duerksen, J.R. and Susanna (Mennonite missionaries), 220–21
Duvewuhioma (Spider clan), 319n.4

Eagle clan, 100, 179, 183, 184, 206, 207
Economy: Bacavi, 137–61; cash, 37, 127, 131, 138, 143–44, 145–47, 154–61, 170, 171, 238, 250; Oraibi, 55–57, 249–50; subsistence, 138, 143–44, 154–61, 163–65, 170, 250
Education, 5, 40, 73–74, 74–75, 76–83, 95, 252, 258, 271. *See also* Schools
Eggan, Fred, 46, 47, 57, 64, 84, 85, 179, 209; on kinship and kin groups, 48, 49, 51, 52, 53, 54, 167–68, 180, 181, 183, 186, 318n.1, 2
Eisenberg, Leonard A., 244
Epp, Reverend J.B., 93, 98, 105, 108, 117, 263–64, 265, 309–10, 313, 314
Escalante, Fray Silvestre Velez de, 23–25, 26
Espejo expedition, 15
Espeleta, Francisco de (Oraibi chief), 19–20
Ethnicity, 140, 163, 195–97. *See also* Clans, at Bacavi
Evans-Pritchard, E.E., 286

Factionalism, 25, 40, 42, 63, 77, 82–83, 86–90, 224–37, 248, 252, 275, 318n.6, 326–27n.12. *See also* Bacavi, politics;

Index

Friendlies; Hostiles; Oraibi, political structure; Progressives; Traditionals/Traditionalists
Fewkes, Jesse W., 78, 329n.9
First Mesa, 23, 25, 31, 48, 53, 78, 140, 142, 148, 193, 196, 200, 214, 225, 259, 319n.3, 320n.12, 324n.5. *See also* Hano; Polacca; Sichomovi; Walpi
Folk models, 286–87, 290
Forde, C. Daryll, 55
Forrest, Earle R., 103, 107, 275, 276, 329n.11
Fort Defiance, 32, 33, 39, 73, 91, 111, 322n.21
Fort Huachuca, 114, 323n.29
Fort Wingate, 39, 79, 111, 301, 305, 321n.14, 321n.15
Franciscans. *See* Missionaries, Franciscan
Frey, C.J. (Mennonite missionary), 220
Frey, J.B. (Mennonite missionary), 220
Friendlies, 5–6, 86, 152, 209, 245, 247, 329n.11; external affairs, 5, 263, 295, 299–301, 307, 321n.16; ideology, 5, 82–83, 252, 263–64, 265, 270; leadership, 66–67, 99, 101 (*see also* Loololma; Tawaquaptewa); population, 326n.6. *See also* Factionalism; Hostiles; Intervillage relations; Oraibi, political structure; Oraibi split
Frigout, Arlette, 57

Garcés, Fray Francisco, 25–26, 27, 318n.4 (chap. 2)
Gardens. *See* Horticulture
Gates, Gertrude P., 95, 96–97, 108, 265
Gathering, 56, 145–46, 165
Geertz, Clifford, 289
Golden, John, 253
Goldfrank, Esther S., 247
Gossen, Walter (Mennonite missionary), 217
Gossett, C.A. (Principal, Oraibi Day School), 117, 314
Gray Flute ceremony/society, 58, 89, 198, 276. *See also* Blue Flute ceremony/society; *Masilelent*
Greasewood clan, 49, 54, 177, 200, 205, 207
Gyashhongnewa (Spider clan), 206

Hamblin, Jacob, 33–35, 41
Hano, 22, 23, 42. *See also* First Mesa
Hargrave, Lyndon L., 13, 29, 252

Havasupai Indians. *See* Indians (non-Hopi), Havasupai
Heevi'ima (*Kookop* clan), 72–73, 77, 82–83, 86, 88, 101, 114, 319n.5, 320–21n.13, 321n.15, 325n.5 (chap. 7)
Hopi Cultural Center, 145
Hopi Indian Agency, 39–40, 123, 129, 133, 134, 138, 139, 145–46, 154, 155, 158, 214, 250, 301. *See also* Moqui Pueblo Agency
Hopi language, 178, 196, 223, 255, 317n.1 (chap. 1)
Hopi Reservation, 3, 42, 323n.2. *See also* District Six; Land disputes, Hopi-Navajo
Horticulture, 56, 121, 156–57, 165
Hostiles, 5–7, 61, 86, 245, 247; external affairs, 78, 79, 81, 82–83, 93, 251, 295–96, 299–307; ideology, 5–7, 27, 82–83, 252, 263–64, 265, 270; leadership, 66, 72–73, 82, 99–101, 209, 258, 272, 319n.3, 321n.20, 329n.9 (*see also* Heevi'ima; Lomahongyoma; Lomayestewa; Patupha; *Pavansinom;* Yukioma); population, 81–82, 264, 305, 326n.6; returned, 6–7, 114–18, 135, 152, 205, 275–76, 300, 305, 307–8, 310–14, 323n.29, 329n.11; Second Mesa, 91, 103–5, 107, 108, 114, 264, 295, 299, 301, 302, 305. *See also* Factionalism; Friendlies; Hotevilla; Intervillage relations; Oraibi, political structure; Oraibi split
Hotevilla: economy, 141, 142, 144, 151, 158, 161; founding of, 6, 109, 110, 112, 113, 114, 116, 117, 323n.9; intervillage relations, 210, 211, 212, 223–37, 326n.9, 330n.15; location, 33, 121, 122, 127; Mennonite church, 217, 220, 221; ritual order, 172, 192, 193, 194, 195, 199–200, 205, 206, 277–82, 322n.22; social organization, 168, 172, 179, 208, 211, 258; sociocultural change, 27, 196, 233, 257, 277–83
Households, 46, 47–48, 49, 55, 140, 164, 165–72, 175, 245, 246. *See also* Clans; Kinship; Lineages
Hubbell, Lorenzo, 103, 158
Hunting, 56, 145–46
Huxley, Thomas H., 34

Indians (non-Hopi): Apache, 26, 42, 144, 188; Comanche, 30; Creek, 188; Havasupai, 27; Keresan, 328n.3; Laguna, 188; Mohave, 188; Navajo (*see*

Indians, (continued)
Navajo Indians); Omaha, 188; Paiute, 33; Papago, 188; Pima, 188; Pueblo, 15, 21, 22–23, 329n.8; Sandia, 23; Shoshone, 188; Tesuque, 31; Ute, 26, 30; Zuni (see Zuni)
Intervillage relations, 223–37. See also Bacavi, relations with Hotevilla; Hotevilla, intervillage relations; Kykotsmovi, intervillage relations; Oraibi, intervillage relations
Ives, Lieutenant Joseph C., 32–33

James, Harry C., 277

Kachina clan, 180, 199, 207
Kachinas: dances, 125, 150, 192–203, 195, 217, 226, 256, 281; religious practices, 125, 126, 206, 261, 266–67; society, 57, 59, 60–61, 274, 322n.24. See also Religious societies; Ritual order
Kampmeier, Herman (Principal, Oraibi Day School), 91, 92, 96, 322n.26
Katsinmana (Eagle clan), 35, 37, 207, 325n.4 (chap. 7)
Kawestima, 112, 232, 257–58, 261, 265, 269–70, 279, 280, 328n.3, 329n.7, 330n.15
Keam, Thomas, 75, 77, 79, 81, 92, 155, 319n.1
Keam's Canyon, 40, 73, 76, 92, 94, 106, 114, 145, 301, 305, 319n.1, 322n.26, 322–23n.29, 324n.5
Keith, Miltona (Field Matron, Oraibi Day School), 93, 108
Kendrick, Major H.L., 32
Kennard, Edward A., 55, 133, 267–68
Kewanhöinim (Coyote clan), 207
Kewanimptewa (Sand clan): in founding of Bacavi, 117–18, 135, 260, 310–14; personal background, 205, 326n.7; role in Bacavi, 123, 125, 131–32, 152–54, 155, 198, 205, 213–16, 225, 256, 274, 326n.9, 328n.5; role in Oraibi (1906–09), 115–16, 300–1; in second Oraibi split, 268–69, 275, 310–14
Kiisonvi (plaza), 58, 123, 125, 128, 194
Kikmongwi, 24, 29, 279, 262; position, 28, 52, 66–67, 88, 151, 204, 208, 213, 214, 216, 230, 231, 267, 277. See also Loololma; Tawaquaptewa
Kinship, 46, 47–55, 162–91, 237, 273–74, 288, 318n.2. See also Bacavi, kinship; Clans; Eggan, Fred, on kinship and

kin groups; Households; Lineages; Phratries; Social structure; Titiev, Mischa, on kinship
Kivas: Bacavi, 125–26, 149, 192, 193, 198, 199, 211, 212, 218; kiva groups, 41, 61–64; Oraibi, 16, 60, 61–64, 84, 116 (see also Sakwalenvi); significance, 57, 165, 257
Kookop clan, 54, 79, 319n.7, 320–21n.13, 322n.25, 327–28n.1; at Hotevilla, 172, 179; role in factions, 72–73, 86, 88, 101, 245, 246, 247, 253
Koyaanisqatsi, 271
Krutz, Gordon V., 328n.4
Kuhn, Thomas, 290
Kwaakwant, 57, 59, 60, 89, 126, 199–200, 205, 329n.12. See also One-Horn society
Kykotsmovi, 5, 123, 141, 151, 211, 217, 223, 224, 257, 274, 327n.13; intervillage relations, 188, 189, 190, 194, 223–37

La Farge, Oliver, 214, 234–36
Lakon (pl. Lalkont), 41, 59, 60, 89, 198, 201, 204, 208, 276, 278
Lamphere, Louise, 238–39
Land disputes: Hopi-Navajo, 103, 161, 230, 234; internal, 86–87, 99, 152, 211, 219, 228, 326n.9
Land rights, 48, 49, 51, 52, 150–54
Lansa, Mina, 225–26
Lawshe, Abraham L. (Agency Superintendent), 152, 277, 324n.5
Lee, John D., 36, 321n.19
Lemmon, Theodore G. (Agency Superintendent), 97, 98, 99–100, 104–5, 105–6, 107, 109, 110, 116, 264, 272, 300, 322n.29
Leroux, Antonie (guide), 32
Leupp, Francis E. (Commissioner of Indian Affairs), 106, 111, 113, 114, 115, 265, 295–97
Lévi-Strauss, Claude, 51, 54, 164
Lineages, 46, 47, 48–51, 55, 56, 68, 167, 169, 171, 237, 273; at Bacavi, 172–77. See also Clans; Households; Kinship
Livestock, 23, 39, 56, 142–44, 148, 154–55, 156–57, 158–60, 324n.5, 324n.6. See also Sheep
Lizard clan, 55, 181–82
Loloma, Charles, 146
Lomahongyoma (Spider clan), 204; role in Bacavi, 125, 198–200, 326n.9; role in

Hostile leadership, 79, 88–89, 92, 99, 100–1, 108, 245, 246, 260, 271, 321n.13; role among returned Hostiles, 114, 115, 116, 276
Lomamsai'ima (Coyote clan), 206
Lomanaksu (Parrot clan), 201, 204
Lomavitu, Otto, 327n.13
Lomayestewa (Spider clan), 101, 104, 199–200
Loololma (Bear clan), 40–41, 63, 204, 269, 271; death of, 99, 101, 105, 322n.27; plans to split Oraibi, 257, 259–60, 261; relations with Government, 5, 72, 73, 75, 76, 77, 81, 252–53; role in Friendly leadership, 42, 82, 88–89
Lowie, Robert, 275
Lummis, Charles F., 95–96

Maasaw (Hopi deity), 79, 228, 271, 322n.25, 327n.1
Maasaw clan (*Masngyam*), 245, 247, 327–28n.1
Malinowski, Bronislaw, 262
Malotki, Ekkehart, 255, 317n.1 (chap. 1), 318n.4 (chap. 3), 328n.3
Maraw (pl. *Mamrawt*), 59, 60, 89, 198, 276, 278, 280, 325n.1
Marrige patterns, 178, 188–91. See also Kinship
Martinez, Phelix (Governor of New Mexico), 21, 26
Masangöntewa (Snake clan), 73, 205, 319n.6 (chap. 4)
Masilelent, 59, 60. See also Gray Flute ceremony/society
Mateer, William R. (Agency Superintendent), 40–41, 318n.7, 320n.12
Mayhugh, John S. (Allotting Agent), 81–83, 321n.14
Mennonite mission, 6, 83–86, 108, 138, 154, 192, 217–21, 250, 279, 310, 313, 327n.13. See also Epp, Reverend J.B.; Missionaries, Mennonite; Voth, Reverend H.R.
Miller, Horton H. (Agency Superintendent), 116–18, 152, 309–14, 315
Mishongnovi, 15, 18, 23, 32, 41, 103, 104, 142, 188, 189, 192, 203, 318n.1, 319n.3. See also Second Mesa
Missionaries, 75; Franciscan, 16–18, 21–22, 217, 262; Jesuit, 22; Mennonite, 83–86, 93, 94, 107, 217–21, 301 (*see also* Epp, Reverend J.B.; Mennonite mission; Voth, Reverend H.R.); Mormon, 33–37, 326n.8 (*see also* Mormons)
Moencopi, 2, 86, 110, 115, 152, 207, 224, 226–27, 257, 303, 310, 321n.19; economy, 138, 141, 249; Lower, 5, 223, 224, 225, 226, 227, 232, 274; social organization, 165–70, 172, 177, 186, 208–9, 326n.11; Upper, 5, 194, 211, 223, 224, 226, 227, 232, 236, 274, 327n.13
Momtsit 28, 61, 65, 66, 72–73, 319n.7, 320n.13. See also Warriors' society
Monongye, David, 231
Moqui Pueblo Agency, 39–40, 73, 91–97. See also Hopi Indian Agency
Morfi, Fray Agustín de, 43
Mormons, 33–37, 86, 138, 207, 249, 250, 322n.23. See also Missionaries, Mormon
Murphy, Matthew M. (Superintendent, Western Navajo Agency; Allotting Agent), 97–98, 110–11, 152–54, 303, 312, 323n.4
Murphy, Robert F., 288
Myron, Nadenia F., 218–19

Naa'usitewa (Greasewood clan), 205
Nagata, Shuichi, 65, 133, 138, 165–70, 180, 186, 224, 226–27, 318n.4 (chap. 3), 326–27n.12
Naquave'ima (Eagle clan), 100–1, 108, 109, 112
Nasimöisi (Greasewood clan), 207–8
Nasingainewa (Eagle clan), 205–6, 209
Nasiquaptewa (Badger clan), 117, 125, 200, 207, 213
Navajo Agency, 39, 40, 73, 111
Navajo Indians, 94, 95, 101–3, 140, 153, 208, 238–39; encroachment, 36, 42, 101–3, 249, 259–60, 323n.2; raids, 26, 29, 30, 31, 34, 35, 144; relations with Bacavi, 143, 148, 158, 188, 212; round-up, 38–39, 40
Nequatewa, Edmund, 29, 103, 107, 259–60, 318n.4 (chap. 3), 322n.28, 330n.15
Niman, 58, 63, 107, 193–94, 198, 200, 205, 278

Oñate, Don Juan de, 15, 16
One-Horn society, 126, 198, 275. See also *Kwaakwant*
Oraibi, 1–118; economy, 39, 55–57, 121, 142, 144, 151, 154, 155, 324n.6; inter-village relations, 12–13, 16, 18, 20, 21, 24, 26, 28, 32, 43, 188–91, 224, 225, 226, 227, 228, 326n.10, 326n.11; politi-

Oraibi, (continued)
cal structure, 23–24, 25, 28, 42, 64–69; prophecy, 270; relations with Anglo-Americans (to 1882), 30–42; relations with Spanish, 5, 15, 16, 17, 18, 19, 21, 22, 24, 26, 28; ritual order, 57–64, 208–9, 275–77, 280, 282, 322n.22, 329n.10; social organization, 44–70, 132, 166–70, 172, 175, 176, 177, 178–79, 185, 187, 239, 318n.1; sociocultural change, 154, 155, 274, 275–77, 288; trade at, 26, 27, 34, 36, 41, 42, 155
Oraibi split: anthropological analyses, 244–54, 283–84; as deliberate act, 151, 274, 285, 289–90; general account of, 5–7, 71–118; Government reactions to, 295–97, 300–5; Hopi analyses, 254–65, 283–84, 328n.4, 330n.15; immediate events, 106–10; 1909 split, 116–18, 268, 309–14
Oraibi Valley, 5, 56, 99, 108, 121, 139, 150, 151, 152–54, 183, 248, 326n.10
Orchards. See Horticulture
Orthography, 317n.1 (chap. 1)
Ortner, Sherry, 164, 289
Owaqöl (pl. *Owaqölt*), 41, 59, 60, 194–95, 198, 199, 276, 278

Pahaana (pl. *Pahaanam*), 34, 224, 270–71, 329n.8
Palengawhoya ("Little Echo," younger War Twin), 28, 67, 328n.13
Parrot clan, 55, 180, 204
Parsons, Elsie Clews, 253, 275–76, 319n.2, 319n.5, 320n.7
pasiuni, 266–68
Pattie, Lieutenant Ohio, 30
Patupha (*Kookop* clan), 72, 77, 79, 82, 101, 319n.3, 320n.11, 321n.13, 321n.15, 327n.1
Pavansinom: actions, 266, 280, 283; among Bacavi founders, 7, 201–10, 258, 282; in social structure, 65, 66, 68–69, 212, 255, 256, 257, 273, 318n.4. See also *Sukavungsinom*
Pavatea, Tom, 325n.5
Perry, Reuben (Supervisor), 111–16, 118, 135, 299–306, 322–23n.29
Peterson, Charles S., 37
Phratries, 46, 47, 51, 53–55, 172, 173, 180–85, 246, 318n.1. See also Clans; Kinship
Piikyas clan: at Bacavi, 179, 216; Piikyas-Patki conflict, 54, 177

Plaza. See *Kiisonvi*
Polacca, 145, 146, 188, 189, 326n.8. See also First Mesa
Polaccaca, Tom, 42, 75
Polanyi, Karl, 290
Polingyaoma (Kachina clan), 126, 150–51, 180, 199, 200, 207
Politics, Hopi: practices, 19–20, 21, 31, 69, 223–37, 253–54, 265–69; structures, 14–15, 16, 28, 64–69, 210–17, 237–38, 249, 260, 285. See also Bacavi, politics; Factionalism; Intervillage relations; Oraibi, political structure; *Pavansinom*; *Sukavungsinom*
Pongyaletstewa (Coyote clan), 206–7, 209
Pongyaquaptewa (Badger clan), 215
Pongyayaoma, James, 230–31
Pöökong (elder War Twin), 28, 67, 320n.13. See also Palengawhoya
Popper, Karl, 286
Population: Bacavi, 127–37, 173–76, 221, 323n.1, 323–24n.4, 325n.6; First and Second Mesa, 90; Hopi (pre-twentieth century), 15, 16, 18, 22, 32, 37; Hostiles, 7, 264, 305; Hotevilla, 221, 227; Moencopi (1900), 249; Oraibi, general, 48, 250–51; Oraibi (1906), 50, 325n.6; Oraibi (nineteenth century), 31, 32, 37, 39, 42, 81, 318n.7; Oraibi (pre-nineteenth century), 15, 18, 27; Shongopavi, 7; Third Mesa, 323n.1
Powamuy ceremony/society, 58, 59, 60, 177; at Bacavi, 192–93, 195, 198, 200, 274; at Hotevilla, 278, 279, 280; at Oraibi, 116, 226, 276
Powaqa (pl. *Popwaqt*, "witch"), 69, 214, 215, 318n.3 (chap. 3)
Powell, John Wesley, 41, 81
Powell, Walter Clement, 41–42
Prescott, Arizona, 38
Progressives, 223–37
Prophecies, 106, 111, 196, 214, 215, 255; regarding Oraibi split, 109, 112, 113, 226, 232, 258–61, 263–65, 269–72, 283
Pueblo Indian Agency, 39. See also Hopi Indian Agency; Moqui Pueblo Agency
Pueblo Indians. See Indians (non-Hopi), Pueblo; Zuni
Pueblo Revolt, 5, 13, 18–19

Qaletaqmongwi (War Chief), 28, 66–67, 73, 319n.7, 320n.13. See also Heevi'ima; War Chief

Index

Qötsaquahu (Sand clan), 205, 206, 209, 280, 281, 325n.3 (chap. 7)
Qötshongva, Dan, 230–31

Rabbit clan, 180, 183
Reed clan, 177
Religious practices, 84, 92–94, 192–210. *See also* Religious societies; Ritual knowledge; Ritual order
Religious societies, 46, 55, 57–61, 68, 73, 202, 210, 273–83, 325n.1. *See also* Religious practices; Ritual knowledge; Ritual order
Ritual knowledge, 84, 249, 257, 273. *See also* Religious practices; Religious societies; Ritual order
Ritual order, 57–64, 86–89, 233, 285, 288, 289; decline of, 257–58, 269, 273–74, 275–83, 290. *See also* Religious practices; Religious societies; Ritual knowledge
Rosaldo, Renato, 254

Saalako, 200–1
Sahlins, Marshall, 12, 243
Said, Edward, 290
Sakwalelent, 58, 59, 60. *See also* Blue Flute ceremony/society
Sakwalenvi, 60, 63, 73, 88, 101, 125, 198, 320n.7. *See also* Kivas
Salt Lake City, 35
Sand clan, 55, 179, 184, 205
Santa Fe, 19, 20, 39
Schneider, David, 45
Schools, 74–83, 90, 91, 104, 111, 138, 221–23, 263–64, 296–97, 300–6, 307, 312, 313, 314; Albuquerque Indian School, 223; Bacabi Day School, 154, 222, 312, 314; Carlisle Indian School, 75, 114, 323n.29; Hopi High School, 222; Hotevilla-Bacabi Day/Community School, 146, 154, 195, 215, 221–23, 227; Keam's Canyon Boarding School, 73–74, 76, 78, 91, 113, 222, 296–97, 302, 305, 306; Kykotsmovi Day School, 222; Mennonite Mission School, 222; Oraibi Day School, 80, 90, 92, 97, 100, 102, 108, 112–13, 115, 153, 300, 302, 305, 306, 312, 313, 314, 322n.26; Phoenix Indian School, 223, 300; Sherman Institute (Riverside), 115, 116, 223, 226, 300, 303. *See also* Education
Second Mesa, 48, 53, 90, 94, 194, 196, 200; economic aspects, 56, 140, 142, 144, 145, 146, 148, 326n.10; Bacavi's relations with, 175, 190, 225. *See also* Hostiles, Second Mesa; Mishongnovi; Shipaulovi; Shongopavi
Sekaquaptewa, Emory, 260–61, 266, 317n.1 (chap. 1), 328n.3, 328n.4
Sekaquaptewa, Helen, 107, 108, 322n.23, 325n.4 (chap. 7)
Sex differences, 163–65, 174–75, 213, 237–38, 324n.2, 325n.1
Sheep, 142–43, 154, 233, 324n.5. *See also* Livestock
Shipaulovi, 22, 23, 103, 104, 198, 272. *See also* Second Mesa
Shongopavi, 7, 13, 15, 16, 18, 23, 142, 188, 189, 318n.1, 326n.10; opposition to Government at, 90–91, 103–5, 113, 271, 295, 296, 299, 301, 302, 305 (*see also* Hostiles, Second Mesa); ritual order, 192, 201, 233–34, 243. *See also* Second Mesa
Sichomovi, 23
Sikyave'ima (Reed clan), 89, 117, 213, 312
Singers' society, 275. See also *Taatawkyam*
Sitgreaves expedition, 32
Slave raids, 29, 39
Smallpox, 15, 26, 32, 90–91, 94, 98
Snake: ceremonies, 58, 93, 103, 107, 116, 275, 278, 279, 280; kiva, 205, 206; society, 73, 89, 195, 278, 280, 319n.5, 320n.13. See also *Tsuutsut*
Snake clan, 55, 73, 79, 86, 141, 179, 181–82, 320n.13
Social dances, 58–59, 62, 187, 192, 194, 195, 226
Social structure, 44–70, 162–91, 245, 254, 273–74, 283. *See also* Kinship; Politics, Hopi; Ritual order
Sopkyaoma, 201
Soyalangw: ceremony, 29, 42, 57–58, 194, 198, 200, 204, 226, 266, 267, 276, 277–78; society (*Sosyalt*), 59, 60, 63, 66, 67, 73, 88, 89, 115, 319n.2, 320n.7, 325n.1
Spider clan: attributes, 53, 86, 104, 177, 319n.7; Bacavi, 172, 184, 199, 212; in Hostile leadership, 42, 72, 88, 322n.26; Hotevilla, 179; in Oraibi split, 117, 245, 246, 247, 253, 272
Squash clan, 179
Stanley, Elizabeth (Principal, Oraibi Day School), 108, 264
Staufer, Peter (Agency Mechanic), 104–5, 107, 116, 300

Index

Stephen, Alexander M., 81, 139–40, 319n.3, 321n.15, 324n.5
Stock reduction, 142–43, 144, 323n.2. *See also* Livestock
Stores, 155–58, 160–61, 250, 313. *See also* Trade; Traders
Suderman, J.P. (Mennonite missionary), 221
Sukavungsinom (sing. *sukavungsino*): *pavansinom* and, 257, 268, 271, 280; in social structure, 65, 66, 207, 257, 318n.4 (chap. 3); status, 235, 255, 273, 278. *See also Pavansinom*
Sun clan, 179, 184
Suukaoma (Snake clan), 206

Taatawkyam, 57, 59, 60, 199, 205. *See also* Singers' society
Talayesva, Don, 169–70, 258, 276, 322n.27, 329n.10
Talaynmptewa, Howard, 216
Talti, 36, 41
Tawahongnewa (Bluebird clan), 103–5, 107, 111, 272, 295, 300, 302, 323n.29
Tawanimsi (Snake clan), 207–8
Tawaquaptewa (Bear clan), 67, 96, 99, 101, 103, 180, 181, 206, 209, 276–77, 328n.5, 330n.15; in Oraibi split, 105, 106, 107, 108, 109, 111, 113, 114, 257, 258, 265, 272, 295–96, 300; relations with returned Hostiles/Bacavi faction, 115, 116, 117, 118, 154, 215, 268, 275, 276, 310, 311, 313–14, 330n.14; successors, 225–27
Tawayesva, Ray, 216
Technology, changing, 147–50
Ten Broeck, Dr. P.G.S., 31
Third Mesa, 2–5, 140. *See also* Bacavi; Hotevilla; Kykotsmovi; Oraibi; Moencopi
Thompson, Lieutenant Robert, 39
Titiev, Mischa, 79, 101, 209, 233, 320n.11, 320–21n.13, 322n.27, 322n.28, 325n.4 (chap. 6); on Bacavi, 198, 216, 325n.2, 327n.13; census notes of Oraibi, 131, 175, 180, 181, 190, 191, 204, 208–10, 321n.16, 324n.6, 325n.5 (chap. 7); on decline of ritual order, 275–77, 329n.10; on economy, 55; on factional population, 264, 325n.6; on kinship, 46, 47, 48–49, 50, 51, 53, 167–70, 180, 182, 183, 185, 246, 318n.2; on Oraibi split, 106–7, 244–47, 252–53; on social structure, 46, 47, 57, 64, 245
Tobacco clan, 180

Tourists, 1–2, 93, 149
Trade, 14, 155; indigenous, 13, 28, 103, 143, 148, 155–56, 158. *See also* Oraibi, trade at; Stores; Traders
Traders, 102–3, 160, 313–14, 319n.1. *See also* Armijo, Antonio; Hubbell, Lorenzo; Keam, Thomas; Trade; Volz, Frederick W. and William
Traditionals/Traditionalists, 27, 223–37, 327n.12
Tribal Council, 2, 65, 145, 151, 210, 213, 216, 221, 223–25, 227, 228–30, 231, 234–36, 323n.3
Tsa'akmongwi (Crier Chief), 41, 66, 67, 177, 207
Tsöötsöpt, 58, 59, 60. *See also* Antelope society
Tsuutsut, 58, 59, 60. *See also* Snake, society
Tuba City, 37, 97, 152
Tuutuspa (Snake clan), 206
Tuuvi (*Piikyas* clan), 35, 36, 37, 41, 86, 318n.5 (chap. 2)
Tuwamöinim (Reed clan), 207
Two-Horn society, 126, 234, 275, 325n.2. *See also Aa'alt*

Upham, Steadman, 20
U.S. government, 30–31, 37–38, 143, 215–16, 220, 221, 228, 235; reaction of to Oraibi split, 295–97, 300, 301, 302, 303, 304, 307, 310, 311, 312, 313, 323n.29; relations of Oraibi with, 72, 73, 77, 80, 252, 253, 264, 272

Vaccination, 90, 94
Vandever, C.E. (Navajo Agent), 40, 75, 324n.5
Viets, A.H. (Principal, Oraibi Day School), 97
Village Chief. *See Kikmongwi*
Vizcarra, José Antonio (Governor of New Mexico), 30
Voegelin, Carl and Florence, 44–45
Volz, Frederick W. and William (traders), 102–3
Voth, Reverend H.R.: on aspects of Hopi life, 18, 88, 89, 98, 209, 262, 319n.5; on religious practices, 57, 174, 321n.17; role in Oraibi, 81, 83–86, 92, 220, 322n.26, 321–22n.21

Wallace, A.F.C., 288
Walpi, 15, 18, 19, 21, 23, 179, 192, 214, 263, 318n.1. *See also* First Mesa

Index

War Chief, 73, 79, 82, 263, 320n.7. *See also* Heevi'ima; *Qaletaqmongwi*
Ward, John (U.S. Indian Agent), 37–38, 39
Warriors' society, 204, 205, 206. See also *Momtsit*
Washington, D.C., 31, 41, 72, 75, 76, 252–53, 259–60, 261, 329n.9
Waters, Frank, 2, 42, 230
Water supply, 16, 30, 42, 48, 98, 102, 248, 249; at Bacavi, 117, 121, 122, 141, 304, 312
Wedding ceremonies, 149, 174
Wheeler survey, 36
Whipple expedition, 32
White, Leslie, 175, 181, 182, 247, 328n.3
Whorf, Benjamin Lee, 255, 328n.6
Williams, Bill, 30
Williams, Captain Constant (Acting Indian Agent), 86–88, 270
Witchcraft, 54, 65, 117. See also *Powaqa*
Wright, Barton, 201
Wright, Margaret, 146–47
Wu'uya (totemic sacra), 47–48, 49, 51, 53, 54, 79, 172, 322n.25, 327n.1
Wuwtsim: Bacavi 198–99, 201; ceremonial practices, 34, 57, 95, 117, 195–96, 257, 275; Hotevilla, 277–79, 280, 281, 282, 329n.12; kivas, 64; power of, 196, 235–36; societies, 59, 60, 68, 73, 89, 271, 274, 325n.1. See also *Aa'alt; Kwaakwant; Taatawkyam*
Wytewa, Benjamin Sr., 279, 281

Yava, Albert, 43
Young, Brigham, 35
Yount, George C., 30
Yukioma (*Kookop* clan): confrontations with officialdom, 88, 106, 295, 297, 300, 301, 302, 303, 329n.9; on Hopi traditions, 67–68, 262, 270–71, 327n.1; in Hostile leadership, 82, 100–1, 104–5, 272, 322n.26; in Hotevilla affairs, 179, 274, 279, 280, 281, 326n.9; imprisonment, 80, 92, 251, 323n.29; in Oraibi split, 109, 111–13, 257, 258, 260; relations with Kewanimptewa, 215, 326n.9, 328n.5

Zuni, 14, 15, 16, 18, 21, 27, 31, 38, 188

PETER WHITELEY holds an M.A. in archaeology and anthropology from Cambridge University and a Ph.D. in anthropology from the University of New Mexico. His interest in the indigenous peoples of New Mexico and Arizona dates from his arrival in the Southwest in 1976. As a result of research into the history of Laguna Pueblo, Santo Domingo Pueblo, the Mescalero Apache, and the Navajo, he has published a number of technical reports and is co-author with Klara B. Kelley of *Navajoland: Family Settlement and Land Use* (Navajo Community College Press, 1988). Since 1980, his primary ethnological and historical interest has been in Third Mesa Hopi. He lived in Bacavi for more than a year in 1980–81 and has returned subsequently on many occasions. From 1983 to 1985 he was Director of the Special Collections Library at Northern Arizona University, Flagstaff. Since 1985 he has been on the anthropological faculty of Sarah Lawrence College, Bronxville, New York.